Human Skills

Wiley Series on Studies in Human Performance

Series Editor

Dennis H. Holding

University of Louisville
Kentucky, USA

Stress and Fatigue in Human Performance
edited by Robert Hockey

Sustained Attention in Human Performance
edited by Joel S. Warm

Noise and Human Efficiency
Michel Loeb

Aging and Human Performance
edited by Neil Charness

Sex Differences in Human Performance
edited by Mary Anne Baker

Acquisition and Performance of Cognitive Skills
edited by Ann Colley and John Beech

Human Skills Second Edition
edited by Dennis H Holding

Further titles in preparation

Human Skills

Second Edition

Edited by

Dennis H. Holding

*University of Louisville,
Kentucky, USA*

JOHN WILEY & SONS

Chichester · New York · Brisbane · Toronto · Singapore

British Library Cataloguing in Publication Data:

Human Skills.—2nd ed.—(Wiley
  series in human performance and
  cognition).
  1. Man. Perceptuo–motor skills
  I. Holding, Denis H. (Denis Harry), *1925–*
  152.3

ISBN 0 471 92076 2

Phototypeset by Input Typesetting Ltd, London
Printed and bound in Great Britain by
Anchor Press Ltd, Tiptree, Essex

Contents

Preface

Research on human performance has made considerable progress during the past forty years, reaching a respectable depth of analysis in several areas while at the same time becoming broader in scope. As a result, there have emerged a number of theoretical ideas which impinge on the general development of experimental psychology and, moreover, a great deal of knowledge has been obtained in ways which encourage direct, practical application. The series of Studies in Human Performance, beginning with this volume, is intended to explain these ideas and their applications in adequate detail.

Approximately half of the books in the series are monographs while the remainder, like the present text, are edited volumes. Although writing a monograph is often regarded as the more difficult assignment, producing an edited volume presents something of a challenge. On one hand, it provides an opportunity to bring to bear a concentration of expertise which is otherwise unattainable; on the other hand, the multiplicity of contributors carries with it a risk that the overall result may be disorganized or, literally, incoherent. In the Human Performance series, every effort has been made to counter the disadvantages attendant on using the edited format, while preserving the advantages of drawing upon special knowledge. The chapters have been commissioned in accordance with an integrated plan for each volume, draft versions of each chapter have been circulated among the contributors in order to ensure cohesion, and editorial control has extended to the level of difficulty as well as to the format of each text.

The result of these preparations should be a series of books which combine readability with high standards of scholarship. The aim has been to supply a good deal of content, but within an expository framework which emphasizes explanation rather than mere reporting. Thus, although each volume contains sufficient material for the needs of graduate students, or advanced undergraduates, in experimental psychology, the books should provide readily accessible information for applied psychologists in many areas. In addition, it is hoped that the books will be useful to practitioners in ergonomics, to persons with interdisciplinary interests in production and industrial engineering, in physical education and in exercise physiology, and to psychologists in other fields.

The analysis of human skills is of central importance to an understanding of the wider area of human performance. Partly for this very reason, the subject of skills is fraught with more theoretical problems than many other topics in human performance; in fact, many of the more applied issues have been quite appropriately reserved for inclusion in the companion volume on *'Training for Performance'*. A further difficulty encountered in dealing with skills is that the relevant research has in many cases reached a stage where some facility with mathematical notation is required for thorough understanding. The policy adopted here has been to grasp the nettle by introducing mathematical concepts when necessary, but always in the context of an explanation. Where the use of a mathematical formula has been unavoidable, the simplest form of expression has always been chosen. We believe that the result is compatible with our overall objective, that each book should be within the grasp of any educated person who has the motivation to study its subject-matter.

Dennis H. Holding
Louisville, 1980

The Second Edition

The present revision differs in several ways from the first edition, although we have attempted to preserve the strengths of the original. Thus, the book remains as thoroughly integrated and cross-referenced as is practicable in a work by multiple authors and as before, except for the introductory and final chapters, sufficient space has been allotted to allow the contributors to provide thorough coverage of each topic at a non-trivial level of explanation. There has been a persistent attempt to maintain a uniform level of difficulty throughout the varied but cohesive chapters of the book. As in the first edition, the content of the individual chapters has been determined by an overall plan for the volume as a whole.

Within this framework, there have been changes in both content and emphasis. Each chapter has undergone some revision, one chapter has been deleted to allow the introduction of another topic, and several new authors have participated in the project. Students of the first edition will notice that the introductory and final chapters have been revised to accommodate these changes. The first major change is that the engineering emphasis of the original feedback chapter has now been replaced by a stress on psychological and physiólogical considerations in a kinesiology-based contribution by new authors. The chapter on motor programs remains appropriate in its present form, but has been thoroughly updated. However, another major change will be seen in what was the chapter on single-channel theory, but now, under new authorship, has become a chapter on attention processes.

The new chapter on discrete movements has also undergone a change of authorship, and is now broader in coverage of fact and theory. It will next be noted that, with some regret, the chapter on motor memory has been removed entirely; research in this area has been sparse in recent years, and the space was needed for other contributions. The most lightly revised chapter is the treatment of sequential reactions, where recent developments are noted in a short, final section. Again, the tracking chapter seems to have required little revision beyond a selective updating. A new author has written on skill learning, in a chapter which now encompasses the entire history of the acquisition of skill. The chapter on cognitive skills is a completely new addition to the book, and concentrates on the processes that control a representative selection of practical skills. Finally, the handicaps chapter, which proved successfully to unify much of the material preceding it, has been retained in its original form, although again with thorough revision.

Apart from these changes in the composition of the book, it will be apparent that there has been a shift in emphasis discernible in almost every chapter. In a word, the new edition is more cognitive. Although the change in emphasis is most readily apparent in the new chapter on attention and the newly added chapter on cognitive skills, there will be found throughout the volume a concern to understand and explain the processes underlying skilled behavior. Such a concern accurately reflects the interests of contemporary skills research in those cognitive processes that have always been required, but less frequently acknowledged, in the analysis of skill. Hence, it may be hoped that the present edition will remain viable for some time to come, and that few changes will be required in any eventual third edition.

Dennis H. Holding
Louisville, 1988

The Contributors

NICHOLAS C. BARRETT   Research Fellow, School of Psychology, Curtin University of Technology, Western Australia, *Australia*.

ANN M. COLLEY   Lecturer, Department of Psychology, University of Leicester, *England*.

DENIS J. GLENCROSS   Professor, School of Psychology, Curtin University of Technology, Western Australia, *Australia*.

M. HAMMERTON   Professor, Department of Psychology, University of Newcastle upon Tyne, *England*.

DENNIS H. HOLDING   Professor, Department of Psychology, University of Louisville, *USA*.

PATRICK M. A. RABBITT   Professor, Age and Cognitive Performance Research Centre, University of Manchester, *England*.

ALAN W. SALMONI   Associate Professor, School of Human Movement, Laurentian University, Ontario, *Canada*.

RICHARD A. SCHMIDT   Professor, Department of Kinesiology, University of California, Los Angeles, *USA*.

CLARK A. SHINGLEDECKER   Senior Scientist, NTI Incorporated, Dayton, Ohio, *USA*.

JEFFERY J. SUMMERS   Senior Lecturer, Department of Psychology, University of Melbourne, *Australia*.

CHRISTOPHER D. WICKENS   Professor of Psychology and Head, Aviation Research Laboratory, University of Illinois, *USA*.

CAROLEE J. WINSTEIN   Postdoctoral Research Associate, Speech Motor Control Laboratories, University of Wisconsin, Madison, *USA*.

Chapter 1

Skills Research

Dennis H. Holding

All human skills involve the coordination of perception and action. However, different types of skill place varying emphases on the contributions required by perceptual processes, cognitive decisions, and motor control. Although research on skills might reasonably cover the entire range of human activities, the work considered in this volume lays most stress on those activities in which there is a significant motor component. Riding a bicycle, for example, or playing a guitar, are clearly examples of skilled performance. So too, in a sense, are achievements like solving a crossword puzzle or delivering a political speech, but these activities make almost incidental use of the subordinate yet crucial skills of writing and speaking. The bicycle and guitar activities differ from one another in some ways, but both are important as instances of perceptual-motor skill. Their skill component derives in a major way from the bodily actions which compose them. This is what distinguishes the majority of the skills covered by this book, setting them apart from the more restrictedly cognitive kinds of performance which puzzles and speeches demand.

It is true that, for instance, learning to read is often considered to be acquiring a skill, or that it is natural to talk of differences in skill at chess. In fact, Bartlett (1958) has gone so far as to argue that thinking itself is a human skill. However, extending the idea of skill in this way introduces quite different research issues, explanatory concepts, and kinds of methodology. Research on chess play, for example, which has been surveyed by Holding (1985), revolves around questions concerning the parts played by pattern recognition or by operations on the search tree in determining the choice of moves, and depends on techniques such as protocol analysis and memory testing. These issues and methods are far removed from those pertaining to more traditional skills, and derive from a different body of theory and experimentation, despite the probability that both groups of activity share cognitive processes in common.

Human Skills. Edited by D. Holding © 1989 John Wiley & Sons Ltd

In consequence, our current concerns are primarily with the kinds of issue raised in studying tasks from sports and athletics, like playing football, sailing boats, or throwing the discus; from the armed services, like piloting aircraft or gun-laying; from business and industry, like key-punching or lathe operation; or from everyday activities, like opening cans or washing dishes. It is to our advantage that these kinds of perceptual-motor performance define a research area possessing both historical continuity and some degree of theoretical coherence.

BACKGROUND

The study of skills began quite early in the history of experimental psychology, perhaps with Bowditch and Southard's (1880) study of motor memory, with Bryan and Harter's (1897) work on Morse code communication, or with Woodworth's (1899) analysis of the characteristics of repetitive, timed movements. After this period, however, research activity was sparse until the Second World War. There had been a number of early finger-maze studies, some industrial studies of time, motion, and fatigue, Thorndike's (1927) demonstration of the effect of knowledge of results on line-drawing, and a sprinkling of relevant papers in the late 1930s; but the real impetus for skills research came from wartime demands for high-speed and high-precision performance.

Tracking skill, which requires the accurate following of a target or course (see Chapter 7), is involved in critical tasks like flying, driving, or aiming. Thus, although many studies of single movements were made, the tracking task became the major skills exemplar. The analysis of tracking entailed the use of formulations from control engineering, which soon led to the first description of the skilled performer as a 'closed-loop' system (Craik, 1947); this approach represents human functioning in the manner of a servo-mechanism with corrective feedback. This kind of engineering analogy, most recently enriched by contributions from modern control theory, led to the introduction of feedback concepts into the study of knowledge of results (with the evental outcomes described in Chapter 2). Further postwar liaisons with engineering led to the growth of applied human factors studies (cf. Fitts, 1951) and, in a different direction, to the adoption of mathematical information theory into psychology (Hick, 1952).

Studies of reaction time attained new importance in the context of information theory and its psychological applications. The finding that reaction times in close succession would interact, coupled with the idea that human servo-action was intermittent, yielded the conception of the human operator as a limited-capacity information channel (see Chapter 4 for subsequent modifications). Together with converging developments concerning the selection of information in perception, these views soon led to more explicit analytic attempts to trace the flow of information through various processing stages (Broadbent, 1958). Coupled with the flow-diagram techniques derived from computer programming, the resulting information-processing approach rapidly migrated into what has become cognitive psychology, later to be reimported into the skills area.

The 1960s were relatively quiescent, perhaps to be characterized as a period of consolidation and are well represented by the Bilodeau and Bilodeau (1969) survey; however, the 1970s and 1980s have seen a resurgence of motor skills activity, prompted in part by the interests of physical education and kinesiology. The newer interests, in process-oriented analyses, have centered on the problem of how motor behaviour is controlled and organized. Discrete movement tasks (of the kind described in Chapter 5), have supplanted the tracking task as the preferred experimental setting; a parallel development has brought sequential, keyboard tasks into prominence (see Chapter 6). Tasks of these kinds lend themselves to studies of the way in which motor memory is organized and to studies of the human programming of motor sequences (Chapter 3).

All of these issues concerning the analysis of skills are discussed in the book, as is the broad outline of our current knowledge concerning the acquisition of skills (Chapter 8). The most recent trends in the long history of skills research have emphasized the importance of studying those cognitive skills with direct, practical relevance. Speech, writing, and music have been chosen (Chapter 9) as representative of those activities in which the motor demands, while still appreciable, are less apparent than the requirement for cognitive processing. Finally, the special insights afforded by the study of handicaps, the consequent deficiencies and mechanisms of compensation, are shown (Chapter 10) to lead to practical contributions.

VARIETIES OF SKILL

A brief, historical outline, such as is presented in the preceding section, must obviously gloss over a number of distinctions concerning the kinds of skill which have been studied. Although we began by excluding purely intellectual skills from consideration, the question remains whether we can make useful distinctions within the central core of perceptual-motor skills. Many classifications have been proposed, mainly on commonsense grounds, but there is a good deal of overlap between them, and rather obscure technical backing for most.

For example, we may order tasks along a continuum from those with mainly perceptual demands, like radar watch-keeping, to those with mainly motor demands like weight-lifting. This distinction seems to overlap with Poulton's (1957a) division into 'open' skills, which require a good deal of interaction with external stimuli, as against 'closed' skills which may be run off without reference to the environment. The terminology is unfortunate since 'closed' skills are virtually 'open-loop' in feedback terms, and vice versa, but the distinction points up a real difference. In fact, we may compare the 'open–closed' distinction in turn with the older dichotomy between skill and habit, since it is only the closed skill which readily becomes habitual.

Yet another comparable distinction is that proposed by Shiffrin and Schneider (1977) between controlled and automatic processing. Controlled processing is supposed to be effortful, to make heavy demands on attention capacity, and to show little improvement with practice, while automatic processing is relatively effortless, unaffected by capacity limitations, and improvable by practice. There are obvious parallels between the controlled –automatic dimension and the open–closed or skill–habit distinctions, although controlled versus automatic processes are operationally distinguished according to whether the stimulus and response elements in a task are variably or consistently 'mapped'. In other words, if the relation between stimuli and responses remains the same then learning can proceed until performance becomes habitual, but if not, not. Viewing the distinction in this way may be too restrictive for the purposes of skill analysis, since other task characteristics than stimulus–response mapping will help to determine the results of practice. For example, Frith and Lang (1979) have shown that practice effects in two-dimensional tracking depend on the predictability of the target course, as might be expected, and might therefore imply either controlled or automatic processing despite the existence of a consistent relation between target stimulus and joystick response.

A different kind of distinction, which we can perhaps consider orthogonal to the group above, begins with the obvious continuum between simple and complex. Open, perceptual, skilful controlled skills can be either simple or complex, as can closed, motor, habitual automatic skills. These differences in complexity, in practice, often run parallel to the difference between gross and fine skills, although the correspondence is far from perfect. Gross skills are those which involve whole-body movement and, barring competition gymnastics, are often less complex than fine skills which require manual dexterity. Finally, tasks of discrete movement, and their sequential counterparts, may be contrasted with tasks of continuous movement. This distinction is not as clear-cut as might first appear, since most discrete tasks involve segments of continuously graded responses rather than simple muscle twitches, but the dichotomy does allow us to distinguish between pushing a button and steering a car. Again, the first is usually simple and the second more complex, so that for many purposes all three distinctions may be treated together.

It seems, then, that we have arrived at an intuitive two-factor classification of skilled tasks or, at least, an analysis in terms of two broad groups of factors. If such a result were to coincide with the outcome of statistical analysis of human abilities, the skills area might be simply partitioned. Unfortunately, those factor analyses of performance abilities which are available tell a much more complex story. In Fleishman's (1958) work, 31 different tasks were performed by over 200 airmen; the tasks included the pursuit rotor, rudder control, dial-setting, and other apparatus tasks, measuring a wide range of different skills. Correlations between these tasks yielded as many as ten different factors, of which seven had some general importance. The most prominent factors were spatial response association, fine control sensitivity, speed of reaction, arm movement speed, arm–hand steadiness, limb coordination, and rate control; in addition, there were factors confined to particular experimental tasks. Later work has revealed many other factors such as manual dexterity, which is separate from finger dexterity and from wrist–finger speed; and whole-body factors like trunk strength and gross body equilibrium (Fleishman, 1966). In all, some eighteen factors have been clearly identified and a number of others undoubtedly exist. Furthermore, the relative importance of these factors changes as a function of the degree of practice an individual has had; one important difference, for example, is that visual abilities give way to kinesthetic abilities as greater skill is acquired.

Later work has attempted to bring order to the situation by searching for more general cognitive abilities whose characteristics are predicted by information-processing analyses. It has been hypothesized that decision-making in highly skilled activities should demand time-sharing ability, or perhaps flexibility in shifting attention from one aspect of a task to another. However, although Keele and Hawkins (1982) designed a number of versions of a reaction-time task calculated to reveal time-sharing ability, the results were essentially negative. The tasks followed a psychological refractory period format in which two signals were presented in rapid succession; the second component could be a letter or a tone, could require a manual or a verbal response, or could be easy or difficult. When any two task versions varied in all these respects, performance on the tasks was uncorrelated, suggesting that no general ability to time-share existed.

Further work gave some evidence for attention flexibility as a general ability, as shown by moderate correlations between two-channel listening and three forms of reaction-time task. However, the evidence was not strong, and it must be concluded that the information-processing approach has thus far added little to the earlier analyses. The same body of work did show that a factor representing speed of repetitive movement gave rise to sizeable correlations between various tapping task and handwriting scores, but this is a relatively specific ability at the same level as those already reviewed above. The same observation may be made of other recently identified abilities, such as dynamic visual acuity. It is certainly of interest to discover that good and poor baseball players may be distinguished on the basis of the acuity differentials produced by varying abilities to perform accurate pursuit eye movements (Horner, 1982), and a factor of this type probably underlies many other skilled activities involving the rapid acquisition of a moving target. Nevertheless, the finding adds yet another item to the already long list of disparate and relatively specific abilities.

This situation is challenging for research purposes, but is impossible to work with as an expository scheme. In order to provide a framework for discussion, therefore, Figure 1 presents a rough classification of a few representative skilled tasks based on the theoretical distinctions discussed above. These distinctions are those most commonly made, and are employed throughout the book. It is obviously an unsophisticated scheme which could be made more accurate, with some loss of intelligibility, by adding further dimensions or by separating out the existing ones. Note that the classification is by type of task rather than by ability factors, although it would make sense to assume that widely separated tasks in Figure 1 would carry quite different loadings on motor ability factors.

With a little thought, and some tolerance for ambiguity, one may easily locate other skills on this surface. Choice reaction tasks, for instance, are relatively simple and about equally perceptual or motor, and are thus placed somewhere above the sorting tasks on the centre axis. For tasks like lathe operation, their placement must vary according to whether the job is simple and repetitive or has special, complex requirements. Certain skills disclose

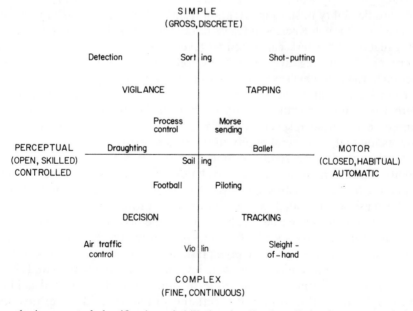

Figure 1. A suggested classification of skilled tasks. Further distinctions are made in the text.

the problem of oversimplifying the major dimensions of the figure. Thus, operating a sewing machine clearly contains a tracking component, which should locate the task below the horizontal axis, but is relatively simple, locating it above the axis. Such minor inconsistencies serve to confirm that the figure is intended only for preliminary orientation. In general, consideration of Figure 1 shows that the interests of this book tend to graduate toward the right-hand and bottom quadrants. The problems of vigilance in particular, in the top left quadrant, raise a number of separate issues which are dealt with in another volume of the series (Warm, 1984).

By and large, the discrete tasks in the upper right-hand quadrant have been represented by a literature separate from the body of work in the lower, tracking quadrant. They are represented by different chapters for convenience although, as the historical review implied, discrete task experiments are beginning to modify the theories originally generated by the study of continuous tasks. Many theoretical problems of skill are common to both areas of research; in fact, the major problems of how motor skills are organized cut across most classifications.

In what follows, we shall neglect questions of individual differences, being primarily concerned with describing average or standard human performance. Nevertheless, it would be unfair to leave the impression that human skills are uniform, since variations in ability are well documented. Noble (1978), for example, has summarized a very large amount of data concerning the effects of age, race, and sex in human skills. The effects of age, throughout the adult lifespan, on various aspects of human performance, are fully documented in another book in this series edited by Charness (1985). Similarly, a volume is available which details the pervasive effects of sex differences on perception and performance (Baker, 1987). However, the kinds of research question which arise in comparing individuals are largely not those whose investigation is relevant here.

BASIC RESEARCH ISSUES

Some of the principal issues concern feedback, programming, timing, and cognitive control. Consider first the performance of a man who has learned to track the excursions of a pointer moving sinusoidally at the fairly fast rate of one cycle per second. If we obscure the display, or simply have him shut his eyes for a period of 5 seconds, a substantial number of times he will be able to continue tracking as accurately as before (Poulton, 1957b). The errors which begin to accumulate, it should be noted, are principally those of timing; his response cycle lags, or more probably leads, out of phase with the target course. However, once the display information is restored, for the part of a second which is long enough for velocity judgements to become reliable, a rapid correction can be made.

This segment of skilled behaviour illustrates a number of performance features. First, the operator obviously could not continue to track in the absence of input from the display unless his performance were maintained by an appropriate motor control program. Such a program must contain anticipatory, predictor components which, in this case, derive more from extrapolating the prior course of the target than from utilizing direct preview of the course. Next, when his performance drifted away from its original level of accuracy, its return to synchrony was dependent upon restoring the visual display, which presented information on the target course and the feedback from his control movements. In fact, feedback from the operator's own motor input, which we might render as knowledge of the results of his own actions, is needed at the very least to 'trim' the values at which his motor program operates. Earlier in learning, before any appreciable skill had been acquired, the need for corrective feedback would undoubtedly have been much greater. As implied by the work on abilities, in most tasks the early stages of skill tend to rely heavily upon visual feedback, with kinesthetic cues from the joints, tendons, and muscles assuming greater importance as skill develops to the point where the learner can 'do it blindfold'.

Any precise, adjustive movement may be regulated by feedback in two different ways. In the form of terminal knowledge of results, occurring at the end of a movement, the feedback information is used to guide the formulation of the next response; it thus tends to be retained and to have a durable effect on skill learning. It is also true that the guidance of a response can be achieved directly; Smyth (1978) confirmed an earlier finding (Holding and Macrae, 1964) that training by repeated movements to a mechanical stop may provide as effective a learning experience as knowledge of results. However, terminal feedback cues are not only sufficient for learning, but are by far the most commonly employed. The other way in which feedback functions has less effect on learning. In its more immediate form, known as concurrent feedback, the information guides the course of ongoing movements, always provided that these are controlled rather than merely ballistic.

This second function is best illustrated by another example, repeating some of the observations originally made by Woodworth (1899). Consider now the performance of a man making a 3-inch movement with a stylus, aimed to finish exactly on a fixed target. He is operating under 'mixed' instructions, to move as quickly as possible, given that the target must be accurately hit. The shapes of two such movements, plotted against time, are shown in Figure 2. The first movement, carried out with eyes open, consists of (a) a brief initial acceleration, (b) a stretch at constant velocity, and (c) a long deceleration phase. The second movement, which is somewhat less accurate, represents a blindfold attempt. The movement begins in the same way, throughout phases (a) and (b), but the deceleration phase (c) is severely curtailed. The average component movement times, taken from unpublished

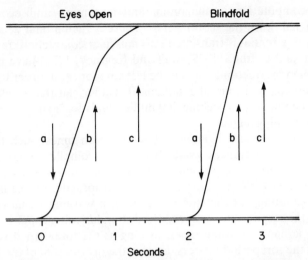

Figure 2. The average time course of visually guided and blindfold hand movements over a fixed distance, based on unpublished recordings. The interval (a) represents initial acceleration (b) is the constant velocity phase (c) is the deceleration phase.

data on eight subjects, are quite instructive. With eyes open, time (a) is 0.14 (b) is 0.59, and (c) is 0.58 second; almost half the time is spent in slowing down. With eyes closed, time (a) is similar, at 0.16 (b) is again similar, at 0.51, but the deceleration time (c) drops to 0.33 second.

The difference in deceleration times is statistically, and practically, significant; the experiment suggests two conclusions. First, the blindfold movement must be the result of a pre-existing program. Second, when visual feedback is available it is used to guide the stylus more accurately, if more slowly, to the target. In fact, the exponential shape of the deceleration curve strongly suggests a servo device homing onto a target by successively reducing the mismatch between the current and the target positions. Like the tracking example, the discrete movement case suggests that both response programming and feedback mechanisms have a part to play in directing skills.

REACTION TIME AND ANTICIPATION

If a person always waited until the appropriate display cue occurred before initiating a response program, his actions would be mistimed or late. A delay might not matter in a simple line-drawing movement, but would be crucial in any continuous or sequential task. The delay comes about because a fixed reaction time must elapse between stimulus and response. A typical reaction time will include several tens of milliseconds while the neural signal is conveyed from the sense organ to the brain, perhaps a hundred or so milliseconds for computation in the brain, and tens more milliseconds for the outgoing signal down the motor nerve. There is then a final delay while the neural action potential is translated into muscular contraction; recent studies (cf. Hanson and Lofthus, 1978; Stull and Kearney, 1978) have made use of this phenomenon, fractionating out the last component in order to distinguish between nervous and muscular fatigue. Together, all these delay intervals will total something approaching 200 milliseconds for a simple reaction time following a warning signal.

An enormous amount is known about reaction times, such that a bibliography of 1000 references would be easy to compile. A good, selective account of the application of reaction time studies to skills research is given by Welford (1968). Without attempting to encapsulate all this information, it is worth pointing out that the presence of a warning signal makes a big difference; the response to an unexpected stimulus will normally take at least twice, and perhaps up to ten times, as long as the forewarned version. The duration of the foreperiod matters, as does the distribution of the foreperiods when many tests are given. Reaction times also depend upon the sense modality which conveys the stimulus cue, the part of the body used for response, and of course the age, sex, and state of arousal or fatigue of the subject.

The reaction time to a highly probable stimulus is much faster than the reaction time to an improbable one; although a complication (Gottsdanker and Kent, 1978) is that low-probability stimuli embedded in blocks of high-probability trials seem to benefit from the subject's general preparedness. When the person has to prepare for a choice reaction, with one from among several possible stimuli to be presented, the probability of any one stimulus occurring is reduced according to the number of possible alternatives. The result, roughly, is that an equal increment is added to the reaction time whenever the number of alternatives doubles. However, the slope of the increase may be flattened or even abolished by extensive practice or by the special kind of compatibility which occurs when the stimuli are signalled by the response keys touching the subject's fingers. Obviously, choice reaction times will particularly affect skills at the perceptual end of the continuum while tracking skills, located in Figure 1 toward the motor end, seems to correlate best with simple reaction times (Loveless and Holding, 1959).

One formulation which fits much of the choice data is Hick's (1952) law to the effect that choice reaction time is equal to $K \log (n + 1)$; here, n represents the number of alternatives, and K is a constant which, when n is 1, will equal the simple reaction time. This formula shows the increase in reaction time from, say, a two-light choice to a four-light choice, as equal to a further increase from four to eight lights, in accordance with information theory. More recently, Smith (1977) proposed modifying the equation to read $K \log (n\, C/E + 1)$; the new variable E is introduced to take into account the strength of the stimulus (reacting to a faint light will take longer than reacting to a bright one). The variable C is important since it draws attention to a feature of reaction times which we have not so far considered: their dependence upon requirements for speed or for accuracy. When the task conditions, or the subject's strategy, emphasize speed, the value of C will be small and the reaction time fast; with a set for accuracy, C will be larger and the reaction time correspondingly slower.

The fact that people may decide to opt for speed or for accuracy, thus modifying their reaction times or movement response times, has attracted a good deal of research. Fitts (1966), for example, showed that monetary pay-offs for speed or accuracy will influence choice reaction times, a set for accuracy inducing a skewed distribution of longer times. Later work has concentrated on the factors affecting individual speed–accuracy tradeoff functions, with accuracy as the dependent variable plotted against constrained changes in reaction time. In tasks which permit a tradeoff, the subject may achieve greater accuracy by the expenditure of more time. The exact form of the function will depend upon the measure of accuracy used, as well as upon extraneous factors. Fortunately, Pew (1969) finds that taking accuracy as $a + b$ log (prob. correct responses/prob. errors) makes the relationship with reaction time approximately linear (a and b are merely the intercept and slope constants). The ways in which reaction times may be manipulated have been discussed by Wickelgren (1977): issuing instructions; offering pay-offs; setting deadlines; setting lower and upper time-limits; synchronizing responses to a second cue. The partitioning of naturally occurring reaction times, without constraints, seems to be the least satisfactory method.

The natural variation of elapsed time may not always reveal a speed–accuracy tradeoff. However, in the case of response times for graduated movements, it will usually be found that slower responding yields higher accuracy (cf. Siddall, Holding, and Draper, 1957). A fairly clear example of the orthodox relationship between speed and accuracy is shown in Figure 3. The mean error and time scores are taken from the study on blindfold line-drawing, reported earlier in connection with the deceleration phase of discrete movements. It can be seen that a straight line produces a good fit to the data, with errors decreasing as the time taken lengthens. While the relationship will take this form for many tasks there are, obviously, some skills like dart throwing, or even bicycle riding, which provide reversals of the relationship such that slow responding leads to increased error.

There are also exceptions in reaction times, which in most cases are found in tasks based upon judgements. Holding and Dennis (1957), for instance, found that shorter times were associated with the correct responses rather than with the errors made in a sound localization task. Presumably the subjects made errors when they were uncertain, and the uncertainty made for delays in responding. Similar effects are to be expected in many cases

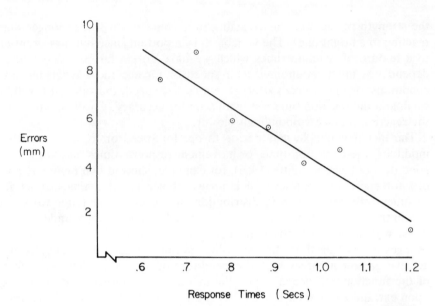

Figure 3. Speed–accuracy tradeoff. Shorter response times are accompanied by larger errors.

where tasks may be varied in difficulty, since it is quite likely that a difficult version will provoke both long reaction times and many errors.

In general, measuring the time elapsing before a response gives a comparatively gross indication of the underlying processes. We may expect a long reaction time sometimes to result from useful processing activity, and thus to accompany accuracy, or else simply to reflect bafflement. Again, a short reaction time may occur because little processing is needed, or because the subject has abandoned any attempt at accuracy in favor of guessing. Thus, speed–accuracy functions will only yield reliable predictions in certain tightly-controlled situations, although the ability to make and to modify the tradeoff will usually form part of the development of a skill.

Whether fast or slow, the existence of a reaction time of any length is a recurring obstacle to a skilled activity, as the smooth performance of a skill is disrupted whenever a response does not occur on time. Thus, achieving proficiency requires that the task cues must be predicted in advance in order to offset the delay in responding which would otherwise occur. For this reason, the most important single feature of highly skilled performance is the development of anticipation. Clearly, the most predictable skilled tasks are those which will yield best learning and performance. In one form, predictability may come about as a result of direct preview of forthcoming cues, as when portions of a tracking course are visible in advance; this has been termed 'receptor anticipation' (Poulton, 1957b).

Predictability in the form of 'perceptual anticipation' may come about as a result of practice with recurring features of a task, as Noble and Trumbo (1967) confirmed in several tracking studies. In one of these, varying the number of repeating, and therefore predictable, elements of a step-tracking course produced differences which remained throughout nine days of practice and a three-month retention interval. It can also be shown that individual skill development accompanies an increasing capacity for anticipation. Pew and Rupp (1971) tested children aged ten to sixteen, who showed consistent age differences, in two measures of tracking ability. Their 'system gain' scores, which imply responsiveness to error feedback, increased with age; more importantly, the older children showed smaller 'effective time delays', having successfully learned to discount their reaction time-lags by making use of anticipation.

As an example from discrete movements, there is the classic demonstration by Leonard (1953) of the effects of advance information in a serial reaction task. In the standard form of the task, the subject moved a lever to one of the outer corners of the apparatus in response to the appropriate signal light. With provision for anticipation, the signal for the next destination was lit while the subject was still returning the lever to its starting point; this procedure led to fast and almost automatic performance. It is clear that such advance cues would permit the early initiation of an appropriate motor program for the control of timing and of spatial movement characteristics. Welford (1968) suggests that the automaticity of performance which advance cues produce results from their pre-emption of the attention normally directed at feedback cues, although it seems sufficient to assume that the programming by past experience of simple movements renders feedback unnecessary.

COGNITIVE CONTROL AND ATTENTION

The preceding sections convey something of the background to research issues considered in the ensuing chapters. In addition, there is a variety of theoretical problems concerning the internal processing and organization of skills. For example, it soon becomes obvious that the individual muscle group is not the appropriate response unit for analysis. Many actions require the coordination of different muscle groups, as in using both hands and feet to play the organ, or one hand and one foot in sawing logs. Again, different muscle groups may produce functionally equivalent results, such that pushing, kicking, or butting may all have the effect of moving an obstruction. The approach taken by Turvey, Shaw, and Mace (1978) is to define the groups of muscles used for a particular purpose as constituting a single coordinative structure. It is presumed that any pattern of activity will be determined by a structural prescription, specifying which group of muscles are required, and by a metrical prescription specifying the relative amounts of necessary muscular activity. Interaction with the environment will have the effect of tuning these prescriptions gradually to produce more successful activities as learning proceeds. Presumably the metrical prescription for an activity is most easily modified, thus leading to positive transfer across related skills.

Other descriptions of the ways in which skills are controlled also have hierarchical characteristics, such that different functions and properties are assigned to higher and lower levels of control. This is the case with Mackay's (1983) model for speech production, for example, which assumes that a mental system is responsible for abstract concepts while a phonological system organizes the relevant muscle groups. A similar distinction between higher and lower levels of organization was already present in Shaffer's (1975b) theory of typing, where an overall structural representation is distinguished from a command representation which controls the movement output. Many questions arise in connection with these hierarchical models, concerning which levels control the timing of actions, how various types of error might be generated, and whether control is passed from one level to another or maintained in parallel. Some of these questions are discussed in Chapter 8, and a more extensive treatment will be found in Colley and Beech (1989).

A different set of questions concerns the amount of information that can be attended and handled at any given time. In executing a skill, cues arising from feedback and from the task itself must be integrated with stored experience, while the demands of decision-making, the planning and command of response sequences, all form an additional information-handling load. The simultaneous load imposed by two such tasks may be impossible to process satisfactorily. This observation gives rise to the common view that processing by the human brain, at least with respect to the upper levels of a control hierarchy, consists of routing information through a single channel of limited capacity. This approach has had some practical success, leading to the design of various dual-task techniques. Thus, in appropriate circumstances, it has been shown that when a person is overloaded his performance on a secondary task will suffer in comparison with performance on a main task of interest. The secondary-task decrement has been used in the assessment of various stresses, such as noise or fatigue, to reveal impairments which would not be apparent in the scores for the main task performed alone.

However, it might be that the capacity limitation occurs at some other stage, perhaps at the level of response selection rather than processing. McLeod (1977), for instance, showed that two different manual responses would interfere with one another but that responses from different modalities, such as manual and vocal, seem to permit 'multiprocessing' to proceed without interference. There are other occasions when two tasks may be performed together without loss of efficiency and, since Allport, Antonis, and Reynolds (1972) demonstrated that paying simultaneous attention to both auditory and visual tasks is quite feasible, it is clear that the single-channel view requires modification. One possibility, raised by Kahneman (1973), is that it is the mental effort required by attention, rather than the computing capacity of the brain, which sets a limit on processing. However, this approach does little to distinguish between those task pairs which do or do not conflict. Hence, in the previous edition of this book, Kinsbourne (1981) suggested as an alternative that the amount of interference between dual tasks depends on the functional cerebral distance separating representations in the brain of the two tasks. Such an account predicts very well the interactions between dual tasks primarily represented in the left or right hemispheres, for example, and has proved quite fruitful.

The current approach, represented in Chapter 4, has the advantage of allowing for the possibility that different pairs of tasks may produce varying amounts of mutual interference. The effects may be demonstrated by inducing subjects in time-sharing experiments to vary the distribution of their attention between the two tasks. If one then plots the scores on one of the dual tasks against the scores on the other, the result is a graph known as a 'performance operating characteristic'. Such a graph will display the degree of interaction between the two tasks. Thus, if both tasks compete for the same cognitive resources, when the subject concentrates on one then the other will suffer, and the graph will show a typical arc. If, on the other hand, the two tasks use different resources, the scores on one will be independent of those on the other, and the graph will be rectilinear. Hence, the degree of 'bowing' of the performance operating characteristic exhibits the degree of interference between the two tasks, and can be used to infer how cognitive resources are allocated. People differ in their abilities at time-sharing, by the way, but can be assisted by appropriate training.

Not only the problems concerning the cognitive control of skills, but all of the basic issues discussed above will be found to recur throughout the text. In addition to the chapters specifically directed to these topics, the treatments of discrete, sequential, and tracking skills, and the discussion of handicaps, all make use of the concepts outlined in this introductory survey. An appreciation of the issues posed by feedback and programming mechanisms, reaction times and anticipation, cognitive control and attention, seems fundamental to the understanding of skilled behavior.

SUMMARY

This chapter attempts to describe the kinds of perceptual-motor skill appropriate to the book, and to introduce in a preliminary way some of the more important theoretical and research issues. The development of the subject is outlined, from its beginnings in the last century, through the wartime expansion, and to its present state of vigor. Distinctions are made between different types of skilled task according to the degree to which they are open, skilled, perceptual, or controlled, and according to the extent to which they are simple, gross, or discrete. The factorial analysis of human abilities shows that skills depend upon a very large number of different factors. Basic research issues first focus upon the concepts of feedback, and of motor control programs, both of which are illustrated in discrete and continuous tasks. Next are the problems of timing, the lags in performance entailed by reaction and response times, whose effects must be circumvented by the development of anticipation. Finally, the issues arising in the control of actions and dual-task performance are briefly introduced as topics which claim increasing attention in the study of skilled behavior.

Chapter 2

Sensorimotor Feedback

Carolee J. Winstein and Richard A. Schmidt

Human beings are capable of highly skilled activities which often involve complex interactions between sensory and motor processes. When we compare the movements of a professional dancer, athlete, or musician with those of an amateur, the differences in smoothness, spontaneity, and facility are obvious, but the underlying control processes responsible for these qualitative distinctions are only beginning to be understood. There has been considerable progress in our understanding of human skills over the last few decades, primarily due to concurrent and often collaborative work in various fields including psychology, engineering, biology, kinesiology, medicine, and the neurosciences.

This chapter is concerned with the use of sensory information, sometimes referred to as *feedback*, for the control and acquisition of skilled actions. The term 'feedback' is used here in a somewhat broad sense to describe incoming information from a variety of intrinsic and extrinsic sources, including vision, touch, and proprioception, all of which could exert important influences on the control of action. Feedback processes are most often associated with mechanical closed-loop, servo-control devices. Such control systems usually consist of a reference mechanism which compares the actual output, sampled by the feedback, to some reference goal or homeostatic 'setpoint'. The difference between the setpoint and the actual output is computed as an error, which in turn is conveyed to an executive level where a new set of output commands are generated. These closed-loop, negative feedback systems have been used quite successfully to model the control of skilled behaviors, particularly those involving continuous movements such as tracking (e.g. Pew and Rupp, 1971; Moray, 1981; also see Chapter 8, this volume). However, as some have argued, 'setpoints', reference mechanisms, and one-to-one mapping of error input into output

Human Skills. Edited by D. Holding © 1989 John Wiley & Sons Ltd

commands in multidimensional systems may have no real biological correlates (e.g. Turvey and Kugler, 1984; Kelso and Kay, 1984).

Evidence from both human and animal research suggests that some actions are organized centrally, and are not critically dependent on peripheral sensory input (see Schmidt, 1988, for review). Nearly two decades ago, Taub and his colleagues (see Taub, 1976, for a review) demonstrated with monkeys that when both forelimbs were deafferented, these monkeys could use their forelimbs nearly normally for climbing, swinging, eating, and grooming. Additional evidence from human subjects deafferented from trauma, disease, or anesthetic nerve blocks further supported the animal findings that purposeful voluntary movement was entirely possible in sensorially deprived conditions (Lashley, 1917; Smith, Roberts, and Atkins, 1972; Rothwell et al. 1982).

More recent evidence for the central generation of action comes from the work on stereotyped innate behaviors such as locomotion, respiration, and ingestion (e.g. Grillner, 1975; Selverston, 1980). Scientists from differing perspectives have characterized the central organization of action by appealing to specialized neural networks which have been variously termed central pattern generators (e.g. Grillner, 1981), motor programs (see Chapter 3, this volume), and coordinative structures (e.g. Bernstein, 1967; Tuller, Turvey, and Fitch, 1982). One consistent finding which emerges from these diverse approaches is that peripheral feedback (e.g. sensory signals) is certainly capable of modifying centrally organized actions, but it is not essential for purposeful movement to occur (e.g. Keele, 1968; see also Requin, Semjen, and Bonnet, 1984). It is the modification of centrally-generated actions by feedback-based processes which is the central theme of this chapter.

The motor behavior literature from the last few decades has generally abandoned the controversial question of whether 'central' or 'peripheral' processes govern motor behavior (see Kelso and Stelmach, 1976; Keele, 1986, for discussion). Instead, it is now generally acknowledged that most skilled actions are accomplished through an integration of open- and closed-loop processes—a so-called 'hybrid control system'—and research has begun to focus on the nature of this integration (cf. Cruse et al., 1988).

The extent to which feedback information is used for motor control depends in part on task requirements such as accuracy constraints, movement duration, attentional requirements, and the degree of training (e.g. Schmidt, 1988). A particularly informative example of the effect of these factors on the utilization of sensory feedback was provided recently by Rothwell et al. (1982). They examined the manual skills of a patient afflicted by a peripheral sensory neuropathy which produced an effective deafferentation of the limbs. Their patient was able to perform a wide variety of finger movements with accuracy, and to produce movements of particular distances and forces, but was unable to use his hands effectively for daily activities such as writing, buttoning his shirt, or holding a cup in his hand without continuous visual monitoring. In addition to these difficulties, the learning of new skills was also impaired. He was able to drive his old car—a well-learned activity—but was unable to learn to drive a newly purchased car. Though this kind of sensory loss would be expected to have much less of an effect on more innate activities (e.g. locomotion), it seems that an account of human skills would not be complete without regard for the feedback contribution to motor behavior.

Feedback contributes to both the control and acquisition of human skills, and accordingly, our discussion is divided along these lines. In the first section, we focus on various ways in which sources of *intrinsic* sensory information are capable of modifying centrally organized actions in order to meet certain environmental demands. We begin with a review of the various movement-related sensory receptors which contribute to the sense of movement called *kinesthesis*. In the second section, we consider issues related to the use of *extrinsic* (or augmented) feedback (e.g. knowledge of results) for the acquisition of skilled actions. A more complete account of other issues related to skill acquisition can be found in Chapter 9 of this volume.

MOVEMENT-RELATED SENSORY INFORMATION

All movement-related sensory (i.e. afferent) information can be thought of as one of two types depending on contiguity of the afferent information with the action. That is, some sensory information is available prior to the action, while other information is available during or after the movement. The former category is included with particular reference to visual signals which work 'ahead' of the action both to regulate and trigger the control of coordinated movements (e.g. Lee and Young, 1985). Sensory information available during or after the action, often termed 'feedback', can be further subdivided into that which is intrinsic or inherent to the action, and that which is extrinsic, or augmented, and supplemental to the intrinsic information. This general classification scheme is outlined in Figure 4. We have assumed a functional use of the term 'sensory' and acknowledge Turvey's (1977) comments that many nervous system descending structures (or so-called 'motor' systems) directly influence ascending structures (or so-called 'sensory' systems) via internal feedback loops (e.g. gamma motoneurons of muscle spindles). Thus, functionally, these 'motor' systems could be considered sensory in nature.

Kinesthesis

The receptors which contribute to one's sense of movement or kinesthesis have typically been thought to be those which are found in muscles, joints,

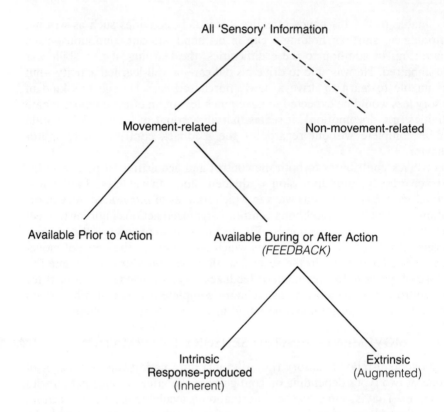

Figure 4. A classification of sensory information.

tendons, and skin. But movement-related information is also derived from visual, vestibular, and auditory input. Originally, the term 'proprioception', as used by Sherrington (1906), described the sensations produced by dynamic action or static position of the body itself, as distinct from 'exteroception' which described the sensations arising from the external environment (e.g. vision). Over the years, the term 'kinesthesis' has begun to replace 'proprioception', and now it is generally accepted that kinesthesis refers to both a sense of movement and to static limb position (Clark and Horch, 1986).

We know that the central nervous system (CNS) can use information from a number of overlapping and often redundant sources to determine movement and position. These sources include (a) the muscle spindle, (b) the Golgi tendon organ, (c) articular receptors, (d) cutaneous receptors, (e) the vestibular apparatus, (f) vision, and (g) audition. We shall briefly discuss these kinesthetic sources as a background for understanding their interaction with central control structures.

Muscle spindle

The muscle spindle is a highly specialized fusiform-shaped receptor which encapsulates several small intrafusal muscle fibers. It lies in parallel with the skeletal or extrafusal muscles fibers enabling it to code muscle length (stretch) and rate of change of length. A critical feature of the muscle spindle is that it has both sensory and motor innervations. Although there are several sensory endings in one spindle, we shall only be concerned with the primary sensory innervation called the Ia afferent. The motor innervation is termed the gamma motoneuron.

Excitation of the muscle spindle's primary sensory receptor occurs when the muscle is stretched. In the spinal cord, the activated primary afferent (Ia) monosynaptically excites an alpha motoneuron which innervates extrafusal muscle fibers from the stretched muscle. Thus, the same muscle which was initially stretched begins to increase its force output. This spinal-mediated reflex is called the stretch reflex, and is the basis behind the clinical knee-jerk tendon-tap test. When the muscle shortens in response to a sudden stretch, the intrafusal fibers are then slackened and the excitatory stimulus to the Ia afferent is removed. Because the stretch stimulus which activates the response causes a contraction in the same muscle which was stretched, this reflex involves *autogenic* facilitation.

If it were not for the gamma efferent montoneurons, when the muscle shortened to a new resting position the intrafusal fibers would slacken and the spindle afferents would be rendered insensitive to subsequent sudden stretch perturbations. The gamma motoneurons, regulated by supraspinal centers, cause the ends of the intrafusal fibers to shorten and thereby re-set a new intrafusal fiber length. This gamma innervation thus enables the muscle spindle to remain responsive over a wide range of muscle lengths.

Initially it was thought that the muscle spindle functioned like a follow-up servo-mechanism to control muscle length (Marsden, Merton, and Morton, 1972). In this way, the intended muscle length would be indirectly controlled by the gamma efferents which directly control the intrafusal fiber length. If the muscle contracted beyond the set intrafusal length, the spindle would become unloaded and diminish its facilitation of muscle contraction. The muscle would stop contracting until the spindle began again to discharge. The critical assumption of the follow-up servo-mechanism notion was that the gamma motoneuron is activated prior to the alpha motoneuron. But experiments done by Vallbo (1971) showed that, in most cases, the alpha and gamma motoneurons are activated together. This process became known as alpha-gamma coactivation.

The exact function of the muscle spindle during voluntary movement remains controversial. Some believe that the muscle spindle discharges only under very specific conditions in which movement is slow or opposed by an external load. Burke (1985) speculated that the muscle spindle could be important in learning a motor task or in performing an unfamiliar voluntary movement, but that in other than these cases the spindle's feedback from the contracting muscle may not contribute to accurate performance.

At one time, muscle spindles were not thought to contribute to one's sense of movement for a number of reasons. First, no one had been able to demonstrate cortical projections from muscle spindles, thus conscious perception from their discharge seemed unlikely. Second, while the spindle discharges could be used by the CNS to compute joint position and movement velocity, the spindle can also be made to discharge by activation of its own gamma efferents, rendering the detection of position or movement ambiguous.

These views were reassessed when, with the development of more precise cortical recording techniques, it was demonstrated that information from muscle spindles does indeed reach cortical somatosensory areas. Also, Goodwin, McCloskey, and Matthews (1972) demonstrated that vibration applied over a muscle tendon in humans produces striking illusions of movement and position of a limb that is actually held stationary (see Sittig, Denier van der Gon, and Gielen, 1985, for more recent evidence). It is believed that the vibration is rather selective for exciting the spindle primary afferents and that this sensory discharge is responsible for the illusion of movement. While there is some concern that the vibratory stimulus is abnormal and therefore may not reveal the normal mechanisms used to sense limb position and movement, empirical evidence from this vibration-induced illusion strongly supports the notion of a conscious, peripherally generated, muscle sense attributed to the muscle spindle.

Golgi tendon organ

Another receptor believed responsible for kinesthesis is the Golgi tendon organ (GTO). GTOs, like muscle spindles, are mechanoreceptors; but unlike muscle spindles, GTOs are sensitive to muscle tension generated through muscle contraction. The GTO is a thinly encapsulated bundle of small tendon fascicles with a fusiform shape, innervated by a single afferent (Ib) fiber. While the receptor endings do respond under high degrees of tendon stretch, they have been shown to respond powerfully to very little tension—even as little as 0.1 g generated by a single motor unit (a small bundle of muscle fibers activated as a unit; Binder et al., 1977). The GTO's location at the musculotendonous junction enables it to sample the overall tension developed in the muscle. Signals from GTOs are relayed back to the CNS via the Ib afferents, which ultimately have an inhibitory effect on the alpha motoneuron of the same muscle which had been contracting (i.e. an autogenic response). This autogenic inhibition is in contrast to the autogenic facilitation associated with the muscle spindle. Some researchers have suggested that together, the muscle spindle and GTO are responsible for the regulation of muscle stiffness, but this is still an issue of debate (Houk, 1979). It seems reasonable to conclude that signals from the GTO inform the CNS about tension in the muscle useful for the regulation of muscle contraction, and are considered to be a viable source of kinesthetic information regarding muscle tension or force.

Articular receptors

Until about 15 years ago, it was believed that kinesthesis about joint position was mainly attributed to the discharges from the receptors located around joints. Articular receptors would change their rate of firing in proportion to the angular velocity of joint rotation, and subsequently adopt different steady firing rates depending on the particular joint angle (Skoglund, 1956). However, later work by Burgess and Clark (1969) revealed that previous recordings from joint receptors had used a biased sample of receptors, and that the majority of these receptors discharged only at the extreme ranges of joint motion. Joint receptors are no longer considered capable of encoding static joint angle. Recent work has revealed that if the muscles around the joint are actively contracting, the tension in the joint capsule is elevated which influences the discharge pattern of the joint receptors (e.g. Grigg, 1976). Thus it appears that the information these receptors are capable of providing can be influenced by the state of active contraction in the surrounding muscles.

Precisely what the joint receptors code is still open to debate. Some researchers ascribe a purely protective function (e.g. preventing hyperextension) to these receptors, while others suggest that, together with information from additional relevant sources (e.g. gamma motoneuron input), joint position information could be 'computed' by the CNS.

Cutaneous receptors

There are nearly a dozen different types of cutaneous receptor differentiated by their locations and response characteristics, but the majority seem to signal the velocity or acceleration of skin or hair displacement. However, some researchers have reported hair follicle receptors discharging in a manner synchronous with joint movement (Appentung, Lund, and Seguin, 1982). In addition, there are two slowly adapting cutaneous receptor types, one of which has been shown to respond to changes in joint position (Knibestol, 1975). The paucity of these latter receptors, relative to the total population in the skin, suggests that joint angle coding might be inadequate, but joint movement coding would be more feasible.

The role of cutaneous receptors may also vary as a function of location. In one study, anesthesia of the skin around the knee joint produced no deficits in knee position sense (Clark et al., 1979). While skin sensation may play only a minor role, if any, in position sense of the knee, a quite different situation prevails with that of the fingers. Skin receptors found in the fingers seem to serve a facilatory or supportive role for kinesthetic sensations elicited from other nearby sources (Clark, Burgess, and Chapin, 1983). These researchers reported that anesthetizing the fingertip, but not the skin around the moving interphalangeal joint, substantially impaired subjects' ability to sense slow joint rotations. Further, anesthetizing the skin on the thumb also diminishes subjects' ability to sense slow displacements of the index finger. In contrast, anesthetic injected into the joint produced no noticeable impairment.

Cutaneous receptors may play an important role in kinesthesis in the hands, feet, and face—regions of skin that have an especially high innervation density compared to other skin areas, and which most often mediate interaction with the environment. Pacinian corpuscles—receptors found on deeper bone and joint tissues and in the dermis of the hands and feet—exhibit acute sensitivity to acceleration (LaMotte and Montcastle, 1975). These same receptors have been shown to respond to low-amplitude, high-frequency vibrations, a capability which is believed to underlie coordinated adaptive responses during precision grip (e.g. Johansson and Westling, 1987; see discussion in section on Triggered Reactions).

Vestibular apparatus

The vestibular apparatus consists of two small sac-like structures called the saccule and utricle, and three fluid-filled semicircular ducts, located in the inner ear. All of these structures contain areas of specialized sensory epithelium with special hair cells. These hair cells in the saccule and utricle are sensitive to various positions of the head with respect to gravity. The hair cells associated with the semicircular ducts are stimulated by movement of the fluid contained inside the ducts. The three ducts are arranged at right angles to each other and thus react to movements in all directions. While the ducts react to movements of the head, the saccule and utricle respond to alterations in head position. The vestibular apparatus is undoubtedly important for balance and posture control (cf. Nashner, Black, and Wall, 1982) as well as head orientation for visual and auditory perception.

Visual proprioception

The sensory receptors discussed thus far are considered proprioceptors—those receptors which process information from within one's body. We now turn to exteroceptors, those concerned with information from outside one's body. Perhaps the most important of these sensory receptors is concerned with vision, which provides information about events in the environment and our own movements within it. So, in a strict sense, the visual system is both a proprioceptor and an exteroceptor (Gibson, 1966, 1979). Indeed, Lee (1978) has proposed a new term, 'exproprioception', which refers to information about the position or movement of the body *relative to* the environment.

Theoretical and empirical support has been offered for the existence of two functionally and structurally different visual systems. Trevarthen (1968) argues that vision involves two parallel processes, one called *focal vision* and the other called *ambient vision*. Focal vision is concerned with events mainly served by the fovea of the eye, its acuity is high, it is specialized for object identification and distinguishing detail, and it seems to make important contributions to tasks involving consciousness (i.e. reading, control of fine movements). In contrast, ambient vision is used for detecting space around the body, including both central and peripheral locations. It provides information about location and movement in space rather than object identity, and seems to make contributions to non-conscious motor activities (i.e. visual orienting).

This two-visual-system distinction seems to have structural correlates represented by the visual cortex and the superior colliculus of the midbrain (Schneider, 1969). Further evidence comes from patients with visual cortex damage (Weiskrantz et al., 1974). These patients, described as having 'blindsight', cannot report seeing a target, but they can accurately point to it if asked to guess where the target appeared.

Gibson (1966, 1979) has described the scatter of light rays from objects in the environment as the optic-flow field. The optical array is the particular pattern of light structured by the various objects in the visual field from which the light reflects. The changes in the optical array when either the observer moves (or something in the environment moves with respect to the observer) produce specific changes in the optical array called *optical flow*. For example, if one moves forward in a stable environment, the optical flow will be an outward expansion of the angles of the rays hitting the retina. In contrast, if one moves backward, the flow will be an inward contraction. If one turns around but stays in the same location, the borders of the visual field will change, but the size of the optical array of an object will not change. Further, if one stands still, but an object in the environment begins to approach, there will be a local expansion in the optic array corresponding to the object.

The importance of the optic flow pattern is that it gives us valuable information about our movements with respect to the environment, a kind of exproprioception (Lee, 1980) or visual kinesthesis. In addition, the optical flow generated as we move tells us about the environment itself in ways which could not be achieved if we remained stationary. In this way, vision and movement are very closely and reciprocally linked. Later, we shall discuss ways in which visual information is used in motor control, and specifically, its role in balance and other skilled activities for which visual input is critical for the initiation and regulation of motor activity.

Audition

The last sensory source we shall consider is the acoustic or auditory mechanism which is a relatively complex system capable of three fundamental functions. It can recognize sound frequency and intensity, as well as localize the source of a sound in space. These functions certainly inform us about events occurring in the environment but, similar to vision, audition can provide us with information about our own movements as well (cf. Henderson, 1977). The sound of our feet contacting the floor as we climb a set of stairs, or the sound of our voice as we speak, are just two examples of how auditory input informs us about our own movements, and may provide valuable information for skilled actions.

We have reviewed the various sources of kinesthesis, the sensory receptors responsible for encoding movement-related sensory information. Now we examine various ways in which this incoming information is used for the modification of centrally organized behavior to produce skilled actions.

MODIFICATION OF CENTRALLY ORGANIZED ACTIONS

The contribution of so-called 'peripheral' input to the production of skilled movements has been an important and controversial issue in the study of motor behavior for nearly a century. Prior to the work in the late 1960s and early 1970s on reflex mechanisms in intact behaving animals (e.g. Pearson and Duysens, 1976), it was generally accepted that modifications that involved a change in behavior required too much time for them to be governed by reaction-time-like processes (Henry and Harrison, 1956; Slater-Hammel, 1960). From an information-processing perspective, it requires several hundred milliseconds for an incoming stimulus to be identified, a new response selected, and that response organized (e.g. programmed) and initiated. Further, these various information-processing stages were shown to be further lengthened by increasing the number of stimulus–response alternatives (Hick, 1952; Hyman, 1953), by lowering the compatibility between stimulus and response (e.g. Leonard, 1959), and by increasing the response complexity (Henry and Rogers, 1960; Klapp and Erwin, 1976), especially when the amount of practice is low (e.g. Mowbray and Rhoades, 1959). Empirical evidence suggests that, in general, the shortest amount of time needed to initiate a voluntary change in behavior is about 150 ms. (Shorter reaction times have been reported for both oralfacial and abdominal muscle responses—e.g. Lansing and Myerink, 1981; Cole and Abbs, 1983). As we shall see, certain types of sensory signal can produce changes in motor output much more rapidly than can be accounted for by these more conscious voluntary processes.

Input-to-output operations

The processing which occurs between the reception of incoming sensory information and a change in motor behavior, the so-called 'input-to-output operations', is thought to involve varying degrees of conscious activity. We can think of these operations on a continuum; 'hard-wired' *automatic* processing such as reflexes is one extreme, where no conscious mediation is involved (e.g. spinal-mediated stretch reflex). These kinds of process are very fast, but the tradeoff is inflexibility with regard to response modification. At the other end of this continuum are voluntary operations where all information-processing stages from sensory identification to response initiation are mediated consciously, called *controlled processing* (Schneider and Fisk, 1983). This type of processing is relatively slow, but the output can be tailored to the specific task demands. In the middle of this continuum are those input-to-output operations which combine fast, automatic, reflex-like processes with slower, controlled, processing operations. This combination is seen in triggered reactions where prestructured responses are elicited by certain patterns of sensory input. Triggered reactions have the speed advantages of automaticity, along with a certain amount of flexibility. This hypothetical continuum is represented in Table 1 and provides a framework for the following discussion.

Table 1
Input-to-Output Operations

Type	Conscious Mediation	Relative Processing Time	Mutability
Reflex (hard-wired)	No	Fast	Low
Triggered	Some	Moderate	Variable
Voluntary	Yes	Slow	High

One fundamental function served by sensory feedback is to inform the system of errors in output so that an adaptive response can be organized and initiated. From an information-processing perspective, it could be reasoned that any voluntary change in behavior would not be possible in a time-duration shorter than that required to go through the stages of information-processing. While limitations in such conscious processing speed may not interfere with movements of relatively long duration, they might provide difficulty for rapid movements or those of short duration. In these short-duration movements, the response would be nearly completed before an error could be detected and a correction initiated consciously. But, the motor control system has a number of 'reflex' or involuntary feedback mechanisms which are not subject to the time constraints nor the attentional requirements necessary for more controlled processing.

Reflex-based modifications

To examine these reflexes, a number of experiments were conducted beginning in the late 1960s in which a subject was asked to maintain a given limb position in the face of an unexpected displacement perturbation which altered the held position. The position of the limb and the electromyographic (EMG) responses from the muscles affected by the perturbation were studied (e.g., Marsden, Merton, and Morton, 1972; Monster, 1973). In general, these investigations revealed that, after various brief delays, the muscle responsible for holding the limb position increased its EMG activity, which increased the torque about the joint, which in turn returned the limb to its original position.

Three distinct EMG responses were identified which differed with respect to latency from perturbation, and the degree to which they could be modified by different instructional sets. The earliest, short-lasting EMG burst, often called the M_1 response, occurred approximately 30–50 ms after the perturbation. It was seen in the stretched muscle, and was associated with the well-known muscle-spindle stretch reflex. The second EMG burst (or M_2 response) was somewhat stronger; it occurred 50–80 ms after the perturbation, and was called the 'long-loop' or transcortical reflex (also called the functional stretch reflex) because it involved cortical, or at least 'higher', CNS centers. Finally, the third burst of EMG activity, referred to as the M_3 response, was seen about 120–160 ms after the perturbation, corresponding to the voluntary response. The M_1 response is essentially unmodifiable by the experimenter's prior instructions that the subject should refrain from resisting the perturbation (e.g. 'let go' or 'do not intervene'), while the M_2 response can be attenuated by such instructions. Further, the number of possible stimulus alternatives affects the latency of the M_3 response, but not the M_2 or M_1 responses. Thus, the least mutable is the fastest (i.e. stretch reflex), while the most mutable is the slowest (i.e. voluntary response) of these responses. There seems to be a tradeoff between flexibility and speed which distinguishes these three responses.

Short-latency stretch reflex (M_1). While the short-latency stretch reflex has been known for many years (see Matthews, 1981, for review), its precise function in human motor control is still unclear and may ultimately be governed by the particular requirements of the motor task (cf. Dietz, 1986). Schmidt (1976b) suggested that under alpha–gamma coactivation, the muscle spindle can presumably detect if the muscle is in a position different from that specified, and then respond with its reflex-based correction if it is lengthened past its specified point. This kind of mechanism was proposed for the regulation of limb movements. However, in postural perturbation and limb displacement experiments, the muscle torque generated by this reflex has not been found adequate to correct the displacement (Gurfinkel, Lipshitz, and Popov, 1974; Crago, Houk, and Hasan, 1976). Indeed, recent investigations have found a suppression of the short-latency stretch reflex during locomotion (Dietz, Quintern, and Berger, 1984). In light of these findings, this fast-acting reflex may only act as a signal to higher CNS centers regarding the type and rate of movement, rather than providing a compensatory force to the system. It may also provide a minor brake to the perturbation so that other mechanisms (e.g. polysynaptic transcortical or voluntary responses) requiring a longer time to be effective can 'catch up'.

While the short-latency stretch reflex does not appear to provide an effective compensation for limb position perturbations, it has been shown effectively to augment the activity of an already active muscle during a rapid response. Dietz, Schmidtbleicher, and Noth (1979) recorded the electrical activity (EMG) of one of the calf muscles (i.e. gastrocnemius) during fast running, finding increased muscle activity within 30–50 ms after ground contact, presumably activated by the sudden calf muscle stretch as the foot contacted the ground. To confirm the contribution of the stretch reflex, they performed a reversible peripheral nerve block using the pneumatic cuff technique. By applying a pneumatic blood pressure cuff around the thigh and leaving it inflated above systolic pressure for 15–20 min, the spindle afferents (and other fibers of similar diameter) are rendered ischemic, but the efferent fibers, because of their larger diameter, are affected little if at all (cf. Laszlo, 1967; but see Chambers and Schumsky, 1978, for a critique of this technique). In this way, the afferent spindle input is temporarily suspended, leaving only the centrally prescribed alpha motoneuron activation. After the temporary nerve block had taken effect, the subjects were tested again. The gastrocnemius EMGs before (A) and after (B) ischemia are shown in Figure 5. Notice that the stretch-induced EMG activity following ground contact is attenuated after ischemia, but the activity prior to contact is unchanged, showing the role of the spindle afferents in this action.

One interpretation of these findings is that the EMG activity prior to ground contact represents the central activation of the muscle; and the activity after ground contract represents central plus peripheral contributions. From a functional standpoint, the feedback provided by ground contact, in the form of a muscle stretch, allowed the precise timing of additional muscle

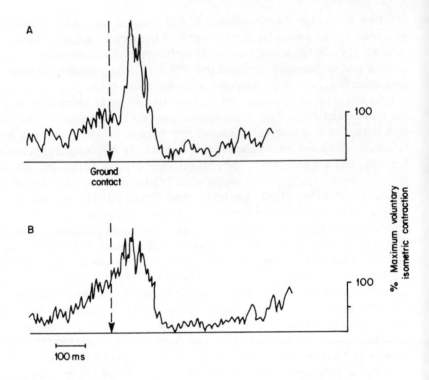

Figure 5. Schematic drawing of averaged muscle activity of right gastrocnemius muscle during running. (A) Activity before the blood-pressure cuff was applied. (B) 20 min after the cuff had been applied, the stretch-induced EMG activity is attenuated, while the activity prior to ground contact remains unchanged. (Adapted from Dietz, Schmidtbleicher, and Noth, 1979).

activation needed for a powerful thrust during the stance portion of the run. Thus, this fast-acting feedback mechanism appeared to adjust the centrally prescribed muscle amplitude, allowing a functional interaction with the environment.

Phase-dependent reflex response. Another example of a more complex but none the less fast-acting feedback mechanism allowing corrections for external perturbations is the phase-dependent reflex response. Researchers using spinalized animal preparations in which the spinal cord is cut below the level of the brain so that higher CNS centers cannot communicate with lower spinal centers, have demonstrated that such spinalized cats, when placed on a treadmill and assisted with balance, can walk or gallop depending on the speed of the treadmill belt. What is of interest to us here is the interaction between this spinally-generated behavior and peripheral input (see Grillner, 1975).

Forssberg, Grillner, and Rossignol (1975a) investigated the capability of chronic spinalized cats to compensate for obstacles encountered while walking. A mild stimulus was applied to the top of the cat's paw as it walked and the corresponding response was analysed. If the stimulus was applied to the paw during the swing phase of walking, the limb would produce an exaggerated flexion motion as if it were lifting the leg over the obstacle. In contrast, if the stimulus was applied during the stance phase when the limb was in contact with the ground, it would push harder into the ground and the stance phase would be shortened. These responses occurred rapidly (i.e. 10 ms latency from stimulus to onset of EMG), and obviously did not involve higher CNS centers because spinalized preparations were used. Thus, the same stimulus elicited two opposite responses (enhanced flexion or extension) depending entirely on the phase of the step cycle in which the stimulus was presented. This phenomenon became known as a 'reflex reversal' because the same stimulus caused two different responses, depending on the phase of the step cycle. These phase-dependent reflex responses are not limited to spinal cat locomotion, as analogous examples have been obtained in humans while standing or walking (Nashner, Wollacott, and Tuma, 1979; Nashner and Forssberg, 1986), and in the control of jaw movements in cats (Lund, Drew, and Rossignol, 1984).

In addition to the so-called 'hard-wired' behaviors such as locomotion and posture, a number of studies have obtained phase-dependent responses in learned behaviors such as speech. Using small displacement disruptions delivered to the lip or jaw during certain speech utterances (e.g. Kelso et al., 1984; Gracco and Abbs, 1985), these studies underscore the flexibility of the input-to-output operations. Compensatory responses to a given perturbation delivered at different points during the response were remarkably rapid (e.g. 30–60 ms), and were unmodifiable by instructions to refrain from resisting the perturbation. In fact, subjects were usually unaware of the perturbations. The compensatory responses involved autogenic or non-autogenic structures depending on the phase of the perturbation within the action, and always tended to preserve the goal-response outcome which usually involved production of a particular utterance that was understandable.

The importance of this kind of central–peripheral interaction rests in its capability to preserve the goal response (i.e. upright posture, specific speech utterance). Clearly, an inflexible response to the same stimulus delivered at different points in the movement sequence could be detrimental to achievement of the movement goal. In the locomotion example, if a flexion response were elicited regardless of the ongoing movement, the animal might fall as the supporting limb suddenly withdrew in response to the stimulus. These reflex-reversals and phase-dependent compensatory responses represent input-to-output processes (i.e. sensorimotor integration) which are rapid, allowing needed error correction, with flexibility preserving the functional goal of the action.

The reflex-reversal in cat locomotion and the phase-dependent compensatory response in human speech are similar in that they both are characteristic of a flexible system which is capable of customizing its adaptive response to the goals of the ongoing action. While it could be argued that the reflex-reversal is inherent, in a sense 'hard-wired' in the CPG network, it is difficult to argue that the compensatory responses to jaw perturbations during (learned) speech actions are inherent. Instead, it is likely that in well-learned responses, as a result of extensive practice, 'learned reflexes' are established (cf. Schmidt, 1987). Indeed, there is some evidence for this speculation which comes from the work on perceptual processing.

Automatic and controlled processing

In an attempt to describe the underlying processes responsible for the difference in motor control between novice and highly practised, skilled performers, researchers as far back as James (1890) have postulated shifts from conscious to automatic processing. As a major by-product of learning, similar descriptions are found in the work of Fitts and Posner (1967), in which the learner begins in the cognitive stage, progresses through an associative stage, and finally reaches the autonomous stage which is characterized by minimal attention to performance. Pew (1966) proposes that skilled actions 'develop with practice beginning with strict closed-loop control and reaching levels of highly automatized action with occasional executive monitoring' (p. 771). Others have characterized the performance of highly skilled artists, musicians, or painters, by emphasizing the automaticity with which movement is accomplished. They argue that, with skilled actions under automatic control, attention is freed for emotional expression (Denier van der Gon and Wieneke, 1969; Schneider and Fisk, 1983). The implied advantage to automatic processing is that it is fast and attention-free in that it does not interfere with verbal-cognitive secondary tasks (also see Chapter 9, this volume).

Recent work done by Schneider and associates (e.g. Shiffrin and Schneider, 1977; Schneider and Fisk, 1982a, 1983) examined changes in visual information-processing strategies across practice regimes involving thousands of trials. In a category-search experiment, subjects had to determine as quickly as possible if either of two presented words was a member of from one to four categories (e.g. is 'parrot' a member of the category 'birds'). The slope of the relationship between reaction time (RT) and the number of categories was considered a measure of processing time for that stage. With extended practice, the slope was reduced from 200 ms/category to about 2 ms/category, indicating a 100-fold decrease in processing time! These and other findings have led these authors to identify two processing strategies which they have termed 'controlled' and 'automatic'. Controlled processing is slow, serial, conscious, voluntary, and is usually employed to deal with novel or inconsistent information. In contrast, automatic processing is fast, nonconscious, and often involuntary, and is invoked to perform well-developed skilled behaviors. Schneider and Fisk (1983) suggest that the interaction between these two processing modes allows both flexibility and speed. There are some interesting parallels with automatic error corrections in movement control such as those seen in the speech perturbation experiments.

We have described three distinct response types: the short-latency stretch reflex (M_1), the long-loop reflex (M_2), and the phase-dependent response. The latter defies the general inverse relationship of speed and mutability outlined in Table 1, for it appears to be highly mutable with regard to the task, yet very rapid. The rapidity of sensory processing in inherent behaviors such as locomotion and posture control has in part been attributed to components of the central pattern generator which functions to modulate incoming signals with little if any involvement of higher CNS structures (e.g. Forssberg, 1979). Well-practised skills such as speech can be viewed in a similar way, except there, the reflex-like automatic processing seems to have developed through extensive practice. We have addressed some of these issues in the last section on the development of automaticity through practice. We now turn to a fourth type of response associated with error correction which combines some characteristics of automatic reflex control and others associated with more controlled processing.

Triggered reactions

The term 'triggered reaction' was first introduced by Crago, Houk, and Hasan (1976) to describe a prestructured, medium-latency (70–200 msec), coordinated response in the same musculature perturbed by a sudden change in muscle length. The difference between these responses and those described earlier (i.e. short-latency stretch reflex, phase-dependent response), is that triggered reactions have been shown to be affected by prior instructions and by the number of potential stimulus-response alternatives (i.e. as in choice RT paradigms). This suggests that these reactions are in some way mediated by at least some of the same information-processing operations underlying conscious voluntary responses.

Recent evidence suggests that in well-practised tasks, these triggered reactions can occur not only in the same muscle affected by the perturbation, but also in distant musculature not directly affected by the stimulus. Of interest to us is that these responses appear to be prestructured, coordinated responses which are triggered by certain learned patterns of sensory stimuli associated with the intended response (Houk and Rymer, 1981).

Precision grip control. In a clever laboratory paradigm, Westling and Johansson (1984; Johansson and Westling, 1987) have shown that, when lifting a small object between the thumb and index finger, if the object begins to slip, a coordinated correction is executed. This correction is manifested by an increased grip force between the fingers, coupled with decreased torque about the elbow joint which precisely offsets the slip. This compensatory response has been shown to occur 60–80 msec after the onset of object slippage.

The evidence suggests that the slippage was detected by the numerous cutaneous receptors located in the fingertips (Westling and Johansson, 1987). The reaction was executed very quickly, fast enough to prevent a noticeable movement of the object, and often the subject did not even know that a slip had occurred. This well-coordinated adaptation response seen in precision grip behavior may represent the triggered reaction described by Crago et al. (1976), but as yet no one has pursued the question of whether these responses are influenced by various manipulations which reflect higher-level conscious processing (e.g. prior instructions, number of stimulus–response alternatives). There is some evidence that the initial increase in grip force elicited by slippage of the object is difficult to suppress, thereby making these responses reflex-like. But the maintenance of such increased forces has been shown to attenuate with prior instructions to let the object drop. This latter mutability is characteristic of volitional rather than reflex control.

Control of posture. Similar triggered responses have been observed in the control of posture. Following an external perturbation which causes a standing subject to sway in the anterior–posterior plane, Nashner (1977) has shown that postural equilibrium is restored by automatic activation of leg and trunk muscles within about 100 msec. This relatively fixed postural strategy is thought to represent a preprogrammed, functionally triggered reaction to a specific pattern of sensory stimuli. The primary sensory stimulus appears to be rotation about the ankle joint, but the coordinated correction response has been shown to occur in leg and trunk muscles not directly affected by the stimulus. In effect, this coordinated postural correction is like the automatic responses discussed earlier which are seen in well-practised activities such as speech and precision grip. Schmidt (1988) has suggested that these triggered reactions are simply a special case of phase-dependent responses.

To this point, we have seen how some forms of sensory input (i.e. unwanted change in joint position, slippage of an object we are attempting to hold), processed by specialized receptors (i.e. muscle spindle, cutaneous mechanoreceptors), are capable of eliciting response modifications rapidly, and apparently automatically with little if any conscious processing. Recent work examining the processing of visual information for motor control suggests that a similar form of automatic or unconscious visual processing may operate. We examine these issues in the next section.

Visual mediation of motor control

Earlier we presented the notion of two functionally and structurally separable visual systems—one primarily for conscious perception, and the other primarily for nonconscious, automatic processing with respect to motor control. Empirical evidence supporting the existence of two distinct systems has been provided by a number of researchers (e.g. Hansen and Skavenski, 1977; Bridgeman, Kirch, and Sperling, 1981). The data suggest that visual information for motor control may involve nonconscious processing as well as well-known conscious contributions from vision.

Bridgeman et al. (1979) used the phenomenon of saccadic suppression to separate the conscious and automatic (or unconscious) visual systems involved with position perception. In this particular experiment (Experiment 2) they asked subjects to press a button if they sensed (consciously) that the position of a visual target changed, and to point to the target's position (a motor task) after the image had been suddenly extinguished. The counterintuitive finding was that pointing accuracy was as good for target displacements which had been detected as it was for those which had not been consciously detected during a saccade. Bridgeman et al.'s results suggested that conscious processing of target displacement was not necessary for the control of pointing. Thus it appeared that unconscious information is available to the motor system for control which is not necessarily available to the cognitive visual system for conscious perception. Schmidt (1988) has suggested that visual information mediated by the ambient system—but not the focal system—may 'bypass' the conscious processing stages and therefore exert more direct control on motor behavior.

Vision and posture. Other evidence that visual information influences motor control in somewhat automatic ways comes from the work with optical flow patterns mentioned earlier (e.g. Gibson, 1966, 1979; Lee, 1980). Lee and Aronson (1974) have shown a powerful relationship between the optical flow patterns from the visual surround and balance control. Their experiment used a 'moving room', where the walls could be made to move toward or away from a standing subject, while the floor remained perfectly stable. In this way, the optical flow pattern could be made to change without actually moving the subject. As illustrated in Figure 6, when the walls were moved

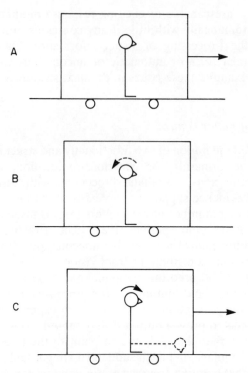

Figure 6. Standing balance as a function of the optic flow created by the moving room. (A) The room is moved forward. (B) The optic flow from the moving room creates an illusion of backward falling. (C) The standing subject compensates by leaning forward. (Adapted from Lee and Aronson, 1974.)

away from the standing subject, an illusion of backward falling was created, and the postural response was to shift the center of support forward for correction. In contrast, when the walls were moved toward the subject, an illusion of forward falling was created and the response was a backward shift of the center of support. Because the floor was not moving, and the subject was in fact stable, the postural correction actually created an imbalance; the subjects, in this case young infants, actually fell over on a third of the trials. Adult subjects do not demonstrate such a dramatic effect, presumably because they are better able to resolve the sensory conflict between proprioceptive and visual information, but a definite increase in postural sway is produced with the same visual stimuli (Flückiger, 1987). Using a slightly different paradigm, Nashner and Berthoz (1978) showed that visual input from the surround could influence automatic postural adjustments within 100 ms of a postural perturbation, further emphasizing the importance of vision in postural control (e.g., Lee and Lishman, 1975; Lee and Young, 1986).

Vision and the timing of motor actions. Visual information has also been shown to play an important part in the timing of motor acts. Lee (1980) has proposed that information derived from the optic flow allows the identification of important external *temporal* events which can apparently be used automatically to control a number of motor activities in humans and animals. First, assume a viewed object which casts an image of size x on the retina. Then, define the *proportionate rate of expansion* of the retinal image as the rate of change in the retinal image (the derivative of x with respect to time, or $\dot{x}$) divided by the image size. At any given distance, a faster-moving object will have a larger $\dot{x}$. Lee (1980) then defines *Tau* as the reciprocal of the proportionate rate of expansion—i.e. $x/\dot{x}$, and showed that *Tau* was proportional to time-to-contact, or the time remaining before the object strikes the eye. For a faster-moving object, the denominator of the reciprocal of the proportionate rate of expansion gets larger and thus, *Tau* will be smaller, indicating that there will be less time until the object arrives.

Data from skilled long-jumpers were consistent with the hypothesis that control of the vertical impulse applied to the ground during the support phase was regulated by time-to-contact with the take-off board (Lee, Lishman and Thomson, 1982; see also Warren, Young, and Lee, 1986, for an analogous discussion of step-length during running). Similarly, in ski-jumping, the optic *Tau* for approach to the take-off point is thought to provide the information for timing the rapid forceful upward thrust of the body. Analogous arguments have been offered to explain how the gannet, as it plummets toward sea with half-open wings for steerage, suddenly folds its wings precisely before hitting the water to spear a fish (Lee and Reddish, 1981).

The significance of these data is that the *Tau* variable, derived from the optical flow, provides an external sensory signal which allows for precise timing of motor actions without much conscious processing. It is true that time-to-contact of an approaching object could be 'calculated' from physical parameters such as object size, distance, and velocity. However, such calculations would undoubtedly take time, require that the object be identified, and its distance and speed computed, and would necessitate a certain level of intelligence. In contrast, *Tau* is specified directly from the visual information, independent from such time-consuming calculations, and appears not to require conscious object identification.

FEEDBACK AND SKILL ACQUISITION

In the previous section, we discussed some of the ways in which intrinsic sensory information contributes to the control of movement, with an emphasis on error correction mediated by relatively automatic, unconscious processes. Now we shift our focus to the research involving the use of extrinsic information, with particular emphasis on the role of augmented feedback as it pertains to the acquisition of human skills.

Augmented information feedback

Aside from practice itself, information feedback provided to the performer about goal achievement is considered to be one of the most critical variables affecting skill acquisition (Bilodeau, 1966; Newell, 1976; Schmidt, 1988). One form of this feedback, termed *knowledge of results* (KR), refers to the augmented information about task success provided to the performer after a practice trial has been completed. It is most often operationalized as a subset of feedback which is augmented, verbal (or at least verbalizable), post-response information about the outcome of the movement response in terms of the environmental goal (Schmidt, 1988). Although there are other forms of augmented feedback (e.g. knowledge of performance; see Gentile, 1972), KR has been the primary focus for research investigating the effects of feedback in motor learning (see Adams, 1987, for an historical review).

In a way analogous to the functioning of intrinsic sensory information, KR can serve as a basis for error correction on the next trial, and as such can lead to more effective performance as practice continues. Because of the importance of feedback, and KR, substantial research has been done in which the effects of a number of feedback variations such as precision, delay, and frequency have been studied (see Salmoni, Schmidt, and Walter, 1984, for a review).

Typically, the research paradigm has been one in which the experimenter uses a relatively simple task (e.g. blindfolded limb positioning) where the usefulness of intrinsic feedback pertaining to movement outcome is effectively minimized. Feedback is then systematically reintroduced (usually in the form of KR) and its effects on the learning process are examined. An implicit assumption underlying this research paradigm is that KR functions with respect to these artificial laboratory tasks in the same way that intrinsic feedback functions in realistic movement situations. While some have criticized the generalizability of this research to real-world, multidimensional, coordinated actions (e.g. Fowler and Turvey, 1978; Newell, 1985), the evidence is extensive that KR is an important determiner of behavioral change in these laboratory settings.

KR affects performance and learning

Scientists have usually found it useful to define learning as a set of internal processes associated with performance or experience, leading to a relatively permanent change in the capability for responding (e.g. Schmidt, 1988). These processes are thought to be complex central nervous system phenomena whereby sensory and motor information is organized and integrated. Operationally, then, learning is inferred from a change in behavior. However, not all changes in behavior reflect learning. Of the numerous variables that determine behavior, some are thought to effect only temporary changes (e.g. drugs) while others are considered to change behavior in more permanent ways.

Because KR is known to influence both performance and learning, it is essential to identify these performance (only) effects before variations in KR on learning can be unambiguously understood (See Salmoni et al., 1984, for discussion). Experimentally, the *transfer design* is a common technique used to obtain a measure of the relatively permanent (i.e. learning) effects of various KR variables. This design typically involves two distinct phases—an acquisition phase in which different groups receive treatments representing various levels of the independent variable, and a transfer (or retention) phase in which all groups are transferred to a common level of the independent variable. The transfer phase is sufficiently separated in time from the acquisition phase, that the temporary effects from the independent variable have had adequate time to dissipate.

In general, KR is considered a practice variable that is capable of effecting both temporary and relatively permanent (i.e. learning) changes in performance. In general, variations which increase the amount of, or 'usefulness of', KR (e.g. precision, frequency, form) during practice are beneficial for both performance and learning (e.g. Bilodeau, Bilodeau and Schumsky, 1959; Newell, 1974; Mulder and Hulstijn, 1985). For example, using a simple line-drawing task, Trowbridge and Cason (1932) examined the effects on performance of three variations in KR precision. While blindfolded, subjects were asked to draw a three-inch line. In the most precise KR condition, the experimenter gave feedback about both the direction (e.g. short or long) and amount of error, in ⅛ inch increments. In a second condition, KR was provided by saying either 'right' or 'wrong'. The movement was 'right' if it was within ⅛th inch of the goal length, and 'wrong' otherwise. In the final and least precise KR condition, the experimenter spoke a different nonsense syllable after the subject finished drawing the line. As illustrated in Figure 7, more precise KR led to more accurate performance during both the acquisition phase and during a no-KR retention test.

While these results and those from a number of other studies (e.g. McGuigan, 1959; Newell, 1974) support the general conclusion that nearly any variation which increases the amount of feedback will lead to beneficial longer-term learning effects, there are a few exceptions to this generalization.

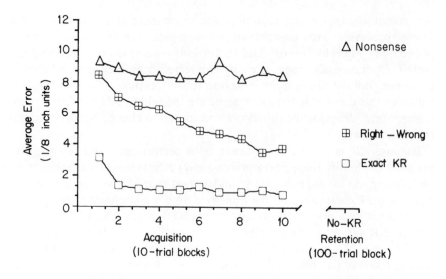

Figure 7. Average error in line drawing as a function of KR precision during an acquisition phase when KR was present and for a no-KR transfer phase. (See Trowbridge and Cason, 1932.)

The guidance hypothesis

Salmoni et al. (1984) have recently proposed that KR functions in a way similar to guidance techniques used in skill learning. With guidance procedures, the learner is literally taken through the task either physically or verbally in order to prevent incorrect responses (Holding, 1970). In general, research with guidance has shown that it is effective—almost by definition—when available, but there seems to be little if any relatively permanent effects on performance remaining once the guidance has been removed (e.g. Armstrong, 1970; Prather, 1971). Salmoni et al. (1984) have proposed that, while KR guides the subject toward the correct response, it can also lead to a kind of dependence on the extrinsic feedback, which *prevents* the processing of other sources of information intrinsic to the task (see also, Holding, 1965; Annett, 1969).

Previous researchers had similarly recognized the detrimental effects of using augmented feedback during training, especially if the subject would ultimately be transferred to a condition without feedback (e.g. Annett and Kay, 1957; Holding, 1965). If KR does function like guidance, it would provide for temporary changes in behavior, but these changes may not necessarily represent learning in the sense of relatively permanent effects.

When temporary performance changes are distinguished from relatively permanent effects using appropriate experimental procedures, variations in

KR which are beneficial to performance during acquisition may actually prove to be *detrimental* for learning as measured on some transfer test. Several such KR variations have been identified, all of which pertain to the scheduling of KR presentations. These variations include: (a) KR relative frequency, which is the proportion of trials receiving KR; (b) summary KR, which provides KR only after a given set of trials has been completed; and (c) bandwidth KR, which provides KR only after trials for which performance is outside a given error tolerance range.

KR relative frequency. The relative frequency of KR is the proportion of practice trials receiving KR, while absolute frequency refers to the total number of KR trials. These fundamental KR variables are relevant to structuring the learning environment, and as such have received considerable attention (see Salmoni et al., 1984). One of the earliest and most influential studies of KR relative frequency was done 30 years ago by Bilodeau and Bilodeau (1958). They manipulated the relative frequency of KR in a simple lever-pulling task, holding constant the number of KR trials (i.e. absolute frequency was 10). By varying the number of interpolated no-KR trials between KR presentations, they produced four relative-frequency conditions with values of 10, 25, 33, and 100%.

Bilodeau and Bilodeau (1958) examined the performance accuracy on the trials immediately following each of the ten KR trials during the acquisition phase; they showed that, even though the 10% group had received ten times the practice as the 100% group, performance was almost identical for the four groups. They concluded that absolute frequency was the important variable for learning and not the relative frequency. However, there were a number of problems with this study, the most important of which was that no retention (i.e. transfer) test was used, so it was not clear whether these performance effects were just temporary in nature, or whether they represented a more permanent effect associated with learning.

Later experiments extended the work of Bilodeau and Bilodeau (1958) by using no-KR retention tests with similar linear positioning tasks, and found that while no group differences were apparent during the acquisition phase, on the no-KR retention tests, groups having practised in low-relative-frequency conditions performed with greater accuracy than those having practiced in conditions with high relative frequencies (Ho and Shea, 1978; Johnson, Wicks, and Ben-Sira, 1981). In contrast to Bilodeau and Bilodeau (1958), these findings suggested that KR relative frequency may indeed be an important variable for learning. Of course, Bilodeau and Bilodeau (1958) had only examined these effects during the acquisition phase where the temporary guiding effects operate.

These later relative frequency findings raise the question of how the interpolation of supposedly neutral no-KR trials could have aided the learning process. One explanation which supports the guidance view described above (Salmoni et al., 1984) is that there are at least two important factors in relative frequency manipulations. First, a condition with low KR relative frequency probably has detrimental effects in that the subject does not have enough information to achieve the proper movement coordination pattern, and has too little information on which to base the next movement. Second, a reduced relative-frequency condition may also have a beneficial effect, in that reduced KR tends to prevent reliance on KR and forces the learner into information-processing operations which provide for independent performance capabilities.

Recently, with a more complex movement task, an attempt was made to optimize the beneficial effects attributed to practice in reduced relative frequency conditions by directly manipulating the distribution of KR and no-KR trials within the practice schedule (Winstein, 1988, Experiment 2). Two groups of subjects practised a discrete arm movement task under either high (100%), or moderate (50%) KR-relative-frequency conditions. In the 50% condition, on each practice day, the proportion of KR trials was relatively high early in practice (i.e. 100%), but was gradually reduced toward the end of practice (i.e. 25%) resulting in an overall relative frequency of 50%. After the two-day acquisition phase, each group was given an immediate (5 min) and delayed (1 day) no-KR retention test. Group mean error scores are displayed in Figure 8 for both the acquisition and retention phases.

There were nearly no differences between groups during the acquisition phase, and only slight differences on the immediate retention test, with the 50% group performing with slightly less error than the 100% group. However, on the delayed retention test, these differences increased, with

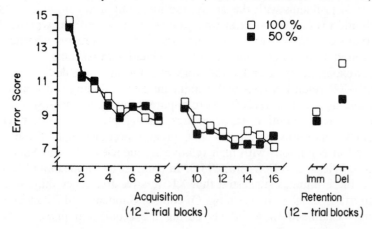

Figure 8. Average error in target movement reproduction as a function of two conditions of KR relative frequency in the two-day acquisition phase (Blocks 1–16), and for the immediate and delayed no-KR retention tests. (From Winstein, 1988.)

subjects in the 50% condition demonstrating 35% less error than those in the 100% condition. These findings run counter to conventional theoretical views (e.g. Thorndike, 1927; Adams, 1971; Schmidt, 1975), which predict that enhanced learning is only affected by increasing the number of feedback presentations, as here more learning was brought about by a *reduction* in the number of feedback trials. The practical implication is that understanding the principles governing the use of feedback for skill acquisition can lead to the intelligent design of feedback schedules for enhanced learning.

Summary KR. Summary KR involves the presentation of KR, usually via a graph of performance against trials, for a set of trials only after the last trial in the set has been completed. It differs from relative frequency in that it provides KR about every trial in the preceding set of no-KR trials, whereas relative frequency provides KR only about the last trial of a set of preceding no-KR trials. Schmidt, Young et al. (1987; Schmidt, Shapiro et al., 1987) have suggested that if the subject in the summary-KR condition only uses the summary information relevant to the last trial in the set, then the summary-KR variation begins to resemble the KR-relative-frequency variation. A number of underlying processes may be shared by these two KR variations.

Over 25 years ago, Lavery (1962) showed that, compared with an immediate condition in which KR was provided after every trial, a 20-trial summary-KR condition was detrimental to performance during an acquisition phase, but was beneficial for performance in a no-KR retention test. Recent experiments examining the effects of different summary lengths found that increased summary lengths generally depressed performance during the acquisition phase. However, Figure 9 shows that with a relatively complex coincident-timing task, subjects who had practised with intermediate summary lengths (i.e. five-trial summary) performed more effectively in a delayed no-KR retention test than either the immediate or the long summary length groups (Schmidt et al., 1987b). A guidance hypothesis predicts such an inverted-U relationship of summary-length to retention performance; extremely short summary lengths provide too much guidance for the development of relatively permanent capabilities for responding, and excessively long summary lengths do not provide enough information for error correction, with some intermediate value being most effective.

In general, these findings are similar to those for KR relative frequency, in that KR variations which were most effective for performance during practice (e.g. 100% KR, immediate KR) were *not* necessarily those which were most beneficial for learning as measured by these no-KR retention tests. These results are contradictory to earlier views regarding KR and motor learning which suggest that KR variations which make performance more effective in acquisition will necessarily benefit learning (e.g. Bilodeau, 1969; Adams, 1971; Schmidt, 1975).

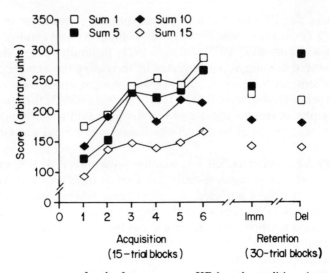

Figure 9. The average score for the four summary-KR length conditions in acquisition and for the immediate and delayed no-KR retention tests. (From Schmidt et al., 1987.)

Bandwidth KR. In bandwidth KR, feedback is given only if the response is outside a given error range. This procedure is quite different from the other KR variations thus far considered in that here, the absence of KR actually informs the subject that the previous response was acceptable and in essence encourages repetition of that response. Sherwood (1988) investigated the effects of bandwidth KR with a ballistic timing task in which a lever was to be moved through a target amplitude in 200 ms. He used 5% and 10% bandwidth-KR conditions and a control condition where subjects received KR after every trial (100% KR). In the 5% bandwidth condition, subjects received movement time KR if their absolute error was greater than 10 ms, while in the 10% bandwidth condition, subjects received KR if their absolute error was greater than 20 ms. He showed no group differences for constant error or variable error during the acquisition phase. However, on a no-KR retention test, subjects in the 10% bandwidth group (average 31% KR trials) were more consistent (i.e. lower variable error) and demonstrated higher overall accuracy (a mathematical combination of constant error and variable error) than either the 5% bandwidth group (average 54% KR trials) or the 100% KR control group.

These retention-test results with bandwidth KR are consistent with those from KR relative frequency, in that overall accuracy was highest for those subjects having practised in conditions with *fewer* KR trials. Since larger bandwidth KR conditions result in reduced KR relative frequencies compared with smaller bandwidth conditions, it is unclear how much of the beneficial effects from larger bandwidths are due to the reduced relative frequency alone. Lee and Carnahan (1985) attempted to unravel the contribution of KR relative frequency from the bandwidth-KR variation by yoking the KR schedules from subjects in the bandwidth-KR condition to a control group. In this way, the relative frequency and distribution of KR trials was exactly the same for both conditions, but the no-KR trials in the bandwidth condition indicated that the response was good and should be repeated, while in the control condition, they were simply trials without feedback. They found that the advantages of bandwidth KR for learning, as measured by performance on a no-KR retention test, were not due simply to the reduced KR relative frequency, but that the customization of the KR schedule to the subject's performance had also contributed to the beneficial effect.

Theoretical implications

Together, the effect of these KR variations suggests that factors other than the number of KR presentations are critical for learning. The emphasis is placed on the contribution of the no-KR trials and what processes they may facilitate. One simplistic view is that conditions with fewer KR trials during acquisition are more *similar* to the no-KR retention test condition than are the 100% feedback conditions in acquisition. This acquisition-test specificity notion described in the motor domain (cf. Henry, 1968; Schmidt, 1988) and the verbal domain (Tulving and Thomson, 1973) predicts that those subjects who practise in the acquisition condition which most closely resembles the transfer test condition will exhibit the more accurate transfer (i.e. retention) performance. Those acquisition conditions with the longest no-KR trial strings (i.e. lowest relative frequency, longest summary length) would most closely resemble the no-KR retention test condition and thus promote the best performance. This interpretation does not account for the superior retention test performance of the five-trial summary-KR group over the 15-trial summary-KR group discussed above (Figure 9). Indeed, the specificity view would predict that a practice condition with all no-KR trials would be best for a no-KR retention test—an outcome which would surely not be achieved empirically. While there may be some beneficial effects from the similarity between acquisition and test conditions, this clearly is not the entire explanation.

A guidance view of KR (e.g. Holding, 1965; Annett, 1969; Salmoni et al., 1984) suggests that the no-KR trials prevent the establishment of dependence on the KR and further, provide an opportunity for alternative information-processing operations which may benefit retention performance. Just what these processing operations are is unclear, but there are several possibilities. First, the no-KR trials may promote response consistency. It has been known for some time that KR encourages response variability (Bilodeau and Jones, 1970), and 'short-term maladaptive corrections' (Bjork, 1987). In contrast, there is also some evidence that during no-KR trials, the subject tends to repeat the previous movement (Ho and Shea, 1978, Experiment 2; Rubin, 1978). Response consistency may be useful at the time of the next KR presentation, whereupon adjustments could be more easily made to a stable response pattern than to one which is more variable. Alternatively, it has been shown that during no-KR trials, performance tends to drift away from the target response. The nature of the drift is obvious at the time of the next KR trial, and this salience may allow effective utilization of KR (Winstein, 1988).

A second possible processing operation which may be facilitated by these KR variations which utilize no-KR trials is the development of error-detection capabilities. During the no-KR trials, the subjects are forced to process their own response-produced feedback and determine the accuracy of their responses. The activities involved in this internal error evaluation process may contribute to the development of an enhanced sensitivity to errors, which would surely benefit performance on a no-KR retention test. There is some evidence that subjective error estimations are enhanced in summary-KR conditions (Schmidt et al., 1987a), but additional work is needed to support these findings.

An understanding of the underlying processes responsible for the beneficial effects from these KR variations will be important for new developments in both theory and practice and these issues offer an exciting frontier for research. Recent perspectives related to the interaction between practice and test conditions from the perspective of transfer-appropriate processes, as outlined in the verbal domain by Bransford et al. (1977), and in the motor domain by Lee (1988), will undoubtedly lead to new insights about the information-processing operations underlying the use of feedback for skill acquisition.

SUMMARY

Movement-related afferent information refers to input which is available prior to the action, and to input which is available during or after the action (feedback). The latter is further subdivided into that which arises from a variety of intrinsic (response-produced) and extrinsic (augmented) sources, that are important for the control and acquisition of skilled actions. Numerous movement-related sensory receptors provide *kinesthesis*—a sense of movement and position. The information these receptors encode also interacts with centrally organized actions, enabling response modifications to meet environmental demands. The automatic nature of these modifications can be seen in reflex-based responses, triggered reactions, and visually-mediated movements. Extended practice facilitates the development of automatic processing of input information, and this capability may underly the triggered reactions which are seen in well-learned skills.

Extrinsic feedback, in the form of knowledge of results (KR), has a role in both temporary performance levels as well as the relatively permanent changes associated with learning. In general, feedback variations which increase the amount of KR during practice benefit both performance and learning. However, there are several feedback variations pertaining to the scheduling of KR presentations which seem to benefit performance, but to degrade learning. In these cases, increasing the amount of extrinsic feedback is thought to promote dependence on that feedback, and thereby prevent the development of intrinsic response capabilities. These detrimental effects have both theoretical and practical implications for the use of feedback in skill learning.

Chapter 3

Motor Programs

Jeffery J. Summers

Skilled performance often requires the organization of highly refined patterns of movements in relation to some specific goal. In the initial stages of skill learning, performance is characterized by slow, jerky movements because of the continuous necessity to use feedback. The unskilled person will make a movement, visually observe the consequences of that movement, make another movement, re-evaluate the results, and so on. With practice, however, the sequencing and timing of movements seem to shift from direct visual control to an internal form of control. As a result performance appears to be rapid and coordinated.

Identifying the mechanisms by which the central nervous system produces a coordinated sequence of movements is clearly an important factor in understanding skilled performance. Historically, two major theoretical positions have been adopted to explain the control of highly practised movements. The first, a closed-loop system, emphasizes the role of sensory feedback in movements, as discussed in Chapter 2. The other stresses open-loop control, and argues that the sequence of movements becomes stored in memory and can be executed without constant reference to feedback. An early closed-loop form of learning theory suggested that, as practice progresses, control of a series of movements passes from visual to kinesthetic control. By means of an associative or conditioning process the kinesthetic feedback from one segment of a movement series was thought to elicit a succeeding movement. According to this response chaining hypothesis, afferent impulses from the various joint, cutaneous, and stretch receptors in a moving limb are necessary for the execution of sequences of movements.

The most detailed application of closed-loop notions to the realm of motor behavior has been made by Adams (1971, 1976). He proposes that at the base of all motor performance is a comparison between a memory of movement (perceptual trace) and kinesthetic feedback from an ongoing response, with any resulting error signal serving as the stimulus for subsequent corrective

Human Skills. Edited by D. Holding © 1989 John Wiley & Sons Ltd

movement. The perceptual trace is formed from the past experience with feedback from earlier responses and comes to represent the sensory consequences of the limb being correctly moved. This view differs from the response chaining hypothesis in that successive movements are not activated by a habit connection but by the error that is sensed (Adams, 1984).

In contrast, open-loop theories of motor control stress the sequencing and timing aspects of skills, which they regard as being governed by central motor programs. Practice on a skill results in the acquisition, by the higher centers of the central nervous system, of a neuromotor program that contains all the information necessary for movement patterning. Thus there is a 'set of muscle commands that are structured before a movement sequence begins' (Keele, 1968, p. 387). Furthermore, once the program is initiated the movement sequence is smoothly and precisely executed without requiring peripheral feedback from prior movements to elicit succeeding movements. This view does not deny the presence of feedback in almost all movements, but suggests that such feedback is usually redundant, since the motor program already contains the information necessary for movement execution.

The major difference between the two theories, therefore, is in the role of feedback in the control of skilled performance. In closed-loop theory response-produced feedback is essential to performance, while such feedback is not necessary in open-loop control.

Clearly, for motor program control to be a tenable alternative to closed-loop control, it is necessary to show that (a) movement can occur in the absence of feedback; (b) that for some movements, even though feedback is present it is not used; and (c) that movements can be structured prior to the onset of movement rather than as the movement progresses.

Let us now turn to a brief consideration of the evidence relating to the three criteria of programmed control.

MOTOR PROGRAM CONTROL

Movement in the absence of feedback

The motor program concept can be considered to have its empirical origins in the work of Lashley (1917), with a patient deprived of sensation as a result of a gunshot wound to the spinal cord. The patient was capable of reproducing active movements in the absence of kinesthetic feedback from the affected limb. This finding led Lashley to propose that such movement was controlled centrally as there was no peripheral information to guide the movement.

Further evidence in support of open-loop control comes from studies in which kinesthetic feedback in animals was surgically eliminated. In general, these studies have shown that movements can be maintained following feedback removal. For example, deafferented monkeys can use the limbs effectively for walking, climbing and reaching movements (for reviews see Taub, 1977; Bizzi and Abend, 1983). Similar findings have been reported in studies on locust wingbeats (Wilson, 1961), birdsong (Nottebohm, 1970) and grooming behavior in mice (Fentress, 1973).

The investigation of movement control in humans without feedback is very difficult because of problems in manipulating kinesthetic feedback without causing permanent neural damage. One potential source of information, however, comes from people who have suffered kinesthetic loss from disease or genetic abnormalities. Rothwell et al. (1982) examined the movement capabilities of a patient lacking feedback from both upper and lower limbs as a result of degeneration of the peripheral neural pathways. Without vision the patient was able to perform a variety of manual tasks such as tapping the thumb repetitively, touching his thumb with each finger in turn, and drawing figures in the air. Furthermore, the patient showed a similar electromyographic (EMG) pattern to normal subjects when making a rapid arm movement to a target (see also Hallet, Shahani, and Young, 1975; Cooke et al., 1985; Forget and Lamarre, 1987).

Although the deafferentation studies provide strong evidence against the view that kinesthesis is necessary for coordinated movement, it does not mean that sensory feedback is unimportant for normal movement control. The movements of deafferented monkeys and humans with sensory loss are never quite 'normal'. In particular, the movements appear clumsy, with a reduction in fine control and precise movement (Bossom, 1974; Rothwell et al., 1982). Rothwell et al. (1982) also noted that their patient's performance on the manual tasks gradually deteriorated and lost their accuracy when he was asked to repeat them for 30 seconds or more. Afferent feedback, therefore, seems necessary to perfect the fine detail of movement, and to monitor the overall accuracy of the motor program.

Central pattern generators

The view that movements produced in the absence of feedback are controlled by some central mechanism, or program has also received support from the work of neurobiologists investigating rhythmic movements in animals (for reviews of this work see Delcomyn, 1980; Grillner and Wallen, 1985). It has been proposed that the central nervous system and spinal cord contain neural circuits called central pattern generators (CPGs) which, when activated, can produce different patterns of interlimb coordination (Figure 10). Evidence for CPGs controlling locomotion has been obtained in a wide variety of species. For example, stimulation to brainstem areas of a decerebrate cat can produce coordinated walking movements, with higher levels of stimulation

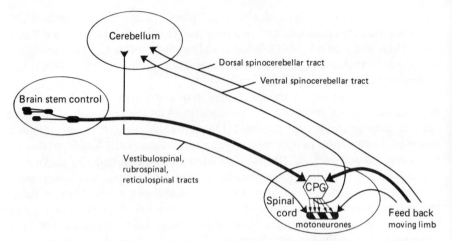

Figure 10. Schematic diagram of the control system for locomotion in vertebrates; CPG = central pattern generator. Source: Modified from Grillner and Wallen 1985, p. 235). Reproduced by permission of the first author and Annual Reviews, Inc.

inducing trotting and galloping (Shik, Severin, and Orlovsky, 1966). It appears, therefore, that a complete program for locomotion is contained within the spinal cord.

Grillner (1985) has also argued that the different limbs are controlled by separate CPGs, each of which can generate the appropriate motor pattern for its limb. Interlimb coordination is achieved through a set of coordinating neurons that combine the limb CPGs in a particular phase relationship. Such a system is extremely versatile, for by changing interconnections between the various components, a variety of locomotor patterns can be produced.

The work on CPGs provides clear evidence for the existence of innate motor programs that can produce complex motor patterns without feedback. However, even for such 'hard-wired' mechanisms sensory feedback signals appear to form an integral and crucial part of the normal control system (Grillner, 1985). Feedback is used to fine-tune the central pattern to prevailing external conditions and to correct for unexpected perturbations to movements. There is also evidence to suggest that the central program may specify how feedback is to be used at particular points in the movement sequence. Forssberg, Grillner, and Rossignol (1975b) examined the effects of applying a tactile stimulus to a cat's hindlimb during locomotion. When the stimulus was applied as the cat was about to lift up the foot to swing it forward, an exaggerated flexion of the foot occurred, as if the animal were attempting to lift the foot over an obstacle. However, when the same stimulus was applied during the stance phase (i.e. when the foot was on the ground) a slight extension of the leg occurred. The same sensory feedback received at different phases of the gait cycle, therefore, resulted in vastly different modifications of the movement pattern.

Is there any evidence for innate motor programs in humans? Recent kinematic and EMG analyses of movements made by young infants suggest that innate central pattern generation mechanisms may also underlie walking in humans. For example, it has been demonstrated that spontaneous kicking movements in the supine position (Thelen, Bradshaw, and Ward, 1981), and 'reflex stepping' (Thelen and Fisher, 1982) in young infants, are identical movement patterns and exhibit a similar spatiotemporal structure to that of mature locomotion. Furthermore, when babies as young as one month old are supported upright and placed on a motorized treadmill they exhibit mature-like alternating stepping (Thelen, 1987). These studies suggest the existence of some innate pattern generation mechanism that undergoes differentiation and integration with other developing systems eventually to produce mature walking (see Thelen, Kelso, and Fogel, 1987).

The literature on central pattern generators provides strong evidence for the existence of innate motor programs in animals and perhaps humans. Motor program theorists, however, wish to extend the concept to the performance of learned acts (e.g. a gymnastic routine).

One interesting speculation is that genetically inherited, or innate, movement patterns may form the basis of learned motor programs. Grillner (1985) has suggested CPG networks may be used in other more complex behavior. Walking, for example, requires the activation of the whole CPG network, but specific movements of individual joints can be produced by activating particular parts of the network (Figure 11). According to this view learning a new movement involves 'learning to combine and sequence specific fractions of the neuronal apparatus used to control the innate movement patterns in a novel way' (Grillner, 1985, p. 148).

Motor program proponents, however, have presented two principal lines of evidence in support of the extension of the concept to learned responses.

Feedback redundancy

It has been argued that feedback processing is too slow to account for the high rate of movement shown in some skilled performance, such as piano playing (Lashley, 1951), typing (Shaffer, 1978) and speech production (Lenneberg, 1967). In many skills the interval between successive movements is often less than 100 msec, yet the time to react to kinesthetic feedback has been shown to be apparently 100 msec or greater (see Glencross, 1977, for a review). Thus, because of the speed of such movements, response-produced feedback would be out of phase with the ongoing movement.

There is, however, increasing evidence that previous work had overestimated feedback processing times. For example, rapid corrections (30–80

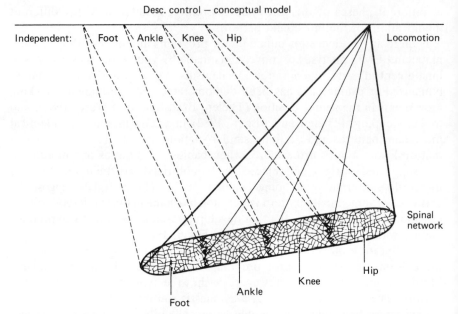

Figure 11. Schematic representation showing how the central pattern generator network for locomotion may be used in other more complex behaviour. Activation of the entire network will give rise to locomotion, but independent control of parts of the network could be utilized to produce specific movements of individual joints. Source: Grillner and Wallen (1985, p. 255). Reproduced by permission of the first author and Annual Reviews, Inc.

msec) of limb movements to unanticipated perturbations have been observed in animals (Evarts, 1973; Evarts and Tanji, 1974) and humans, (Marsden, Merton, and Morton, 1972; Carlton, 1983). Even saccadic eye movements traditionally considered to be under open-loop control (e.g. Festinger and Canon, 1965) have been shown to be modulated by sensory feedback (Fuchs and Kornhuber, 1969; Morasso, Bizzi, and Dichgans, 1973).

The presence of fast-acting peripheral feedback loops, however, does not necessitate the rejection of the motor program concept, as some have argued (e.g. Adams, 1977). These fast feedback processes operate to correct for minor perturbations to the ongoing movement, without changing the basic movement pattern that was initiated to achieve a particular goal. Large errors in movement that may result from the selection of an inappropriate motor program or an unexpected occurrence in the environment, however, cannot be corrected until the program has run its course for at least one reaction time (about 200 msec). In this case central decision-making processes are required to select a new spatiotemporal movement pattern.

It appears, therefore, that there are at least two levels at which movement can be controlled. At the highest level are voluntary decisions based on a comparison in the brain between feedback from the actual movement and the expected feedback from the intended movement. This system is used to detect gross errors in performance, or as Schmidt (1976a) has defined them, 'errors in response selection'. Such errors arise when something in the environment informs the individual that the movement selected was inappropriate. For example, the tennis player may have swung the racket too early to contact the ball correctly. As it requires about 200 msec to initiate a new program, the intended movement is often carried out as planned, even though the feedback might indicate that it is going to be incorrect.

At the same time a lower level of control is operating involving spinal-level feedback mechanisms. Fast-acting muscle spindle-initiated feedback loops act to smooth out movement by correcting small, unexpected disturbances to the intended movement (see Keele and Summers, 1976; Evarts, 1981; Schmidt, 1982, for a detailed discussion of this mechanism). This lower level of control is a very rapid (30–80 msec), subconscious and automatic process that ensures the original program is executed as planned. Thus errors in response execution (Schmidt, 1976a) can be detected and corrected very quickly in contrast to the long delays required to change the goal of the movement. The presence of these reflex-based corrections led Schmidt (1976b, p. 59) to redefine the motor program as a set of prestructured motor commands that, 'when activated, result in movement oriented toward a given goal, with these movements being unaffected by peripheral feedback indicating that the goal should be changed.'

Pre-programming of responses

A different approach to the assessment of programmed control focuses on the idea of organizing the motor command sequence prior to the onset of movement, and considers the possibility that such organization may take measurable time. The time required for programming has been investigated in experiments which measure reaction time prior to the beginning of the response as a function of the nature of the response to be made. Changes in reaction time as a function of response parameters are interpreted as reflecting changes in the time to construct the appropriate motor program (see Sternberg et al., 1978, Rosenbaum, Inhoff, and Gordon, 1984; Monsell, 1986; for models of the motor programming process).

One of the predictions from the pre-programming concept is that there should be a longer reaction latency for a complicated movement than for a simpler movement since a more comprehensive program would be required for the complex response. A number of studies have reported increases in reaction time with increases in movement complexity. Programming time has been shown to increase with the physical length of movements, the temporal duration of movements, the number of movements required, and the complexity of the timing requirements for the components of a movement (see Kerr, 1978; Marteniuk and MacKenzie, 1980, for a review). For example, the time to initiate the first word in a pre-cued string of words to be pronounced (i.e. Monday, or Monday–Tuesday, or Monday–Tuesday–Wednesday) increases with the number of words to be uttered (Sternberg et al., 1978).

Recently, the movement pre-cuing technique has been developed to examine the organization of the processes involved in the selection of response parameters (e.g. arm, direction, and extent) prior to movement execution. In this technique subjects are presented with advanced information (pre-cue) about the required movement. By comparing the effects on reaction time of providing complete, partial, or no information about the dimensions of the forthcoming response, the temporal organization of the planning and preparation processes can be ascertained (see Rosenbaum, 1983, for review).

There are a number of problems in this area, such as in the use of simple or choice reaction time paradigms (e.g. Klapp, 1981; Marteniuk and MacKenzie, 1981), the assumptions of pre-cuing methodology (see Zelaznik and Larish, 1986), and the extent to which the external task parameters usually manipulated (i.e. movement extent, direction) are the same as those used by the central nervous system in organizing a movement (Kerr, 1978; Marteniuk and MacKenzie, 1980). However, the studies do lend some support to the concept of pre-programming inherent in motor program theory. In particular, recent evidence (e.g. Klapp and Greim, 1979; Heuer, 1984; Rosenbaum, et al., 1984; Ivry, 1986) suggests that the organization of the timing aspect of a response is a critical determinant of initiation time.

A number of physiological changes during the preparation for movement have also been observed. Through the use of electroencephalographic and EMG measurements changes related to the preparation for movement have been reported at both cortical and spinal levels (see Evarts, 1984; Requin, Lecas, and Bonnet, 1984; Brunia, Haagh, and Scheirs, 1985, for reviews). Requin, et al. (1984) have proposed that movement organization involves three stages: goal planning, motor programming and movement execution respectively, and each stage is associated with a particular neuronal system and preparatory process (Figure 12).

A particularly interesting form of preparatory activity are postural movements that occur prior to voluntary movement in humans (e.g. Belenkii, Gurfinkel, and Paltsev, 1967; Bouisset and Zattara, 1981). When standing subjects are asked to raise an arm to point at a target a sequence of postural movements occurs 40–80 msec prior to movement of the limb. Furthermore, these anticipatory movements are modified according to the characteristics of the movement (e.g. single arm versus double arm raise) to be performed

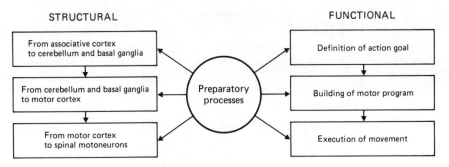

Figure 12. Schematization of a three-stage model of motor organization. Each stage (on the right) is associated with a particular neuronal system (on the left) and preparatory process. Source: Requin, Lecas and Bonnet (1984, p. 261). Reproduced by permission of the first author and Lawrence Erlbaum Associates, Inc.

(Bouisset and Zattara, 1981; Zattara and Bouisset, 1986). It appears that these postural changes are pre-programmed and serve to compensate, in advance, for displacement of the centre of gravity due to the forthcoming movement. These anticipatory effects provide further evidence for the idea of central representations of actions.

In this section I have reviewed some of the evidence for motor programs. The main conclusion that can be drawn from this review is that at least some skills appear to be under motor program control. As we have seen, however, the view that such skills are 'uninfluenced by peripheral feedback' (Keele, 1968, p. 387) is clearly incorrect. Feedback is essential for monitoring the movement to ensure that performance is progressing as planned and for updating or changing programs as required.

Motor program acquisition

Keele and Summers (1976) have also stressed the importance of feedback in the development of a motor program. The initial stage in the learning of a motor skill is seen as involving the development in the learner of a template or model of how the feedback should appear if the skill is performed correctly. At the beginning of the learning process the individual will probably use an external model to guide performance. For example, watching another person perform the desired skill would provide an external model against which the feedback from the learner's own movements can be compared (see Carroll and Bandura, 1982, 1985). Eventually, however, it is likely that a permanent representation of the model becomes stored in memory. Evidence for the existence of such internal models has come from studies on the development of birdsong (see Keele and Summers, 1976; Konishi, 1985, for a review).

A series of movements is then produced by a motor program via motor

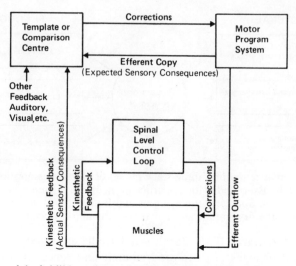

Figure 13. A model of skill learning and a mechanism for the detection and correction of errors. Source: Modified from Keele and Summers (1976, p. 122). Reproduced by permission of Academic Press, Inc.

commands to the muscles. The kinesthetic and exteroceptive feedback (i.e. vision and audition) arising from these movements is matched to the template (the expected sensory consequences) and any resultant error leads to a modification of the motor program (see Prinz, 1984; Henry, 1986, for a discussion of the matching process). In time the motor program will produce an appropriate spatial-temporal pattern of movements, and with further practice on the skill the program will become stabilized. The process of motor program development is illustrated in Figure 13. Once the motor program has been established performance can be maintained by a close interaction between program and feedback in the manner previously described.

This model of skill learning is similar in many respects to closed-loop accounts of skill development (Adams, 1971). In closed-loop theory, feedback is also compared to a template of expected feedback established during training, and any discrepancies between current feedback and the template are the basis for corrections.

THE SCHEMA CONCEPT

A problem for any theory of motor control is to account for the tremendous flexibility evident in human skill. Human skills are seldom performed in exactly the same way twice. A movement can be small or large, such as signing your name on paper or on a blackboard; there may also be differences in speed, exact sequencing, orientation, etc. The motor system, therefore, can produce the same or similar movement outcomes through a variety of movements and muscle combinations. Cinematographic and EMG analyses have also shown that even the same movements performed under identical environmental conditions result is slightly different movement patterns (Higgins and Spaeth, 1972; Glencross, 1980; Moore and Marteniuk, 1986). A further characteristic of motor performance is its modifiability. The particular spatial and temporal pattern of muscular contractions can vary depending on the task demands, initial configuration of the body, and the state of the environment.

These features of skilled behavior present difficulties for the traditional open-loop and closed-loop theories of movement control. Basic to the operation of both programmed and closed-loop control modes is the assumption that stored in memory is some representation of past successful responses. It would seem, however, extremely cumbersome and inefficient for the nervous system to store a separate motor program or reference of correctness for all the possible variations of every movement we can produce. Furthermore, under either scheme it would be impossible for an individual to produce movements that have never been performed previously.

Yet despite the amazing flexibility evident in the movements people produce, an obvious feature of skilled performance is the consistency and stability of action (Glencross, 1980). Although the micro-details of a movement may vary on different occasions, the overall spatial and temporal structure of the action remains consistent. A person's characteristic style of handwriting is evident for words written with the right and left hands, with a pen taped to the right foot, and with a pen held in the mouth (Raibert, 1977). Shaffer (1984) has also shown that a skilled pianist's idiosyncratic style of playing a piece of music is remarkably consistent across performances given a year apart. The consistency and stability of action indicates that there must be some underlying memorial representation of a movement pattern.

The generalized motor program

In an attempt to deal with the problem of skill variation, motor control theorists have moved away from the idea that the motor program specifies every detail in the response and toward the view of a multi-level or hierarchic system. The production of action is seen as a constructional or generative process in which abstract descriptions of an action at the high levels are transformed into specific patterns of movement at lower levels (Glencross, 1980; Keele, 1981; Summers, 1981; Shaffer, 1982). According to this view the motor program contains the general characteristics about a movement that then must be organized to meet specific environmental demands and the goal required by the performer.

Schmidt (1975, 1976b), in an application of schema theory to motor learning, developed the concept of a generalized motor program. The generalized motor program is an abstract memory structure that 'governs a given class of movements that requires a common motor pattern' (Shapiro and Schmidt, 1982, p. 115). Variations in the movements within a movement class are produced by the application of certain parameters (e.g. speed and force) to the generalized program prior to movement execution.

The selection of appropriate movement parameters is accomplished through a motor memory called the recall schema, 'which is a rule based on past attempts at running the program' (Shapiro and Schmidt, 1982, p. 116). Although Schmidt maintained that the recall schema is responsible only for parameter selection and not program selection, Zanone and Hauert (1987) have proposed that it can perform both functions.

A second memory state, the recognition schema, is responsible for the generation of the expected sensory consequences that should arise if the movement is performed correctly. A comparison between actual and expected sensory consequences forms the basis for error detection and correction (see Schmidt, 1975, 1976b, 1982) for details of the operation of the recall and recognition schemas).

Memory structure of movements

The concept of a generalized motor program has led to a consideration of the content and structure of such programs. Attempts to answer these questions have focused on identifying the invariant features of a movement that are represented in the generalized program and those features or parameters that can be varied to meet specific task demands.

There is considerable evidence from a wide variety of movement behaviors that the temporal structure, or relative timing, of movement is an invariant property of the generalized motor program (see Schmidt, 1984, for a review). Armstrong (1970b), for example, had subjects learn a sequence of forearm movements containing an inherent spatial-temporal structure. He noticed that although on some trials subjects' total movement time was too fast or too slow, they tended to compress or extend the entire sequence proportionally in time. That is, the relative timing of the submovements making up the task was maintained across variations in movement speed. Similar invariance in relative timing has been observed in studies of typing (Terzuolo and Viviani, 1979, 1980), handwriting (Viviani and Terzuolo, 1980; Stelmach, Mullins, and Teulings, 1984), drawing movements (Lacquanti, Terzuolo, and Viviani, 1986), speech (Tuller, Kelso, and Harris, 1982), locomotion (Shapiro et al., 1981), and reaching (Jeannerod, 1981).

Further evidence for the view that relative timing is intrinsic to the generalized motor program has come from studies in which subjects were encouraged to change the learned phasing of a series of movements. For example, Summers (1975), using a sequential finger-tapping task, trained subjects to execute a sequence of key presses with a particular time structure. By the end of training subjects were able to reproduce both the correct sequence and time pattern entirely from memory. Subjects were then told to execute the movement sequence as rapidly as possible and to ignore the timing imposed during training. Although under speed instructions the entire sequence was speeded up, performance was still influenced by the learned timing pattern. This was particularly true for subjects who had learned a rhythmic timing structure (see also Summers, Sargent, and Hawkins, 1984). Similar results have been obtained in lever rotation tasks requiring forearm supination and pronation (Shapiro, 1977; Carter and Shapiro, 1984). Furthermore, the invariance of relative timing under speed instructions is apparent not only in kinematic description of the movement, but also in the pattern of EMG activity (Carter and Shapiro, 1984). These and other studies (e.g. Summers, 1977a; Williams and Churchman, 1986) suggest that the sequencing and timing of movements are invariant features in the program, whereas the overall execution speed of a skill is a parameter that is input to the program prior to movement initiation.

Studies of bimanual coordination also suggest that the two hands are controlled by a single timing mechanism. Kelso, Southard, and Goodman (1979) examined the ability of subjects to make two-handed movements to separate targets that differed in size and in distance from the resting position. Under these conditions, the hands appeared to move in synchrony, so that they arrived at their respective targets at the same time. Thus even though the spatial demands for the two limbs were quite different, the timing relations between them remained constant (see, however, Corcos, 1984; Marteniuk, MacKenzie, and Baba, 1984, for other interpretations of these data). Studies using bimanual tapping tasks have also shown a similar disposition toward simple timing relations in the coordination of the two hands (e.g. Klapp, 1979; Yaminishi, Kawato and Suzuki, 1980; Kelso et al., 1981). Subjects have little difficulty in producing two isochronous sequences in parallel, one with each hand, when the sequences have identical or harmonically-related time intervals (e.g. 2:1, 3:1, 4:1, etc.). However, great difficulty is experienced in the concurrent performance of non-harmonically-related motor sequences, such as polyrhythms (e.g. 3:2, 4:3, 5:4, etc.). It has been argued that the temporal constraints evident in the performance of concurrent movements by the two hands result from the interaction of lower-level neural oscillatory mechanisms during execution (e.g. Kelso et al., 1981). Recent studies using the pre-programming paradigm (see p. 55), however, suggest that intermanual interactions may also arise at a more central level when movements are programmed (e.g. Klapp and Greim, 1979; Heuer, 1984, 1986; Rosenbaum et al., 1984).

The specification of timing, therefore, seems to play a special role in programming which is not shared by other components of a movement sequence, such as the spatial and muscular aspects. Some motor program theorists have argued for the existence of a subordinate timekeeper or clock, not directly involved in movement production (e.g. Keele 1981; Shaffer, 1982, 1984; Rosenbaum, 1985). Keele (1981), for example, proposed that the motor program specifies a time for action and the time is read from some sort of internal metronome. (For a discussion of processes by which information from the abstract program and clock pulses are associated, see Shaffer, 1982; Rosenbaum, 1985).

In addition to the ordering and relative timing of events being represented in the generalized motor program, Schmidt (1982, 1984) has argued that the relative force with which the events are to be produced is an invariant feature of movement. The overall duration of the movement, the overall size of the movement and the muscle (or limb) that is used to make the movements are seen as parameters that allow variations in the movements produced from the abstract program.

Problems with generalized motor programs

The importance of finding invariances in motor behavior lies in the possibility that they provide information about 'the underlying control processes for skills, in terms of how skilled movement behaviour is represented in the CNS, and what aspects of muscular contraction are controlled' (Schmidt, 1984, p. 189).

The evidence suggesting that relative timing is an invariant feature of many motor tasks and that overall force and movement duration are parameters led to a theory of motor programming (the Impulse-Timing model) in which the intensity, timing, and duration of muscular contraction are controlled by the program (see Schmidt et al., 1979; Schmidt et al., 1985).

There is increasing evidence, however, to suggest that the invariant features of movement may vary according to the task to be performed, the specific task demands, and the stage of learning. Studies of simple arm movements, for example, indicate that movement endpoints may be represented in the motor program. Bizzi and his colleagues (e.g. Bizzi, Polit, and Morasso, 1976; Bizzi et al., 1978; Polit and Bizzi, 1979) trained monkeys to make unseen arm movements to briefly illuminated visual targets. Some of the movements were unexpectedly perturbed either by displacing the arm prior to movement initiation or by the application of a load during the movement. Despite these perturbations both normal and deafferented animals were able to make accurate pointing movements. The importance of the final position of a movement has also been shown for human subjects in studies of motor short-term memory (see Laabs and Simmons, 1981), and rapid arm movements (e.g. Schmidt and McGowan, 1980). It appears that, at least for discrete unidirectional movements, the motor program need only specify the terminal location of the intended movement.

It has been argued that final location is defined as an equilibrium point (i.e. a particular length–tension relationship) between agonist and antagonist muscles involved in the movement (Asatryan and Feldman, 1965; Bizzi, Polit, and Morasso, 1976). This hypothesis, known as the mass-spring model, holds that once a particular equilibrium point has been specified, the inherent spring-like properties of the muscles will ensure that the correct final position is reached regardless of external perturbations to the movement (see Feldman, 1986, for a detailed discussion of the model). One obvious advantage of having the motor program specify only movement endpoints is that the same outcome can be achieved in a variety of different ways through the use of the same program.

Recent evidence, however, suggests that location programming may only apply to discrete unidirectional movements, involving a single joint. Analysis of hand trajectories for two-joint arm-reaching movements, for example, indicate that the trajectory of the movement is controlled, in addition to final location (Bizzi and Abend, 1983; Atkeson and Hollerbach, 1985).

The above studies strongly suggest that the muscle properties controlled by the central nervous system vary as a function of the type of movement to be performed (Stein, 1982). In tasks where the maintenance of a particular temporal structure is necessary for successful performance (e.g. music) relative timing may form part of the high-level representation of action. In other tasks, such as simple pointing movements, however, phasing need not be represented in memory at all. Even the assumption that relative timing is a fundamental characteristic of the representation of sequential motor tasks has been challenged (e.g. Gentner, 1982, 1987; Rumelhart and Norman, 1982; Langley and Zelaznik, 1984).

The questions of what features of a movement are represented in the generalized motor program, and what are the mutable parameters, are clearly issues requiring further research. For example, there may be fundamental differences in the invariances observed when the same movement is performed in a closed or open environment (Zelaznik, 1986), at different stages of learning (e.g. Marteniuk and Romanow, 1983; Moore and Marteniuk, 1986) or across different age groups (e.g. Burton, 1986).

The concept of a generalized motor program poses a number of other questions that future research must attempt to answer. One important problem is the definition of a class of movements that is represented in the abstract program. Related issues are the amount of variation in behavior governed by a single motor program, and how motor programs are learned (see Shapiro and Schmidt, 1982).

CURRENT VIEW OF MOTOR CONTROL

The previous sections were concerned with the structure and contents of motor programs. Although these issues are still the subject of much debate, there does appear to be general consensus that the motor program should be viewed as a multilevel system in which an abstract representation of action is elaborated into its more specific components at lower levels. There is less agreement, however, on the exact definition and nature of the various levels involved in motor control (e.g. Hinton, 1984; Zanone and Hauert, 1987). In Chapter 9 Ann Colley discusses in detail how the concept of multilevel hierarchical control has been applied to models of handwriting, speech, and typing.

One advantage of multilevel systems is to reduce the computational burden of higher control centers by allowing the details of movement to be specified by subordinate structures (Stelmach and Diggles, 1982). There is now considerable evidence for the existence of relatively autonomous units of activity that may be used as components for more complex motor behavior. These lower-level organizations or neuromotor synergies (Wynne, 1984), may be built-in structures such as reflexes (Easton, 1972), oscillator mechanisms (Craske and Craske, 1986), central pattern generators (Grillner, 1985), or they may be functional groupings of muscles constrained to act as a single unit (coordinative structures) that can be organized temporarily to accomplish a particular behavioral goal (Turvey, Shaw, and Mace, 1978).

The concept of a neuromotor synergy has important implications for the question of how motor programs are translated into action. It suggests that the programming process may involve the coordination and integration of appropriate subsystems to achieve a particular behavioral goal (Greene, 1982). The motor program is responsible for the selection, ordering, timing, and parameterization of lower-level organizational units. The higher levels of the motor system, therefore, are concerned only with the general aspects of a movement (i.e. the effector units and their coordination) and are not involved in specifying the micro-details of movement execution. Rather, the fine structuring of a movement is left to autonomous subsystems. The mechanism by which the higher centers organize the lower centers for the anticipated movement has been termed 'tuning' (Greene, 1972; Turvey, 1977; Easton, 1978; Arbib, 1980; Kelso and Tuller, 1981). The anticipatory effects previously described (see p. 56) are examples of tuning processes.

The existence of relatively autonomous subsystems is also incompatible with a strict hierarchical view of movement control. The problem with a hierarchically organized system is that interactions between processes can only occur in one direction: from higher to lower levels (Turvey, Shaw, and Mace, 1978). Thus there is no provision for communication between processes at the same level nor can there be input from a lower to a higher level. It is clear, however, that movement organization and execution involve multiple feedback and feedforward interactions at various levels of the central nervous system concurrently (Brooks, 1979; Stelmach and Diggles, 1982; Pew, 1984). To overcome the limitations of a rigid hierarchical organization, distributed control systems have been proposed. Rather than having decision-making invested in one high-level executive system, distributed control systems allow control to shift between levels or even appear to reside at several levels simultaneously, with processes occurring in parallel at different levels. For example, Arbib and his colleagues have proposed a distributed control model incorporating perceptual and motor schemata, and coordinated control programs (Arbib, 1980, 1981; Arbib, Iberall, and Lyons, 1985). Some recent versions of motor program theory have stressed the on-line use of feedback and feedforward information in the control of multimovement behaviors (e.g. Abbs, Gracco and Cole, 1984; MacKenzie and Marteniuk, 1985). Abbs et al. (1984), for example, suggest that:

> . . . a program is more likely the representation of the dynamic processes whereby the appropriate sensorimotor contingencies are set up to ensure cooperative complementary contribution of the multiple actions to a common, predetermined goal. Included within this hypothesized program are representations of the mechanisms for achieving an intended motor goal via (1) a general activation of appropriate muscles, (2) adaptive preadjustments based upon the state of the periphery, and (3) setting up sensory evaluation— motor translations for appropriate compensatory adjustments among multiple synergistic movements as the action unfolds. (p. 215)

According to this view the motor program only sets up the correct patterns of interaction among the submovements of a particular motor task. Through such a dynamic system the same intended motor outcome can be achieved in a variety of different ways.

Interim summary

The current view of a distributed motor organization makes it difficult to identify any part of the total control system as a motor program in the traditional sense. The term motor program has also been defined in a variety of different ways, ranging from such general statements as 'motor programs are communications in the central nervous system that are based on past experience and that can generate postural adjustments and movements' (Brooks, 1979, p. 1) to the concept that motor programs are descending force signals from the motor cortex (Evarts, 1968). Other writers have chosen a particular level in the motor system, such as the abstract plan of action, as a motor program (Miller, Galanter, and Pribram, 1960; Bernstein, 1968), or have defined the program as a mechanism that controls a particular aspect of motor behavior, such as movement timing (e.g. Rosenbaum, 1985). Still others have abandoned the concept completely (e.g. Kelso, 1981; Saltzman and Kelso, 1987). One could argue that the recently identified lower-level control mechanisms come closest to the original concept of a motor program. However, as Hayes (1978) has pointed out, the movement-specific pattern of spinal tuning is always necessary prior to movement initiation, indicating a central 'model' of the intended movement. Perhaps, as Pew (1984) has argued, 'we should not be searching for a unitary integrative concept of a motor program: It may have different representations at different levels in the motor system' (p. 26). Another issue that must be addressed by researchers in the area is whether the term motor program should be regarded as a metaphor or a literal description of motor organization (Stelmach and Hughes, 1984).

Clearly, considerable work is still needed in the area of motor programming. At this stage it may be best to view a motor program simply 'as the central representation of a sequence of motor action' (Keele, 1981, p. 1400). The representation is seen as being abstract in nature similar to the concept of the generalized motor program (Schmidt, 1975, 1976b). The important aspect of the program is that it allows the organism to organize, through a sequence of operations, a series of movements in advance of movement execution. Furthermore, these movements can be carried out without requiring feedback from one movement to elicit a succeeding movement. Feedback, however, is constantly being monitored during program operation and is used to update and modify well-learned movement patterns.

In the execution of any perceptual-motor skill, the ultimate way in which a skill is performed would be to have it almost completely programmed so that very little conscious attention is required. In general, the greater the ability of the central nervous system to 'predictively determine' a motor response, the less is the need for peripheral feedback. It seems likely, therefore, that closed skills involving the execution of relatively long sequences of movements in a static environment can be almost completely programmed in advance with a minimum of feedback involvement. In contrast, the performance of skills demanding high accuracy or where the environment is constantly changing involves both program and feedback control. In such skills an individual may make short programmed movements followed by an evaluation of response-produced feedback. It is possible that the central representation of such skills contains instructions for sensing and responding to feedback at particular points in the movement sequence (Sternberg et al., 1978).

The maximum length of a motor program is difficult to estimate. The size of motor programs may be limited by the duration over which pre-programming can extend (Schmidt, 1982), the span of a special motor-command buffer (Sternberg, et al., 1978), the number and complexity of the components (Rosenbaum, et al., 1984; Monsell, 1986), the predictability of the environment and the stage of learning.

IMPLICATIONS FOR SKILL LEARNING

It has been argued that at the base of all skilled performance is the ability to generate an appropriate sequence of motor commands from a generalized source of movement information, the motor program. The initial problem facing the learner, however, is the establishment of a template or model of how the feedback should appear if the skill is performed correctly. The acquisition of the skill is then accomplished by a matching process in which the feedback from the movements generated by the subject is compared to the template. The system that generates movements (the motor program) and the system that evaluates feedback (the template and comparison center) are seen as separable units. Once the motor program has been established, feedback can be eliminated and the program can produce the learned movement in open-loop fashion.

One implication of this formulation is that 'an artificial template and feedback source can be used for the learning phase to build an appropriate program' (Keele, 1977, p. 9). Such feedback substitution techniques have been used as aids in the learning of a foreign language (Kalikow, 1974) and in training the deaf to speak (Nickerson, Kalikow, and Stevens, 1976; Lippman, 1982; Povel and Wansink, 1986). In these studies visual displays present transformations of the learner's speech to be compared with a model (Figure 14). Other techniques that have been investigated in skill learning are loop films and videotape (see Holding, 1965). Generally, such systems have been found to be of little use (Newell, 1981). However, most studies have used only loop films, while others only video feedback. According to motor program theory both techniques should be used together—loop films to portray a model, and videotape to provide feedback for use in the comparison process. Keele (1977) reports two attempts to apply this idea to the skills of discus-throwing and flycasting.

The independence of feedback and program also suggests that for certain skills the template may be established prior to actually performing the skill. It has been suggested that the acquisition of an auditory template prior to movement production may be the basis of the Suzuki method of violin teaching (Keele and Summers, 1976; Keele, 1982). In addition to storing a template prior to actual movement, it also may be possible to store part of the motor program itself. One way of accomplishing this may be through the use of mental practice, a technique that has been shown to improve perform-

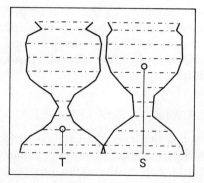

Figure 14. A visual display used in teaching the deaf to speak. A teacher's vocalization of the ē sound from the word 'be' is shown on the left, and a student's attempt to produce a match is portrayed on the right. The vertical dimension represents voice frequencies and the width of the shape is determined by the energy at each frequency. Voiced and voiceless sounds are represented by the presence and absence of the horizontal lines, respectively, and voice pitch corresponds to the height of the 'lollipop'. Source: Modified from Nickerson, Kalikow, and Stevens (1976, p. 122). Reproduced by permission of the first author and the American Speech-Language-Hearing Association.

ance on a variety of skills. The introspective or covert rehearsal of the required movements would aid the establishment of the movement sequence in memory. This idea was tested by Summers (1977b) using a task in which subjects were required to respond as rapidly as possible to events that tended to occur in sequential order. Mental rehearsal of the event order was found to be effective even when movements were not used until later in the task.

The motor program concept, therefore, suggests several ways in which skill learning might be improved. The central element in the acquisition of a skill is the comparison process between response-produced feedback and a model or template of expected sensory consequences. The training techniques described are aimed at improving the quality of the match between feedback and model.

It has previously been noted that one of the distinguishing characteristics of a highly skilled performer is the ability to perform the skill in a number of different ways according to variations in environmental demands. This flexibility in motor behavior was seen as resulting from the acquisition of a motor schema for a given class of movement. The teaching of a motor skill, therefore, can be viewed as a 'two-stage process'. Initially, the teacher or coach much direct the learner in the acquisition of the correct sequence and timing of the movements that comprise the skill, through the use of such training techniques as previously described. Once the performer is able to perform the skill correctly, the next stage is the development of a motor schema containing all the parameters that are needed to generate a unique movement to meet each situation in which the skill is performed. This can be accomplished by providing the learner with practice in a wide variety of situations that not only allow many variations of a movement to be produced, but also require the learner to produce movements that meet the exact environmental demands. For example, in teaching the jump shot in basketball, once the player can perform the shot correctly, little is gained from continually practising it in isolation without someone guarding him or her. Placing the learner in a 'gamelike' situation will allow for the development of a diversified schema from which the player will be able to generate a particular sequence of motor commands to meet the specific game situation. The acquisition of a diversified schema is particularly important in the learning of open skills that are performed in a constantly changing environment. Closed skills, on the other hand, because the environment is relatively static, demand a more precise and invariable motor schema that allows for the generation of the same movement sequence over and over again. In such skills practice should involve repeated attempts to reproduce exactly the correct movement sequence.

SUMMARY

In this chapter I have attempted to contrast the two major theoretical approaches to motor skills: motor program control and closed-loop control. Evidence has been presented that many motor skills are centrally represented in memory as a motor program. It has been argued, however, that the control of skilled movement requires the integration of both feedback and program processes. The concept of a generalized motor program was then discussed as a possible solution to some of the deficiencies evident in the traditional view of programmed control. Next, the current trend in motor control theories to delegate greater responsibility to progressively lower levels of the system was reviewed and its implications for the motor program concept discussed. Finally, some of the implications of motor program theory for skill learning were outlined. More information on skill learning will be found in Chapter 9.

ACKNOWLEDGEMENTS

The preparation of this chapter was supported by the Australian Research Grants Scheme, Project No. A78115899.

Chapter 4

Attention and Skilled Performance

Christopher D. Wickens

People are often called upon to do more than one thing at a time. The secretary continues transcribing a manuscript (reading while typing) even while carrying out a conversation with the boss; the quarterback deftly evades the oncoming rushers while locating the open receiver and calculating the right trajectory to launch the football for an easy catch; while controlling your car along the crowded freeway, you are able to tune the radio dial to your favorite music, while still planning what you will say in the forthcoming job interview. Some situations lend themselves quite easily to successful time-sharing—listening while driving, for example. But others, like listening to two voices, do not. Correspondingly, some people are very good at time-sharing, while others are not, a difference that clearly defines a skill of time-sharing.

In an effort to understand these differences between situations and between people, the current chapter first provides a fairly comprehensive model of the different phenomena and mechanisms that are involved in complex multi-task performance. This model focuses on the mechanisms of attention, as manifest in skilled performance. The corresponding chapter in the previous volume accounted for these differences in terms of functional cerebral distance (Kinsbourne, 1981). In the present chapter we account for them in terms of four mechanisms: switching, resources, confusion, and integration. As these different mechanisms are introduced, the evidence that shows that a given mechanism may be trained will be described. Finally, the chapter will conclude with a close look at data pertaining to two aspects of differences in attentional behavior: the changes that result from practice under dual-task circumstances, and the differences between individuals in dual-task performance.

Human Skills. Edited by D. Holding © 1989 John Wiley & Sons Ltd

A hybrid model of multiple-task performance

The history of attention theory has been replete with various arguments for one theoretical position versus another. For example, arguments have been made as to whether selective attention occurs 'early' or 'late' in the sequence of information-processing stages (Norman, 1968; Treisman, 1969; Keele, 1973) whether time-sharing may be best accounted in terms of task structure or task demand (Kerr, 1973; Kahneman, 1973); whether there exist one form of attentional resource or several (Norman and Bobrow, 1975; Navon and Gopher, 1979; Navon, 1984); whether information-processing is serial or parallel (Townsend, 1974; Kantowitz, 1985); and whether task interference may be related to the competition for scarce resources or to the conflict between incompatible outcomes (Navon, 1984; Navon and Miller, 1987). In the current chapter, we reject this emphasis on validating one versus another theoretical position. Instead, our view is that the issue of multiple-task performance is sufficiently complex to allow several different mechanisms, some associated with one theoretical position, others associated with different positions. Therefore, there need be no 'right' or 'wrong' position. Rather, the important goals for analyzing skill behavior are to identify the environmental or antecedent conditions that make one mechanism more likely to be brought into play than another one.

Figure 15 presents a global representation of three mechanisms of multiple-task performance and defines those conditions that determine when each of these mechanisms should operate, along with the consequences or the data that may be observed when each comes into force. Across the top are three different conditions, or characteristics of the tasks that are to be time-shared. On the left is represented the global similarity between tasks: their similarity in terms of a few global structural characteristics such as their stages of processing, or whether they are verbal or spatial, auditory or visual. On the right side is represented the *microsimilarity* between tasks. This refers to similarity that can be expressed in a quantitative scale such as the closeness in space, similarity of color, or similarity of meaning. In the middle is represented a third characteristic; the difficulty, demand level, or complexity of each task in a time-shared combination. While difficulty is a feature of each task within the pair, the two aspects of similarity may be thought of as 'emergent features' of a pair of tasks.

In the next level of the table are described the different mechanisms by which the tasks interact. Global similarity will produce resource competition. For example, the tasks of driving a car, while trying to recall a poorly memorized map, place common demands upon spatial resources, forming a source of interference. Such competition is an intrinsic characteristic of the task combination and cannot be easily modified by adopting different strategies. In contrast, the difficulty of the task determines the amount of

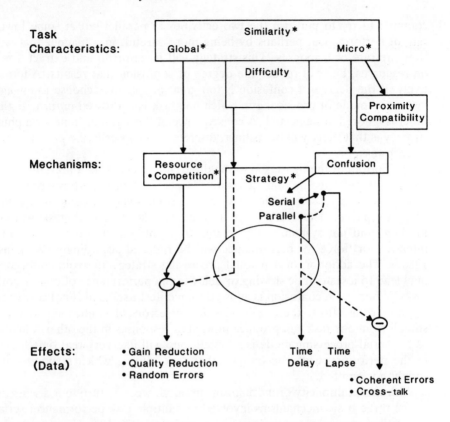

* Emergent Feature of Dual Task.

Figure 15. A hybrid model of multiple-task performance, described in the text.

resources or effort an operator must invest to obtain a given level of performance. Hence, there is an input to the box marked *strategy*. The level of dual-
task performance will then be a joint function of the amount of resources
invested, as determined by the difficulty, and the degree of resource competition between the tasks within a pair. If the difficulty of one task in a pair
becomes too great, subjects may simply abandon any efforts to time-share it
with another, and adopt a strict 'serial' mode of performance. Thus, we see
the combination of these two factors to the lower left.

The micro-aspects of similarity may lead to confusion between the elements
of the tasks, much as two simultaneous conversations about the same topic
may get 'mixed up' in the listener's mind. On the one hand, this confusion
may directly lead to systematic or coherent errors in one task that are directly
related to events in the other. On the other hand, people may adopt different
strategies in an effort to reduce this confusion. One such strategy may be to

continue to try to perform the two activities in parallel but at some lower rate of performance, perhaps by being more careful, in a manner that will slow the rate of responses. This strategy will be effortful and extract a toll on resources, but will reduce the degree of confusion that results. Alternatively, if the degree of confusion is too great people may choose to engage in a serial mode of processing in which one task is addressed in turn, as the other is ignored or neglected. A consequence of the serial or 'time-swapping' strategy is that there will be distinct, discrete time-lapses in the performance of each task.

The bottom of the figure shows the different effects of the different mechanisms, as reflected in the qualitative aspects of task performance. For example, resource competition will lead to some overall loss in the quality of performance. The errors that may be produced in each task will be random, and not systematically related to events on the other. The gain, intensity, or 'force' of performance will be reduced accordingly (Wickens, 1986a). The adoption of a parallel processing strategy to avoid confusions may lead to a systematic slowing or delay in the performance of one or both tasks. Where such confusion is allowed to manifest itself and is not corrected by mobilizing effort, there will be *coherent* errors of confusion, in which stimuli from one task will produce unwanted responses in the other. Finally, as the serial processing mode is adopted, one will find very real time lapses in the performance of one or the other task, during which responses are simply not emitted.

With this multiplicity of mechanisms in mind, we now turn to a discussion of the three basic mechanisms involved in multiple task performance: serial processing, resource competition, and confusion, the latter leading to the closely-related characteristic of task integration.

SERIAL PROCESSING

When the demands imposed by one task become excessive, then it simply cannot be shared in time with another, and it is necessary to engage in some sort of sequential sampling, or serial 'time-swapping' behavior, as shown at the bottom right of Figure 15. This process describes many aspects of the sampling of visual information, because the range of foveal vision necessary for object recognition is so restricted. Hence, visual scanning behavior is a potent way of assessing the serial aspects of human skilled behavior in such tasks as looking at a scene, driving an automobile, flying an aircraft, or scanning a nuclear power instrument panel (Moray, 1986). If the sequence of visual fixations can be tracked, then the sequential allocation of attention over time can be effectively understood. Investigations by Senders (1966, 1983) in a basic laboratory task, by Fitts, Jones, and Milton (1950), Harris and Christhilf (1980), and Harris and Spady (1985) in studies of aircraft instrument scanning, and by Moray, Richards, and Low (1980) in a study of radar monitors, have examined these serial components of attention allocation through visual fixation (see Moray, 1986, for a summary of much of this work).

It is also possible to model these serial aspects at the coarser level of description of the *task*, rather than the finer level of the visual sample. At this level of scheduling task performance, the limited mechanisms that are sequentially allocated, may be either the hands and arms necessary to perform one skill that are unavailable to the other, or the full allocation of cognitive processes. Thus, when scheduling study time during final exam week, the student cannot easily study for two classes simultaneously, but must establish the relative priorities of when one class or the other must be dealt with or 'attended'.

The research on selection between serial processes has produced a number of general conclusions concerning the degree of 'optimality' of human sampling behavior. Optimal behavior refers to performance when we attend to those things at a time that will produce the greatest benefit and ignore those things during times when ignoring them will lead to the smallest cost. Research that has been summarized by Moray (1986) and Wickens (1984) has identified four important characteristics of such behavior.

(1) The internal model. Sampling and scheduling is fairly well modeled by the human's *internal model* or mental model of the statistical properties in the environment. That is, channels or locations at which relatively frequent events will occur will be sampled more often than those channels in which events occur only rarely. Furthermore, Senders (1966, 1983) has found that the frequency with which visual channels in different locations are sampled (visually fixated) is nearly directly proportional to the frequency of events occurring along those channels.

(2) Departures from optimality. There is, however, some departure from optimality as events occur very frequently, in which case they are sampled less often than optimally; or very rarely, in which case they are sampled slightly more frequently than optimally (Senders, 1983). The oversampling of rare events appears to be a result of human memory limitations as described next.

(3) Memory limitations. Restating characteristic (1), how often we should sample or attend to a particular channel depends in part upon how frequently the events occur in that channel. For continuously changing information, like the position of a car on a highway, sampling should be related to how rapidly the signal is changing. Consider the meter that slowly oscillates between two critical 'danger values'. If our job is to keep an eye on the meter, or to

sample it in order to make sure that it does not cross into a danger zone, we shall be likely to sample it more frequently if it oscillates rapidly (Senders, 1966). Furthermore, if we have sampled the meter once and found it right in the center range, we shall feel that it is safer, and therefore we shall be able to wait longer before we sample again, than had we sampled and found the meter to be only a millimeter away from the danger zone. This indeed defines one aspect of an optimum sampling prescription (Sheridan, 1972). That is, how long we wait till the next sample should depend, in part, upon what we saw the last time we sampled. However, human memory is fallible, and we may forget that, when we last sampled, the meter was in the middle. Now to be on the 'safe side' we may take our next sample sooner than had we remembered the precise location of the meter at the previous sample. In fact, as time passes since our last sample, a spreading 'haze of uncertainty' clouds our memory of where things were and causes us to sample at shorter intervals than is 'optimal'. In one sense, however, this behavior is actually optimal by compensating for our known failures of memory.

Sheridan's analysis has pointed out that we may remember what we have forgotten, in terms of learning *when* to sample. However, there are also times when we are not aware of what we have forgotten in terms of *what* to sample. For example, Moray (1984) has voiced concern over the representation of nuclear power instruments on a single centralized video display, to which the operator must address requests in order to view a particular instrument. Moray notes that on the display board of a conventional instrument panel the reminder of what instruments to look at is represented by their physical presence. In the computerized panel, however this physical cue must be replaced by the memory reminder of when each instrument needs to be inspected. Without the visual reminder (or some other automated assist), subjects may simply forget the existence of an instrument altogether and inspect it much less frequently than is optimal.

(4) Planning prediction and preview. Suppose the several events or tasks that drive this selective aspect of attention were given some preview so that we could see when each of several events are about to occur. Such preview is quite helpful for planning and makes it easier to predict when attention will be needed where, and thereby align it accordingly. The situation however is made more complex (and the optimality of human performance reduced) as certain other variables and constraints are added. For example, events may differ in the benefits to be gained by attending to them or the costs to be imposed by their neglect. The restaurant chef may be little concerned by a burnt dinner roll but may have his career ruined by the overcooking of the elegant soufflé even though each event may be caused by the same one-minute delay in attending.

Secondly, there is often a cost imposed in *switching* from one event to the next. There is some 'overhead' or 'switching time' necessary to disengage from one activity and engage in another. For example, when writing papers for two different courses it is not easy instantly to stop writing one and pick up the other, without spending some time to begin thinking about the topic area of the second paper. Together, these factors make the attention allocation problem, even with preview, a somewhat challenging one. Does one stay on a relatively low-benefit activity, or does one switch to a higher-benefit activity knowing that it may take a while to switch over there, and one may not have much time to deal with the second activity once the switch is made? Tulga and Sheridan (1980) have investigated human performance under these circumstances in a simulated scheduling task. They found that humans can effectively use the preview to direct attention to optimum channels and maximize their expected earnings, as long as the number of different channels on which events arrive is small. As this number grows, however, their planning horizon decreases and performance becomes far less optimal.

Efforts to understand and to model these effects of serial processing have focused on two major characteristics. First, what is the logic that should and does drive human sampling, and what accounts for the departures from optimality described above? Secondly, what is the 'cost of neglect' of an unperformed task during the period while other tasks are processed? Sometimes this cost may simply be predicted by the amount of time that passes until the task is again dealt with and responded to. At other times, however, there may be failures of memory between when a task is once attended and when it is next picked up, and these memory failures will add to the overall performance loss. This would clearly be the case, for example, if a mental arithmetic task is time-shared with a verbal task. Momentary switching from the former to the latter at the wrong time may cause critical subtotals to 'decay' from working memory to a level where they are no longer usable.

The previous section has focused on the 'destination' of the attention switch and the logic governing this switching process. A somewhat different issue relates to the dynamics of the switching process itself. How rapidly can attention move from one source of input to another, or alternatively from one cognitive process to another? The speed of this switching process, and the fact that it is little influenced by other variables, suggests that switching speed is probably not a highly important variable necessary for skilled performance nor one that is greatly modifiable through training and practice. Perhaps the only direct relevance of switching dynamics to skilled performance is a finding that pertains to the next section on resources. That is, there appears to be a greater cost to switching between input modalities, (i.e. from audition to vision or from vision to audition) than to switching between two channels within a modality (LaBerge, VanGelder, and Yellott, 1971).

In contrast, the implications for training and skill acquisition of the logic of attention switching are substantial. Major differences between novice and skilled pilots, for example, may be found in the pattern of instrument scans (Harris and Spady, 1985); and a fundamental component of pilot training is focused on teaching the optimal scan patterns. The optimal internal model revealed by Senders (1983) appears to be one that only emerges with high levels of skill, characterizing implicit knowledge of the frequency of different events in the world (Moray, 1986). Furthermore, although little systematic research has been done in this area, it would seem that substantial benefits in time-sharing many complex tasks might be obtained by teaching subjects when to ignore certain channels, at times when less critical information is presented. In reading while listening to a conversation, for example, one might 'tune' to attending to highly informative content words, while returning to the written text as the more redundant function words that often follow are spoken.

RESOURCE COMPETITION

While many aspects of information-processing are serial, there are nevertheless numerous others that are carried out in parallel. Common examples of parallel processing are walking and talking, driving and listening, jogging and thinking, scanning the horizon while engaged in some sort of control manipulation, or identifying objects in foveal vision, while processing peripheral motion cues to guide one's egomotion. The analysis of skilled performance in such situations must be concerned with the factors that allow this time-sharing or parallel processing to be carried out with greater or less efficiency. It is important here to emphasize that parallel processing does not imply perfect time-sharing (i.e. at a level equal to single task performance), but only that the information-processing system is engaged in handling and transforming information for two tasks simultaneously, even though there may be some cost to this simultaneity. It is also important to emphasize that the term *time-sharing* indicates a true sharing of time between two activities as distinct from *time-swapping* or switching which describes the more serial aspects of performance discussed in the previous section. Finally, it must be acknowledged that very rapid aspects of time-swapping may in fact be indistinguishable from true time-sharing (e.g. Townsend, 1974). However, this inability to make a distinction is not particularly critical from the point of the view of skilled performance, as long as changes in the efficiency of both processes (parallel processing and rapid switching) can be accounted for by the resource-like mechanism described below.

The construct underlying the concept of resources is that of *scarcity* of a fixed capacity (Gopher, 1986; Wickens, 1986a). It is a concept used to describe how the increases in demand of one activity will disrupt the performance of another. The increased need for resources of the first activity must be met at the expense of their availability to the second activity. There are two fundamental characteristics underlying resources, their availability (or demand) and their multiplicity, and each of these will be dealt with in turn.

Resource availability: single resources

The concept of resources is an *energetic* one (Hockey, Gaillard, and Coles, 1986). This 'mental energy' of limited availability can be manifest in three independent psychological phenomena. First, the effect of the difficulty of a task on its own performance; second, the physiological or subjective manifestations of increasing task difficulty; and third, the interference with concurrent activities. Both of the first two phenomena are definable concepts in a single task domain, that are used then to predict performance in a dual task domain.

The concept of difficulty itself may be defined both in terms of task characteristics and of the development of automaticity. For example, task characteristics that require more complex mapping from stimuli to responses impose greater demands upon working memory, greater need for prediction, greater involvement of attentional focusing, or greater complexity of response coordination may all be assumed to be more difficult. So are tasks that are less practised. This increase in difficulty is typically reflected by a reduced quality of performance. Furthermore, converging evidence that such manipulations have increased the difficulty or resource demands may be obtained either by assessing subjective measures (Gopher and Braune, 1984; Vidulich and Wickens, 1986; Yeh and Wickens, 1988), or by examining the cost to the processing system reflected in physiological measures such as heart rate variability or pupil diameter. For example, investigators have nicely illustrated the sensitivity of heart rate variability measures to increases in cognitive task difficulty (Mulder and Mulder, 1981), tracking stability (Derrick and Wickens, 1984; Hart and Hauser, 1987), or perceptual-motor load (Kalsbeek and Sykes, 1967). Other investigations summarized by Beatty (1982; Richter, Silverman, and Beatty, 1983) have nicely illustrated the sensitivity of pupil diameter to manipulations of task demand. These studies then suggest a direct physiological cost to these manipulations. Studies by Kramer, Wickens, and Donchin (1985) and by Wickens et al. (1983) have illustrated that the amplitude of evoked brain potential components provides a direct index of the resources invested into more difficult tasks.

A second source of variance in single-task resource demands results from the development of automaticity, that is a characteristic of high levels of skill development. While the concept of automaticity has been defined by a number of different attributes (Fitts and Posner, 1967; Kahneman and Chajczyk, 1983; Logan, 1985), the most important of these from the current perspective is the characteristic that automatic processing may be carried out without the allocation of attentional resources. In an extensive program of research, Schneider and his colleagues (Schneider and Shiffrin, 1977; Schneider and Fisk, 1982a; Schneider, Dumais, and Shiffrin, 1984; Schneider, 1985a) have illuminated the conditions under which this automaticity is most likely to develop. These are conditions when *consistency* is maintained in the mapping of one element of the task to another. For example, in the letter categorization task used by Schneider and his colleagues, the automatic perceptual processing of letters occurs only if a set of letters is consistently assigned to a target class, and never to a non-target class.

In summary, converging evidence from manipulations of task characteristics, observations of performance changes, assessment of physiological and subjective measures, and the development of automaticity all point to the underlying construct of resource demand. The relevant issue for theories of attention is how much this variance in resource demand can account for variance in dual-task interference as increased demands by one task leave fewer resources available for performance of another. The answer is that in some circumstances it can account for this variance very well. For example, it is well established that the development of automaticity in skill learning will decrease the amount of interference with a concurrent task (Bahrick and Shelly, 1958; Schneider and Fisk, 1982). Furthermore, many secondary task measures of workload have nicely illustrated a sensitivity to manipulations of primary task demand Rolfe, 1971 Ogden, Levine, and Eisner, 1979).

There are, however, a number of instances in which this reciprocity between the difficulty of one task and the performance of another is not observed. Such a circumstance might simply imply that the manipulation of difficulty has not in fact required or produced the allocation of more resources. Subjects may have simply let their performance deteriorate on the primary task whose demand is increased. It also may reflect the fact that subjects still have ample resources available to perform the concurrent task even as the primary task has reached its most difficult level. This would suggest then that the concurrent task was automated as described in the preceding paragraphs, and required few resources to attain maximum performance. Both of these cases can be described with reference to the performance-resource functions, shown in Figure 16, which is a hypothetical mapping of the relation between the resources invested in a task, and its level of performance (Norman and Bobrow, 1975).

There are, however, a number of instances in which the same manipulation of primary task difficulty can produce a deterioration in the performance of one concurrent task but no change in performance with another. The question we then ask is, what is different about the primary task or the difficulty manipulation between these two situations? In previous reviews of the literature and in experimental programs, I have determined that this difference seems to result from the sharing (when there is a deterioration) versus separation (when there is insensitivity) of different global task characteristics,

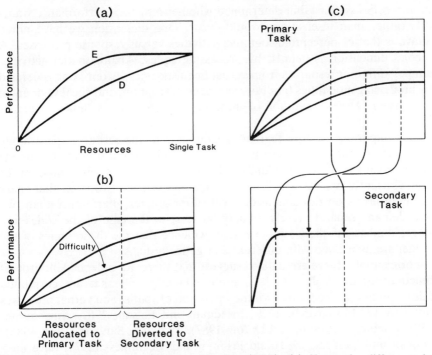

Figure 16. The performance resource function (PRF): (a) Shows the difference in the PRF between an easy (E) and difficult (D) task. Note the greater efficiency of performance obtained per unit resource invested in the easy task. The easy task is said to be 'data-limited'. (b) Shows the effect of increasing difficulty of a primary task when the subject does not change the allocation of resources between tasks. Hence the secondary task would not be expected to deteriorate although the primary task would do so. (c) Shows a PRF for both a primary and secondary task when the secondary task needs only minimal resources to attain perfect performance. It is trained to automaticity. Here again, one expects little reduction in secondary task performance, as primary task demands increase.

energetic systems or *resources* (Wickens, 1980, 1984). For example, a diffi- culty–performance tradeoff is more likely to result when two tasks both require heavy involvement of perceptual/cognitive activity or both demand heavy involvement of response processes, but not when one is perceptual/ cognitive and the other is response-related. These phenomena require that the identity of the different resources be formally specified, which brings us to the second attribute of resources—their multiplicity.

Resource similarity: multiple resources

An initial analysis of the literature (Wickens, 1980) suggested that three dichotomous dimensions could be used to define the differences in resource or energetics systems that determined whether difficulty–performance trade-offs rather than insensitivity would occur. One dimension we have noted above is that of perceptual/cognitive activities versus response processes. A second dimension is defined by processing codes: Analog/spatial activities employ different resources from verbal linguistic ones. A third one is defined by processing modalities (auditory vs. visual perception, and vocal vs. manual responses). A representation of these three dimensions is shown in Figure 17.

It is important to note that the partitioning of the resource space along these dimensions is not established by these findings of differential tradeoffs and insensitivity alone. In addition, the dimensions also seem to account for how efficiently two tasks will be time-shared. That is, two tasks that share common levels on the dimensions will suffer greater interference than two that demand separate levels. Finally, at least in the case of the codes and stages dimensions there is convergent evidence that the dichotomies of the model are associated with different energetics systems.

For example, there are data to suggest that there are independent arousal functions of the right and left cerebral hemispheres that are correlated (although not perfectly so) with the operation of spatial and verbal processes respectively (Moscovitch, 1979; Friedman and Polson, 1981; Kinsbourne, 1981; Friedman, Polson, and Dafoe, 1987). Similarly, Sanders (1983, 1986), Gopher and Sanders, 1983) and Pribram and McGuiness (1975) have integrated a large amount of date to suggest the existence of a distinction between arousal states related to perceptual, cognitive, and response processes. Thus, the concept of multiple resources does not hinge upon one phenomenon alone but rather is built upon the convergence of several phenomena into a

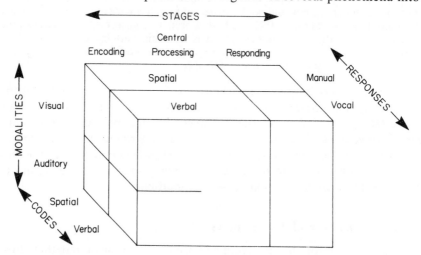

Figure 17. The structure of multiple resources. (From Wickens, 1984.)

single 'construct'. Concepts of difficulty, performance, subjective experience, and physiological cost converge to define a single task manifestation of resources, while phenomena of physiological energetic brain systems, difficulty insensitivity, and time-sharing efficiency converge consistently to identify the nature and multiplicity of these resource systems.

The particular multiple resource representation presented in Figure 17 has close parallels with the theoretical positions proposed by other researchers (Polson et al. 1987, in press). For example, the concept of functional cerebral space proposed by Kinsbourne and Hicks (1978; Kinsbourne, 1981) also associates the sharing of brain structures with the competition for or scarcity of processing availability. Kinsbourne and Hicks (1978) emphasize the importance of the processing code dimension (defined in their model by cerebral hemispheres) as a major component of functional cerebral space. Their model also makes finer discriminations between other dimensions of task similarity that will lead to performance interference. For example, they draw the distinction between bimanual performance (two responses that are close) and manual and foot performance (two responses that are relatively more distant in the functional cerebral space). A closely allied model is one proposed by Friedman and Polson (1981; Friedman et al., 1982; Friedman, Polson, and Dafoe, 1987), who have placed greatest importance on the separate resources defined by the two cerebral hemispheres.

Finally, the efforts of Baddeley and his coworkers to define two functionally separate working memory systems—a phonetic rehearsal loop and a visual/spatial 'scratchpad'—are closely related to the multiple-resource concept (Baddeley and Hitch, 1974; Baddeley and Lieberman, 1980; Farmer, Berman, and Fletcher, 1986). Baddeley's data suggest that two tasks using the different memory systems will be carried on more efficiently in parallel than two tasks using the common memory systems.

There exist numerous laboratory demonstrations of the increases in interference—and in demand reciprocity—that result when tasks share code and stage-defined resources (Wickens and Kessel, 1980; Friedman et al., 1982, 1987; Wickens and Weingartner, 1985; Wickens et al., 1985; Wickens and Liu, 1988). Rather than summarizing the basic laboratory experiments which document these effects, we shall instead describe certain phenomena in the world of skilled performance, for which these resource dimensions can account. For example, suppose a motor skill is to be mentally rehearsed by imagining the temporal-spatial sequences of activities. How would such a sequence best be studied—by printed words or by oral instructions? The perception of print, initially requiring visual registration, would be more likely to interfere with the visual-spatial rehearsal than would be the processing of the spoken word. In the world of human–machine interaction, Wetherell (1979) found that navigational instructions for driving an automobile through a 'maze' were better retained when they had been presented in the format of a verbal 'route list' of turns, than in terms of a visual-spatial map. This difference, he concluded, was due in part to the greater resource competition between the spatial map, and the spatial task of driving.

The role of processing stages in 'real world' interference is a little more subtle. But an example would be the air traffic controller whose task is heavily demanding of perceptual cognitive resources—trying to maintain an accurate visual-spatial 'mental picture' of the airspace from the evolving multi-element display. Which additional task, each of the same difficulty, would disrupt performance more: requiring the controller to retrieve from long-term memory and speak a sequence of commands or call signs (a response load), or requiring that an auditory sequence be listened to and remembered (perceptual cognitive load)? Multiple resource theory predicts that the first of these secondary tasks will be more efficiently time-shared, given that the resource demands (difficulty) of the two tasks are equal.

Misconceptions and qualifications of multiple resources

In interpreting the multiple resource model and applying it to predict and describe complex task performance, it is necessary to call attention to certain misconceptions that are sometimes held. First, it *cannot* be assumed that two tasks which use different resources will be perfectly time-shared. For example, two tasks may use different resources along one dimension (i.e. one visual and one auditory) and yet still share common levels along the other two dimensions (Herdman and Friedman, 1985). This latter sharing will indeed produce a substantial degree of interference. An example here would be time-sharing the tasks of understanding speech while reading. Thus, the model will rarely go so far as to predict 'perfect' time-sharing in the absence of some level of automaticity, because almost any pair of tasks will involve some degree of resource overlap along at least one of the dimensions (but see Allport, Antonis, and Reynolds, 1972, for a nice example of how perfect time-sharing between piano sightreading and verbal shadowing can be predicted from the model). Instead, what the model predicts is a monotonic decrease in time-sharing efficiency, and an increase in difficulty–performance tradeoffs, as progressively more levels are shared along the three dimensions (Derrick and Wickens, 1984; Tsang and Wickens, 1988).

The model is also not intended to account for all sources of task interference, as described in the introduction. For example, when extreme levels of difficulty make time-sharing impossible and invoke the serial processing or time-swapping strategy as described earlier, it is clear that multiple resources are silent as to predictions of task decrements. If time-sharing is not going on, then resource-sharing (or separation) simply has no relevance. Furthermore, as we shall see in the next section, other dimensions of similarity besides the three global dimensions used in the multiple resources model, may account for variance in task interference.

Finally, it is possible that there may indeed be other 'resource systems' with the resource properties described above that can be used to account for differences in task interference. One logical candidate would be the dimensions contrasting foveal and peripheral vision. Leibowitz and Post (1982) have argued that these two visual subsystems—designed for object recognition, and spatial orientation respectively—operate in a truly independent, parallel fashion, akin to the other dichotomous dimensions. In any case, it is important to set a fairly strict criterion as to what dimensions may truly be labeled resources. The model was not designed to account for all sources of interference but was developed as a tool that could predict a reasonably large portion of variance and be relatively parsimonious.

In order to be viable, however, the model must not only be parsimonious but also robust. That is, it should predict differences in interference as a function of resource overlap across a wide variety of different task configurations. While the stages and codes dimensions have passed these 'tests' relatively effectively, there is less certainty regarding the status of the modalities dimension. A careful analysis of a number of studies in which the competition for input modalities (visual vs. auditory) has been manipulated has called into question the viability of this dimension as defining separate resources (Wickens, Webb, and Fracker, 1987; Wickens and Liu, 1988). This analysis suggested that two other processing phenomena–pre-emption and attention-switching—may characterize performance distinctions when a visual/visual combination (resource overlap) is compared with a visual/auditory combination (resource separation).

First, when a visual tracking task is time-shared with a discrete reaction-time task that may be auditory or visual, the consequence of using the auditory rather than the visual modality for the discrete task is not to increase the overall level of time-sharing efficiency—a resource explanation—but rather it is to pre-empt processing of the continuous visual task. That is, when an auditory stimulus is used for the discrete task it calls attention to itself, reducing the decrement in processing that stimulus relative to a visual stimulus, but at the same time increasing the amount of disruption with the continuous tracking task, as if the auditory stimulus pulls resources away from tracking to produce its faster processing, while the discrete visual stimulus does not. As such, the auditory modality appears to change the bias between tasks rather than changing their level of time-sharing efficiency. An analogous form of pre-emption seems to occur when a manual, rather than a voice response is used for a discrete task which is time-shared with a continuous manual control task (e.g. McLeod, 1977; Wickens, Sandry, and Vidulich, 1983). The manual response preempts the continuous tracking. The voice response does not.

Secondly, when two discrete task are time-shared as, for example, two Sternberg memory search tasks (Wickens, Webb, and Fracker, 1987), the consequence of using the auditory rather than the visual modality appears to be a reduction in time-sharing efficiency, rather than an increase. The data suggest that this increased cost in the cross-modal condition is a result of the extra time required for cross-modal attention-switching (LaBerge, VanGelder, and Yellott, 1971). Thus, careful scrutiny suggests that modalities may not behave like resources from a processing standpoint. Nevertheless it is still appropriate that this dimension be used to define resources for the engineering and task-analysis applications of the model; that is, when the model is used to predict when tasks will and will not interfere. The reason is that in most real-world situations the time-sharing of two visual channels requires a fair degree of visual scanning. This scanning in turn almost always imposes a cost to performance in a visual/visual condition that is not present in a visual/auditory condition. It is a safe assumption that this scanning cost usually outweighs or dominates the relatively small switching cost for the auditory/visual condition. In less controlled environments, cross-modal presentation will usually be superior. Hence, all three dimensions of the model remain valid as an engineering design tool.

Relevance to skilled performance

How are multiple resources relevant to skilled performance? The most direct linkage is with the concept of automaticity. As noted above, automaticity is defined in part by the reduction in resource demands that occur with practice on tasks in which there is consistent mapping between different components (Schneider and Fisk, 1982a). A second linkage concerns the skill in allocating resources. If two tasks are time-shared and A requires 70% of the available resources to obtain perfect performance, while B only requires 30%, it is then clear that a strategy of allocating 50% resources to each task (e.g. equal priority) will maximize performance on task B but not on task A. However, a strategy in which 70% resources are devoted to A and 30% to B will be sufficient to yield the perfect performance on both tasks. These two strategies are shown in Figure 18. One might say that the first strategy 'wastes' resources to task B.

The research that has dealt with this aspect of skill and resource-allocation has not been extensive. Schneider and Fisk (1982a) have shown that subjects may not spontaneously adopt the optimal allocation strategy when two tasks are shared, such as A and B above. They tend to 'waste' resources on the more automated tasks like task B. However, they can be instructed to allocate more optimally and improve their performance as a consequence. Gopher and his colleagues (Gopher and Brickner, 1980; Gopher, Weil, and Siegel, 1986) go further to show that training subjects to perform a complex skill under conditions in which first one task and then the other is emphasized (i.e. training a skill of variable resource-allocation) leads to better transfer to complex task performance under conditions of fixed priorities, than does

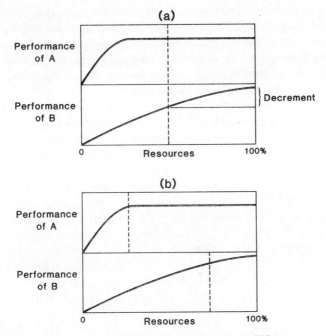

Figure 18. (a) An example of 'wasted' resources on task A. Fifty per cent of resources are allocated to each task. The decrement in task B is shown. (b) A more optimal allocation of resources, yielding nearly perfect time-sharing.

training under fixed priorities. Tsang and Wickens (1988) have found that training and instructions of explicit strategies for allocating resources between a primary and secondary task, when the demands of the former are constantly shifting, can have some benefit. The data then suggest that learning to allocate one's resources in graded quantities between tasks is an important component of complex task skill that will allow the subjects to reallocate or reschedule priorities at times of increased demands on one component or the other. This component of skill is not far removed from the component of scheduling and optimal selection described in the previous section.

There is yet a third potential mechanism whereby the resource concept is relevant to skill acquisition. This mechanism is inherent in the potential for subjects to learn to perform the same task with different strategies, which in turn demand different resources. When placed in a time-sharing situation, subjects can learn to adopt the strategy that will impose minimum resource demands with the concurrent task. Some limited experimental evidence for this flexibility in dual-task performance is available. For example, Parks et al. (1972) had subjects retain letters in working memory in silence and under conditions of intense auditory distraction. (The latter condition may be defined as a dual-task condition if one assumes that the second task is ignoring the distraction.) The investigators found that subjects were able to change the nature of the rehearsal code used in working memory to minimize interference from the auditory distractor task. In silence they used the more natural phonetic-acoustic code, while under the noisy condition they rehearsed the letters in terms of visual images.

As a second example, Wickens and Goettl (1985) trained subjects to perform a tracking task with acceleration dynamics (see Chapter 7) using either a continuous control strategy requiring relatively high-precision manual responses, or a discrete double-impulse 'bang-bang' control requiring 'hard over' responses with minimal response demand (Kerr, 1973). Examining the interference of these two tracking strategies, with concurrent performance of a reaction-time task using either auditory or visual presentation, Wickens and Goettl found some evidence that the strategy adopted influenced the resource cost. The bang-bang strategy, requiring greater cognitive involvement but minimum motor demand, showed greater interaction with the display modalities of the reaction time task. Performance with the continuous strategy, hypothesized to place heavier demands on response processes, was insensitive to the manipulation of input modality competition.

MICROSIMILARITY

Representational similarity: confusion and cross-talk

Recently, Navon (1984), and Navon and Miller (1987) have called into question the usefulness of resource competition as an explanation for task interference. In particular, Navon has argued that an alternative mechanism, that of *outcome conflict*, may provide a better framework for understanding, predicting, and describing dual-task interaction. Outcome conflict results when the internal processes activated by performance of one task represent unwanted intrusions into the performance of a concurrent task. Therefore, as shown in Figure 15, the concurrent task will either be disrupted by these intrusions—producing errors—or must be postponed or reduced in its quality, as strategies are adopted to suppress the intrusions. One well-known example of such outcome conflict is seen in the Stroop task in which the subjects, trying to report the color ink of printed color names, find that the response tendencies activated by semantic content of those names interfere with the desired outcome of reporting the ink color (Stroop, 1935; Keele, 1972).

While the Stroop task represents a failure of focused, rather than divided attention, Navon and Miller (1987) have illustrated the role of outcome conflict in a dual-task reaction-time task. In their experiment subjects monitored four visual channels. Two of these channels, defining one task, presented the names of boys or girls, and two channels defining the other task presented the names of either cities or states. Subjects made two-choice classification responses for each task, and performance was measured in both single- and dual-task conditions. Navon and Miller showed that increasing the difficulty of monitoring one channel by itself (i.e. increasing resource demand) did not influence the amount of interference in the dual-task condition. Furthermore, they showed systematic effects of outcome conflict. For example, when a target relevant to one channel appeared on the other channel, processing of the first channel was delayed. The authors also demonstrated a pattern of outcome conflict in responses such that giving two positive or two negative responses on both hands was easier than giving a positive response on one hand and a negative response on the other.

This then is the role of *microsimilarity* in task interference, which is distinguished from the global aspects of similarity defined by multiple resources. Increasing microsimilarity may cause outcome conflict or, in the terms we prefer here, will cause confusion and cross-talk between channels or tasks. The importance of microsimilarity is revealed in the review of the following studies, all of which are compatible with an outcome conflict or confusion point of view. Consider first the Stroop task. Kahneman and Chajczyk (1983) have shown that the Stroop effect may be 'diluted', by 'pulling apart' the semantic (color name) and physical (ink color) aspects from a single object into two different objects. Increasing distance (one object to two objects) reduces interference. The effect of similarity on interference also is observed with respect to 'semantic distance'. The Stroop effect is strong when the irrelevant (semantic) component of the stimuli are color names, but it will be diluted if they are simply words with strong color associations (i.e. 'sky' or 'grass'; Klein, 1964) and will be eliminated if the words have no color associations whatsoever. In an analogous manipulation with a different sort of task, Treisman (1964) reports that the ability to shadow a message is disrupted by increasing the semantic similarity of a competing message which is to be ignored. Employing a task similar to that used by Navon and Miller (1987), Hirst (1984) reports that the ability to shadow or process two messages in parallel is disrupted by increasing semantic similarity between the two. The author identifies the important skill of 'segregation' as being a necessary component of efficient dual-task performance in this situation.

The identification of confusion and cross-talk, as an interference source, should be accompanied by some direct assessment of confusion between responses to the two tasks. The dual-axis tracking task provides a nice paradigm in which such information is directly available in the measure of *contralateral coherence* (Damos and Wickens, 1980; Fracker and Wickens, 1988). This measure describes the control responses on one axis that are linearly related to (and therefore is presumably directly caused by) error on the other axis. An experiment by Fracker and Wickens (1988) employed this tool, along with the measure of total tracking error, to examine the relative contributions of resource competition, and confusion and cross-talk, to dual-task tracking interference as the difficulty of each axis and the similarity between axes were varied. Difficulty was increased by raising the order of control, from first (velocity) to second (acceleration). Similarity was increased by integrating the display into one two-dimensional cursor, and the control into one two-axis joy stick.

Three important conclusions emerged from Fracker and Wickens' data. First, increasing the order of control on one axis led to increasing interference on the other. Yet this increase in error was *not* accompanied by any increase in confusion and cross-talk (measured by coherence), suggesting that resource competition was primarily responsible. Second, increasing the similarity between the two tasks by integrating the displays and controls did indeed increase confusion and cross-talk, as measured by contralateral coherence. But *this* effect was divorced from any increase in error. Thirdly, a second source of confusion and cross-talk appeared to result from the incompatibility between control and display integration. When there was a mismatch between these two levels of integration (i.e. tracking two cursors with one two-axis stick, or tracking one two-dimensional cursor with two sticks) there was evidence for confusion and cross-talk. While not accompanied by a rise in tracking error, this incompatibility was nevertheless accompanied by an increased delay in processing each response and by a reduction in control energy, as if subjects dealt with the potential for confusion and cross-talk by adopting a different, more cautious processing strategy.

In summary, representational similarity, inducing confusion and cross-talk, or outcome conflict, is certainly a potential source of interference under some circumstances. Yet its effects do not appear consistently, and the increases in interference that occur with increasing task demand continue to point to resource competition as a major source of dual task performance decrements.

Processing similarity: cooperation and compatibility

In the previous section, increased similarity of stimulus channels or semantic representations has been seen to produce greater interference. There is, however, another sense in which increased similarity will lead to better, not poorer performance. This is the role of what we may describe as 'mapping similarity', 'processing similarity', or 'task similarity'. Here we find cases in which increased similarity leads to a 'sharing' or 'cooperation' between the two tasks. For example, Duncan (1979) reports an experiment in which subjects are asked to time-share two reaction-time tasks. Both tasks could have compatible S-R mappings, incompatible mappings, or one could have a compatible and the other an incompatible mapping. A resource competition explanation would predict that poorest performance should result when both mappings are incompatible, each thereby imposing the highest demands. However, Duncan found that this combination actually provided better performance than the heterogeneous situation in which one mapping was compatible and the other was incompatible.

Analogous findings have been reported in dual-axis tracking. Chernikoff, Duey, and Taylor (1960) had subjects time-share two tracking tasks that were either both zero-order (position control)—and therefore quite easy— both second-order (acceleration control)—and therefore quite difficult—or one zero- and one second-order control. Again, resource theory would predict poorest performance in the dual second-order task. However, performance was actually poorest in the condition with heterogeneous dynamics. Other studies of motor performance have observed superior bimanual tapping performance when the tapped rhythms are similar (Peters, 1977), and improved bimanual target acquisition when the index of difficulty of the two movements are identical (Kelso et al., 1979). In all of these cases, there seems to be some beneficial cooperation that results when the two tasks employ common processing routines or response mappings. This benefit will outweigh the resource costs that result when both tasks are difficult.

Thus, we have seen that representational similarity disrupts performance, while processing similarity may facilitate it. The linkage between these two phenomena may be loosely described as a *compatibility of similarity*. That is, when there exists similarity of processing routines, then the harmful effects of representational similarity (confusions) may be reduced, whereas when there exists high representational similarity, the benefits of processing similarity may be enhanced. Two investigations of multi-axis tracking, both comparing tracking with similar dynamics (processing similarity) to dissimilar dynamics (processing distance), provide evidence supporting this principle. In the first, a study by Chernikoff and Lemay (1963) employed a design similar to that used by Fracker and Wickens (1987) described in the previous section. They compared performance of two-axis tracking tasks of homo- geneous dynamics and heterogeneous dynamics that also had either close (a single two-dimensional cursor) or distant (two one-dimensional cursors) displays and were controlled by either a single two-axis stick (close) or two separate sticks (distance). Chernikoff and Lemay observed a compatibility of proximity interaction such that the cost of heterogeneous dynamics was increased when a single control stick was employed relative to the condition when two separate sticks were employed. Second, the results of Fracker and Wickens' (1988) study indicated that the cost of processing heterogeneity interacted with the proximity of the display rather than of the control. Heterogeneous dynamics were better served by two separate displays, and homogeneous dynamics were better served by an integral display, an interac- tion which will have important echoes below.

Microsimilarity and confusion: implications for skill acquisition

There is little evidence as yet for the relevance of confusion, cross-talk, and cooperation effects to the development of learnable, trainable skills. One may speculate that different strategies may be learned which can serve either to integrate central processing requirements or to segregate them in order to be compatible with display or response components that are themselves either integrated or separated. Hirst (1984) has reported that training will improve the ability to separate or segregate two channels of information that may otherwise be similar, thereby avoiding confusion effects. It is possible that a major component of complex skill learning may be involved in developing automaticity for processing the critical perceptual or semantic features that discriminate one task channel from another, when these channels are not discriminated by other physically salient cues (e.g. by spatial separation). The development of automaticity is critical here, for it will not be sufficient to know what those cues are, but rather, one needs to respond automatically to them in discriminating the task channels. This clearly represents a fruitful area for future research.

INFORMATION INTEGRATION: SIMILARITY COMPATIBILITY REVISITED

The preceding discussions have focused either on situations in which there is independent processing required between two or more tasks, or a need for focused attention on one task while ignoring irrelevant information from another perceptual channel. These two situations are shown in the top half of Figure 19, and we have noted in the top half that the advantage of separate or dissimilar displays or controls may be reduced by increasing the similarity of central processing activities. However, many aspects of complex skill do not maintain this independence between the two activities. For example, the skill of flying an aircraft may be broken down into two separate axes of control: movement of the yoke back and forth pitches the airplane's nose up and down to achieve vertical control, whereas rotation of the yoke banks the aircraft to the left or right to achieve heading or lateral control. However, these two axes are not independent. Banking to the left or right will also cause the nose to pitch downward, producing a vertical error which must be compensated by pitch control (i.e. pulling the yoke back). Thus, the situation of flying an aircraft is like that shown in the third panel of Figure 19 in which cross-talk is an inherent and integral part of the two tasks, rather than an unwanted side-effect. One may say that there is not so much two tasks here as, perhaps, '1.5' tasks.

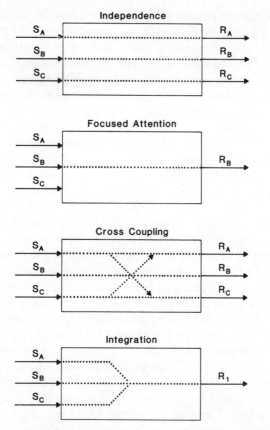

Figure 19. Four representations of information processing tasks. Row 1: Dual (independent) task. Row 2: Focused attention task. Row 3: Partial information integration or cross-coupling. Row 4: Complete information integration.

Compatibility of proximity

Sometimes a complex skill may be represented as in the bottom panel of Figure 19. Here two or more relevant channels of information will be funneled into only a single mental representation or a single response. For example, in driving an automobile, the driver will perceive both the heading error of the vehicle and its lateral deviation off of the desired middle of the lane. These two channels of perceptual information become integrated into only a single control response—the movement of the steering wheel. In a different domain, the skill of reading involves the simultaneous integration of the different letters of one word, along with the overall 'shape' formed by the word (Wickelgren, 1979; Broadbent and Broadbent, 1980).

Recently we have proposed that independent and focused attention tasks, shown in the top half of Figure 19, may be distinguished from partial and complete information integration tasks, shown in the bottom half, in a way that directly maps onto the compatibility of the similarity principle. That is, tasks at the top preserving separate tasks or independence of channels are best served by separate or distant information displays, while tasks at the bottom demanding greater 'mental closeness' are better served by more similar displays of the information sources (Wickens, 1986b; Carswell and Wickens, 1987; Boles and Wickens, 1987, Barnett and Wickens, 1988). Much of this work has been carried out in paradigms in which display similarity has been defined by the several dimensions of a single object (Goldsmith and Schvanveldt, 1984). An example of these studies is provided by Carswell and Wickens (1987) who had subjects monitor two chemical process control systems represented either as two sets of three separate bargraphs or as two integrated triangles. When the task required them to integrate information across the three dynamically changing variables in each system in order to detect failures in the simulated process, performance was better served by the integral triangle displays. However, when the task forced subjects to remember the value of a particular input (focused attention), or to respond independently to each of the six inputs (independent processing) performance was better served by the separate bargraph displays.

Of course there are many forms of 'information integration' which take the form of the third row of Figure 19. In these circumstances, where multiple stimuli and responses are required but there may be some partial integration of the streams, the relative difference between object and separated displays is not as strong (e.g. Casey and Wickens, 1986).

The compatibility of similarity principle has been demonstrated with other dimensions than object integrality. For example, Andre and Wickens (1988), and Harwood et al. (1986) showed that both color and spatial similarity could facilitate information integration. Boles and Wickens (1987) manipulated similarity in terms of representational similarity of display codes in the multiple resource model. Subjects performed either of two tasks on pairs of displayed numbers. They 'integrated' the two digits, making a single response on the basis of the pair, or they processed each independently in a dual-task configuration. The integration task was performed best when the representational format of the two digits was identical (both printed or both bargraph). The dual-task configuration was performed best when each task had its own representational format.

Integration as a skill

As was true with confusion, there are no extensive data on the skill learning implications of information integration. Presumably, however, the key to such skill learning is in identifying the relevant perceptual features that may help to integrate the separate components of the displays as task demands require. For example, it is evident that 'emergent' features (Pomerantz, 1981) may be a salient characteristic of information integration. If an emergent feature formed by the combination of two elements of a display into an integral representation directly serves the integration task at hand, then performance will benefit by this integration. For example, combining two linear dimensions into the height and width of a rectangle will produce an emergent feature—area—which will directly serve any task that is dependent upon the product of these two variables, like rate and time combining to produce distance or amount (Barnett and Wickens, 1988). To the extent that subjects can be trained to search for and find these emergent features where they may not already be obvious, a fundamental component of skill learning has been identified.

TIME-SHARING SKILLS

Training

As each of the mechanisms for multiple-task performance was reviewed in the previous pages of this chapter, such evidence as existed was brought to bear on whether or not the particular components could be trained. In other words, we discussed a 'part-task' training procedure for attentional skills. This raises a number of issues, not dealt with in Chapter 8. In the current section, we address this issue from a slightly different perspective, namely, what are the attentional implications of training complex multi-task skills? We see that this emphasis invokes attentional mechanisms in two respects: (1) what is the importance of a time-sharing skill? and (2) what is the importance of attentional resources to learning? As discussed by Lintern and Wickens (1987), these two concerns in turn have implications for two tailored training procedures: part-task training and adaptive training.

Part-task training

The various forms of time-sharing skills such as those described above related to switching of attention, allocation of resources, and perceptual focusing or segregating elements of an array, may be described as *emergent features* of the multi-task situation (Duncan, 1979). To the extent that these skills are learnable through training, then if one wanted to train the learner to a high level of expertise in a multi-task environment, a disservice would be done by training the component tasks independently as shown in the first row of Figure 20. The reason, of course, is that training on the components in isolation from each other allows no opportunity for the emergent time-

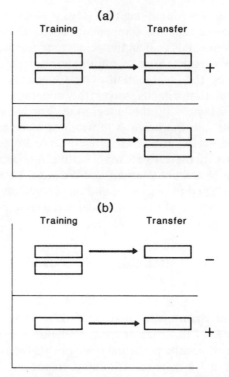

Figure 20. Two different representations of complex task training and transfer. Each block represents a task. Row 1: Transfer to a dual-task condition with whole and part-task training. Row 2: Transfer to a single-task condition with single- and dual-task training.

sharing skills to be practised. Studies by Damos and Wickens (1980), Rieck, Ogden, and Anderson (1980), and Connelly et al. (1987) have all demonstrated this point. All three investigations found that when subjects transferred to a dual-task condition, those who had also been trained under a dual-task condition learned the skill better than subjects who had received training on each component task by itself. The results of all three studies thereby clearly implicated the importance of training in time-sharing skills. Furthermore, Damos and Wickens (1980) applied a fine-grained analysis of the task components in an effort to determine what skills in fact were learned and therefore were more facile for the whole task training group. They discovered converging evidence from two sets of dual-task configurations, that subjects improved their abilities to parallel process the task streams of information.

It should be noted that part-task training will do further harm to transfer to a complex scenario to the extent that the task components in the complex scenario are inherently linked as in the third row of Figure 19. Not only will subjects who are part-task trained fail to learn the time-sharing skills necessary to coordinate the component activities, but they will also fail to learn the necessary relations whereby the input of one component is tied to the processing of another. A specific example of this failure is revealed by the comparison of two conditions in a study of complex skill learning performed by Naylor and Briggs (1963), who examined subjects' abilities to predict stimuli on two different channels. When information on the two channels was correlated (i.e. there was linkage between the two tasks as in row 3 of Figure 19), training was disrupted when performance on each channel was practised independently. When such correlations were absent (as in row 1), learning was as proficient with part-task as with whole-task training.

Resources and learning

The research discussed in the preceding section all argues that the training for complex tasks should take place in the whole- or complex-task environment and that the components should not be broken down for the purposes of training. However, to the extent that effective learning depends upon attention, or the allocation of resources, then a force is generated that pushes in the opposite direction, in favor of part-task training. It is reasonable to assume that learning a skill does require some resources allocated to the learning process. Therefore, diverting the resources needed to learn component A to the concurrent performance of component B, should in fact decrease the efficiency of learning of component A, relative to single-task learning of A. This representation is shown in Figure 20b. This force toward training with full resources available to learning has implications both for part-task training and for adaptive training. Simply put, it indicates that task components should be trained in part, rather than in whole. It also indicates that the demands of the task component itself should not be so high that its performance requires all resources, and no resources are left over for learning the structure underlying those task components. This then is the argument for *adaptive training*, a technique in which the difficulty of a task is gradually increased as its performance is mastered.

The evidence for this reverse force for reduced-demand training (part-task and adaptive) comes from a number of sources. First, there is strong evidence that learning under dual-task conditions does a disservice when this skill must transfer to single task condition (this is shown in Figure 20b). For example, Nissen and Bullemer (1987) had subjects learn a repeated sequence of ten stimuli in a four-choice reaction-time task. Some subjects practised the task alone, while others practised while concurrently maintaining a running count of discrete auditory events. When single-task performance of both groups was evaluated at transfer, a clear advantage for single-task training was evident.

Secondly, when the target task for transfer is in fact a dual-task condition (row 1 of Figure 20a), there is, as we have noted, a tension between the advantage of dual-task training (facilitating the development of time-sharing skills) and the advantage of part-task training (focusing attention on learning the individual components). Lintern and Wickens (1987) have found evidence to suggest that this tension or force may be stronger in one direction or the other depending upon the nature of the tasks. Specifically, to the extent that the component tasks contain consistencies—repeated or learnable sequences of events—rather than simply random input, they will benefit relatively more from part-task or adaptive training. A difference, for example, may be cited between learning to perform a tracking task with repeated or semi-predictable inputs (consistencies) and learning to perform the same task with random input. An example of this contrasts the effects of reduced-demand training in studies by Noble, Trumbo, and Fowler (1967) and by Eysenck and Thompson (1966). The former study, employing inputs which had repeated characteristics, produced relatively greater advantages for reduced-demand training than did the latter which involved a more random sequence of inputs. More recently, Schneider (1986) has made a similar point in noting that it is impossible for automaticity to develop even when categorizing consistently mapped targets, when subjects are initially forced in training to divide their attention between the categorization task and a concurrent activity.

The previous paragraph has described how the learning of consistent patterns will benefit more from the allocation of attention than will the learning of random patterns. An interesting expression of this same phenomenon is a finding by Pew (1974) that learning to track a consistent spatial-temporal pattern demands more resources, and therefore diverts more from a concurrent task, than learning to track a random pattern. In Pew's study subjects practised for twenty sessions on a tracking task that had three segments. The first and the last segments involved random input, while the middle segment involved a repeated input which the subject experienced on every single trial. Subjects were not told about the repetitive nature of the repeated segment and in fact only a few of them ever realized that it was different from the random segments at the beginning and the end. However, the learning curves suggested that subjects were in fact acquiring the consistencies of the repeated segment, in that tracking error for this segment decreased significantly faster over practice than did tracking error for the random segments. Of relevance to the current hypothesis, however, was the fact that when a secondary task was performed concurrently with the primary task, the secondary task was more disrupted by the repeated segment than by the random segments. This result suggests that the repeated segment was draining additional resources away from the secondary task as the consistencies were being learned. Stated in other terms, the learning of consistencies requires more resources than does the processing of random information.

While the previous discussion has focused on part-task training, similar arguments can be directed toward adaptive training. While adaptive training has not generally proven to be very successful (Lintern and Gopher, 1978), the conditions under which relatively greater success has been found can be characterized by the same presence of consistent learnable characteristics of the task, that favor part-task training. That is, when these learnable characteristics are a part of the target task, and the target task itself presents very complex information-processing demands, then there will be some benefit for training the target task at a easier level (e.g. slowing it down; Mane, 1984) as long as those consistent elements remain unaltered. Otherwise the resource demands of performing the task will compete with those of learning its consistencies, and learning will be slow and ineffective. Of course, the inherent danger of adaptive training is that at the easier level subjects may learn habits that need to be unlearned at the more difficult levels. To be effective, an adaptive variable must be chosen in a way that prevents this from occurring.

It should be noted that the task conditions identified here that do or do not benefit reduced-demand training are quite analogous to the distinction made by Schneider (1985a) regarding the conditions under which automaticity will develop. Schneider and Shiffrin (1977; Schneider, Dumais, and Shiffrin, 1984) have argued that automaticity will be developed through extensive training only to the extent that there are consistent characteristics within the task. We argue here that the allocation of attention to learning through part-task or adaptive training will also have its greatest benefit to learning to the extent that consistency is present.

Individual differences in attention

There are tremendous differences between people in the efficiency with which they can time-share. One obvious source of these differences is simply related to the automaticity of the component tasks. For example, differences between flight instructors and student pilots in their ability to fly while performing a secondary task are clearly related to the automaticity with which the flight instructors carry out the flight task (Damos, 1978; Crosby and Parkinson, 1979). Our interest in this final section is not in differences attributable to single-task automaticity (that is, task-specific differences resulting from practice), but rather in operator-specific differences in time-sharing that may apply across tasks, independent of the level of single-task skill achieved on those task. Two general sources of differences in time-sharing efficiency will be considered: differences in the mechanisms of resource allocation and switching, and differences in the amount or availability of resources.

Differences in mechanisms

The idea that people may differ in their ability to allocate resources or to switch attention is an appealing one. However, there remains surprisingly little firm evidence that this is a consistent enduring ability. Gopher and his colleagues (Gopher and Kahneman, 1971; Gopher, 1982) have observed that a measure of attention-switching in a dichotic listening paradigm successfully predicts performance of bus drivers as well as airplane pilots. Keele and Hawkins (1982) have also found modest evidence that a switching measure of attention seems to be correlated across a variety of different tasks manifesting that switching. However, the evidence has been mixed. Other researchers have failed to find that dichotic listening tasks predict time-sharing performance with other tasks (e.g. Braune and Wickens, 1985, 1986). Lansman, Poltrock, and Hunt (1983) have found that attention-switching, as a measure, seems to be specifically related to the modality of the input and is not a more general processing characteristic. Furthermore, Braune and Wickens (1985, 1986) looked explicitly for switching as a general ability, and designed a number of task configurations that would demand switching between visual and auditory channels, to be performed along with the standard dichotic listening test of auditory switching. Although individual differences in each specific measure were observed, there was no general correlation of switching ability across the different measures to suggest that this is a general task characteristic.

Differences in resource availability

An alternative but not a mutually exclusive view is that people may differ from each other in terms of the total amount of resources they have available for performing a task. This resource model of differences may be contrasted with the 'skills' model of differences which suggests that people differ from each other in terms of the efficiency with which those resources are deployed; that is, the slope and intercept of the performance resource function. These two models are shown in Figure 21 in which each panel shows PRF representations of an individual of high (dashed line) and low (solid line) ability. An implication of the skills model (Figure 21b) is that the withdrawal of the same amount of resources (diverted to a concurrent task) by an individual of high and low ability will lead to a small decrement for the individual of high ability and a large decrement for the individual with low ability. That is, there will be a negative correlation between the absolute level of single-task performance and the size of the dual-task decrement. In contrast, the

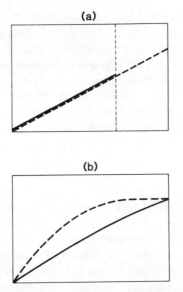

Figure 21. Two models of individual differences in time-sharing. Each figure shows the performance resource function of a low (solid line) and high (dashed line) skilled individual: (a) capacity model, and (b) skills model.

capacity model (Figure 21a) predicts that withdrawal of the same amount of resources will lead to the same loss in performance for the individual of low and high ability. That is, the capacity model predicts a zero correlation between performance level and the size of the decrement.

Hunt and Lansman (1982), and Lansman and Hunt (1982) have argued for the capacity model. They argue that if people differ in the amount of resources available, then the level of performance on single tasks that are difficult, and therefore resource-limited, should predict the size of the decrement on easier dual-task conditions when resources are at a premium because they have to be divided between tasks. Their predictions are shown in Figure 22, which depicts the resource characteristics of two people (S1 and S2) performing each of two tasks: one easy and one difficult. The PRFs of the person with the smaller capacity are shown at C1, those for the individual with the larger capacity are shown at C2. These two functions are also represented by the solid and dashed lines, respectively. Looking at the easy task (light lines) which generates a high level of performance and a data-limited PRF, it is apparent that for the low-ability, low-capacity subject there will be a few residual resources available to perform a secondary task (R_1) and the dual-task decrement on that task should be large. For the high-ability subject, there are more resources available (R_2) and the decrement should be small. For the difficult version (heavy lines), however, the amount of residual resources is small and equivalent for both subjects, and so the dual-task decrement should also be equivalent, although single-task performance will be better for the higher-capacity subject. Thus, this sample of two subjects would generate a low correlation between performance on an easy task and the dual-task decrement with that easy task; a low correlation between the same measures with the difficult task, but a strong negative correlation between the level of performance on the difficult task and the dual-task decrement with the easy task. To evaluate this prediction Lansman and Hunt (1982) had subjects time-share a running paired associated learning (PAL) task with a choice reaction-time task. The PAL task could be either easy or difficult, and was performed under single- or dual-task conditions. In support of their predictions, Lansman and Hunt indeed found that the decrement in reaction time when performed with the easy PAL task correlated negatively with the level of performance on the difficult PAL task when performed by itself. They also found that the level of single-task performance of the difficult PAL task did *not* correlate at all with the decrement in reaction time when time-shared with the difficult PAL task. This finding again is consistent with capacity representation shown in Figure 22. Both S1 and S2 will show the same level of decrement in the difficult task, when the same amount of resources (R_2) are withdrawn.

While these data were supportive of the capacity hypothesis, Lansman and

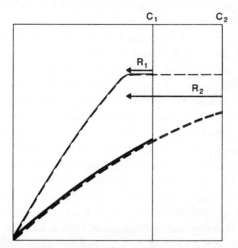

Figure 22. The assumed PRFs underlying Lansman and Hunt's study of individual differences in time-sharing. C_1 and C_2 are the capacity of the low ability (solid line) and high ability (dashed line) subjects, respectively. R_1 and R_2 represents the amount of resources that may be diverted to a side task. The light lines represent the PRF for the easy primary task, the heavy lines represent those for the hard task.

Hunt made no effort to identify whether the 'good' and 'bad' performers on the PAL task truly had more resources available for that task or whether they were simply more skilled performers. A different study by Wickens and Weingartner (1985), however, suggested that high- and low-ability groups do differ in the amount of resources available. They assessed individual differences on generic spatial abilities using standardized spatial aptitude tests. On the basis of these tests, they also concluded that those of higher spatial ability had 'more' spatial capacity. This extra capacity benefited them when performing an information-processing spatial task (filling in an imagined matrix). However, Wickens and Weingartner also found that single-task performance on the spatial task did not correlate with the size of the decrement produced when this task was time-shared with a concurrent difficult spatial task of monitoring a simulated chemical process, thereby replicating the finding from Lansman and Hunt's study, with the difficult task.

One final piece of evidence in support of a capacity model of individual differences was provided by Braune and Wickens (1986) in a study of dual-axis tracking. They observed that the correlation of single-task tracking performance with the dual-axis tracking decrements was approximately zero and perhaps was slightly positive, whereas a negative correlation is predicted by the skills model. Thus, collectively, these three correlational studies seem to reject the 'skills' model of individual differences in time-sharing which associates better performance with smaller decrements, in favor of a capacity model. This does not, of course, imply that zero correlations between decrements and performance levels will not be found. Correlations depend upon the constitution of the sample, and if the sample includes people who vary widely in the skill or automaticity of component tasks, then such correlations, predicted by the skills model, will, of course, be in evidence.

The previous discussion suggests that individual differences may be reflected in terms of overall level of capacity, and this difference in turn is related to some fundamental differences in cognitive abilities. More capacity available will mean better single-task performance but will not necessarily mean a smaller loss in performance when a fixed amount of resources are diverted to a concurrent task. Does this general phenomenon pertain to the separate resources within the multiple-resource space? Although the data are not extensive on this issue, the answer that is suggested is negative. In Braune and Wickens' (1986) study, dual-task tracking decrements were correlated across different task combinations. Surprisingly, the lowest correlation was found between a tracking/tracking decrement and the decrement of tracking time-shared with a visual/spatial reaction-time task. That is, the lowest correlation was found between two task combinations sharing many similar resources. The correlation was relatively higher between the tracking/tracking task decrements and the decrements of tracking time-shared with an auditory/verbal reaction-time task (sharing fewer resources). In fact, the correlation was highest between the tracking/tracking decrements and a time-sharing combination of two totally different tasks: a digit-processing task time-shared with a Sternberg memory search task. According to the multiple-resources model, these two task combinations share none of the specific resources in common.

What then causes the substantial shared variance in performance between the two very different time-sharing combinations? That is, what is responsible for the 'g' factor of time-sharing? One possibility is that there may be competition for some general processing resources that are available to all task operations, no matter where their loading is in the multiple-resource space. A second alternative is that the 'g' factor may represent a particular time-sharing skill of scheduling, allocation, or switching as described above. This conclusion was supported by a factor analysis performed by Braune and Wickens (1986) on different components of dual-axis tracking.

In summary, different task combinations produce variance in time-sharing efficiency. So do different people. But the mapping between the patterns of correlation in task performance on the one hand, and the specific efforts to identify processing mechanisms in dual-task performance on the other, remains poorly understood.

SUMMARY

A hybrid model of multiple-task performance is presented that describes four mechanisms governing task interaction as complex skills are performed. The implications for skill learning of each of these mechanisms is discussed. The first of these relates to the discrete and serial process of attention-switching between information sources or tasks. With sufficient skill, operators become fairly proficient at sampling optimally according to the frequency of events on different channels, and expected benefits of attending to them. However, their sampling is limited by memory failures.

The second mechanism relates to resource allocation. Resources are a hypothetical construct that reflect the demand which tasks impose on the limited human processing system as a function of their difficulty. Multiple resources are defined by a small number of global structures related to processing stages, processing codes (spatial-verbal), perceptual modalities, and possibly visual fields. Tasks interfere more to the extent that their difficulty is increased (demanding more resources), and their global structures are shared (competing for more resources).

A third mechanism relates to the confusion and cross-talk resulting when task elements are quite similar to each other in terms of such features as spatial location, color, or meaning. The final mechanism is a positive one that relates to the compatibility of similarity. If there are similar information-processing requirements between two tasks, then this will also lead to a benefit for similar stimulus or response features.

A final section discussed the issues related to the acquisition and training of time-sharing skills, and to the differences in time-sharing ability between people. It is concluded that time-sharing skills may indeed be learned, and probably relate to scanning, selection, and resource allocation. The implications of these skills for part-task and adaptive training are discussed, and it is noted that such techniques are most beneficial when task components contain learnable consistencies. Finally, the nature of differences between individuals in time-sharing ability is discussed. The data suggest that these differences may relate to the capacity that individuals have available, as well as to strategies in resource allocation.

ACKNOWLEDGMENTS

This chapter was written in part while the author was supported by a grant from NASA Ames Research Center (NASA NAG 2–308), and many of the concepts discussed resulted from research carried out on this grant. Sandra Hart was the technical monitor.

Chapter 5

Discrete Movements

Denis J. Glencross and Nicholas Barrett

The investigation of what on the surface seem to be relatively simple and 'uninteresting' movements such as reaching, tapping, and aiming has been a very significant chapter in the study of motor control mechanisms and human skill in general. Historically, these discrete movements, as they are called, have been the cornerstone of the systematic investigations of the organizational principles underlying human skill.

Indeed, it has been the study of discrete movements that has forged the essential link between psychology, physiology, and cognitive science, highlighting the convergence of physiological and behavioral evidence.

Woodworth (1899), in his classic study on 'The accuracy of voluntary movement', emphasized what has become a central issue in cognition and human skill, that is, the notion of levels of control. In short, there is an automatic or programmed phase (the 'initial impulse') and a sensory control phase ('current control').

In a similar way Bryan and Harter (1899), in a study of the temporal organization of discrete finger movements in learning the skill of typewriting, demonstrated the transition from the sensory control of individual effector units (the fingers) to the control of larger units, each unit controlled as a whole (or as a program). This mode of organization was referred to by Bryan and Harter (1899) as a hierarchy of habits, again emphasizing the hierarchical organization of levels of control. Thus, the study of discrete movements has been a useful heuristic for the investigation of more complex skills and behaviors.

But what do we mean by discrete movements? Discrete movements can perhaps be best understood in terms of both the type of movement and the end-point target:

> *Single Discrete Movements* involve a single reaching movement to 'hit' a stationary target, as in pointing, reaching for a cup, or tapping a key on a typewriter.

Human Skills. Edited by D. Holding © 1989 John Wiley & Sons Ltd

Repetitive Discrete Movements involve a repetition of this single movement 'back and forth' to a stationary target of targets as in tapping a morse key, or in hammering.

Sequential Discrete Movements involve discrete movements to a number of stationary targets, regularly or irregularly spaced, e.g. climbing stairs, serial RT task.

Complex Discrete Movements involve a number of different effector units (e.g. the fingers) reaching for several stationary targets, as in typewriting or playing the piano. Of course, many complex skills are made up of such phased sequences of single discrete movements.

In this chapter we shall concentrate on a description of the first two categories—single discrete and repetitive discrete movements—but not forgetting that these are the bases for many complex skills which are discussed in other chapters in this book (see Chapters 2, 4 and 8).

THE EARLY STUDIES

Two phases of movement

Woodworth (1899) deployed 'various forms of the graphic method' enabling a variety of movements to be made at any desired speed and interval. Subjects made movements in time with the beat of a metronome, and thus varying and controlling the speed between 20 and 200 beats per minute. In this fascinating and extensive series of experiments, Woodworth compared movement of the right and left hands at varying speeds with and without vision, to movements of the foot, the movements of bending and swaying of the body, and the effects of practice and fatigue. However, of particular interest in the present context was his work on aiming movements, at various speeds, with and without vision. When vision was available, there seems to be a linear relationship between error and speed at 40–140 beats/minute (viz. 1500–430 msec per tap). This relationship broke down at very slow and very fast movements (see Figure 23). On the other hand, when vision was removed (the eyes closed condition), error was independent of speed and the level of accuracy was about the same as that for the very fast speeds (< 500 msec per tap) of the vision condition.

From these and related studies Woodworth concluded that there were two phases to the control of voluntary movements: (1) the 'initial adjustment' or original impulse phase; and (2) the 'current or contemporary control' phase in which a number of finer adjustments brings about the end-point accuracy.

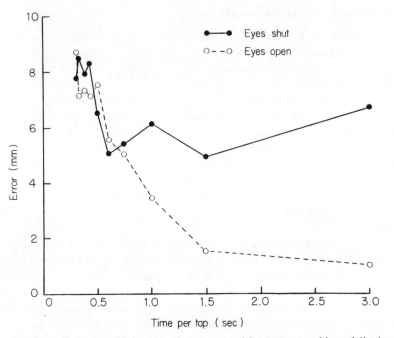

Figure 23. The effects of tapping speed on error with eyes open (dotted line) and eyes closed (full line). Woodworth's (1899) data replotted in terms of time per tap.

The period of current control was related to the accuracy or precision required as specified by the target constraints. The smaller the target (greater accuracy required) the longer the period of current control needed to achieve this accuracy. However, of course, the greater the speed of movement (and hence restricting the time available for current control) the larger the error.

We shall come to discuss these two phases recognized by Woodworth as the initial 'programmed' phase and the later 'sensory' controlled phase, although, as we shall see, this distinction is not as apparent as has been assumed for so long.

What has happened in the intervening, three-quarters of a century of research that has extended our knowledge and understanding of discrete 'voluntary' movements? Three major issues have emerged:

1 How much detail (precision) can be programmed in advance of execution?
2 How much time is needed for current sensory control and feed-back-based adjustments?
3 What 'other' forms of rapid error correction, and amendment mechanisms contribute to control?

Ballistic and tension movements

The essence of the early approaches was to investigate those phases of discrete movements which were under automatic control and to ask which details were under current sensory feedback control, and what was the time-course for such processes.

The issue became translated into the question, How much time is needed to use the sensory (visual) information upon which movement control is dependent? Experimental procedures manipulated the speed of movement, and the availability of visual information ('vision' versus 'blind' movements) and end-point accuracy was measured, as well as in some cases other electro-myographic and/or kinematic details for the movement. For example, as we have seen in the Woodworth (1899) study, accuracy was related to movements of varying speeds (controlled by the beat of a metronome) performed with and without vision.

Stetson and Bouman (1935) emphasized the kinematic and electromyo-graphic detail in highlighting the distinction made by Woodworth (1899) but with respect to two different classes of movement, and modes of organization of muscle activity, namely 'ballistic' and 'tension' movements. In the former the agonist initiates the action, then there is a period of quiescence, and then the antagonist arrests the movement, the timing of these phases being critical. On the other hand, with the tension movements the agonists and antagonists are continually 'playing' against one another (see Figure 24).

Clearly what is significant here, although not emphasized by Stetson and Bouman, is the complexity of the temporal patterning required to coordinate the sets of muscles and the time-scale for such control to occur. They conclude, 'The regulation of the ballistic movement both in variations of force and variation of timing is remarkably precise' (p. 254).

Kelso (1982) has recently readdressed this approach in calling for a process-oriented approach to the study of human skills and re-establishing the emphasis and lead given by Woodworth, 'we should look at the movement _itself._' Displacement, velocity, acceleration, and electromyographic records must reflect the intricate temporal patterning of the forces in space and time and hence the details of the control processes. It is such details which cannot be fully described by reaction time, movement time, or error scores of performance.

Acceleration and deceleration phases

An analysis of kinematic data in rapid discrete movements reveals that there appear to be two main phases of movement—an initial rapid acceleration and a final period of deceleration. Depending upon the speed and extent of movement, there may also be a period of little or no acceleration (viz.

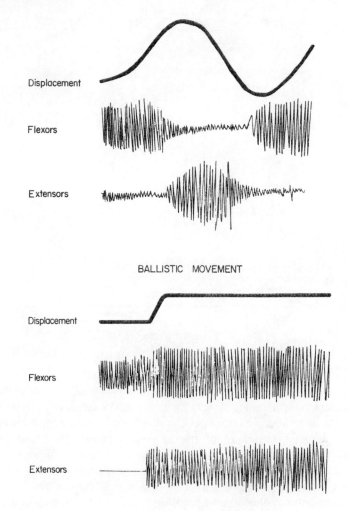

Displacement

Flexors

Extensors

BALLISTIC MOVEMENT

Displacement

Flexors

Extensors

TENSION MOVEMENT

Figure 24. Diagrammatic representation of EMG activity during a ballistic movement (top) and tension movement (bottom). (After Stetson and Bouman, 1935.)

constant velocity) in the mid-section of the movement as seen in Chapter 1. If we plot the extent of the movement (distance traveled) against the movement duration (time) then the curve represents the 'S-shaped' normal ogive. In fast movements not requiring great end-point accuracy, the acceleration and deceleration phases are approximately equal. Stetson and Bouman (1935) have described the typical agonist, then antagonist muscle firing pattern of these rapid ballistic movements (see Figure 24), the antagonist burst bringing

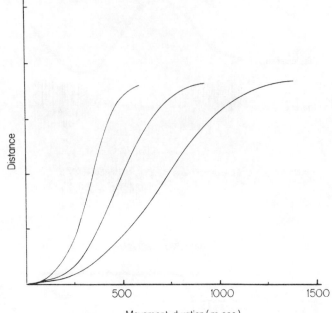

Movement duration (m sec)

Figure 25. Typical acceleration–deceleration functions for movements of varying speed (duration) over a fixed distance.

the movement to a halt. However, for movements requiring a high degree of end-point accuracy, the final deceleration phase may be prolonged and consume a larger component of the movement time. This final phase is associated with homing in on the target, the adjustments assumedly being made on the basis of sensory (visual) information, arising during the movement, about the likelihood of hitting or missing the target. This, of course, is the current control phase to which Woodworth (1899) refers. Stetson and Bouman (1935) have clearly illustrated the simultaneous co-contraction and interplay of the agonist and antagonist muscle groups during this slow 'homing' phase of the movement. Peters and Wenborne (1936) reported that the acceleration–deceleration phases were quite consistent across a range of movement extents and directions. Further, when these movements were speeded up, the phases retained their relative temporal relationship.

As with the earlier studies, the kinematic analyses reflected a relatively fixed and stable programmed initial phase of movement, followed by a more variable 'homing' phase, the sensory control phase of the movement. Such kinematic data can indicate the phase structure of the corrections and amendments, based on visual information arising during execution. At this stage in our story on discrete movements, there seems to have occurred a major shift of emphasis, which coincided with developments in communication theory and, in particular, with the emergence of the study of man as an information processor.

Information processes

A series of publications immediately following World War II were significant in highlighting the three major issues and rekindling the interest in human skills and the discrete movement paradigm. Coincident with the publication of Wiener's *Cybernetics* (1948) and Shannon and Weaver's *The Mathematical Theory of Communication* (1949), I believe the seminal paper of Karl Lashley (1951) 'The problem of serial order in behavior', and the stimulating investigations and ideas of Kenneth Craik, were most influential. Craik's (1947, 1948) tracking studies and those of Vince (1948) emphasized the discontinuity of movements in which corrections in tracking, based upon visual information, were delayed some 300–500 msec. These studies became the springboard for what came to be known as 'Limited Capacity Theory', influential over a wide range of approaches and investigations into human skill and human performance, emphasizing the discontinuous nature of information processes.

The limitations of time

Although we can produce and achieve amazingly complex performances—witness the concert pianist or Olympic gymnast—there are limitations to the processing of information upon which these performances are dependent. Keele (1973) makes a useful distinction between the limitations of 'time' and the limitations of 'space'. Briefly, the limitations of 'time' refer to the time to access, retrieve, and process information, and this is our main concern in this chapter. However, 'space', or capacity limitations, the restrictions to performing several operations and tasks simultaneously, has relevance later in the chapter when we consider the amendments to on-going discrete movements.

Reaction-time procedures, later elaborated by Posner (1979) as the chronometric techniques in his book, *Chronometric Explorations of Mind*, have provided the basic research tool for investigating these time and space restrictions to human information-processing. As far as discrete movements are concerned, the limitations of 'time' highlighted two major issues, first, the time taken to initiate the movement was related to the complexity of the ensuing movement; and secondly, the time taken to process sensory (visual) information arising during execution, restricted the nature and extent of any correction or amendment and hence accuracy of the movement. These became the two major themes in the investigation and study of discrete movements.

THE PROGRAMMED PHASE

If at least the first stage of a discrete movement is 'ballistic' or, as we shall call it, programmed, then it was argued that the latency or RT to initiate the movement could be used as an index of the complexity of this program. In other words, the more complex the program, the longer the time needed to assemble or structure the components of the program. Reaction time, it is assumed, reflects the complexity of this process. The promise of the reaction-time techniques was that they could be used to unravel not only the complexity of the response but indeed the dimensions of this complexity. Unfortunately, this promise has not been fulfilled although there have been some valuable contributions. Part of this difficulty has arisen because of the paradigm itself and the confusion that has arisen from the use of a single versus choice RT procedure. Secondly, the nature of complexity has remained elusive. Remember also that we are making reference only to that part of the discrete movement which is programmed in advance, we need to consider later how the programmed and sensory control phases are integrated, particularly in movements which require a high degree of spatial accuracy.

Reaction-time procedures

Simple and choice reaction-time procedures have been used extensively to investigate the organization and control of discrete movements which may be programmed in part at least in advance of the imperative stimulus. Although there was some early work of this nature, Brown and Slater-Hammel (1949) reported that the time taken to initiate a discrete movement was independent of the distance moved and direction; it was Henry and Rogers (1960) who proposed a 'memory-drum' theory, in which it takes longer to 'compile' a more complex movement before the execution phase, and this would be reflected by the reaction time. In their original study Henry et al. (1960) found reaction-time differences for three discrete movements each varying in spatial complexity, viz. a finger lift, a reaching movement, and a multi-planar arm movement. Glencross (1972) investigated horizontal discrete movements 'built up' systematically by adding similar movement components, viz. one-tap, two-tap, three-tap movements. The respective reaction latencies were 242 msec, 276 msec, and 291 msec. However, in none of the above studies was the target or accuracy constraint very precise.

Controlling for accuracy, Klapp (1975) reported that over very short distances (2 and 11 mm) reaction time was longer for small targets of 2 and

4 mm, compared with the larger targets of 32 and 64 mm. Assumedly over such short distances the whole movement was programmed in advance. Klapp did not find the same pattern of results for longer movements of 70 and 333 mm to the same sized targets.

However, overall, the pattern of results has been equivocal, partly due to use of either simple or choice reaction-time procedures, and partly a result of the 'uncontrolled' manipulation of movement parameters.

Let us add a brief comment about simple versus choice reaction time. With the simple reaction-time procedure, it is likely that some, if not all, of the programming can be prepared in advance of the imperative stimulus and then just 'triggered' into action when the stimulus eventually occurs. Why should more complex programs take longer to 'trigger' into action? Perhaps the program is 'unpacked' prior to execution—in which case the latency may reflect the complexity of the program. On the other hand, the choice reaction-time procedure restricts the specification of which response is to be made until the occurrence of the imperative stimulus. Only then can the compilation of the motor program take place and only when this is completed will execution occur. Thus programming complexity is more likely to be reflected by the latency in choice reaction-time situations.

Finally, many of the reported studies employed movements which were comprised of arbitrary components of direction, extent, sequence, and accuracy. Further, the duration (which is important for the purpose of sensory control) was often not controlled. However, when these details are controlled it seems that two 'dimensions' are consistently reflected by increases in reaction time, rapid temporal (rather than spatial) sequences, and rapid aiming movements to targets requiring a high degree of precision to be programmed in advance. However, in many instances such parameters are confounded with movement duration and this is a critical factor, for movements of duration longer than 250 msec may be subject to sensory control, certainly in the final stages of the action. One of the difficulties in using RT procedures as an index of programming in these long-duration movements is that it is unclear what portion of the movement remains under motor program control. The dominance of the visual system for motor control may well subjugate even the programmed phase.

Probe reaction-time procedures

The probe reaction-time procedures overcome some of the difficulties confronting simple and choice reaction-time techniques. This procedure is a refinement of the dual-task technique. Essentially what is involved is that whilst the subject is performing the required discrete movement (the primary task), a secondary task is superimposed.

With the probe reaction-time technique the primary task may be a discrete movement, and the secondary task usually a single stimulus and a single hand, foot, or vocal response. This stimulus, called the probe, is 'inserted' precisely at any phase of the primary task. The lengthening or delay in probe RT at the various probe positions has been taken as an index of the on-going processing or attention associated with the organization and control of the primary task.

In the investigation of discrete movements the probe RT procedure will reflect the attention demands not only of the preparatory and programming stages, but also the 'capacity demands' during execution, and will 'detect' if sensory feedback is being used for guidance and/or correction. For example, Posner and Keele (1969), Ells (1973), and Kerr (1975) have shown that probe RT is lengthened during the initiation of the movement, during the approach to a target, and to directional changes of the movement path. In a related series of studies in which the sequential complexity of a discrete horizontal arm movement was systematically varied, Glencross (1980a) reported length-ening of probe RT to the number of sequential 'instructions' in the move-ment, but the type of instruction was not important. For example the length-ening of probe RT was similar in a 'one-tap' movement compared with a

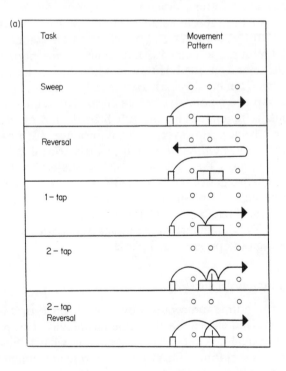

Figure 26. (a) Patterns of movements investigated in probe reaction time studies. (After Glencross, 1980a.)

reversal movement over the same distance. Again, a 'two-tap' movement caused similar probe RT delays as a 'two-reversal' movement. However, the probe RT delays were longer than in the previous single-instruction conditions. In all movements, the probe RT was lengthened during the latency of the movement and at the initiation and mid-phases of the movement, reflecting both programming and execution complexity (see Figure 26a and b).

Although the probe RT technique has been used extensively, it has not been without its critics. Kantowitz (1974) has argued that it is difficult to relate the probe RT and hence the attention demand at the 'point' where the probe was inserted. McLeod (1980) extends this criticism, arguing that probe RT needs to be plotted not on the basis of the time of arrival of the stimulus, but rather in terms of the time of response production. It would seem that to provide an overall picture of the capacity demands, then, probe RT should be plotted both as a function of stimulus arrival and as a function of response production.

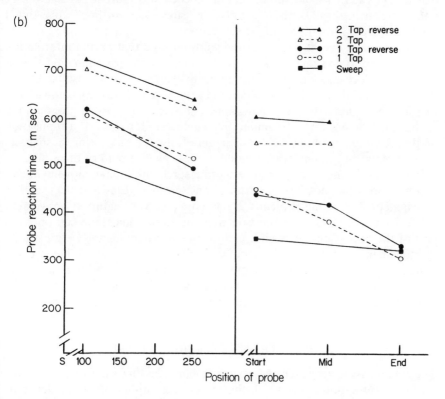

Figure 26. (b) Delays in probe reaction time at various stages before and during movements of varying sequential complexity. (After Glencross, 1980a.)

Pre-cuing techniques

Pre-cuing procedures are a further development and refinement of reaction-time techniques. Basically, this procedure provides the subject with partial information (the cue) prior to the initiation of the movement. This partial information could indicate which arm was to be used, or the distance or extent of the movement, or the direction of the movement. The imperative stimulus, of course, completed the information needed to make the response. How much programming in advance could occur given the different details about the required response? The reaction time, it was assumed, should indicate the time needed to complete the programming of the movement and hence reveal the time saved because of the information provided by the advance cue.

Rosenbaum (1980) reports a number of studies using the pre-cuing technique. In one of the studies subjects were required to make any one of eight movements. There were three movement dimensions: arm, direction, and extent. On each trial the subject could be cued with partial information of none, one, two, or all of these details. The subsequent or imperative signal gave all of the information and the subject was required to respond as rapidly as possible. The overall results of the study showed that partial information could be used to do some advance programming for the upcoming movement and thus reduce the latency of the movement. The specific results showed that reaction time was longest when the arm required was not known, and was shortest when extent was not known, and hence had to be programmed at the last moment after the imperative stimulus. However, in a replication of the Rosenbaum study, Goodman and Kelso (1980), using a spatially compatible arrangement, were unable to replicate the pattern of results.

In retrospect, the reaction-time era of research into human movement and motor control has not been as fruitful and productive as had been earlier anticipated. Part of this difficulty is related to the very nature of movement itself. That is, measures of reaction time and movement time can only tell part of the movement story and, as Kelso (1982) reminds us, we must look at movement itself: what is happening prior to execution? What are the kinematic details during movement? 'If we are to understand the manner in which the outcome was attained, we need to analyze the kinematics of the movement. That is . . . the movement process' (Kelso, 1982, p. 12).

THE CURRENT CONTROL PHASE

The second issue to which we now turn concerns the time to process the sensory information upon which the target or end-point accuracy depends. We now turn our attention to the 'current control' phase of the discrete movement. How do we eventually hit the target? If a movement is made slowly enough, we can 'always' thread the needle, we can always hit the target. But as speed of movement gets faster and faster, accuracy falls off. In all aspects of human performance, the operator is confronted by this speed–accuracy tradeoff. It was Paul Fitts who grappled with this problem and provided a direction for motor control research as significant as that made by Woodworth half a century earlier.

Speed–accuracy tradeoff

Fitts in 1954 discovered a meaningful relationship between speed (time), distance, and accuracy for discrete repetitive movements (Fitts, 1954) and later for single discrete movements (Fitts and Peterson, 1964). This relationship, which became known as Fitts' Law, can be expressed as:

$$\text{MOVEMENT TIME} = a + b \, \text{Log}_2 \frac{2 \, (\text{Distance})}{\text{Target Width}} \text{ (a and b are constants)}$$

Equation 1

The essence of Fitts' Law is that movement time increases logarithmically as the ratio, distance/width increases (see Figure 27). If the ratio remains the same (viz distance doubled, but the target width also doubled) then the time remains the same. We shall return to Fitts' Law later in the chapter, but one of the consequences of this interest in the speed–accuracy problem was to direct our attention to those processes which ensure target accuracy. If target accuracy is not or cannot be built into the initial program, how then is sensory information used to amend or correct the movement? Let us now consider these error-correction processes.

Minor error correction processes

Both Woodworth (1899) and Welford (1968) viewed the initial response as a ballistic movement and argued that the relatively long duration for the final portions of the limb trajectory could be related to the time needed for visual control and 'homing' in on the target. Carlton (1981) has shown that if you preclude visual information from the initial 75% of the distance to be traveled in an aiming movement, the final accuracy achieved is not affected. Such findings suggest an initial movement brings the limb to the correct 'ballpark', whilst additional control processes then modulate the trajectory so it eventually comes to rest within a specific target area. Indeed, Glencross and Barrett (1983) reported that removing vision during a repetitive tapping task had little effect on the subject's ability to produce movements of the desired

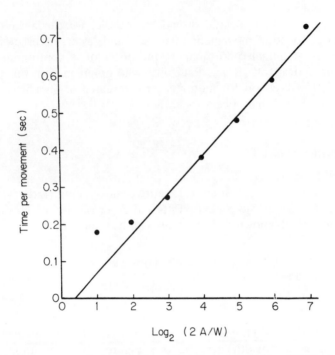

Figure 27. Time per movement as a linear function of the Index of Difficulty expressed in the form $\log_2$ (2A/W). (After Fitts, 1954.)

amplitude. It is the precision of such movements that is greatly affected by the removal of vision (see Figure 28).

The understanding of visually-based error-correction mechanisms, however, should not be limited to the analysis of homing-in processes. On some occasions, the initial response will not bring the responding limb to the correct ballpark. Examples of 'ballpark incorrect' responses occur naturally in the directional errors of step tracking (e.g. Higgins and Angel, 1970), or may be artificially induced in a double-step tracking paradigm (e.g. Gottsdanker, 1966). A full account of the control principles underlying discrete aiming movements must consider amendments to both 'ballpark correct' and 'ballpark incorrect' responses. Are there different modes of error correction? What conditions presuppose a shift from one mode to another? What implications do the error-correction processes have for the relationship between speed, distance, and accuracy of a movement? Let us consider initially those discrete movements that are in the right 'ballpark', but still require amendments to the target, based on visual information arising during execution.

Crossman and Goodeve (1983) and Keele (1968) proposed that these visually-based amendments were processed intermittently at several points during the trajectory. On the other hand, Beggs and Howarth (1970)

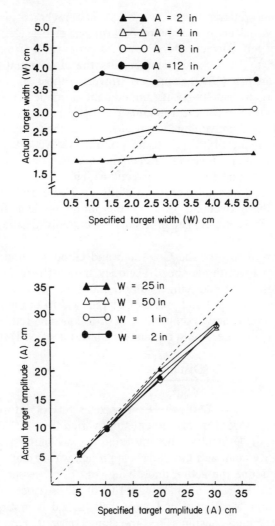

Figure 28. The effects of tapping blind on target width and target amplitude in a Fitts-type task. (After Glencross and Barrett, 1983.)

suggested that there was only one correction prior to target impact. Let us now discuss these two proposals in some detail, for they lie at the heart of our understanding of the speed–accuracy tradeoff in discrete movements.

Multi-correction models

Crossman and Goodeve (1983) and Keele (1968) have suggested that a movement to a target consists of a series of submovements each of a duration '*t*' and the same relative accuracy '*k*'. A submovement is an impulse in response to visual error that helps reduce that error. The variability of the end-point of any correction is a constant proportion (from 4% to 7%) of the distance to be moved. This means that the initial programmed phase, as Woodworth (1899) supposed, traverses most of the distance to the target before a visually-based amendment is made. A series of corrections then follows until the remaining error is reduced to ½W (target width), when a final movement is produced that makes contact with the target. A basic tenet of the Crossman and Goodeve (1983) and Keele (1968) models is that precision affects the *number of corrections* to be made, and not the time for these corrections. This time is presumed to be in the order of 250 msec, based on a study by Keele and Posner (1968). Consequently, the movement time of the initial movement is independent of target precision. Target precision affects only the number of submovements.

An interesting feature of the Crossman and Goodeve model is that it is consistent with a logarithmic speed–accuracy tradeoff (see Equation 1). It will be recalled that an underlying assumption of Fitts' Law is that the effects of the distance (amplitude) and precision (target width) of the movement on the movement time exactly compensate. For a constant ratio of amplitude to width, movement time should remain constant. Fitts (1954) further argued that the quantity

$$\text{Log}_2 \frac{2 \text{ (Distance)}}{\text{Width}}$$

represented an Index of Difficulty expressed as bits of information to be processed. Since, moreover, movement time varied linearly (see Figure 27) with the Index of Difficulty, the information was being processed at a constant rate. Crossman and Goodeve's approach was so important because it attempted to define the actual underlying control processes, and it did so with reference to the way in which visual feedback is processed. Initially it seemed to account for Equation 1 very well. a and b in Equation 1 are empirically determined constants. b is the slope constant. Fitts and Peterson (1964) reported an average for constant b of +74 msec. Remarkably, this estimate is equivalent to that arrived at using the assumptions of the Crossman and Goodeve, and Keele models. An estimate for a was in the order of −70 msec, measured from the intercept. At the heart of the discussion is whether visual feedback processing underlies the logarithmic speed–accuracy tradeoff. If we are to understand the logarithmic speed–accuracy tradeoff we must ask, what are the characteristic conditions under which Fitts Law is observed and under what conditions does it break down? We are, therefore, concerned with the generality of Fitts' Law.

The generality of Fitts' law

Fitts' Law has been generalized to a wide variety of tasks; it has, for example, been observed across species. Brooks (1979) observed the relationship in the movements of monkeys just as readily as those of humans. It is possible, furthermore, that Fitts' Law may predict movement time in a range of other species, thus permitting neurological investigations of this phenomenon but using a subhuman model. Within the human species, Fitts' Law has been observed for a number of situations. Fitts' (1954) initial study involved repetitive tapping movements. Perhaps the most basic replication has been by Fitts and Peterson (1964) who observed that the Fitts relation applied equally to both repetitive and single-aiming movements. Other studies have examined different groups of people. Wade, Newell, and Wallace (1978; cited in Schmidt, Zelaznik and Frank, 1979), for example, examined retardates. Though retardates display the logarithmic speed–accuracy tradeoff, they also display a steeper slope than for age-matched 'normals'. Welford, Norris, and Shock (1969) report Fitts' Law for older people. At the earlier stage of the lifespan, Sugden (1980) reports very slow movement times in young children at each amplitude–width ratio examined. However, Fitts' Law was maintained. Fitts' Law also holds across different muscle groups, including head (Jagacinski and Monk, 1985) and feet (Drury, 1975) movements. Presumably it would hold, too, for the mouth or any other organ possessing the necessary mechanical degrees of freedom. Movements of a different character to Fitts' original linear arm movements have also been studied. Knight and Dagnell (1967), for example, observing the rotary movement of the wrist, and also Kerr and Langolf (1977) observing back-and-forth motions like dart-throwing, confirmed the generality of Fitts' Law.

Fitts' Law also extends to different environments. Kerr (1973, 1978) reported the Fitts relation for underwater movements; Jagacinski et al. (1978) for the remote manipulation of a joystick; and Langolf, Chaffin, and Foulke (1976) for the microscopic analysis of wrist and finger movements.

Despite the wide variations of the slope relating movement-time to the logarithm of the ratio of amplitude to target-width for these different situations, Fitts' Law very accurately described the movement time variations. The Crossman–Goodeve model thus seems to predict a general law governing human behavior. However, the generality of the law is not support of the model.

A feature of the 'Fitts' tasks we have examined so far is that they all involved spatial and not temporal constraints. That is, the subject was required to produce an aiming movement that would come to rest within a precisely defined target area but was free to vary the movement time. In addition, movement times greater than 200 msec were examined. What happens when the bandwidth of possible movement times (i.e. temporal precision) is specified? Under these conditions the speed–accuracy tradeoff is no longer logarithmic. Furthermore, this research questions the importance of visual feedback as a basis for the logarithmic speed–accuracy tradeoff. What then, is the precise role for visually-based error detection mechanisms? This issue is now addressed from the perspective of the impulse variability model.

Impulse variability

The foregoing discussion has highlighted the remarkable generality of Fitts' Law. Fitts' Law does, however, break down at movement speeds of 200 msec or less (see Figure 27) and it is to the implications of this observation that we now turn. Indeed, Schmidt, Zelaznik, and Frank (1979) have observed a linear speed–accuracy tradeoff for such rapid movements. These authors required subjects to move at precise movement times (i.e. temporal precision) with effective target width (W_e) as the dependent variable (i.e. spatial variability). Note that this procedure is different from the Fitts paradigm where the required target precision is specified but the movement time is free to vary. Schmidt et al. (1979) observed that W_e increased linearly with the ratio A/MT (see Figure 29). The essence of Schmidt's Impulse-Timing

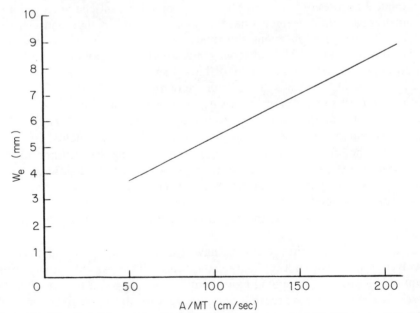

Figure 29. The linear function relating the effective target width (We-extent) to the average velocity (A/MT). (After Schmidt et al., 1979.)

model is that the distance and direction of a discrete movement (and hence the final end-point location) is specified by the force–time integral of the impulses that accelerate and decelerate the limb. Further, the model proposes that there is no reference to feedback-based corrections.

It is interesting to note that the range of movement times (< 200 msec) studied by Schmidt et al. (1979) were too rapid to permit the processing of visual information associated with each corrective submovement according to Crossman and Goodeve's (1983) and Keele's (1968) models. For this reason Schmidt et al. (1979) toyed with the idea that the logarithmic and linear speed–accuracy tradeoffs could be accounted for by fundamentally different mechanisms related to whether the processing of visual feedback was possible. Recently, however, it has been proposed that though the speed–accuracy tradeoffs for slow (> 200 msec) and fast (<200 msec) movements may indeed differ quantitatively, 'related versions of the same mechanism may underly both of them' (Meyer, Smith, and Wright, 1982, p. 469).

Meyer et al. (1982) extended the model, first proposed by Schmidt et al. (1979) to account for the linear speed–accuracy tradeoff, to account also for the logarithmic trade off. The essence of these models is the nature of the force pulse that generates an aimed movement. Schmidt et al.'s (1979) seminal impulse-variability model sought to explain muscular control in relation to physical principles. The limb is initially accelerated by the force produced from the first agonist burst and decelerated with the help of the major antagonist burst. The output of the human muscular system is contaminated, however, by 'noise' (within subject variability) and this variability is assumed to be related to the nature of the movement (i.e. to its amplitude and speed). The essential point, then, is that the magnitude of error in producing a response increases in proportion to the magnitude of forces being attempted. Slower movements are more accurate, quite simply because they involve smaller forces. Meyer et al. (1982) argue that the temporal precision but spatial variability of Schmidt et al.'s (1979) movements meant that these movements would be mediated by a single pair of large force pulses which results in the linear tradeoff.

Meyer et al. (1982) propose that if the aimed movement is generated by a series of 'miniature' overlapping force pulses rather than a single large pulse, then a logarithmic speed–accuracy tradeoff will result. They propose, moreover, that the conditions under which overlapping pulses may be observed are spatial precision and temporal variability. This, of course, is the situation for Fitts' paradigm where subjects move to precisely defined targets but establish their own movement times. So in Meyer et al.'s (1982) approach there is a unifying theory that accounts for both a linear and logarithmic tradeoff. It must be stressed, furthermore, that this 'temporal precision' hypothesis allocates no explanatory power to error detection and correction processes (cf. Crossman and Goodeve, 1983) in deriving the tradeoff function. Wright and Myer (1983) subsequently demonstrated that a linear speed–accuracy tradeoff could be obtained even when ample time was available for the processing of visual error information, so long as the movements were precisely timed.

The detection and correction of errors is, nevertheless, crucial to movements requiring a degree of spatial precision. Crossman and Goodeve (1983) argued for a multicorrection control model. Alternatively, Beggs and Howarth (1970, 1972a, b) have suggested that visual feedback information is sampled only once toward the end of a movement, and a single amendment initiated. This approach, detailed in the first edition of this book, did not address the issue of a logarithmic speed—accuracy tradeoff. Moreover, it was derived from an experimental paradigm in which temporal, not spatial, precision was specified.

Single correction model

Howarth, Beggs, and Bowden (1971) and Beggs and Howarth (1972a,b) have proposed a theory of intermittent visual control, in which terminal accuracy is controlled by a single, visually-based correction, taking in the order of 200–300 msec. This time is similar to that proposed by Keele (1968) for the multicorrection model. When greater accuracy is required, velocity throughout is reduced so that the subject is close to the target when time for one correction is left. The underlying assumption is that the closer to the target at the time of correction the less will be the outcome error. In short, response accuracy is proportional to the distance remaining at the time of correction. As Keele (1980) points out, however, Beggs and Howarth's model does not incorporate a prediction for the effect of movement amplitude on total movement time and precision. The experimental paradigm underlying the model, however, invoked a linear speed–accuracy tradeoff. Since these authors constrained movement time this is precisely what might be expected according to Meyer et al.'s (1982) temporal-precision hypothesis.

The fact that Beggs and Howarth's arguments were derived from circumstances conducive to a linear tradeoff does not, nevertheless, detract from the generality of the model in terms of feedback processing, in view of Wright and Meyer's (1983) observation that visual feedback is not the crucial source of the speed–accuracy tradeoff. Presumably, the principles underlying the processing of visual feedback information will be the same whether temporal precision is required or not.

How well, then, do the single-correction and multicorrection models compare? Those studies showing evidence for corrections—for example, from the high-speed cinematographic analysis of aimed movements—suggest that, typically, only one correction may occur instead of a series of corrections, although two may sometimes be seen, often associated with relatively narrow target constraints (Carlton, 1981). For discrete aiming movements, further-more, Carlton (1981) has demonstrated that visual error information is sampled close to the target. Blocking visual information related to stylus position for the first 75% of the distance to be traveled by the aimed limb did not disrupt performance. It must be asked whether vision is not used in these early stages because of a refractory state, or alternatively because of the magnitude of the error. Crossman and Goodeve's (1983) model, however, assumes that the movement error is detected at the initiation of the move-ment. This must, as Schmidt et al. (1979) point out, be the case since the first corrective submovement is assumed to appear in the order of 190–250 msec into the movement. For this to be feasible additional assumptions would have to be made. For example, it is possible that a prediction of the resultant amplitude of the initial submovement is derived from some central 'reference' in the brain which, in turn, generates a predictive error from a comparison with incoming visual information regarding the target position only. Such a mechanism has been proposed to underlie saccadic control (e.g. Becker and Jurgens, 1979). However, as will be argued later, the prediction of response-unit position via a central or efference copy is not as likely for the limb system as it is for the saccadic system. If not, what is the basis for this assumed early detection of movement error in the Crossman and Goodeve (1983) model?

A further issue is whether the restraints placed on the number of visually-based corrections by the time delays in processing the error information could adequately account for the continuous changes in movement times that occur as a function of distance and precision, if a multicorrection model is proposed. Fitts and Peterson (1964), for example, varied movement ampli-tude from 3 to 12 inches and target-width from 0.125 to 1.0 inch. Movement times ranged systematically from 150 msec to a maximum of 500 msec, thus restricting corrections to two or three at the most. In reference to Crossman and Goodeve's argument, then, whilst precision may affect the number of corrections, this number is too restricted to account for the smooth and continuous changes in movement time observed as a function of distance and precision. It is interesting to note that there is, as Sheridan (1979) points out, a curving of the 'straight'-line Fitts relationship graph in tasks where there is a high index of difficulty. Yet it is for high Indexes of difficulty where one might expect to observe more than one corrective component to the limb trajectory. It appears that the logarithmic speed–accuracy tradeoff which the multicorrection model strives so hard to explain actually 'breaks down' when eventually more than one correction is possible or likely. This, then, is a serious difficulty for the Crossman and Goodeve model.

There is, however, one essential agreement across the single- and multicor-rection models. Both propose that visual feedback takes in the order of 200–300 msec to be processed. It is this common assumption to which we now turn. This processing time is assumed to be the critical restraint on movement speed if the movement is to be performed accurately. The control principles underlying the processing of visual information are, therefore, a major concern.

Visual feedback processing time

How can we determine the processing time for visual information arising during the ongoing movement? The estimate of 200–300 msec is in agreement with a large number of studies (e.g. Craik, 1947, 1948; Henry and Harrison, 1961; Pew, 1966; Keele and Posner, 1968; Beggs and Howarth, 1970; Christina, 1970) that have sought to measure the processing time of such visual information. Only these confirmatory studies will be referred to here. Other studies which have contradicted this finding are discussed later in the chapter.

In their seminal study, Keele and Posner (1968) required subjects to make discrete aiming movements to a 0.25 inch diameter circular target, six inches distant from a start position. They trained subjects to move at different rates ranging from 190 msec to 450 msec. On some trials subjects were denied visual feedback for movement guidance, by switching the light off as soon as the subject lifted his stylus from the homeplate. Movements of about 190 msec duration yielded similar accuracy levels (assessed by hits or misses) irrespective of the presence or absence of visual feedback. Accuracy was enhanced for movements of about 260 msec duration by the presence of visual feedback. Keele and Posner (1968) interpreted their data to suggest that between 190 msec and 260 msec was needed for a visually-based amendment. Unfortunately, a more precise estimate could not be determined from their study. Of course, if visual information is not used in the initial portions of the movement (Carlton, 1981) this technique may overestimate the processing time. In addition, the estimated time includes the movement time of the final corrective response. These issues are taken up later.

If, for the moment, one accepts a visual processing time in the order of 200 msec, then Schmidt et al. (1978) suggest a number of factors which may actually increase the correction time beyond a normal reaction time. They suggest the performer is essentially faced with two problems: (i) overcoming psychological 'refractoriness', and (ii) reducing the number of error alternatives. These problems must in turn be addressed by the single- and multicorrection models.

'Refractoriness'

It has been consistently reported that a response to the second of two closely presented stimuli is delayed due to the so-called 'psychological refractory period'. This has important implications for the Crossman–Goodeve model.

A central theme for this model, it will be recalled, is that movement time is occupied by a series of 200–300 msecs corrections. The subject may, therefore, need to respond to two consecutive stimuli spaced by approximately 250 msec. It is well documented (see Bertelson, 1966, for review) that in responses using two separate anatomical units (e.g. the right and left hands) to two consecutive stimuli spaced between 50 to 500 msecs apart, the reaction time to the second of the two closely-spaced stimuli will be delayed considerably relative to the stimulus presented alone. The delay has been related to a limited channel capacity in the information-processing system and is, for the double-response unit situation at least, discussed in a number of texts (see chapters by Glencross, 1979; Schmidt, 1982).

Schmidt et al. (1978) extended the notion of a psychological refractory period to responses to consecutive stimuli in the Crossman and Goodeve situation. For movements in the order of 500 msec the multicorrection model assumes the subject responds to two consecutive error signals in attaining accuracy. Since these stimuli are closely spaced, Schmidt et al. (1978) argue that the total reaction time for the second stimulus should take in the order of 500–600 msec, thus exceeding the specified movement time. Perhaps, using these arguments, it may also be inferred that the late sampling of visual information by Carlton's (1981) subjects reflects refractoriness during the initial 75% of the trajectory rather than other factors, for example, the magnitude of the error to be corrected. Indeed, this is the underlying assumption of a model for discrete saccadic aiming movements proposed by Young and Stark (1963). These authors proposed that once target eccentricity is sampled, a corresponding saccade is programmed and executed whilst the system enters a refractory phase. At the termination of the saccade, target eccentricity is sampled again.

Schmidt et al.'s (1978) argument, however, was derived from results to the double-response unit paradigm where two hands typically respond to the double stimuli. In the discrete aiming movement situation the subject responds to successive errors, but with the crucial difference that only a single response unit is employed. It must, therefore, be asked whether the results to the double response unit situation do indeed generalize to the single response unit situation. As early as 1966 Gottsdanker argued 'no', and his position will be examined later.

The number of error alternatives

The second problem discussed by Schmidt et al. (1978) concerns the number of likely error alternatives. Schmidt et al. argued that intermittent control models assume that only one visually detected error has to be corrected. Information theory, however, suggests that reaction time increases with the number of stimulus alternatives (Hick, 1952). In an ongoing movement there may be several error signals. The number of ways in which an error may occur within a movement, in terms of the metrical or scalar details, the spatial features, and also in terms of phasing and timing of the response (e.g. Glencross, 1979), presents the subject with a substantial choice amongst stimulus alternatives. When viewed in relation to the temporal and spatial uncertainty, a corrective reaction time of 200–300 msec would underestimate the complexity of the movement situation, according to Schmidt et al. (1978).

Contrary to the above predictions, however, high-speed cinematographic analysis of aiming movements suggest that the visual processing time may actually be shorter than 200 msec. Not only did Carlton (1981) block off vision of the stylus from the initial 75% of the movement distance of a discrete aiming movement, but he was also able to measure the delay between the first appearance of the stylus and initiation of the final movement. This period represents the visual processing time which, in this study, was in the order of 130 msec. Interestingly, this time corresponds to the intersaccadic pauses that have been observed as the eyes foveate a visual stimulus (Henson, 1978). Carlton (1981), in line with Henson (1978), argues that a general control principle may exist across systems where the subject produces an initial response with a deliberate error. For example, the subject may deliberately undershoot the target. In this way the subject would know in advance the direction and approximate amplitude of the final corrective response. One might expect the magnitude of the error to increase as well.

From this viewpoint, then, the corrective response could actually be programmed largely in advance whilst the initial response process is ongoing. As Becker (1976) argues for eye saccadic movements, the final decision for the correction depends on confirmation of the actual amplitude of the corrective response via visual afferents and this occurs once the initial portions of the movement have been completed. Discrete aiming movements may therefore be considered as composed of overlapping programs. This is an interesting idea since it bears similarities to the notion of overlapping force pulses developed by Meyer et al. (1982) to explain the logarithmic speed–accuracy tradeoff. For the manual system then, the processing time might be expected to vary with the precision required of the final corrective response (i.e. target width) and also show considerable variation within a condition. This was indeed the conclusion arrived at from Langolf, Chaffin, and Foulke's (1976) observation of a standard deviation of 55 msec (range 80–360 msecs) for breakpoints in a repetitive tapping task. Wallace and Newell (1983), furthermore, demonstrated a greater involvement of vision for smaller target-widths. The essential point here, nevertheless, is that the subject is able to reduce the number of stimulus alternatives by producing a deliberate error.

DIRECTIONAL ERRORS

We now move on to examine large magnitude errors, the errors of trajectory. In the previous section small amendments to a correct ballpark response served to 'home' the response onto the target. On the other hand, trajectory errors (incorrect ballpark responses) demand a modification that must get the limb back onto the right trajectory again so that the homing-in procedures can then begin. In the following sections modifications to directional errors in single-step tracking tasks and the artificially-induced errors studied in discrete double-step tracking tasks will be examined.

Single step analyses

How can we study the situation where the subject makes or programs a wrong response? Let us consider the situation where the subject has to align a cursor or pointer with targets, located to either side of a homebase. Thus, there is directional uncertainty of which target will appear and hence which response will be required. We can call this a single-step choice reaction-tracking task. Higgins and Angel (1970) employed such a procedure in a study in which the subject was required to position a cursor on an oscilloscope screen, by manipulating a joystick. In a similar study by Megaw (1972), the subject had to align a pointer with a target neon light positioned along a track. These studies, furthermore, encouraged errors by using an incompatible arrangement between the control and the display. That is, the correct response is always in the direction opposite to that indicated by the target stimulus. Our interest in these studies is when a wrong response occurs and, hence, a movement is initiated in the wrong direction (in the 'wrong ballpark'). What is the mechanism that detects and corrects such displacement or directional errors in these 'single-step' situations?

Central and peripheral mechanisms

The possible error-detection mechanisms can be inferred from the onset of the incorrect response and some measure of the displacement, velocity, or acceleration records and, in some cases, electromyographic detail.

One of the difficulties in interpreting evidence in this area is that different studies have used different measurements for this interval which is referred to as the error correction reaction time (ECRT). Figure 30 gives an example of the displacement, acceleration, and velocity profiles for an incorrect velocity response.

The reaction time (RTI) to the step stimulus is measured from stimulus onset to response onset. Figure 30, however, illustrates the different measurements for the ECRT which have been used. Gibbs (1965), for example, defined ECRT to the initiation of the corrective response. Angel and Higgins (1969) shortened the interval to the time when velocity becomes zero, that is, when the incorrect response was actually halted. Higgins and Angel (1970), on the other hand, defined ECRT in relation to the instant when acceleration begins to decrease. It is this later measurement that will be adopted here since it allows a ready comparison with the processing times for alternative sources of error information.

Higgins and Angel (1970) themselves preferred to explain their data in terms of a central source of error information. This is an important devel-

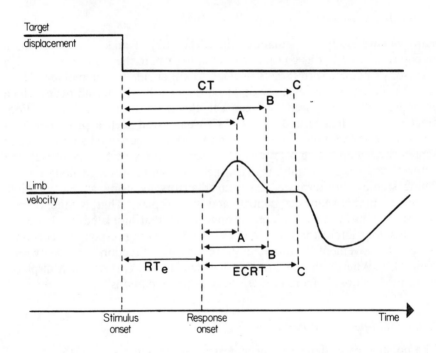

Figure 30. A schematic representation of a directional error response to a position step of a target. The top trace illustrates the displacement of the target. The bottom trace represents the corresponding velocity trace of the cursor. The subject makes an initial movement in a direction opposition to the target step direction. This error response is subsequently amended. RT:e: Reaction Time of the Error Response; CT: Correction Time; ECRT: Error Correction Reaction Time. Both CT and ECRT are variously measured in relation to A: the onset of deceleration; B: the onset of zero velocity; or C: the initiation of the corrective response. See text for further explanation.

opment for it introduces the notion of some central error correction mechanism (as opposed to peripheral mechanisms) and suggests that subjects are able to monitor their own actions internally, comparing the actual motor commands with some reference value, which is the correct command under the given conditions. If there is a discrepancy between the actual command and the correct command, the response can be arrested prematurely (Higgins and Angel, 1970). We will discuss such central mechanisms again a little later. Higgins and Angel (1970) have argued that peripheral sources of information were too slow to account for their findings. The ECRTs reported by Higgins and Angel (1970) are faster than the corresponding proprioceptive reaction times, thus attesting to the relative speed of these amendments.

Earlier, Gibbs (1965) had considered the possibility that proprioceptive feedback sources were involved. Using Chernikoff and Taylor's (1952) paradigm, Higgins and Angel (1970) compared the proprioceptive reaction times (PRTs) of their subjects with their corresponding ECRTs. A joystick was held in a central position with two equal (5 lb) and opposite forces pulling to the left and right. Removing a force meant the joystick would be pulled in the direction of the unopposed force. The subject was required to arrest this movement by applying a counter-force emerging from a proprioceptive-based reaction of the limb. In line with Chernikoff and Taylor (1952), PRT was measured from the appearance of a movement until a decrease in acceleration is observed. Note that this measurement is directly analogous to the measurement of ECRT adopted by Higgins and Angel (1970). Higgins and Angel (1970) found that for every subject the mean ECRT (range: 83–122 msec, mean = 98 msec) was smaller than the obtained PRT (range: 108–146 msec, mean = 136 msec). Of course, recent findings of Zelaznik, Hawkins, and Kisselburgh (1983) suggest, nevertheless, that visual information can be processed in a time similar to an ECRT.

A number of studies (e.g. Angel, Garland, and Fishler, 1971; Megaw, 1972; Angel, 1976), however, have directly controlled the visual information available. Angel (1976), for example, obscured the response cursor from view until it had moved more than half the distance to the target positions. Under these conditions, a large proportion of false moves could still be corrected whilst the cursor was hidden. This implies that direct sensory information about the direction of travel of the cursor is unimportant for an error amendment to occur. Indeed, a correction may even commence prior to any displacement of the limb. Cooke and Diggles (1984) and Morris (1981) demonstrated by means of electromyography that an error may be corrected before instigation of the wrong response. If this is the case, then the role of peripherally-based feedback information is seriously questioned.

There are a number of difficulties with the central monitoring viewpoint. One problem is the specification of the reference value or intended plan of action. Presumably, this value is retrieved from memory. At issue, then, is whether a separate reference value for every possible movement exists in memory. A specific reference value would have the effect of restraining the flexibility typically observed for the human motor system. Motor constancy phenemona, for example, illustrate that the motor system may generate a wide range of movements, each involving the exercise of different musculature, which may each subserve an identical goal or outcome (Greene, 1972). Glencross (1980b) has argued, furthermore, that the analysis of discrete action patterns indicates that they are not an identical map of preceding patterns, as evidenced by performance scores and also the fine-grain displacement, velocity, and electromyographic recordings. Just as it is unlikely that the precise spatial, temporal, and parametric details of the response are stored centrally ready to be triggered into action, it is also unlikely such details should be stored in the reference value.

Kelso and Stelmach (1976), furthermore, present a strong argument against sensing limb location on the basis of an efference copy since the limb does not move under a constant set of forces. Since these forces are modified from movement to movement, prediction would be difficult. At least, it must be stressed, prediction of the limb within a relatively specific location would be difficult. In the situation to which Higgins and Angel (1970) applied the notion of an efference copy, however, the error is in the wrong choice of muscles altogether to subserve antagonist/agonist roles. The error appears to be one of muscle or response unit selection. On the basis of differences in the reaction time to directional-certain extent-uncertain and directional-uncertain extent-certain conditions, Megaw (1972) has proposed that muscle-selection and parametric-specification are subserved by different levels of the response organization process. The efference-copy may, therefore, be restricted to the detection of errors in the selection of the appropriate muscles (response units).

Finally, if the error movement command is structured when the target displacement occurs, as the single-step viewpoint suggests, then the reaction time of error responses might be expected to be equal to that of correctly programmed responses. A cause of concern has been the observation that where a directional error occurs, the reaction time (RTI) to that trial is relatively short compared to correct trials (Megaw, 1972). The reduced reaction time suggests anticipation of the stimulus event and has formed the basis of an alternative description of the double-step viewpoint. This viewpoint is discussed later within the context of the discrete double-step tracking paradigm.

Central monitoring

Before proceeding, it is necessary to relate the present notion of a central efference monitoring device (e.g. Higgins and Angel, 1970) with 'inflow efference copy' (e.g. von Holst, 1954) and 'corollary discharge' (e.g. Sperry, 1950). Kelso (1982) has recently emphasized their conceptual distinction. Higgins and Angel (1970) denied the importance of proprioceptive sources in the error correction process and, as a result, their model has been designated an 'outflow' model (Jones, 1971, 1974; Schmidt, 1975, 1976). The efference copy and corollary discharge models, on the other hand, depend on proprioceptive feedback and have been referred to as 'inflow' models (Jones, 1971, 1974). von Holst (1954) defined an efference copy as an 'image' which is held in temporary storage and, if the incoming efferent impulses match with the efference, then the subject will conclude that the motion was self-generated. Likewise, any mismatch would indicate an error in the system. Sperry (1950), on the other hand, coined the term 'corollary discharge' to refer to a discharge prior to the emergence of an eye movement that subsequently allows any visual input to be intepreted.

Teuber (1972) extended the notion to voluntary movement. Teuber argued that, along with the neural discharge to the musculature, there is, centrally, a simultaneous or corollary discharge from the motor to the sensory systems that presets the sensory system to handle the response-produced feedback. Whereas the efference-copy is specified in a motor language, the corollary discharge specifies the sensory consequences of the planned movement. The conceptual difference relates to whether motor or sensory information is stored. The corollary discharge sensitizes sensory areas such that afferent information is subject to facilitated processing (Kelso, 1982). As Kelso points out, not only does the corollary discharge signal active movement but, as with the efference-copy, it may also subserve an error-correction function. However, the efference copy and corollary discharge notions can only inform the subject that the movement is going as planned and not whether the initial plan or program is the correct response. These notions are, therefore, not relevant to the forms of error detection being discussed here.

Directional errors—double-step analyses

In this section the 'double-step' viewpoint of directional errors is developed, and is then evaluated against results from double-step tracking studies. By double-step we mean that first the target steps to one position (requiring a response) and then the target steps to a second position (requiring an amended response).

The finding that directional error responses have relatively short reaction times provoked Schmidt and Gordon (1977) to explain the rapid amendment of directional responses in terms of a double-stimulus (refractory) situation. They point out that these relatively short reaction times suggest the subject is anticipating incorrectly on error responses. Moreover, most of the earlier experiments showing 'rapid' error corrections have used stimulus sequences that had constant fore-periods. This evidence suggests that the subject is able to anticipate both the time when the stimulus will arrive and also its direction. This is then the mechanism for generating an error. Whether or not the error will be detected depends on the generation of the expected sensory consequences of the stimulus display. These sensory consequences of the stimulus display are generated prior to the movement and are fed forward in a manner analogous to the expected sensory consequences of response-produce feedback proposed for 'corollary-discharge' notions (e.g. Sperry, 1950). In this way the anticipated stimulus event and actual stimulus event can be compared and any impending errors registered. If an error is revealed the subject must, therefore, initiate a corrective response. 'Because the initial (incorrect) movement has already been activated, the initial segments of the incorrect movement do not appear until the corrective response appears' (Schmidt and Gordon, 1977, p. 103).

The initial response, then, is programmed to an anticipated stimulus or target step (i.e. a first step). The corrective response is programmed to the actual stimulus and may be viewed as presenting a target at a new step position (i.e. a second step). Hence, this approach is described as a 'double-step' viewpoint. Since, furthermore, the subject anticipates the stimulus on an error response, the reaction time will be shorter than normal. Schmidt and Gordon (1977) propose, on the other hand, that the corrective response will be initiated after one reaction time plus a delay due to psychological refractoriness. Schmidt and Gordon (1977) are, therefore, proposing that the true corrective reaction time should be measured from the onset of the target stimulus. This value is termed the 'correction time' (CT) and its relation to be ECRT can be seen in Figure 30 earlier.

Double-step tracking

Schmidt and Gordon's (1977) anticipation hypothesis makes a number of assumptions regarding the processing of sequential stimuli in a discrete aiming movement, where the response to both stimuli is produced using the same response-unit. In particular, borrowing from principles derived from the double-response unit paradigm, they proposed that a psychological refractory period exists during the programming of a response to an initial step stimulus. This issue is directly examined in the double-step tracking paradigm where the second target step may be viewed as an artificially-induced movement error. As such, the initial step response is equivalent to a ballpark incorrect response. Double-step tracking responses have recently been analysed around the notion of an amplitude transition function.

The amplitude transition function

A consistent finding in the manual double-step tracking literature (e.g. Gottsdanker, 1966, 1973; Georgopoulos, Kalaska, and Massey, 1981; Gielen, van der Heuvel, and Denier van der Gon, 1984) has been that the reaction time to a second-step stimulus presented during the reaction time to an initial step stimulus will be equivalent to a single-step reaction time. That is, the psychological refractory period phenomenon does not generalize across the single- and double-response unit situations. In an attempt to understand the processes underlying manual double-step tracking, Barrett and Glencross (1988) have interpreted the results in terms of an Amplitude Transition Function (ATF), a notion which they borrowed from the oculomotor double-step tracking literature. First stated by Becker and Jurgens (1975, 1979), the ATF specifies the relationship between the amplitude of an initial step response and a determinant time-interval (D).

The principle of the ATF is illustrated in Figure 31. The determinant time-interval is the interval between the onset of a second target step and the initiation of a response. Becker and Jürgens (1979) observed that at short determinant time-intervals saccades were produced that went directly to the initial step position (i.e. Initial Amplitude Responses, IARs). At very long values of D a saccade could be produced that went directly to the final target step position (i.e. Final Amplitude Responses, FARs). At intermediate values of D, Intermediate Amplitude Responses (IMARs) were produced which formed a gradual transition between IARs and FARs. In a similar vein, Barrett and Glencross (1988) noted that constant amendments of manual double-step tracking responses varied with the determinant time-interval. The constant amendment specifies the mean signed distance of a double-step response relative to the mean signed distance of single-step responses to the initial step position.

It should be realized that the construction of an ATF for the very rapid (<150 msec) movements in Barrett and Glencross (1988) would not be possible if a psychological refractory period cloaked the reaction time to the initial step stimulus.

Although the principle of an ATF characterized double-step tracking across the oculomotor and skeletal-muscular control systems, the control principles underlying its construction appear to be fundamentally different. Across a number of stimulus patterns, for example, Becker and Jurgens (1979) noted that the transition time (T_w in Figure 31) remained constant (approximately 110 msec). They argued that the transition phase of the ATF represented an averaging window of duration T_w. All error signals falling across the time

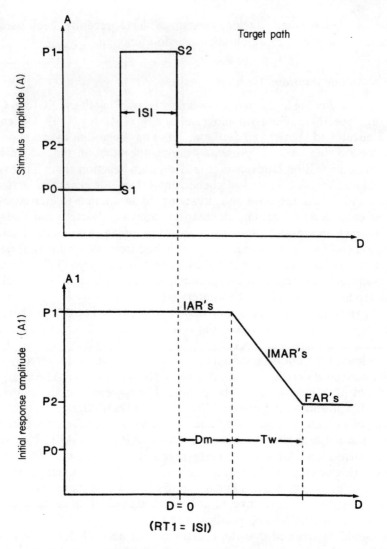

Figure 31. The amplitude transition function (ATF) for a family of possible initial response amplitudes to a double-step target, as a function of the delay (the determinant time interval, D) between the occurrence of the second target step (S_2) and the commencement of the initial response.

S_1	= First Target Step		IARs	= Initial Amplitude Responses
S_2	= Second Target Step		IMARs	= Intermediate Amplitude Responses
PO	= Home Base Position		FARs	= Final Amplitude Responses
P1	= Initial Step Position		D_M	= Modification Time
P2	= Second Step Position		Tw	= Transition Time
ISI	= Interstep (Interstimulus) Interval		RT_1	= Initial Reaction Time

(See text for full explanation.)

window would receive a weighted average of their distances from the home-base and a saccade of corresponding amplitude would be initiated by a neural pulse generator once the time window was closed. If the second step occurred prior to opening of the time window (at long values of D) only the second step position would be implicated in the amplitude calculation leading to an FAR. If, however, at short values of D, the second step is presented following the closing of the averaging window, the initial amplitude is determined by the first step position and an IAR results.

The value Dm in Figure 31 refers to the modification time, the time at which a step response can be modified by the presentation of a second-step stimulus. Within the saccadic system, a minimal value for the modification time has been reported in the order of 80 msec (e.g. Becker and Jurgens, 1979; Deubel, Wolf, and Hauske, 1984; Findlay and Harris, 1984). Where the averaging of errors across a time window is assumed, the minimal modification time is interpreted in terms of the summation of efferent and afferent delay times.

Barrett and Glencross (1988) also report a modification time in the order of 80 ± 20 msec for manual double-step tracking. Their data, however, suggested a fundamentally different interpretation. They observed, for example, a concave function relating the standard deviation of movement end-points to the determinant time-interval. In addition, the electromyographic analyses of Gielen et al. (1984) suggest the initial manual response on a double-step trial is not a discretely structured response carrying the amended amplitude. Instead it appears to be interrupted in 'mid-flight' by the response to an amending stimulus. Manual double-step tracking, then, is characterized by overlapping and parallel programmed responses. Whereas for the error averaging model Dm was understood in relation to the efferent and afferent delays associated with the initial reaction time, for the overlapping response model Dm is understood in terms of the reaction time of the response to the second stimulus. Dm reflects the determinant time interval one reaction time prior to the completion of the unamended initial response. Despite differences in the control processes underlying the ATF across the saccadic and manual systems, the ATF, nevertheless, remains a valuable conceptual tool for the integration of findings across different control systems.

The findings discussed in relation to the ATF suggest that the sampling strategy adopted by ballpark correct responses reflects the magnitude of the error and not refractoriness associated with the initial reaction time. A multicorrection model (e.g. Crossman and Goodeve, 1983) would, therefore, not be affected by psychological refractoriness.

Georgopoulos et al. (1981) report brief delays at short interstimulus intervals (ISI = 50 msec) for a stimulus that stepped first to one side of a homebase and then to the other side. These delays were too brief to be considered as refractory delays. On the other hand, there is a large variability of end-points for directional errors. Angel, Garland, and Fischler (1971) excluded view of the cursor until it had traveled half the distance to a target position. Out of 24 false moves 16 were arrested while the cursor was hidden. This finding implies that the amplitude of the initial response may vary quite substantially. The variability of end-points is consistent with an 'overlapping' response to a second step located during the transition phase of the ATF. Future research must determine whether the amending of a directional error can indeed be understood in terms of an ATF which has emerged from the double-step analysis of the manual control system. The parallels between directional errors and double-step tracking is an area that merits further systematic investigation. Already, Georgopoulos et al.'s (1981) research shows that a subhuman model exists with parallels to human step-tracking performance. Finally, the control we have over discrete movements and its components makes such movements ideal for this analysis.

Let us now integrate the foregoing discussions into a description of the different modes of error correction.

MODES OF ERROR CORRECTION

The idea that there may be different modes underlying the processing of visual error information has recently been expressed for both the manual (e.g. Zelaznik et al., 1983) and oculomotor (e.g. Becker and Jurgens, 1979) control systems. Before examining Zelaznik et al.'s (1983) viewpoint it is first necessary to highlight the three modes of error correction already identified in the present chapter. These are the intermittent sampling mode, the continuous updating mode, and a mixed mode. The modes noted by Becker and Jurgens (1979) for the oculomotor system have clear parallels with the present scheme. Subsequently, Zelaznik et al.'s (1983) automatic mode is discussed. Finally, mention is made of a mode of error correction where any afferent-efferent distinction is superfluous.

The intermittent sampling mode

This mode is reserved for responses which are initially in the correct ballpark but require minor adjustments to home in on the target. The adjustment must be relatively precise and, at least for manual responses, the nature of the error cannot be predicted in advance. The analogous oculomotor control form is the retinal mode (e.g. Becker and Jurgens, 1979). Here the magnitude of a predictive error assessed via an extraretinal feedback pathway is small (<3 deg) and the intersaccadic latency equals a normal saccadic reaction time. Likewise intermittent sampling models of manual control propose a sampling pause equivalent to a visual reaction time.

The continuous updating mode

Large magnitude errors, on the other hand, like the artificially-induced errors in a double-step tracking task, are responded to immediately. A number of studies (e.g. Georgopoulos et al., 1981; Gielen et al., 1984) now indicate that the corrective response to a second step of the target can be programmed in parallel with the initial step response and without delay. It appears, therefore, that responses to double stimuli in the single response-unit situation are not characterized by a psychological refractory period so typical of the double-response unit situation (e.g. Bertelson, 1966). The response program initiates a movement as soon as possible without awaiting visual confirmation.

Again, a similar situation exists where oculomotor control is concerned. Large errors (>15 deg) in the saccadic system are, according to Becker and Jurgens (1979), processed in an extraretinal mode. Here the decision element immediately triggers the preparation of a second saccade whilst the primary saccade is still ongoing. It does not wait for retinal confirmation on the basis of visual afferents. Likewise, the large magnitude directional errors in manual step tracking could be detected by an efference copy which triggers immediate reversal of the movement direction and does not wait visual confirmation at the completion of the error response that the error actually exists. Such movements, nevertheless, are followed by a reversion to the intermittent sampling mode as the limb homes in on the correct target.

The mixed mode

High-speed cinematographic analyses of discrete aiming movements (e.g. Carlton, 1981) suggest that the sampling interval between responses may be reduced where some features of the impending error can be predicted in advance. The initial response is again in the correct ballpark but some programming of the final corrective response can be done in advance. Carlton (1981) even suggests that this is the 'preferred' strategy of the manual control system. By producing a deliberate error the corrective reaction time is, accordingly, reduced. The deliberate error would be of some intermediate magnitude. Given the magnitude of the final error, however, a sampling period is required prior to target contact. Becker and Jurgens (1979) have also proposed a mixed mode for the correction of saccades with errors ranging in magnitude from 3–15 deg. The mixed mode, likewise, considers retinal as well as extraretinal information. It must be noted, however, that this mode of error detection has not been as extensively investigated for the manual as it has for the oculomotor system.

An automatic mode

Some very rapid 'visually'-based corrections have also been reported (e.g. Smith and Bowen, 1980). In keeping with the present theme, these rapid adjustments must be understood in relation to the specific error amendment they achieve. Each mode is attuned to a specific situation and will step aside as the situation changes, in favor of alternative modes. Zelaznik et al. (1983) proposed an 'automatic' processing of visual information in addition to the intermittent sampling mode discussed above. Rapid amendments are illustrated in a study by Smith and Bowen (1980). They used a videodisc and playback system to analyse the effects of delaying the view of the hand for 66 msec during target directed movements of 150, 250, 350, 450, 550 and 650 msecs duration. Basing their results on constant errors, they reported a difference in errors between delayed trials and undistorted trials at movement times of 150 msec. If a movement of 150 msec duration is affected by a visual delay of 66 msec, Smith and Bowen (1980) argue that the processing time for visual feedback must be somewhat less than 100 msec. Smith and Bowen (1980) reported a minor undershoot (-1.50 mm) for undistorted trials and an overshoot ($+3.20$ mm) for delayed visual feedback trials.

More needs to be known regarding the processes underlying these rapid amendments. In particular, what is the nature of the error they subserve? Perhaps this rapid processing is of value only where a gross adjustment is called for? Indeed, very little precision appears to be built into the amendment. Whereas constant error indicates the tendency of performance, variable error indicates the consistency of performance. Standard deviations increased from 2.87 on undistorted trials to 6.16 on delayed trials in Smith and Bowen's (1980) study. That is, the overshooting was associated with a doubling of the variable error, indicating that the success of an amendment varied from trial to trial. To interpret this finding more also needs to be known about the actual movement times in each condition. Subjects were encouraged to perform at 150 msec $\pm$ 40 but unsuccessful trials were not excluded.

Zelaznik et al. (1983) have also indicated that visual information may benefit movements as rapid as 80 msec. Since for rapid movements subjects demonstrated an equivalent error difference between non-visual and visual conditions at all movement times, whereas for movements slower than 200 msecs the difference in error with and without vision increased with the movement time, these authors argued for different modes of correction. Again, more must be known regarding the nature of the error itself that is corrected. For example, on slow movements is visual information used to build in a higher level of precision to the response on *each* trial? On the other hand, for fast movements does visual information instigate only a gross correction on *specific* trials where the error is of a comparatively large magnitude? Is the system in some way preset for such corrections? The notion of an automatic processing of visual information requires further research with specific attention to the nature of the error itself that is amended.

The present discussion has concentrated on modes of error correction where an error is signalled via afferent pathways and the correction signalled via the efferent pathways. It must be remembered that the question of how errors are corrected is important since it reveals underlying control principles. We now address a situation where adjustments to artifically-induced movement errors are produced and yet there is no clear afferent–efferent dichotomy. This research is associated with the mass-spring model. This research further highlights our argument that the processes underlying error correction may be influenced by features of the error, such as its magnitude.

Mass-spring model

One explanation of how the final position of the movement can be achieved without reference to feedback is the mass-spring model. The notion is very simple—it proposes that the end-point location is specified by a new 'balance' of forces between the agonist and antagonist muscles. Technically, this balance or equilibrium is specified by a specific tension–length relationship of the muscle groups controlling the limb. Every point in space can be specified by such a unique tension–length ratio. According to this mass-spring model, as it is called, movement, and the achievement of the final direction and location are a consequence of the physical properties of the muscles, acting like springs in moving the mass of the limb.

Support for the mass-spring model comes from the work of Bizzi, Polit, and Morasso (1976), using normal and deafferented monkeys in a head alignment task. The animals had to learn to rotate their heads to a specified location in space. It was found that without visual, kinaesthetic, and vestibular feedback the animal could rotate the head to a specified location. When a load was applied the head overshot the learnt location, but adjusted and returned to this position when the weight was removed. The same result occurred when a spring resistance was applied to the monkey's head movement. Thus, it is clear that the final head position was achieved without reference to any sensory feedback.

Further support for the mass-spring model over the impulse-timing model comes from the work of Kelso (Kelso, 1977; Kelso and Holt, 1980). Removing visual and proprioceptive information, subjects were able to relocate a specified finger position, even though the starting position was surreptitiously changed by the experimenter moving the finger passively to a new starting position. The subject, of course, was unaware of this maneuver. Thus, it seems that this final end-point location is achieved automatically, independently of the starting position. This, indeed, is a simple but elegant solution to the 'limitations of time' in the processing of sensory feedback for on-going control purposes.

Pertubations to the trajectory of rapid on-going movements may therefore be amended without the involvement of any sensory feedback or central processing. The foregoing discussion indicated, however, that different modes of error correction could be related to the magnitude of an error. Likewise, the adjustment to a pertubation is related to the magnitude (i.e. duration) of the perturbation. Carlton (1983), for example, has demonstrated that at long durations of a perturbation the system reverts to the central processing of the movement error. Again, there is no single mode for error correction. Instead, the system is attuned to the specific nature of the error to be corrected.

It is clear that the processes underlying the correction of movement errors are influenced by features such as the magnitude of the error and the precision required of the amendment. It is no longer plausible to expect that a single mode of correction should encompass all types of error in discrete movements. The classification of various error-correction modes is an initial step. The direction for future research must ultimately be a comprehension of how these different modes interrelate.

FUTURE DIRECTIONS

It may be difficult for the reader to appreciate the rapid developments in the field of motor control over the last twenty years. In particular, there have emerged several new directions reflecting quite dramatic changes in approach and conceptualization of the issues. Two such initiatives relate first to the way in which we view the 'informational units' upon which movement is based, and secondly, to the organizational principles underlying motor control.

Coordinative structures

Perhaps the most influential work in establishing this new direction was that of Nicoli Bernstein (1967) in his book, *The Coordination and Regulation of Movements*, in which he suggested that the 'informational units' are not muscles or even forces, but rather synergistic functional units of action characterized by invariant relationships between certain kinematic (force) parameters (Bernstein, 1967; Saltzman and Kelso, 1987). The description and understanding of such coordinative structures, as they have been called (Turvey, Shaw, and Mace, 1978), have important implications for the way in which we view discrete movements. In a limited-capacity control system, where the limitations of 'time' and 'space' impose severe restrictions to the on-going control mechanisms, any means of reducing the large number of individual elements that need to be organized, provides a partial solution to our control problem. Functional synergies, as coordinative structures, are one such solution. In discrete movements of the arm, for example, in spite of the large number of muscles, and possible joint movements and joint/ muscle combinations (a large number of degrees of freedom), are there just a few coordinative structures which need to be organized, in which several invariant properties are already 'preset'?

Task-dynamics

Saltzman and Kelso (1987) have extended the new approach further, suggesting that coordinative structures could be described in terms of a so-called 'task-dynamic' framework. The essence of this approach is that the action units are specified not in terms of muscular or even kinematic details, but rather in the language of dynamics (p. 843). Thus in discrete movements, instead of specifying a biphasic, programmed and feedback control system, the task-dynamic description is based on inherent properties which are implicit consequences of the task's underlying dynamics. As such advance programming and reprogramming do not need to be specified, and action is a consequence of spatial trajectories along straight lines with spontaneous adjustments inherent in the system. This latter proposal, that of automatic adjustments without the need to detect or attend to the error, has far-reaching consequences not only in the understanding of discrete movements, but, for example, in the design of robotics. Are such 'automatic' adjustments the basis of the very rapid amendments frequently reported in the literature?

SUMMARY

We have seen that the study of relatively simple discrete movements involves rather complex control and organizational principles. The recent investigations of discrete movements has centered on the understanding of the processes underlying such movement organization. Thus, the early notion of a 'ballistic' phase of movement has been transformed into an understanding of the preparatory or programming processes which precede execution. Further, the 'current control' phase of movement has been specified now in terms of the time to process (visual) information upon which amendments and corrections are presumably based.

Discrete movements, particularly rapid movements, necessitate the advance programming of part of the action. It is likely that movements of a duration of less than 200 msec are programmed completely in advance, and run their full course uninfluenced by sensory feedback (even though we know that there are fast 'specialized' amendment processes). Chronometric techniques have begun to unravel some of the mysteries of setting up motor programmes, particularly as we now start to understand and define some of the dimensions of response complexity. But clearly we must clarify further these parameters of extent, direction, and the like as functional units, perhaps in terms of force and time specifying how functional synergies are integrated to produce meaningful velocities of movement, in desired directions to intended targets or equilibrium points.

The investigation of the current control phase of discrete movements has revealed the possibility of a number of sophisticated error detection and correction mechanisms. We can no longer be satisfied just with the description of functional relationships as with Fitts' Law, but we must pursue the processes underlying such 'mathematical descriptions'. The recognition of different amendment mechanisms for minor 'homing-in' adjustments compared with large 'incorrect ballpark' amendments is important. Again, the understanding of some very rapid amendment and automatic adjustment mechanisms still awaits further systematic investigation. There seems to be value in the comparison of the manual and oculomotor systems, and as such, this may provide a level for the understanding of the interaction between peripheral and central mechanisms, not only for the control of discrete movements but for the understanding of control principles in general.

Chapter 6

Sequential Reactions

Patrick M. A. Rabbitt

Tasks of sequential reaction, such as keyboard tasks, present both timing and accuracy problems. As it will appear, the problems of accuracy and its relation to speed have been relatively neglected. However, concern with reaction-time issues goes back to the beginnings of modern psychology.

Wilhelm Wundt set up the first laboratory for the study of human experimental psychology in 1879, in Leipzig. His main research program was to continue the studies of simple and choice reaction time begun by F. C. Donders ten years earlier. In one form or another this program has been energetically pursued for the last 100 years in all the major psychological laboratories of the world. Yet in all this time the simplest possible question about human performance at reaction-time tasks has hardly ever been asked and has never satisfactorily been answered. We still cannot explain why people become faster and more accurate when they are practised on very easy choice reaction tasks, and indeed we have no useful models to explain any kind of change in performance at any simple psychomotor task.

This is a curious neglect since practice probably has more effect on mean reaction time (RT) than does any other variable so far investigated. For example, I, like many other investigators, have collected a great deal of data on the effects of prolonged practice on choice reaction times (CRTs) which I have not published because there is no useful model to interpret them. A group of subjects was practised on two-choice, four-choice, and eight-choice task in which S–R compatibility (spatial mapping of signal lamps onto response keys) and signal discriminability were varied. Changes in RT due to twenty days' practice were four times as great as any changes due to variations in the number of signal and response alternatives (information load), S–R compatibility, signal discriminability, or any interaction between these variables. Indeed after forty days' practice, involving some 40,000 responses on each task, speed and accuracy continued to improve while variations in CRT due to variations in information load, compatibility, and

Human Skills. Edited by D. Holding © 1989 John Wiley & Sons Ltd

signal discriminability had little or no effect. It is possible that if I had been able to practise my subjects for longer, I should have replicated Mowbray and Rhoades' (1959) classic results and found that CRT no longer increased as the number of signal and response alternatives rose from two to eight. I might also, eventually, have confirmed Crossman's (1956) hypothesis that, if subjects are given enough practice, effects of particular variations in S–R compatibility may be entirely abolished.

It has been obvious (to all of us) for the last twenty years that variations in the number of signal and response alternatives, S–R compatibility, signal discriminability, signal repetition effects, and sequential effects usually studied in CRT tasks (Bertelson, 1965; Rabbitt, 1968a) account for a much smaller fraction of RT variance than does extended practice. There is also excellent reason to suspect that the effects of all these other variables are evanescent if enough practice is given. Yet all existing models for choice reaction time still concentrate only on these relatively trivial and temporary sources of variance. The trouble seems to be that all current models for human performance are descriptions of a system in a hypothetical 'steady state'. None describes systems which are subject to any sort of *change*, whether change brought about by practice, by maturation, by ageing, by diffuse brain damage, by disease such as schizophrenia, by stress, or by ingestion of drugs. The main models now debated allow us no way to discuss any of these effects (e.g. see Henmon, 1911; Audley, 1973; Stone, 1960; Falmagne, 1965; McGill, 1967; Snodgrass, Luce, and Galanter, 1967; Laming, 1968; Welford, 1968; Vickers, 1970; Pike, 1973; Theios et al., 1973; Audley et al., 1975): they are all essentially 'static' models.

LIMITATIONS OF STATIC MODELS

In my view the trouble can be traced back to the uncritical, tacit adoption of the assumption of sequential, independent, successive processing stages made by F. C. Donders in 1868 to justify his decomposition of measured mean CRTs into additive components. The class of models resting on this assumption may be termed linear independent sequential process systems (LISPS).

Donders (1868) felt it reasonable to suppose that a subject required a certain measurable period of time to identify any signal presented to him as a particular member of a set of signals between which he had to distinguish. He further supposed that until the subject had completely identified a signal he could not begin the process of selecting an appropriate response to it. It followed that overall mean RT represented the sum of the latencies of at least these two successive and independent processes. This assumption allowed Donders to compare RTs in three tasks. In task (a) only one signal was ever presented and subjects always made the same response to it. In task (b) any one of five signals might appear and subjects had to choose the appropriate one of five different responses accordingly. In task (c) any one of five signals might appear, but subjects had to respond only to one of them and to ignore the onset of the others. Donders argued that the difference in RTs for tasks (a) and (b) gave an estimate for the time required to choose between five different possible responses rather than to make the same response; while the RT difference between tasks (c) and (a) gave an estimate of the time required to identify any of five different signals rather than simply to register the onset of a signal repeated on every trial. Note that Donders' assumptions were quite arbitrary, and could not be tested by his experiments. Note further that the logic of his experimental manipulations was faulty on two grounds. First, aside from problems of signal recognition, the mean RT would be shorter in task (a), in which subjects might expect a signal to respond on every trial, than in task (c), when a signal requiring a response occurred only on one trial in five. Second, in task (b), subjects indeed had to discriminate each signal from each of four other possible signals since they had to select an appropriate response to each of them. In other words they had to discriminate a set of five signals into five subsets of one signal each. However, in task (c), subjects only had to discriminate one critical signal from four other possible distractor signals. They did not have to discriminate the distractors from each other. Thus, they only had to discriminate a set of five signals into two subsets of one signal and of four signals. Consequently, difficulties of discrimination between signals in tasks (b) and (c) were not comparable and the equation $XRTb - XRTc$ = response choice time was invalid (see Rabbitt, 1971).

Models of this kind can serve as extremely sophisticated frameworks (e.g. Briggs and Swanson, 1970) within which data from CRT experiments can be analysed. Because they are based on very rigid and clearly stated assumptions, they allow us to construct intricate functional descriptions of hypothetical perceptual-motor processes. I shall nevertheless argue that the simplicity and rigidity of the assumptions on which they are based prevents them from handling aspects of CRT data which are more informative than simple mean RT, prevents them from giving any account of the way in which subjects control their performance in CRT tasks and, consequently, prevents them from discussing the most critical aspects of *changes* in performance within or between individuals.

Failures to consider accuracy

A first limitation of all the models we have discussed is that they are based only on computations of arithmetic means of overall observed CRTs. They take no account of accuracy. Indeed a necessary condition of application of Sternberg's (1969, 1975) techniques for decomposing RTs is that error rates should be minimal, and identical in all conditions compared, even if this means that subjects must be given more practice at some conditions than at others. Note how this demand actually obliges us to disregard any *other* effects which practice might have beyond increasing accuracy. Overall mean RT is partitioned to give estimates for each of a number of hypothetical sequential processes (signal encoding time, memory search time, response selection, and production), but there is no rationale for deciding that particular errors represent failures at one point rather than another in this chain of hypothetically independent events, nor even any way of comparing the contributions made to overall errors by each of these independent events. Obviously, if any one process in a linear sequence fails, input to all succeeding processing stages will be corrupt and identification of any unique point of failure in the chain will be uncertain.

More seriously, Sternberg's and Brigg's decomposition models do not predict the large differences between mean RTs for correct and incorrect responses usually observed in CRT tasks. In most tasks mean RTs for errors are much faster than mean RTs for correct responses. This difference is usually explained by the assumption that people need some minimum time to identify a signal correctly and to select an appropriate response to it. Errors are assumed to become increasingly probable as RTs fall below this necessary minimal time, so that on average error RTs will be faster than correct RTs. Over some critical band of RTs speed and accuracy appear to trade off against each other (Schouten and Bekker, 1967; Pachella and Pew, 1968; Pew, 1969; Rabbitt and Vyas, 1970). Distributions of RTs for correct and incorrect responses can be compared to derive speed–accuracy tradeoff functions for various tasks and for various subject populations, and there is a choice of several plausible models to explain such functions (Ollman, 1966; Yellott, 1967).

The linear independent sequential process (LISP) models which we have discussed treat overall RT as the simple sum of independent latencies for successive processes. The existence of speed–error tradeoff functions (SETOFs) makes it questionable whether this assumption can be correct, or even useful. For example, we must assume that each of these hypothetical independent processes will require its own characteristic minimum time for successful completion. Each process may also have a different *range* of latencies over which speed and accuracy can be exchanged (i.e. a different SETOF with possibly a different slope constant (see Rabbitt and Vyas, 1970).

We have seen that the critical assumption for LISPS is that processing times are independent for each stage. This can be true only when all stages have more than enough time for completion—that is, when speed and accuracy are not traded off. Where speed and accuracy are traded off two things may happen. First, subjects may set themselves to complete all stages in some fixed time. In this case any increase in the time taken by one stage, on one trial (due, perhaps, to random fluctuations in processing time from trial to trial) must reduce the amount of time available for successful completion of all other stages. Processing times for stages will, therefore, not be independent. Second, each stage may be completed after consuming some criterial time for accuracy, and it may be argued that these times will be independent because processing at each stage must terminate in order for processing at the next stage to begin. That is, each stage may be regarded as having, and observing, a separate and independent SETOF. This will not do either. Rabbitt and Vyas (1970) point out that subjects *cannot, ab initio*, recognize their SETOFs but must make and detect errors before they can learn to recognize and avoid the fast, limiting RT bands at which errors become intolerably frequent. Thus, in order to adjust performance and to avoid errors, subjects must adjust RT from trial to trial. If overall SETOFs are determined by a sheaf of SETOFs for each of a number of independent component processes, subjects must not only learn to control overall RT but also to partition overall RT so as to preserve the accuracy of each of a number of processes, all of which take different times to complete. In order to distribute overall mean RT among component processes in this way, subjects would have to be able to monitor accuracy of each component process independently in relation to its own, idiosyncratic, mean completion time and SETOF. In short, they would not merely have to know whenever errors occurred *somewhere* in the train of successive processes, they would also have to know *in which particular process* the failure occurred. There is no evidence that this is possible.

Note that any other line of explanation sacrifices the assumption of independence on which all such models depend. If we assume that subjects do *not* discover and set lime-limits for accurate completion of *each independent* process, but rather discover, set, and adjust time-limits for the completion of *all processes*, it follows that time-limits for individual processes are not independent because they are set in relation to a common criterion for accuracy.

Failures to discuss changes in distribution of RTs from trial to trial

LISPS are based on obtained differences between mean RTs and do not predict changes in trial-to-trial variance in RT within or between subjects and tasks. This greatly limits their usefulness because task variables such as the number of signal and response alternatives or S–R compatability and signal discriminability, intrasubject variables such as practice and fatigue, and intersubject variables such as age or diffuse brain damage, all affect RT variance much more strikingly than they affect mean RT.

In particular, shifts in computed arithmetical means of RT, on which LISP models are based, typically do not reflect any shift of an RT distribution along the RT axis. They rather merely reflect changes in the positive skew of distributions; e.g. practised subjects make fewer very slow responses and more fast responses, but the latencies of the *fastest* responses which they make may remain invariant with practice. The picture is, therefore, of a system which improves average performance by reducing trial-to-trial variation rather than of a system which alters its maximum capabilities over time.

Failures to describe accurate regulation of set to respond to discrete continuous tasks

In real life people often have to respond to continuous series of events rather than to discrete signals. These events may occur at more or less predictable intervals. To perform optimally a man must learn the characteristics of such sequences and accurately predict and estimate time intervals in order to prepare himself to respond at precisely the moments when signals fall due (see Rabbitt, 1969, 1979a, b). Even in simple RT tasks, when fore-signals are used, subjects seem to need a fixed, minimum time (fore-period) to prepare themselves adequately for onset of a signal to respond (Klemmer, 1956; Davis 1957; Nickerson, 1965; Karlin, 1966). As fore-periods grow longer they become less accurate at estimating fore-period duration and so predicting the moment of signal onset. At all fore-period durations they make effective use of sequential properties of sequences of successive fore-periods in order to optimize their prediction (Nickerson, 1965; Possemai et al., 1975). To do this people cannot behave like the simple, passive information-processing channels assumed by LISP models. They must rather actively and flexibly control their sets throughout long series of events. LISP models do not allow for control of this kind. They rather consider each transaction of signal identification and response production as a passive, independent process without considering that subjects may use overall supervisory control to order these transactions in time so as to anticipate events and so maximize sensitivity of signal detection and facilitate response production. In short, even in very simple RT tasks, subjects can be shown to exercise a degree of the predictive control which is so important in tracking (see Hammerton, Chapter 7, this volume).

This is an important limitation, since recent work shows that changes in the variance of CRT which are brought about by differences in the efficiency with which temporal control of set can be established are quite as great as those introduced by most other parameters which have been investigated (Rabbitt, 1969, 1979a).

Failures to describe control of information encoding and response production

Subjects can exercise very flexible control over the units in which they encode information and the complexity of the response sequences which they emit.

For example Christovitch (1960) and Christovitch and Klass (1962) showed that people who shadow speech adopt various strategies at various times, monitoring and reproducing individual phonemes, words, or entire phrases as best suits task demands. Both the size of the 'chunks' in which they encode input (deduced from the lag between received and emitted messages) and the complexity of the sequences emitted (judged by units of output) vary with message speed, with experimental instructions, and with message discriminability.

Subjects are able to exert flexible control of input and output in this way by reference to information available in long-term memory which allows them to recognize and use redundancy in continuous input, and provides them with motor programs for the emission of complex response sequences rather than merely for discrete motor acts. The best examples of this are a series of brilliant studies by Shaffer (see Shaffer and Hardwick, 1970; Shaffer, 1973, 1975a) who investigated how highly skilled typists transcribe continuous text. He showed that they exercise adaptive control by determining the rate at which they process input, by choosing the size of unit in which they sample this input, and by alternating sampling of input with emission of responses in order to achieve a remarkably fast and very constant rate of responding.

The point, once again, is that LISP models do not consider how subjects exercise this complex control let alone how they *learn* to do so. Shaffer's elegant studies show that this control improves with practice and so must be learned. We may go beyond these experiments to suggest that breakdown of performance with brain damage or in response to stress may reflect loss of this high-level, learned control. Let us consider how far LISP models can account for change in performance with practice, and what additional assumptions may be necessary to explain the data we have discussed.

Descriptions of practice effects by LISP models

As we have seen, LISP models assume that in order to identify a signal and choose a response to it a person carries out a fixed series of processing operations $P_1 \ldots P_2 \ldots P_3 \ldots P_n$, each of which takes a finite time $T_{P1} \ldots T_{P2} \ldots T_{P3} \ldots T_{PN} \ldots$ so that

$$RT = T_{P1} + T_{P2} + T_{P3} \ldots + T_{PN}$$

Thus, if total observed RT reduces with practice this can only be because some or all of these or all of these component processes take less time. If performance becomes more accurate with practice this can only be because some or all of these processes improve in accuracy.

This is a very simplistic model of practice since it assumes that early and late in practice precisely the same events occur in precisely the same order, the only difference being that they occur faster and more accurately. Models of this kind can be made slightly more sophisticated if we adopt a suggestion by Crossman (1959) that the sequences of events which occur between reception of a signal and emission of a response to it may be regarded as activating 'pathways' through a hypothetical information coding network. Crossman's suggestion is that early in practice any one of a number of different pathways through a network may link a particular signal to the particular necessary response. Some of these pathways will be slower than others. Thus, early in practice, when all pathways are employed with equal probability, variance in RT from trial to trial will be great and overall mean RT will be slow. Crossman (1959) suggests that as practice proceeds, a mechanism (which he does not discuss) causes 'more efficient' (i.e. faster) pathways to be selectively preferred to 'less efficient' (i.e. slower) pathways. Both RT variance and mean RT are thereby reduced. Further, the asymptotic shape of practice curves can be predicted from these assumptions.

This is an ingenious and useful concept which may well guide later thinking, but it needs to be greatly extended before it can account for many results. First, it is precisely the *active* selection of 'more efficient' rather than 'less efficient' techniques of information processing ('pathways') which a good model of practice should describe. If this is left as an *ad hoc* postulate we do not get very far. Second, Crossman's model does very well as an account of how an individual may improve with practice, attain greater speed and accuracy and so contribute less to overall RT variance. But many recent studies show that with extended practice subjects do not simply carry out the same information-processing transactions faster and more accurately in the same way, but rather find new and more efficient ways to identify signals and select responses to them.

Fletcher and Rabbitt (1978) found that after practice subjects cease to identify the symbols to which they respond as particular entities and begin, instead, to respond to constancy and change between successive displays. This of course carried the important corollary that a response is always selected in relation to the last response made (same or different to last response) and not merely as a particular motor act triggered by a particular signal. Kristofferson's (1977) data from signal classification tasks show that subjects cannot use the same cues in order to discriminate complex signals from each other both early and later in practice. Rabbitt, Cumming, and Vyas (1979a) obtained similar results in a series of visual search tasks. They also showed that as practice proceeds subjects may change their perceptual encoding strategies and identify signals by two successive decisions rather than by a single decision. Signals are first identified as members of a particular class (target class rather than background class) and only when once located are they further analysed to determine which particular target set member they are. Even if we only consider how particular signals are recognized it is clear that subjects do not simply retain and improve the same strategies of signal recognition, but rather develop new and more efficient ways of dealing with particular discriminations.

In all the cases which we have considered it is clear that changes in performance with practice must be regarded as active progressions toward determined goals rather than as gradual improvements in the passive system which Crossman's (1959) model describes. This realization is unhelpful unless it provokes us to put forward, and test, active rather than passive models. Let us consider a very simple control process model which explains some data from elementary, self-paced, serial choice response tasks.

A 'TRACKING' MODEL FOR MAINTAINING SPEED AND ACCURACY

Shaffer's typing studies are concerned with tasks in which skilled subjects clearly learn to exercise adaptive control over very complex performance (Shaffer, 1973). They learn to determinate the rate at which they process input (text) and to use, or discard, redundancy which determines the size of perceptual samples which they take of that input. Their improvement with practice is partly due to the fact that they learn to alternate sampling of text with production of responses. They learn to emit responses at a very fast, and remarkably regular, rate irrespective of variations in redundancy of input. In order to explain how these complex activities are integrated with each other we must postulate overall control and time-sharing. It may seem that we do not need these complex assumptions if we consider very simple tasks in which signals occur one at a time, and a discrete response is made to each before the next appears. Here the unit of input (one signal) and the unit of response output (a single finger movement) are determined by the task. Straightforward LISP models may seem quite adequate to described such situations.

In fact, even very straightforward serial self-paced tasks present subjects with problems of active control over their performance. In all such tasks the invariable experimental instruction is, 'Go as fast as you can and make as few errors as possible.' In the author's experience 95% of subjects immediately retort to this bland instruction, 'Yes, but which matters more—speed or errors?' The author is ashamed to have ignored this excellent question for over fifteen years. Subjects who ask it precisely define the control problem which they face in such tasks. They are concerned to point out to the experimenter that they can *actively choose* whether to respond fast and make more errors or to respond slowly and improve accuracy at the expense of speed. In formal terms they are saying that they can *actively choose* how to structure their RT distributions in relation to their SETOFs. This implies that either know, or can discover, what their SETOFs may be for a particular task.

This last point is critical since SETOFs will vary from task to task (Pachella and Pew 1968; Pew, 1969; Rabbitt and Vyas, 1970). Faced with a novel task a subject cannot, *ab initio*, deduce his SETOF for that particular situation. He must rather *discover* just how fast he can respond without making an error. It is useful to consider just what a subject needs to know, and just what control he must have over his own behaviour in order to do this.

Subjects need at least two different kinds of information in order to adjust their performance to task demands. First they must know when they make errors, otherwise a SETOF could never be recognized. Second, to profit from their recognition of errors, they must know just how fast each incorrect response was. They must also be able to vary their response speed accurately to respond a little slower, or a little faster, than a response which they have recognized as fast but inaccurate or accurate but unnecessarily slow. They must be accurate in estimating, reproducing, and adjusting their brief reaction times.

In a number of discrete RT tasks, as in continuous self-paced serial choice response tasks and in continuous tasks with preview (e.g. typing) subjects very rapidly detect most of the errors they make (e.g. Burns, 1965; Rabbitt, 1966a, b, 1968b, 1978b; Rabbit and Vyas, 1970; Long, 1976). Subjects can even detect errors which have occurred two or more responses previously (Rabbitt et al., 1979a) and, apparently, can detect some errors due to failures of perceptual analysis as well as errors due to failures of responses selection and execution (Rabbitt, Cumming, and Vyas, 1978).

It is interesting to arrange computer printout of trial-to-trial variation in CRT during continuous, self-paced serial response tasks so that response speed is plotted as a function of trial number. From such graphical plots it is immediately apparent that subjects respond faster and faster from trial to trial until an error occurs. They must then immediately recognize the error because responses following errors are typically very slow indeed (see Rabbitt, 1969). After an error, slow responses continue for three or more trials. Responses then again speed up to approach the risky, fast RT band at which errors are likely to occur (Rabbitt and Vyas, 1970). The general picture is of a system which gradually reduces RT from trial to trial until an error occurs, then slows RT to avoid this limit to accurate performance, and then once again 'tracks' a critical RT band at which speed can be maximized without risking accuracy. Thus the SETOF for any particular task is actively *discovered* by commission and detection of errors and is subsequently 'observed' by adjusting response speed so that RTs approach, but do not transgress it. The system is not concerned to control overall mean RT directly. Mean RT is controlled by adjustment of RT variance between a lower limit determined by the SETOF and an upper limit determined by an internal 'clock' which warns the subject when he is responding unnecessarily slowly.

This is a description of a system which actively adapts to improve its performance with practice. We have not merely described a system which can 'learn', but have suggested *what* it learns, *how* it learns, and *what information it needs* in order to learn. The model makes predictions for the effects of prolonged practice on the *distributions*, as well as the *arithmetical means* of RTs, and makes further predictions for changing relationships between the distributions of RTs for correct responses and the distributions of RTs for incorrect responses. On the first point we must predict that as subjects become more practised, they learn more precisely to estimate their safe lower limit of responding and more precisely to control their RTs from trial to trial to observe this limit, but not to rise far above it. This is just what happens. On the second point we have assumed that subjects establish their SETOFs for particular tasks and then learn to avoid those rates which cause errors. It would follow that they would transgress SETOF limits early but not late in practice. As a consequence, if we derive SETOFs by *post-hoc* comparisons of the distributions of subjects' correct and incorrect responses (as we must; Rabbitt and Vyas, 1970), SETOFs should be obtainable from RT distributions early in practice when subjects make fast errors, but not late in practice, when they avoid making fast errors. To put this another way, the difference in the means of RT for errors and RTs for correct responses must reduce with practice. Again, this is what happens (Rabbitt and Vyas, 1980). Finally, on the model we have proposed, subjects can regulate their lower limits of RT by identifying and so observing their own SETOFs. When a SETOF is transgressed there is likely to be immediate feedback, since an error will probably occur. There is no such precise feedback when subjects respond unnecessarily slowly. They can only compare response speeds against some internal clock which tells them when they are taking too long to respond. It would follow that subjects have precise feedback from which they can judge when they respond too fast, but that their recognition that they are responding too slowly depends upon the accuracy of an internal 'clock' (i.e. on time estimation). Two consequences follow. First, RT distributions should be markedly skewed, with a sharp cut-off for fast responses and a straggling 'tail' of slower responses. This is the case. Second, if subjects are provided with external feedback (such as an elapsed time signal) which informs them when they are slow, they should be able to shape the RT distributions accordingly and reduce arithmetical means of RT, without increasing errors, by shaping the distribution of RTs to avoid unnecessarily slow responses. Again, this is just what happens (Rabbitt and Vyas, 1979).

It is important to recognize that the system we have described is flexible, and can adapt equally well to a variety of different task demands other than those expressed by the curiously ambiguous instruction, 'Go as fast as you can and make as few errors as possible.' If speed is stressed, and errors are in consequential, subjects may abandon error detection and simply respond more or less at random approaching their limiting rates of response production (Rabbitt and Vyas, 1979). If accuracy is stressed and there is no demand for speed, subjects are faced with a new control problem. They can no longer 'track' the lower limit of accurate RT in order to maintain a distribution of RTs with the least possible variance avoiding errors. Since the task now demands that they never transgress the fast RT band at which errors become more probable they must restrict the speed of their fastest responses, not by detection of errors and avoidance of the RT band in which they occur, but rather by reference to some independent internal timing device or 'clock'. In consequence, we might expect that the sharp lower cut-offs to RT distributions observed under speed–accuracy optimization instructions will be replaced by a straggle of RT variance representing uncertainties as to which cautious 'clock-settings' are most appropriate for the task (see Figure 32). In fact this is just what happens (see Rabbitt and Vyas, 1979).

As we have seen, this model is specifically derived to describe how extended practice at a task changes performance. It is important to note that it can also describe the way in which performance changes as a result of intrasubject variables such as fatigue or stress and intersubject variables such as chronological age.

Old people have considerably slower mean RTs than the young. The surprising point is that old and young people may have almost identical mean RTs for errors (Rabbitt and Vyas, 1979). Previous models have concentrated on the first detail but ignored the second (e.g. Birren 1977). If we consider only the first detail we might assume that old people respond more cautiously than the young, seeking to avoid their SETOFs by a larger margin so as to guarantee high accuracy at the expense of speed. However, their error RTs show that this is not the case and we may be tempted to conclude that old people are, in fact, much more brash than their juniors and attempt to reduce their RTs by responding as fast as possible irrespective of increases in error rate. But this does not do either since old people, on average, do not make more errors than the young.

In terms of the model which we have discussed, a further possibility is that old people, unlike the young, cannot recognize the errors which they make and so do not know when they sacrifice accuracy by responding too fast. However, their low error rates contradict this, and Rabbitt and Vyas (1979) find that old people detect their errors as accurately as their juniors. The key seems to lie in the fact that trial-to-trial *variance* in RTs greatly increases as people grow older. It seems that old people lose precise control over their response speed and that when they attempt a slight increase in speed to

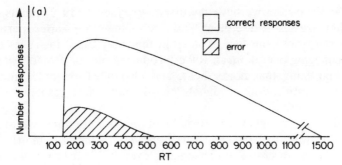

Figure 32. (a) Typical RT distribution where speed is stressed, curtailed at fast reaction times by observation of SETOF limits.

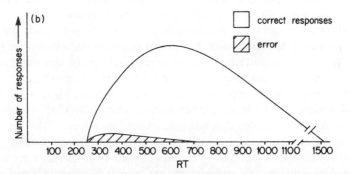

Figure 32. (b) Typical RT distribution when extreme accuracy is stressed and subjects avoid the SETOF limit, thus having no feedback to shape the fast tail of their RT distribution.

reduce RT without sacrificing accuracy they begin to respond much too fast, overshoot their SETOFs by a large margin, commit errors, detect their errors, and react to them by immediately responding much too slowly. Thus, they add responses to the lower and upper limits of their RT distributions. Their fast errors are much too fast and their cautious responses are unnecessarily slow. Thus, this model suggests the particular change with age which reduces flexibility of adaptation and optimization of performance.

It is also possible to reinterpret classical data on the effects of various stresses on performance of continuous self-paced choice response tasks with the context of the same model. Wilkinson (1959) pointed out that subjects suffering from loss of sleep may occasionally make single, very slow responses (blocks), but their overall mean RTs do not increase as performance continues over a half-hour run. They seem to 'spurt' between blocks to maintain a relatively constant overall mean rate of responding. This picture of increasing drift from a fast, tight optimal RT distribution with intermittent attempts to maintain constant mean response rate would be well described by the simple system we have discussed. Broadbent (1972) points out that three other stresses—noise, heat, and alcohol ingestion—affect performance in a different way from loss of sleep in that they cause increases in errors without changing overall mean RT of producing blocks. Broadbent explains this by suggesting that noise, heat, and alcohol all degrade processes of perceptual identification of signals but do not affect response selection, timing, or execution.

Since the experiments which Broadbent quotes were done without benefit of apparatus now available *error RTs were never measured*, and the changes in RTs which he discusses are changes in overall RT during a run. Thus the data for noise, heat, and alcohol are consistent with the idea that under the influence of these stresses SETOFs remain stable but subjects lose time control of their response speed. *RT distributions* may be affected, and errors may increase while mean RTs remain approximately constant.

The difference between predictions from Broadbent's and the present hypothesis lies in his contention that input from signals will become poorer, or will become intermittent, because of distraction. In this case a SETOF obtained from distributions of correct and incorrect RTs produced by subjects who suffer from the effects of heat, noise, or alcohol should be displaced towards a slower RT band in comparison with a SETOF obtained from subjects responding under optimal conditions (see Figure 33).

This is to say that if subjects suffering from the effects of noise, heat, or alcohol consumption attempt to respond at their normal rate they will make more errors. This can be checked by examining RT distributions obtained in all these conditions, calculating SETOFs from them, and examining the spread of the actual distributions of correct RTs in relation to the derived SETOFs. If RT distributions under normal and stressed conditions are the same, while SETOFs differ, this will be evidence that Broadbent may be right. In this case we may further check to see whether heat, noise, or alcohol reduces the efficiency of error detection so that subjects suffering from these do not discover that their SETOFs have shifted.

An alternative possibility is that heat, noise, and alcohol, like old age, deprive people of fine control over the timing of their responses. In this case errors might occur because subjects under these stresses behave like old people and when trying to track their SETOFs respond much too fast and so tend to make fast errors (see Figure 34). Once again, examinations of the distributions of actual RTs against derived SETOFs would show whether this is what happens. SETOFs would be identical for stressed and unstressed conditions, but stressed conditions would show much greater RT variance and much poorer control of RT from trial to trial.

Note that these hypothetical models for changes in performance under different stresses are not mutually exclusive. It is quite possible that both changes in response timing and changes in observation of SETOFs occur

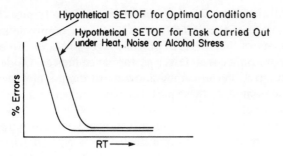

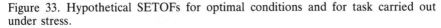

Figure 33. Hypothetical SETOFs for optimal conditions and for task carried out under stress.

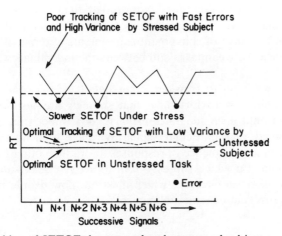

Figure 34. Tracking of SETOFs by stressed and unstressed subjects.

concurrently, but in different degrees for different stresses. This might at last allow us to distinguish between the effects of noise, heat stress, and alcohol in ways which Broadbent's model does not allow. This would be a relief because it offends intuition and common sense that we still cannot distinguish the effects of three such dissimilar conditions on a simple task.

Two further general points can be made. First, in order to describe the effects of practice, old age, fatigue, noise, heat stress, or alcohol consumption any model must incorporate the idea that these conditions change the efficiency of one or more parameters of human performance. Current models of performance on simple tasks have considered only two possible changes in performance parameters—mean RT and accuracy. The present model substitutes for these a wider range of more sensitive parameters, i.e. $\bar{X}$ correct RT, $\bar{X}$ error RT, SETOF, relation of the fast tail of the correct and error RT distributions to the calculated SETOF, and degree of positive skew of the entire distribution of correct and incorrect RTs. It must be emphasized that the advantage of the SETOF model does not simply lie in the fact that it allows 'profiles' of the effects of practice, age, stress, etc. to be constructed in terms of more rather than fewer performance indices. Models of this type should be preferred because they allow us to discuss how people *adapt* to changes in one or more of these performance parameters in order to maintain as high a level of efficiency as possible.

The second point is that if we discuss human beings as purposive systems which strive to maintain performance between defined parameters, or as systems which exercise choices between various optional strategies of adaptation to task parameters, or which adapt to their own changing efficiency, we do not therefore move further from our data. On the contrary, models of this kind oblige us to consider *more* rather than *fewer* data, they make more rather than fewer predictions for empirical results, and they allow us to design a wider range of convergent experiments in terms of which we can assess differences between tasks and between the individuals who carry them out.

We may now go on to consider other details of performance in simple tasks which oblige us to recognize that subjects are not simple, passive systems which emit each separate response as a direct transform of information conveyed by a particular signal. We have seen how the timing of each of a continuous sequence of responses, more than other factors, creates control problems for which subjects have to actively seek solutions. Let us consider two other simple tasks which illustrate how people meet different forms of this problem of temporal control.

MANAGEMENT OF TEMPORAL CONTROL

Adaptation to irregularities of signal onset

In most simple, serial, self-paced tasks subjects can accurately predict the moment at which each signal will arrive. This is because the interval between successive signals (S–S interval) or the interval between each response and the next signal (R–S interval) is very precisely controlled by the experimental equipment and remains constant throughout a task. Rabbitt (1969) held R–S intervals constant during runs of 300 successive signals and responses, but varied R–S interval duration from 20 msec to 200 msec between runs. He found that overall mean RT reduced by 30 msec to 60 msec as R–S intervals increased between these limits. This regression of RT on R–S interval duration was strikingly similar to that observed in simple RT tasks in which intervals between warning signals and signals to respond (fore-periods) were varied over the same range (see Davis, 1957; Nickerson, 1965). It seems that both in simple RT tasks and in choice RT tasks with R–S intervals subjects require a minimum time, greater than 220 msec, to prepare optimally to respond to each signal. When fore-periods or R–S intervals are as short as 20 msec subjects cannot attain optimal preparation by the moment of onset of the response signal. However, as R–S intervals or fore-periods increase to 220 msec preparation gradually approaches optimum and RTs decline.

In most real-life tasks signals do not occur at constant, predictable intervals and subjects have to keep pace with irregular series of events. Rabbitt et al. (1979a, b) investigated the effects of varying R–S intervals unpredictably from trial to trial within the range of 20 msec to 200 msec and the range 20 msec to 1600 msec. He found that the negative regression of RT on R–S interval duration between 20 msec and 200 msec remained exactly the same whether R–S intervals were constant and predictable or variable and unpredictable during a run. However, when R–S intervals were 800 msec or longer subjects responded faster when successive R–S intervals were identical than when they were different.

Rabbitt et al. (1979b) pointed out that the absence of any effect of R–S interval irregularity over the range 20 msec to 200 msec was consistent with the idea that subjects need at least 220 msec to attain optimal preparation for an expected event. If R–S intervals are shorter than this it does not matter if they vary unpredictably from trial to trial because subjects can gain nothing from being able to predict correctly or to time accurately the next R–S interval. All they can do is to mobilize their preparation as fast as possible on each trial. The level of preparation they attain at the moment of signal onset will simply depend on the speed of this mobilization and cannot be improved by prediction.

In contrast, when R–S intervals or fore-periods are 800 msec or longer we must assume that subjects always have enough time to maximize preparation for each signal. Since, presumably, maximum preparation once briefly attained cannot be indefinitely maintained, RTs will be fastest if subjects can arrange to attain their point of maximum preparation to coincide precisely with the moment of onset of the signal they expect. To manage this they must:

(a) correctly predict the moment of onset of the next signal;
(b) accurately estimate the passage of time so as to achieve the necessary coincidence.

If all fore-periods or R–S intervals used during a task are equiprobable subjects can manage prediction (a) with only a chance level of accuracy. In this case they can only optimize time estimation (b), and any prediction strategy which helped them to do so will optimize performance. In this case it may be strategic for them to expect fore-periods or R–S intervals to repeat on successive trials. This is because this expectation will prove false no more often than any other. However, when it proves correct, it may have the advantage that a subject can most accurately estimate a time interval which he has just experienced. A number of experiments on the effects of repetitions and alternations of fore-period durations in simple RT tasks can also be interpreted as demonstrations that subjects use this strategy to optimize time estimation when accurate prediction is impossible.

Several features of this model must be contrasted with other, passive, models of human performance. First, a number of experiments show that the efficiency of information processing is not invariant at any moment, but changes with momentary fluctuations in arousal and attentional selectivity. In order to optimize performance subjects must plan ahead to ensure that their information-processing systems are maximally efficient at the moments when signals occur.

A second point is that to achieve this advance planning subjects must store and use a great deal of information. For example, subjects must be able to sample long sequences of events in order to recognize, and use, complex properties of the distributions of time intervals between them; (see Nickerson, 1965). Subjects must also be able to make accurate estimates of the durations of different time intervals, store this information about relative and absolute interval durations, and access it as necessary in order to control the timing of their expectancy.

A final, most crucial, point is that the system we have described to account for the results of these very simple experiments is adaptive in one unique respect. It adapts to its own limitations. It bases optimization of performance on optimization of one parameter (time estimation) when optimization of another (accurate advance prediction) becomes impossible. If accurate advance prediction becomes possible the advantages of accurate time estimation may be abandoned in order to capitalize on this. An interesting experiment would be to arrange sequences of R–S intervals or fore-period durations so that alternations between two different interval durations are more common than repetitions of interval durations. As bias shifted in this direction we would predict that RTs for particular R–S intervals or fore-periods would become faster on alternations than on repetitions. In brief, faced with a situation in which its own limitations as a statistical predictor, or as a clock, force the system to abandon the possibility of optimization in terms of both parameters, the system adjusts and does the best it can by trading off one against the other.

Adaptive time-sharing of signal identification and motor programming

We cannot describe complex real-life skills such as driving or air traffic control without discussing how subjects manage their allocations of attention over time in order to interrogate a number of different sources of information in a strategic order and with strategically biased frequencies (Baron, Kleinman, and Levison, 1970; Moray, 1978). It is less generally recognized that accurate time-sharing of this kind, particularly time-sharing between the identification of signals and the control of responses made to them, is necessary even in very simple tasks.

Rabbitt and Rogers (1965) showed this in a task in which subjects made reaches of varying extents to press touch switches mounted immediately below signal lights on a console 45.7 cm long. Two conditions of a continuous task were compared. In the first condition the sequence of events began with the ignition of a signal lamp (A) on the extreme left of the console. As soon as the subject had switched it off by touching the switch immediately beneath it, either lamp B (48cm to the right) or lamp C (45 cm to the right) came on. These events occurred unpredictably with equal frequency. The subject then had to move his hand as fast as possible from A to switch off either B or C as necessary. As soon as he did this lamp A lit again, he moved his hand to switch it off, and the cycle continued in this way for 300 trials. In a comparison, condition lamp A was followed by either lamp B or lamp D (10 cm to the right), and the same cycle of events occurred.

The point was to compare RTs for moves from A to B between the first condition, where this required a choice between two, very similar reaches (i.e. 48 cm and 45 cm) and the second condition where this required a choice between two very different reaches (i.e. 48 cm and 10 cm).

Early in practice young subjects showed no difference in RTs to initiate reaches to B between these two conditions. However, as practice progressed RTs to initiate reaches to B became faster when the choice was between similar reaches than when the choice was between different reaches. This happened because when the choice was between very similar reaches, as soon as a subject touched A he could begin to make a reach of correct amplitude to get to the general vicinity of B or C without waiting to discover which of these lights had, in fact lit up. They could then decide which light was on during the course of this ballistic movement, and to modify the termination of the movement to home in on the correct touch switch. In the second condition they could not do this since they had to discover which lamp had lit before they could begin to program an appropriate response to answer it.

Subjects required practice to achieve this precise alternation between initiations of a reach, identification of a signal, and modification of the reach to touch the correct switch. Old subjects carrying out the same tasks never learned this skill, and took the same time to initiate reaches to B in both conditions.

Thus we have an example of a system which learns to program itself to use dead time during a ballistic movement to identify a signal and to begin to direct the termination of that movement. Apparently, young subjects shifted with practice from this sequence of events:

1. identify signal;

2. initiate ballistic reach to terminate precisely at signal;
3. terminate reach at signal;
to the more efficient sequence of events:
1. initiate ballistic movement of approximately the right amplitude;
2. identify signal during movement;
3. modify termination of movement to touch key.

Again we see that as subjects become practised they do not merely improve their performance by going through the same information-processing transactions in the same order, ever faster and more accurately. Even in this very simple task they improve by exercising adaptive control over the sequence in which they perform successive transactions, and actively seek out new and more efficient ways of scheduling sequences of operations. Good examples of other ways in which people reschedule the order in which they make a series of component decisions, so as to improve the efficiency with which they make very simple choices, appear when we consider how they decide which of two limbs to use to make a simple reach.

Attentional control and choice between limbs

Rabbitt (1978a) found that people can respond to signal lights on a console faster when they make all reaches with the same hand than when they have to answer some lights with the right hand and others with the left. Subjects also respond faster when they have to make successive, different movements with the same hand than when they make a movement with one hand followed by a movement with the other (Rabbitt, 1965, 1978a). When successive movements are made with the same hand both right- and left-handed subjects respond equally fast with either hand. In contrast, when successive movements are made with different hands, all subjects respond slightly faster with their dominant hands.

Instructions	*Instruction content*
Step 1	Is key in range of dominant hand?
	If yes, go to Step 3
	If no, go to Step 2
Step 2	Is key in range of non-dominant hand?
	If yes, go to Step 4
	If no, go to Step 1
Step 3	Complete reach to key abd go to
	Step 1 to test new event
Step 4	Complete reach to key and go to
	Step 1 to test new event.

Rabbitt (1978a) suggested that these effects can be explained if we assume that repetition of a response facilitates only those processes responsible for its execution. With this assumption choices between responding limbs may be made by a sequence of decisions which can be conveniently illustrated as a sequence of instructions such as that found on computer programs.

A system controlled by such a sequence of instructions would show 'dominance' in the limited sense that each new sequence of tests would always begin with a test to discover whether the dominant limb could be used. This would be quite an adaptive way to control decisions since apparently the choice between limbs takes a finite time and by developing the habit of using the same hand (or paw) for most responses an animal would save time and increase efficiency.

For our present purposes this is another demonstration that human beings can adapt to their own limitations in order to increase their efficiency. On the model we have discussed they do not do this merely by increasing the speed and accuracy with which they carry out in turn each instruction in a hypothetical sequence, but also by altering the sequence in which decisions are taken and by *altering the conditional branching of the sequence* in order to initiate some tests before others. Changes in the efficiency of such a system, whether these represents improvements in efficiency due to 'learning', or loss of efficiency due to old age, stress, or injury, are likely to appear as new patterns of regularity in performance rather than as simple changes in speed or accuracy.

We have seen that even in the simplest perceptual-motor tasks decisions necessary to produce appropriate responses may be made in more or less efficient sequences. The effects of such variations in planning of overall control of response sequences appear when we consider how people produce length sequences of familiar responses which must be 'played off' from information stored in long-term memory.

Control of responses by information stored in long-term memory

Consider how people produce very familiar sequences of responses—for example, how they manage to recite the alphabet aloud. The problems here are rather different from those considered in the previous chapter. Obviously the names of letters of the alphabet, and their conventional ordering, are stored in a man's long-term memory and he can access them whenever he wishes at any moment throughout a long lifetime. In order to recite this familiar sequence correctly he requires two different kinds of information. First, as we have seen, information about the entire sequence must be available, and must be accessed in long-term memory. Second, he requires some prompt from short-term memory to tell him what he has just done so that he can index long-term memory picking up the point he has reached in the sequence and deciding what letter to name next.

Each letter of the alphabet is unique so that in order to decide which letter to produce next a person need only remember the last letter he spoke. However, not all sequences are of this type. If sequences contain recurrent elements the problem becomes much more difficult. For example, consider a sequence of this kind:

$$A, B, C, D, B, E, D, B, F \ldots$$

Here, even if a man can recall that he has just uttered 'D' he will not know what letter to name next unless he can remember the last two letters he spoke. If he just uttered 'B' he will be able to continue unless he remembers his last three responses.

With Anderson and Heptinstall I have carried out pilot experiments which suggest that young adults can maintain very accurate performance on sequences of the first kind in spite of very high levels of distraction (successive serial subtractions from large numbers). However, while sequences of the second kind were flawlessly reproduced without distraction, they could not easily repeat them when distracted by subsidiary tasks. They paused after repeated items and often went into recurrent 'loops' (e.g. from the example above 'B, C, D, B, C, D, B, C, D . . .') These delays and failures seem to indicate that the process of 'running control', or 'indexing' of an overlearnt sequence held in long-term memory by means of information held in short-term memory had failed due to attempts to keep up with a subsidiary task. Increased demands on short-term memory load bring about failures in performance. Time-sharing of the interlocked processes we have discussed remain to be investigated. Once again it is obvious that we cannot discuss even commonplace, and apparently very simple tasks in terms of rigid sequences of operations. We have to assume dynamic, active, adaptive control of a number of interlocked systems all of which, acting together, must adjust to any change in task characteristics. It follows that changes in the efficiency of any one of condition, short-term memory capacity, speed and accuracy of short-term memory indexing of long-term memory programs, etc., will not result in a readjustment of an integrated system. The point is that this readjustment will occur as the response of an entire adaptive system to some particular change in its efficiency. It will not occur, and may not be recognized, as a change in efficiency of any single parameter of performance.

RECENT DEVELOPMENTS

The tracking model described earlier implies that fast reaction times generate error feedback, thus enabling subjects to shape their own RT distributions. Illustrations of the typical distributions obtained with instructions for speed or for accuracy are given in Figure 32a and b, where it can be observed that both the shapes and the cut-off points are represented as changing in accordance with the imposed requirements. In addition, the text implies that subjects presented with a demand for accuracy, for example, will be able to maintain the least possible variance compatible with avoiding errors.

There is a difficulty with this account that remains to be resolved. Recent, unpublished work has examined large numbers of responses to sequences of stimuli in order to establish the empirical characteristics of such distributions. It now appears that the obtained distributions have systematic statistical properties other than those described above. To wit, the standard deviations of sequential RT distributions vary with the means of these distributions. Thus, a set of fast responses shows little variability while a slower set shows higher variability.

The implications of these findings are both far-reaching and subtle. It is clear that some modifications to the tracking theory for sequential responses are entailed by the findings, but it is not yet clear exactly what final form must be taken by an amended model. Since devising and presenting an amended theory must be deferred to a later occasion, the purpose of including the new information at this time is simply to enter a caveat with respect to the details of the exposition presented above. It remains true, however, that useful models must make provision for subjects to monitor and modify the characteristics of their own performance.

SUMMARY

Over the last 100 years models for the processes by which people recognize signals and make responses to them have failed to consider how performance may change. The most striking instance of this is the absence of any discussion as to how performance on very simple tasks improves with practice. Absence of models for change has also prevented discussion of improvement of performance with maturation, or the gradual impairment of performance by old age, by the onset of illness such as schizophrenia, by diffuse brain damage, and by a variety of stresses.

One reason why models for simple tasks have been so limited is that they have, either tacitly or overtly, considered human beings as linear independent sequential process systems of limited capacity. To discuss changes in performance in terms of such systems we are forced to make the very crude assumption that particular, independent component processes become faster or slower, or become more or less accurate. Models of this kind do not allow us to discuss how the systems which they describe may adapt to task demands, *and to their own changing limitations*, so as to maintain optimal performance. A large number of experiments show that human beings actually do adapt in this way. The recognition that people can learn to monitor and select their own speed–accuracy tradeoffs, and can achieve high-level control of other information processes, makes possible a new class of adaptive models.

Chapter 7

Tracking

M. Hammerton

When you drive a car along a road, avoiding alike the kerb and the center-line, you are carrying out a typical tracking task. It is typical in all the definitive respects: the path, the control, and the 'score'. The road is outside your control: it imposes a demand upon you; and you may have much (as on a motorway in daylight) or little (as in a country lane at night) forewarning of what that demand may be. You are producing your response via a mechanism—the steering of your car—which is characterized by some precise relation between the movements you make and the response of your vehicle. Your object is at all times to keep your error—which may roughly be defined in this case as the extent to which you overrun either kerb or center-line—at zero.

These three characteristics were used by Adams (1961) to define, more formally, the class of tracking tasks. In his words:

'(1) A paced (i.e. time function) externally programmed input or command signal defines a motor response for the operator, which he performs by manipulating a control mechanism.

(2) The control mechanism generates an output signal.

(3) The input signal minus the output signal is the tracking error quantity, and the operator's requirement is to null this error . . . The measure of operator proficiency ordinarily is some function of the time-based error quantity.'

This definition stands.

Investigations into tracking began with severely limited and practical aims in view. Although there is a 'pre-history' of tracking dating back to the 1930s or earlier, it was not until the demands of war became pressing that the systematic study of tracking problems was vigorously pursued. The object of these early studies was simply to find how to make it as easy as possible for

Human Skills. Edited by D. Holding © 1989 John Wiley & Sons Ltd

operators to point guns in a desired direction. The urgency of this problem was especially pressing in air warfare, where targets move very rapidly and guns have to be swung correspondingly fast; and the Second World War saw a number of studies of this kind (e.g. Tustin, 1944).

However, narrow and immediate though their aims were, these early researchers found themselves at once faced with problems of more general interest. The attention of academic psychologists was drawn to those matters largely by the work of Craik (1947, 1948), since when both theoretical and immediately applied work has continued in parallel.

A little reflection will soon produce a number of reasons why tracking studies have theoretical interest. A tracking task may be devised to require almost any degree of visual-motor skill from trivial simplicity to insuperable difficulty. Further, the task is definable in strictly mathematical terms (of which a little more later) and the subject's performance is measurable to any desired degree of precision. Both track and response may, in principle, be approached and described in terms of information load and of control theory—branches of applied mathematics combining great power and elegance. The task may readily be combined with others (see Chapter 4), to enquire whether and how far subjects can combine performance of more than one task at a time, and, if so, how this is done. Also, the laboratory task may often be given a large measure of face realism, a characteristic beloved by both naïve subjects and by grant-awarding bodies.

TYPES OF TRACK

Although the possible variety of tracks which might be presented to subjects is infinite (for once the word is used literally) laboratory workers have generally found that a small number of types is adequate for their purposes; and some account of the main ones is called for. First, let us consider an ultra-simple tracking apparatus. Let us suppose that a roll of paper has some curve drawn along it, and that the roll can be made to move beneath a sheet of board, in which is a slit of variable width (see Figure 35). The subject is asked to keep the point of a pencil on the curve as it passes under the slit. The curve (track) can be so prepared as to have any desired degree of complexity and predictability; and, by varying the width of the slit, the extent of foresight allowed the subject can be controlled at will. The speed with which the roll moves, and the nature of the excursion of the track also affects the task difficulty.

Nowadays, electronic devices of more or less complexity are used to present points or lines on a cathode ray oscilloscope (CRO), whereon the subject controls another spot or line; but the idea is essentially the same.

The simplest type of track is the *ramp*. This is a simple line, usually straight (see Figure 36); and when pursued through the slit in the basic equipment

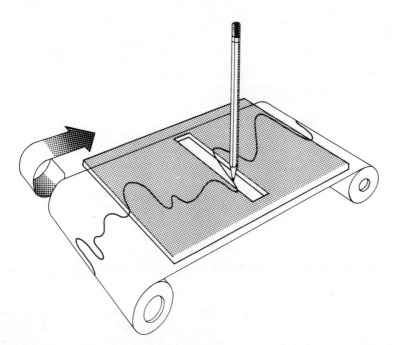

Figure 35. A very simple equipment for tracking studies. A subject tries to keep the point of his pencil on the track drawn on the roll of paper.

we described would require a simple movement at constant speed. Ramp tracking is rare in the real world: Poulton (1974) mentions the operator of a TV camera in the centre of a circular race-track. It is, however, of theoretical interest in that, since it requires a constant response, any alterations in response characteristics must reflect limitations in the operator.

A *step function track* is more complex. Here the track consists of segments parallel with the overall direction of travel joined by segments at right angles to it (see Figure 36b). Again in our basic equipment, the task presents itself as a series of abrupt jumps spaced by fixed-position waiting periods.

The *sine-wave track* is outwardly simple, but of great and subtle importance. This is the indefinitely repeating waveform shown in Figure 36c. The lateral distance between peaks and troughs is called the amplitude (*a*) and the distance between corresponding points on repeating waves is called the wavelength (λ). (It is often more useful to use the frequency (*v*) than the wavelength, the frequency being the number of wavelengths which pass a given point in unit time.) In our simple equipment, the required response is a back-and-forth movement of smoothly and continuously changing speed.

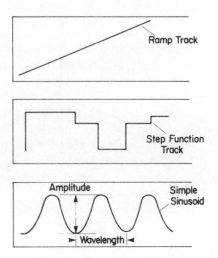

Figure 36. Three basic types of track. For explanation see text.

Sine waves are of basic importance, partly because they enable performance to be studied when variable rates of response are required, but more
because—as was shown by the great French mathematician Fourier, in the
nineteenth century—*any* curve can be produced by combining a sufficient
number of sine waves of various λ and *a* values. Complex sine waves,
therefore, include all real-world tracking situations; and tracks of any degree
of complexity and (to the subject) predictability can be produced by such
combinations.

Pursuit and compensatory displays

In the equipment we described above, the arrangement is of the kind known
as *pursuit*. In this type of display the subject simultaneously observes the
track, his own output, and his error, if any: if the task were presented on a
CRO he would see a moving (target) spot, the spot he controls, and the
distance between them—i.e. the error. However, another form of display is
possible: he could be shown the current error only. On the CRO there would
be a mark, usually in the middle of the screen, representing the position of
zero error, and a moving spot whose distance from the zero point represents
the current state of the error. A display of this kind is called a *compensatory*
display.

Numerous studies, pioneered by Poulton (1952) have attempted to decide
which form of display produces the best results—i.e. the smaller overall error
measure. The results of over forty such studies, tabulated and discussed by
the same writer (Poulton, 1974) unequivocally point to the superiority of

pursuit displays. The only caveat which has to be entered is that, as Poulton himself remarks, not every possible variety of task has been examined; but the presumption is strong that pursuit is always to be preferred. This conclusion is not *a priori* surprising, for two evident reasons. In the first place, the pursuit display provides the subject with more information at all times: he sees, as we have remarked, both input and output; whereas in a compensatory display only the difference between them is shown. Secondly, as the reader will readily discern, in the compensatory mode he has to make apparently reversed control movements. Suppose his track is veering to the right of where it should be. He will then observe a spot moving to the right of center of the screen, which will demand a leftward movement from his control. This can be disturbing.

More elaborate modes of display will be adverted to later.

Order of control

So far we have only discussed the simplest kind of linkage between the subject's movements and his output—namely a pencil. Real systems—such as a car's wheel—are usually more complex than this; and the degree of complexity is broadly indicated by what is called the *order of control*. What is meant by this can best be understood by considering the control movements required by the different orders in a specific case.

Let us suppose that a subject sits facing a CRO upon which is a movable spot of light and two fixed vertical lines a fixed distance apart. Initially, the spot rests upon one of these lines; he is required to move it to the others, and to do this he uses a control in the form of a joystick. The order of control decides the movements which have to be made to achieve this end; and for the moment we shall assume an ideal subject who acts with perfect economy and precision.

Suppose that the deflection of the joystick from center directly controls the position of the spot, i.e. for any value of deflection of the stick there is a corresponding position of the spot. This is called *zero order* or positional control. In this case (see Figure 37) the operator makes a single movement of his stick, from its initial to its final position, and keeps it fixed there.

Secondly, suppose that, if the stick is held in its central position, the spot remains stationary wherever it happens to be, and that it moves away from that position in the direction in which the stick is moved and at a speed proportional to the extent of the deflection: twice the deflection produces twice the speed. This is called a *first-order* or velocity or rate control; and, as appears in Figure 37b, it requires at least two movements for the same task. The first deflection gives the spot a velocity in the required direction; the second, back to centre, stops the spot when it has reached its target.

Thirdly, let us consider the more complex and difficult situation known as

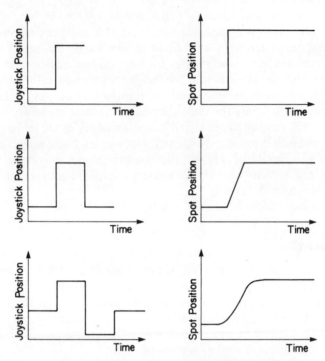

Figure 37. Movements required to move a controlled spot from one position to another with three orders of control. Position control (a) requires a single movement; velocity control (b) requires two; acceleration control (c) needs three.

second-order or acceleration control. (British students especially often find this confusing, because of our unfortunate habit of calling the speed control of our cars an 'accelerator'. It is, in fact, a velocity control with variable lag.) In this case, when the stick is in the central position, the spot keeps the velocity which it already had: this may be, as in the case we are imagining, zero. Any deflection of the stick produces an acceleration of the spot, i.e. a change of velocity, in the direction of, and proportional to that deflection. Thus, if the stick is held in some deflected position, the spot will steadily increase its velocity in the direction of that deflection, and will soon disappear off the screen. A minimum of three movements is therefore required for our task (see Figure 37c). The first step will cause an acceleration in the desired direction. If the stick were then merely returned to its central position, the spot would go on moving past its target with the speed it had attained; i.e. the stick must be given a deflection equal and opposite to its first one. If the operator's judgement and timing were exact—which we are supposing—the spot would just have stopped as it reaches its target, when he will return the stick to center, having the spot stationary where it ought to be.

Augmented displays

In the discussion so far, we have tacitly assumed a single display of a straight-forward type, be it pursuit or compensatory. However, the skill of a modern instrument designers, with the resources of advanced electronics at their disposal, can provide a variety of displays for special purposes.

We have remarked that second-order controls are very difficult to master; but sometimes their use is unavoidable: the dynamics of the machinery involved allows nothing less. Even more complex controls are compelled in some cases: the steering of a submarine, e.g., is essentially a lagged third-order system. When this cannot be avoided, it is as well to provide the controller with more information. This is generally referred to as an 'augmented' display; and two kinds are especially to be recommended, namely rate-augmented and predictor displays.

In a *rate-augmented display* the controller sees not only the current state of things (either in pursuit or compensatory form) but also the rate at which it is changing. Thus, in one of the most familiar applications, the pilot of an aircraft who wishes to reach or maintain a particular height will have not only his altimeter—giving the current state of affairs—but also a rate-of-climb indicator. This latter gives the rate of change of the situation, which greatly helps in smoothing out the approach to the desired value. It is not intended here to go into any mathematical detail; but we will merely observe that if the 'output' is x, then the rate of change is dx/dt. This is always one control order down from x, so that an operator who finds x peculiarly difficult to handle may find the rate much easier to handle.

A predictor display, as its name implies, shows the operator his current position and the way that position will change over the next few seconds (or longer period in a slow-responding system). This can only be done with the help of advanced electronic equipment. It requires a special-purpose computer which holds a mathematical representation of the system, and continuously calculates the effect of current operator behavior very much faster than the actual effects take place. This calculation has to be performed in a time which is negligible compared to system or operator response, hence the need for a computer. Since this effect will itself be a function of any changes in the operator's behavior, the predictor usually has one of two assumptions built in: either it assumes that the operator slowly returns his control to the central position during the time of the prediction, or it assumes that the operator keeps his control where it is at the current instant. The writer does not know of any experiment which investigates which of these two is the better; but Kelly (1962) convincingly demonstrated the advantages of a predictor display in a complex system.

Present-day predictor displays usually look something like Figure 38 with time as one axis and system state (or error, in a compensatory display) as the

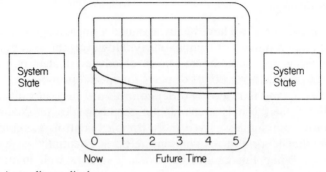

Figure 38. A predictor display.

other. However, there is no reason why future systems should not incorporate holographic presentation in three dimensions, with two output variables in a viewing plane and the future represented as increasing depth. The idea is attractive.

Preview

Common sense and experiment alike affirm the value of preview, i.e. of being able to see what is coming next. Poulton (1957c) showed that the more preview of a track an operator got, the less his error. He also speeded up when the experimental conditions allowed it. The desirability of supplying any controller with the maximum amount of information on forthcoming demand is evident.

The reader will already have thought that no real system has such perfect and immediate response as we have supposed (though purely electronic systems can approach it very closely indeed). Neither do real operators possess such immaculate skill and judgement. Real systems exhibit some degree of lag. Some finite time elapses before the demand signaled by the control movement is achieved: this has the effect of rounding and slightly flattening response curves such as those shown in Figure 37. Also, however, they make the judgement of when to make or cancel a demand more difficult; and this is especially the case if the lags are long. This naturally brings us to another question.

OPTIMAL CONTROLS AND DISPLAYS

We have talked about controls which produce movements or change in velocity in proportion to the extent of their deflection. Clearly, a control can be very sensitive indeed: we may imagine a first-order control such that the merest touch gives maximum velocity. Such a device would be pretty useless;

for few if any operators could refine and control their movements enough to halt movement with sufficient precision. On the other hand, supposing that we were using a wheel rather than a stick, we could arrange matters so that a couple of full turns were necessary to obtain a moderate velocity. Such a control would present no difficulty; but equally we could hardly expect subjects to perform their tasks at record speed, because of the time taken to get things going. It would seem reasonable, therefore, to suppose that some intermediate level of sensitivity were optimal. But there is a catch here: in presenting our imaginary extreme cases, we changed from a joystick-type control to a wheel; and if we do not, we are forced to other conclusions. Let us examine our task with more precision.

Let us define the sensitivity of the control as the movement produced (cm for a zero order, cm sec^{-1} for a first order, and so on) divided by the movement made (cm deflection, e.g., for a stick). This value is variously named 'gain' or—which I prefer—display/control ratio (D/C ratio). Let us consider the elements of the simple acquisition task we have discussed already. The operator has to get his spot to the target area, and there to stop it. Assuming a first-order control with a particular maximum velocity (and all real systems have such an upper limit) it is evident that the more rapidly the operator can reach maximum velocity, the more rapidly will the gross movement—i.e. the movement to the target area—be accomplished. Thus the gross movement requires a high D/C ratio. However, he there has to stop; and every real operator has a certain amount of tremor and a certain liability to positioning error; and if every such slight error or movement sets his spot in motion it will take a long time to settle down. Thus the settling or adjustment phase calls for as low a D/C ratio as possible. The result of those two conflicting requirements can be seen in Figure 39.

This diagram appears in many textbooks and is part of the 'received wisdom' of the subject. It is also highly misleading.

A joystick can have only limited travel—say 30°–40° upon either side of centre at most. Therefore, with any real system, there is a downward limit to the D/C ratio given by maximum deflection for maximum output. Moreover, the rapid flick required to reach maximum deflection is virtually constant, unless the stick should have very heavy spring or frictional loading. In other words, for a joystick control, it is not possible to move down the D/C axis below the flat part of the travel-time curve. The curve therefore, is of the truncated, roughly J-shaped form of Figure 40; and we assert that, for all controls of joystick type, the lowest possible D/C ratio is best (see Hammerton, 1963; also Poulton, 1974).

It is surprising how persistent is the misleading conclusion of Figure 39; though the writer doubts whether any other reason needs to be cited than the sheer inertia of the printed word. An unfortunate consequence is that

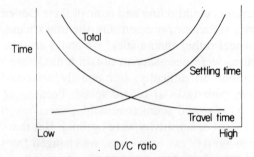

Figure 39. The components of acquisition time. When the D/C ratio ('sensitivity') is indefinitely variable, there will generally be an optimum value in the roughly U-shaped relationship between acquisition time and this ratio.

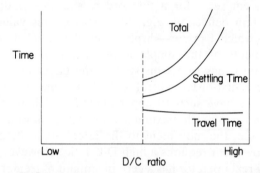

Figure 40. When D/C ratio has only a limited possible range (as is the case with many practical controls, such as joysticks, levers and pedals) the optimum value is generally the lowest obtainable.

the very conclusion offered has to be rediscovered again and again: this is still being done (Labuc, 1978).

We have discussed in a little detail the arguments related to optimum sensitivity for controls of the joystick type; but this by no means exhausts the optimization questions which might be asked. For example, are joysticks best? If they are, are movement or pressure sticks best? Is thumb control to be preferred to hand control, or vice versa? What is the optimum order of control? Further, do these optima vary with the task (remember that we have only discussed a very simple one-shot target acquisition)?

Only tentative answers can be given to some of these questions. Chernikoff, Duey, and Taylor (1960) present data which strongly favor first-order control systems, which is entirely in agreement with the present writer's observations; but their experimental design was open to criticism (Poulton, 1973). Thus we can only assert the superiority of first-order controls as probable; though it must be added that its superiority over higher-order systems is hardly open to doubt. That human beings find great difficulty in predicting and judging accelerated motion has been notorious for a century (Gottsdanker, 1956). Similarly, as has been pointed out by Poulton (1974), it is possible that continuous tracking of very rapidly swinging paths may be easier with a slightly higher than minimum D/C ratio: the matter has yet to be studied.

The quite general argument adumbrated above seems to require the superiority of joysticks over almost any other kind of control; and the present writer, together with the late A. H. Tickner, looked into the type of joystick which is to be preferred (1966). We concluded that hand controls were marginally better than thumb controls, which were vastly better than large sticks swung by the whole forearm. This is entirely in accord with common sense, of course; but it deliberately and specifically ignored the possible need to apply brute force: such a need should be eliminated in any well-designed modern system.

We referred above to pressure controls. These may not be as familiar to all readers as others; but their name is in fact self-descriptive. A pressure control is one which does not move and whose output is proportional to the force exerted upon it by the operator. It invariably (as far as the writer's experience goes) incorporates a form of spring centering—i.e. it returns to an equivalent of zero position when force is removed—and is generally operated by means of a piezoelectric crystal. The obvious advantage of such a system is that its D/C ratio is almost indefinitely variable; its drawback is that pressure feedback—i.e. the sensation of effort the operator is exerting— is almost certainly less precise than is the visual and positional feedback available with moving controls. Evidence carefully amassed and weighed by Poulton (1974) appears to indicate the superiority of pressure controls, especially in more difficult tasks—a conclusion emphatically endorsed by Mehr (1970).

Another question which arises, and which has given rise to some curious confusion, is that of display compatability: what is the best relationship between movement of (or direction of pressure on) a control and the movement of the display? The answer is entirely conformable to common sense, and has been known for a long time (e.g. Regan, 1959): move the control right and left to move the display right and left, move the control forward and back to move the display up or down. This unsurprising conclusion often draws the query: 'What about aircraft?'; but it should not be forgotten that aircraft are controlled from inside; and the horizon, which is effectively the display, does indeed move up as the stick moves forward.

These comments, of course, apply to a sensibly arranged system where the operator sits with his control before him and facing his display. Not every system is sensible (alas); and there are cases where an operator has no choice but to look at a display which is not in the same direction as his control. (A military application at once springs to mind here. The controller of a guided

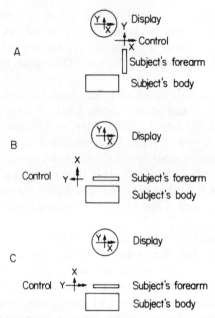

Figure 41. Schematic plan view of an experimental set-up to investigate the relative importance of space — and body — frames of reference in control tasks. In A, the control (a thumb joystick) is correctly oriented both to the spatial frame (the face of a CRO) and the body frame (the subject's forearm). In B, orientation is correct for body but not for space; in C, orientation is correct for space but not for body.

anti-tank missile may be in a helicopter with his control-stick in front of him and his target well off to one side.)

This question has theoretical as well as practical interest, and that in a different field of psychology. The question is: what is the preferred frame of reference for skills learning: is it spatial, or located in the operator's body? Put differently, would it be better to have to move a control parallel to the desired display movement irrespective of the location of the display, or if the display has to be moved left (say) in space, should the control be moved to the left of the operator's body? (See Figure 41.)

For simple situations at least, it seems that the body frame is what matters: the operator should always have to move his hand to his left in order to move the display to its left.

Alternative presentations

All the studies we have discussed involve the operator watching a display at the centre of his visual field, and doing something about it. This is not always possible; e.g. a pilot bringing his aircraft in to land may not wish to take his eyes off the runway to monitor his instruments more than he can possibly help. The change in accommodation of the eyes takes time, and therefore results in a dead time of 1–2 sec. One method of dealing with this which modern technology can supply is the 'head up' display. Here the necessary data are projected either upon the aircraft's windscreen or on the pilot's helmet and focused at infinity: he should be able to keep them in view while watching the ground. (Test pilots have assured the writer that this does not wholly solve the accommodation problem: it is difficult to see why not.) Another method is to use peripheral vision.

If you are looking at a display in front of you, you will not find it easy to read a dial (say) out of the corner of your eye. It is relatively easy, however, to note whether and how fast a light is flashing, or how bright it is. Only a few studies have been conducted to look into the effectiveness of such peripheral markers (e.g. Ziegler, Reilly, and Chernikoff, 1966), but they seem to indicate that some coded flashing system (e.g. the faster the flash rate, the larger the error) could function satisfactorily. Perhaps this possibility merits further study.

A little work has been done on using auditory instead of visual demand signals in tracking. As we all know, we can (roughly at least) localize the unseen source of a sound; and the human auditory system is highly sensitive to changes in the pitch and quality of a sound. Also, simple reaction time to an auditory stimulus is much shorter than to a visual stimulus (this makes good evolutionary sense: if you can hear something, it must be nearby). The possibility of using an auditory display for the second of two quantities which have to be followed simultaneously has, therefore, found some advocates.

Ellis, Burrows, and Jackson (1953) had their subjects track one variable visually, while a second was presented by representing upward errors by a high note (2.3 kHz) and downward errors by a low note (170 Hz). The magnitude of the error either way was represented by the rate at which the tone bleeped. The results indicated that satisfactory performance could be obtained in this way. It will be remembered that the German wartime *Knick-ebein* aircraft guidance system operated on a similar basis: to the right of the path the pilot heard a stream of Morse dashes, to the left a stream of dots, along the correct path a continuous note (Jones, 1978). It seems to have been entirely satisfactory, so long as no one was interfering.

It seems, then, that subsidiary tracking tasks can well be monitored by hearing. Little use of this is at present made in practical systems; but, again, the matter might be worth pursuing.

A variety of other forms of subsidiary tracking have been tried from time to time; Poulton (1974) refers to skin vibration and mild electrical stimulation. Not surprisingly, perhaps, they have attracted little attention; though there is no *apriori* reason to doubt that a more intense electrical stimulation could be, at least, an infallible emergency signal.

It is worth noting that all the moderately successful non-visual tracking systems which have been tried are analogous to compensatory rather than to pursuit tracking. It is reasonable to suppose that this is because the non-visual senses have insufficient discrimination to keep simultaneous track of both target and current status: at best they can apprehend the direction and approximate magnitude of an error.

MEASUREMENT OF TRACKING PERFORMANCE

In order to make statements about 'better' or 'optimal' tracking controls and devices, it is necessary to have some measure of performance. In the very simple acquisition task discussed above, nothing more complex is required than the time required, after leaving the initial position, to come to rest on the target. However, in more complex continuous tracking tasks time measures are rarely satisfactory. For example, suppose we used time-on-target as our measure (i.e. the actual length of time, or the proportion of the operating time, for which the subject is on or within a permitted distance from the target track). This has only one virtue—that of simplicity. It has, however, the fatal drawback of showing no difference between an operator who is (say) on target half the time and very near it the rest, and one who is on target half the time and wildly out for the rest. Clearly, a better measure must be sought.

Consider the imaginary data presented in Figure 42. With modern electronic equipment it is a simple matter to keep continuous track of the subject's error and present an integrated value (in cm^2) at the end of the experiment. This again, however, does not differentiate between the operator who makes one huge error but is otherwise perfect and the one who is never far off but never quite on. Two measures are generally used which provide the bulk of the information required: these are the modulus mean error (MM) and the root mean squared error (RMS).

In MM, no account is taken of the direction of error; but the value of the error (cm) is measured at successive time intervals, and the mean of all these values is taken. In formal notation, if an error at some measured instant is $\pm x$, and n such measures are taken,

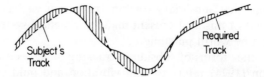

Figure 42. In general, a subject's track will differ from the required one. Here we see a reasonable effort, error being shown by vertical hatching: there are problems in producing a measure for the overall error.

$$MM = \frac{\Sigma|x|}{n}$$

In RMS, each error is squared, and the square root of the mean of the squares is taken. With the same notation,

$$RMS = \sqrt{\frac{\Sigma x^2}{\acute{n}}}$$

These two measures correlate very highly together, and either is very useful and valid. For certain statistical purposes, RMS is to be preferred, for it lends itself more readily to use with parametric statistics, but there is usually no compulsion to use such statistics; so the student may please himself. Poulton (1974) recommends the use of *relative* RMS or MM error scores. These are defined as the error (RMS or MM as the case may be), divided by the error that would be obtained if the operator simply did nothing, and multiplied by 100. In other words, the ratio of actual to zero-action error expressed as a percentage. This clearly has utility in comparing the results of different experiments and different equipments.

In all these measures, only one error quantity is considered at any instant—what we have termed x. However, it is sometimes the case that a subject may be following a track well-nigh perfectly, but a trifle late. If we follow the ultra-simple experimental picture we started with, we would observe, in such a case, that his error in a direction at right angles to the direction of movement of the roll (x as we have called it) would vary a lot, while his error along the direction of movement (y, let us say) would be a small constant. The former (x) may be called amplitude error, the latter (y) tracking lag. It may be desirable to measure them separately; in which case the experimenter will produce two values, either of MM, RMS, or relative errors.

MODELS OF TRACKING BEHAVIOR

By this time the reader may have thought that these several findings are no doubt interesting, and very useful if you wish to design a control system, but that they are lacking in generality. Is there not, he may well ask, some adequate theory of tracking behavior which would enable us, having measured, perhaps, various constant terms, to predict the outcome of all these experiments? Unfortunately, there is not; though not for want of heroic efforts.

Most of the efforts to reach a theoretical understanding of tracking behaviour have stemmed from two extra-psychological areas, namely the theory of servo-mechanisms and information (or communication) theory. The immediate attractiveness of the servo-mechanical approach is obvious (and is endorsed in Chapter 2). To say that a human being controlling a mechanism is acting as part of a closed-loop servo system is, in a sense, trivial. (Poulton, 1974, refers to compensatory control systems as 'open loop'—a terminology which seems to the writer to be slightly misleading.) Some part of the world— i.e. the system—is not as desired; the human operates upon it; he perceives the effects of his operation as the display; and performs a further or different operation, and so on. The system or device he is using will generally have some definable characteristics of its own, which may be very simple—as, for example, a hammer—or of the greatest complexity, as in some advanced vehicles. This state of affairs can quite validly be portrayed in the kind of diagram shown in Figure 43; and the servo language is clearly an acceptable one. But that alone is not enough.

Each of the 'boxes' in Figure—or any like it—has the characteristic of changing its output systematically in response to a change of input—as, for example, the flow of electric current in a circuit will change as a controlling resistance is altered. The theory of servo-mechanisms (see e.g. Brown and Campbell, 1948) is a branch of applied mathematics which offers a powerful set of techniques—technically known as transfer functions—for describing such changes and hence for describing and predicting the behavior of the systems they make up. Also, when an element is a 'black box', as a human operator is, methods exist for deriving its transform by examining its response to a known input or sequence of inputs (see e.g. Teasdale and Reynolds, 1955).

In the first flush of enthusiasm for servo methods, much research was directed toward finding 'the transfer function of the human operator'—note the confident definite articles. Tustin (1944) wrote: 'The object . . . was to investigate the nature of the subject's responses . . . and to attempt to find the laws of relationship of movement to error. In particular it was hoped that this relationship might . . . permit the well-developed theory of linear servo-mechanisms to be applied to manual control.' Such an aim, if achieved, would not only make it possible to synthesize optimal system designs, but on a theoretical plane it could have immense value in guiding studies of brain

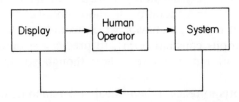

Figure 43. Any tracking task can be treated as a closed-loop control set-up; and (in principle at least) the mathematics of control theory can be applied.

functioning and the search for the physiological mechanisms involved. Alas, the attempt failed.

The first important catch lies in the use of the word 'linear' in Tustin's remarks above. It means, simply, that the transform must be of the type which can be described by a class of mathematical functions known as 'linear differential equations'. This type of expression cannot cope with an intermittent response; and it soon became evident that, in many cases, human operator responses are intermittent (Poulton, 1950).

There are, indeed, methods for coping with non-linear systems. They involve finding the best linear equation—i.e. the one which leaves the least amount of the data unaccounted for—and adding a 'remnant' non-linear term for the rest. These methods have neither the beauty nor the generality of linear equations, but they can, nevertheless, be very useful in particular cases.

This has been particularly urged by McRuer and his several co-workers (e.g. 1967), who were able to construct reasonably successful descriptions of their data. However, in order to do this, expressions of considerable complexity were required, involving at least five, and in some cases nine undetermined constant terms. Now an expression with nine undetermined and independent numbers in it can be made to fit just about anything after the fact, but can predict nothing before it. (In this context Poulton, 1974, approvingly quotes the common saying that 'an equation with 2 constants in it can be made to fit an elephant, and one with 3 constants can make its tail wiggle'.) It is therefore difficult to argue that our general understanding has been advanced by these studies, impressive though their mathematical sophistication undoubtedly is.

There are further difficulties. In almost any situation, human operators display a remarkable ability to learn at least the overall statistical characteristics of the task. They can also learn to master control systems which, at first, were insuperably difficult; but such learning tends to be unstable. Thus, Garvey (1960) showed that subjects could, in effect, acquire an extra order of integration—enabling them to cope with an order of control one higher than they could before—but that they lost this ability when their attention had to be divided. Similarly, the learning of general task characteristics may, in any particular trial, be counteracted by fatigue and boredom. Thus, it would seem, one cannot hope to do more than find the transfer function (be it never so complex) of a well-practised, well-motivated operator who is not yet very tired or bored. It is hard to avoid the conclusion reached more than thirty years ago by Birmingham and Taylor (1954) that '*The* human transfer function is a will-o'-the-wisp, which can lure the control system designer into a fruitless and interminable quest.' This is yet another problem which will be adverted to below.

Both the track and the operator's output can be treated as signals or messages received and transmitted over time. It is not surprising, then, that a number of workers have tried to see whether information theory could help our theoretical understanding. During the 1950s many psychologists became very enthusiastic about the application of this theory to their subject. This was not at all unreasonable; for, after all, a very great deal of human activity may validly be described as the processing of information of more or less complexity. However, the theory of information (or communication, as it is more properly called) has certain constraints which make its application to psychology very difficult (see, e.g. Pierce, 1962), and most of the attempts to use it proved sterile.

Nevertheless, its application to tracking studies seemed *a priori* reasonable, since both input and output take a form which seems to lend itself to information measures. However, despite some ingenious attempts and a lot of disputation, no formulation has succeeded in commanding general acceptance. It is perhaps significant that in his formidable survey of the area, Poulton (1974) did not even index information theory.

Why should so many attempts to find a generally applicable and acceptable theory have failed to deliver the goods? Consideration of an experiment which was actually conducted for another purpose (Hammerton and Tickner, 1970) may help to cast some dark on the matter.

In this study subjects sat facing a TV screen, which bore on it a central vertical graticule. They used a thumb joystick which controlled the movements of a TV camera which could move back and forth parallel with and facing a horizontally moving target. The control was a first-order one with a small lag, which was not difficult to use; and the movements of the target were determined by the sum of three sine waves: this pattern of movement repeated after about 2 min, which was a good deal longer than each testing run.

Before and behind the target were screens. In one condition these were painted with a landscape, so that the target seemed to be running along the top of a cliff, backed by rolling downland; in the other condition they were matt white. This was the *only* difference between the two conditions: the target courses were statistically identical in the two cases; and identical responses were available, which would have produced identical data. Nevertheless, the results of the two conditions were very markedly different. It therefore seems to the writer that any comprehensive theory of tracking behavior, in whatever terms, must take account of the purely local characteristics of the visual background of the input. The literature of the field is far too extensive for any man to be able to claim with confidence that he has not overlooked any relevant paper: the writer can only aver that he knows of none which attempts this.

What may turn out to be a powerful approach has been adumbrated by Pellionisz et al. (1982), and by Churchland (1986). Their argument may be rendered, somewhat simplified, as follows. The instantaneous position and velocity of the subject's input signal must be representable as a vector. A vector is a segment of a straight line having specific length, direction, and location in space: in this case it might be either in real space or in the subject's visual space. Similarly, the response required must also be representable in this way, though generally in a different frame of reference—usually the subject's own body. The mathematical function used for transforming one vector into another, whatever their frames of reference may be, is called a *tensor*; and hence it is possible that tensor calculus may provide the appropriate tool for a deeper understanding of tracking behavior. It might well be, indeed, that such a technique could get round the difficulty raised above, since a subject's visual space may differ according to the current background texture (cf. Julesz, 1981). It must be emphasized, however, that at the time of writing, this approach remains a suggestion to be pursued.

What of computer models? The amazing power and versatility of modern computers has naturally attracted persons interested in tracking problems; but simulations so far lack generality. Given an ingenious programmer (and many members of that respected profession are very ingenious indeed) a machine can be made to mimic any particular piece of human tracking behavior. The programs produced so far, however, do not generalize to other tasks and other operators. In any case, the criticism advanced above also holds.

Virtually all the studies we have referred to so far were laboratory studies, using more or less artificial situations and displays, all of which were a few tens of centimeters from the subject. How well do these results apply to real-world tracking situations? Also, since the use of simulators for training is becoming ever more important (Institute of Measurement and Control, 1977), how much does a skill learned in a restricted 'artificial' environment help in coping with the 'real thing?'

TRANSFER OF TRAINING

There can be little doubt that the optimizing conclusions cited above hold, at least as rank orders; although a caveat has to be entered to the effect that the real world seems to be rather a good place to do tracking in. Steering a ship is, after all, a heavily damped third-order system; but it is not usually of insuperable difficulty. The questions which arise concerning applying a skill learned on an indoor simulator to a real situation, however, involve psychological problems of deep significance. Suppose that it is indeed the case that persons who master task A subsequently master task B more rapidly than those who have never attempted A (an effect known as the transfer of training); why should it be, and what conditions may enhance the effect? Like many interesting questions in psychology, this one is difficult: the phenomenon itself it not easy to measure; more than one possible explanation is in the field; and these answers, further discussed in Chapter 8, are not necessarily mutually exclusive.

It should be made clear that we are not, in general, concerned with starting with an easy task and proceeding to a less easy one. Indeed, Holding (1962) concluded that 'task difficulty' was not a useful concept at all for examining transfer between tracking tasks: it is doubtful whether it ever is.

Consider a 'typical' transfer experiment. A control group, which we shall call C, learns some task B, their initial and final performances providing by subtraction or ratio a measure of skill acquired. A matched experimental group, which we shall call E, learns some task A, and then learns task B. Evidently we need some formula for comparing E's performance on task B with that of C. We may, as we shall remark in a moment, require other information, but let that suffice for the moment.

Simple and straightforward though this seems, literally hundreds of formulae have been proposed (e.g. Murdock, 1957). Broadly, however, they fall into two classes: there are those which are concerned with *savings*, and there are those which are concerned with initial or '*first-shot*' transfer performance. Saving measures answer, more or less directly, the question: how much training time (or how many training trials) are saved in learning task B by the prior learning of task A? First-shot measures answer the question: how does the prior learning of task A affect *initial* performance on task B?

It is important here to remember that these classes of measures really are dealing with different things. It has usually been tacitly assumed—though not, so far as the writer knows, explicitly stated—that the two classes correlate almost perfectly one with the other—that a very high savings measure automatically implies a very high first-shot measure. Unfortunately, as the writer showed (1967), this is not the case: it is possible to combine a saving of some 70 per cent or more of training trials with a *negative* first-shot measure. In other words, though E-group trainees may take less than a third as long to attain proficiency in task B as do those from group C, their initial performance can be worse than if they had no prior training at all.

It is evident upon very slight reflection that there are some practical situations in which this would be disastrous, and others in which it would not be a serious drawback. Thus it is necessary to be very clear about what we need from a simulator, and hence what measure of its performance is appropriate, and to design the simulator so as to maximize its effectiveness. 'Effectiveness' in any real situation is, of course, an economic as well as a purely technical matter; and the costing is far from being a simple exercise. It is necessary to ask: what is the running cost per hour of the simulator as compared to that of the real equipment? Does even a poor operator of the real equipment produce some useful output which can be set against cost?

Is he, on the other hand, likely merely to waste raw materials, or even damage the plant itself? And so on. It is considerations of this kind which decide whether the user is after a very high 'first-shot' transfer, or whether he will be satisfied with a substantial saving of training time.

When the need has been established, the simulator must be designed; and there is now a good deal of information available to guide the designer. Much, though not all, of this information derives from studies of aircraft cockpit simulators, for the very obvious reasons that aircraft are very expensive to build and run, that their misuse can be disastrous, and that, consequently, funding for research into training methods has often been generous. The results may be summarized quite simply: very simple devices can produce remarkably good savings measures; but if you want good first-shot transfer, then you must pay for it in terms of more complex fidelity to the real situation. Curiously, perhaps, this result is more unequivocally shown by laboratory than by field studies.

Let us consider the question of what is transferred in a visual-motor skilled task. The trainee learns to make some set of appropriate motor responses to various discretely or continuously varying signals, which are usually visual. Let us suppose that a simulator has been made which presents the 'bare bones' of this situation—for example, a particular dial with a pointer as the input signal and a lever to move in response. In general, the real situation will be more complex than this; and the trainee, when first he uses the real equipment, will be getting a whole host of other signals, many of them unfamiliar. These will include the relevant signals; and he has to learn to ignore and discard a lot of others among which they are found: this situation is known as 'stimulus compounding'. The need to cope with it probably accounts for the poor, or even negative first-shot transfer which can, as we have noted, sometimes be associated with very good savings measures.

Where savings are the chief requirement, it is remarkable how simple some effective devices are. Even in flying, noticeable reductions in dual-control hours were reported (Flexman, Matheny, and Brown, 1950) using nothing more elaborate than an 'artificial horizon' consisting of a line on a board held up by an instructor. Not unreasonably, though, we might expect that, if we want good first-shot transfer, we must provide *in the learning situation* a fair sample of those irrelevant 'compounding' stimuli with which the trainee will eventually have to live. Such an expectation was amply borne out in a series of studies the writer conducted some years ago (Hammerton, 1967). Precisely comparable field data are hard to come by. There is, indeed, ample evidence (e.g. Caro, Isley, and Jolley, 1975) that elaborate simulation—including such refinements as projected scenery and multiple-axis cockpit motion—produces very good transfer indeed. A strict comparison with less complex devices is, as far as the writer's knowledge goes, wanting. The reasons for this are very simple: it has become usual, when introducing a new type of aircraft, to make the most complete and elaborate simulator possible, so that no one even tries a simpler one; and, when an elaborate simulator is used to replace a simpler one, the amount of training time used on it is promptly cut down—without first carrying out the expensive comparative study. One must suppose that the responsible authorities are so convinced by the laboratory studies already cited that they do not consider more extended tests to be necessary. If they are so convinced, they are probably right, for once.

What light do these several findings cast upon the theory of transfer? Three theories have been propounded at various times. The traditional view was that the training task (task A in our summary) exercises some part of the brain, just as lifting weights exercises sets of muscles; and in consequence the subject approaches task B with a stronger, fitter brain. However, other alternatives are now more popular.

Thorndike (1903) propounded the most extreme view: task A can help with task B only in so far as there are elements of performance which are common to them both. There is an attractive simplicity about this, as about so many of the ideas propounded by the early behaviorists. However, it rules out—or seems to—any notion of 'generality' in learning; and a contrary view is that it is precisely such general principles, explicit or implicit in task A, which are of use in task B. The celebrated study of Hendrickson and Schroeder (1941) may be cited as supporting this view. They found that a prior study of refraction did not show any advantage when aiming at underwater targets; but that an advantage did show when the depth of water was changed: subjects with knowledge of refraction adapted more rapidly than those without.

(There is also what may be called the cynics' or 'test' view: task A is not the slightest use in learning task B; but it is a good test of potential for task B. In other words, in order to do well at task A, you need the very abilities that will stand you in good stead when tackling task B.)

At first sight, it might be argued that the 'common element' theory is supported by the data we have discussed. However, it is worth noting that the poor 'first-shot' transfer recorded in some experiments indicates that it is precisely these common elements that the learner fails to extract from the second situation. It cannot be claimed that these results are decisive; but, besides bringing to light the previously unsuspected phenomenon of different savings and first-shot transfer, tracking studies give some support to the 'general principles view'. It should not be forgotten, however, that the traditional or 'exercise' theory has never, to the writer's knowledge, actually been disproved. It has only become unfashionable.

TRACKING AND CHANNEL CAPACITY

A vital question (already raised in Chapter 4) for those who wish to understand human skill is: to what extent can we do two things at once? Put more formally, what are the limitations on our rate of processing input demands and output responses? For many years, the view which was most generally accepted was that of Broadbent (1958), which suggested that all these operations passed through a single central channel, whose capacity had, naturally, some upper limit. This model held that we can indeed do only one thing at a time; and that when we appear to do more we are either switching smartly and economically between tasks, or are leaving one of them, which must be highly overlearned (e.g. riding a bicycle) to a purely automatic system. Later work modified this view to suppose that there is indeed a single limited channel, but that it can, as it were, be divided between various tasks, provided none of these is overwhelmingly difficult.

Continuous tracking tasks afford an elegant means of testing this theory. A fairly difficult task of low predictability certainly absorbs a great deal of capacity, but uses as input only the eyes (vision) and for output only one hand. The subject can still hear, speak, make one-handed gestures, or otherwise respond to a variety of visual stimuli. These facts were utilized by McLeod (1977) in a study which should become a classic.

His subjects were presented with a decidedly difficult second-order tracking task, for which they used a hand joystick. The difficulty was increased by making the control asymmetric: the D/C ratio in one direction was less than in the other by 20 per cent. At the same time a second task, easy in itself, was presented: this was to decide whether a short bleep of sound was of middle (1 kHz) or high (3 kHz) pitch. One experimental group indicated this decision by pressing an appropriate button with their free hand; another simply stated which sound it was.

The beauty of this experiment is that in stimulus or perceptual uncertainty the two groups were identical; the only difference was in the modality of the output of the second task. However, it was found that there was a marked decrement in tracking performance when, but only when, the choice response was made manually.

In a further experiment, the same tracking task was performed simultaneously with mental arithmetic (questions and answers being spoken) of two levels of difficulty. It appeared that performance on the tracking task was independent of the difficulty of the arithmetic.

The conclusion appears to be compelled that two processes employing the same output mode (manual, in this case) are indeed on a single channel; processes involving different output modalities are on separate channels. A multiprocessor, as opposed to a single-channel model seems required by these data: a result of fundamental importance.

THE STATUS AND FUTURE OF TRACKING STUDIES

Some years ago the writer wondered whether tracking studies were in the process of being automated out of existence. To some extent this has happened. The progress of microelectronics has made it possible to eliminate human controllers from many situations where, a few years ago, a highly trained operator was essential. The difference between the command-guided Soviet SAM-2 missiles and their SAM-7 and SAM-9 successors, or the US 'Stingers', which only need to be launched in the general direction of their target, will come immediately to the thoughts of the informed.

There remain, of course, wide areas where the controller has not been, and for some time is not likely to be, eliminated: road transport and air transport are the most obvious and numerically the most important cases. Yet even here, we may ask, are there problems sufficient to justify prolonged research programmes? After all, the major prescriptions, as we have seen, can already be given; and it would be difficult to justify, on straightforwardly applied grounds, elaborate investigations of new systems, unless they contained features thought likely to modify available conclusions, or to be of a nature where even the faintest improvement must be sought. For example, the peculiar difficulties of using complex controls in a ship, itself subject to lively motion, raises some interesting problems (McLeod et al., 1986).

Are there applied areas where more needs to be known? The only one which seems important, other than tying up some of the loose ends we have already indicated, is the effect of prolonged vigilance upon tracking skills. The extensive literature on vigilance studies suggests that operators may modify their criteria of being 'on target' over time. How this tendency may best be met and overcome has not yet received much attention.

However, the function of science, as has justly been observed, is not to make things, but to make sense of things. It cannot be pretended that anything like a full theoretical account of tracking behavior can be given. For reasons given above, the writer does not believe that a full account can be attained in terms either of control theory or of information theory. It is a challenge to control theorists to extend their theories to include intermittent or variable systems within their range; but even if success crowns such an enterprise, it must be combined with an account of how human beings incorporate background features into their assessments of speed and relative position. At present this can be done only in general terms, which it would be difficult to combine with formal control equations.

Advantage may be taken, however, of the large empirical body of data on tracking tasks, and of the powerful and informative measures which exist for assessing performance on them. We have already adumbrated the way in which these have been used to settle an important issue in the study of channel capacity. It needs little imagination to see that they might be used in such areas as attention and motor learning. They are already being used in studies of the sequelae of some neurological diseases; and it is reasonably hoped that they may pinpoint the nature and area of deficiencies which afflict some sufferers.

If such studies appear auxiliary and tangential, they may nevertheless prove valuable.

SUMMARY

Tracking studies began in the 1940s with the most strictly practical ends in view. These early studies, however, raised questions of great theoretical interest concerning the functioning of human beings as elements in closed-loop control systems, and as processors of information. High hopes were entertained that formal descriptions of human behaviour in servo- or information-theoretical terms would enable optimal designs to be derived mathematically and would cast an important light on central human functioning. These hopes have not been realized to more than a very limited extent; and there is reason to suppose that they cannot be, with the mathematical tools now available.

Nevertheless, the original object of tracking work—the finding of specifications for optimal control orders, displays, and sensitivities—has substantially been achieved. It is evident that zero or first-order control systems are to be preferred wherever possible. The superiority of pursuit over compensatory displays is firmly established, except where a non-visual auxiliary system is contemplated. Hand controls are in general to be preferred; and with the possible (and somewhat doubtful) exception of pressure-operated controls following a complex track, the lower the D/C ratio the better. Ordinary control systems can therefore be optimized virtually by rule of thumb.

Some tracking tasks, especially piloting aircraft, necessarily involve some difficulty, and the consequences of failure are grave. Great attention has therefore been paid to the design and use of tracking training devices and simulators. This work has produced important results in the measurement and understanding of transfer of training; and, again, enables broad rules to be laid down for the design of simulators.

It is not clear whether classical tracking studies will retain their importance in applied psychology: automation and microelectronics have enabled the human controller to be removed from many advanced systems. The established knowledge and informative measures available, however, can be used to investigate many fields of general importance. They have already made substantial contributions to our knowledge of human channel capacity, and may prove useful in a number of other areas.

Chapter 8

Motor Skill Learning

Alan W. Salmoni

The purpose of this chapter is to convey to the reader a general appreciation of the area called 'motor skill learning' and of some of the research topics and issues therein. Historically, researchers in this area began with a broad view of skill and an interest in learning, only to have the view of skill narrowed to movement skill and research on learning dropped. In more recent times however, skill is again being viewed in a broader context and the study of learning or acquisition is again in vogue.

THEORIES OF LEARNING

The first section briefly reviews those theories which I have judged to have had the greatest impact on the research in skill learning.

Thorndike's connectionism

Although Edward Thorndike (1874–1949) was not a behaviorist, Hilgard and Bower (1966) credit him with being the first S–R psychologist. Thorndike (reviewed in Hilgard and Bower, 1966) believed that learning was the strengthening of associative bonds between the stimulus and response and his greatest impact on skill learning was his 'law of effect' and 'law of use/disuse' (or exercise). Somewhat characteristic of a behaviorist, however, he believed that the formation of these S–R bonds was not mediated by thoughts or ideas, but that learning was basically a trial-and-error process. The law of effect stated that if a connection is made and accompanied or followed by a satisfying state of affairs, the connection is strengthened, while if it is followed by an annoying state, the strength will be weakened. Although Thorndike did not place theoretical importance on the information content of the reward (e.g. saying 'right' or 'wrong' after a response) which might be satisfying or annoying, these notions formed some of the original theor-

Human Skills. Edited by D. Holding © 1989 John Wiley & Sons Ltd

etical bases for the area of knowledge of results to be reviewed below. The law of exercise stated that an increase in practice led to an increase in the strength of the connection; however, Thorndike later denounced this idea, as he concluded that only a trivial amount of learning could be accounted for by mere repetition. For example, Trowbridge and Cason (1932) showed that repeated attempts to draw a three-inch line failed to cause an improvement in performance unless the attempts were followed by some type of reward. Thorndike believed this law was most relevant for muscular skills and although disclaimed by him, ideas concerning the role of repetition in skill learning still remain today. The other theoretical idea of importance was Thorndike's 'identical elements' theory of transfer. Any transfer from original to novel learning was thought to depend on the presence of identical elements in the two situations and these identities could be either of substance or procedure. Thus, learning was always specific. Thorndike has had a huge effect not only on psychology in general and skill learning in particular, but also in the field of education. Although most of the specifics of his theoretical ideas have disappeared from the current literature, his influence has not.

Hull's behavior theory

Like Thorndike, Clark Hull was considered to be an S–R psychologist and according to Hilgard and Bower (1966), was responsible for moving psychology to an S–O–R model, such that many organismic variables were postulated to mediate performance. Both the major strength and weakness of Hull's theory was its quantitative-deductive nature. He defined many variables affecting behavior, which were subsequently set into a list of postulates, which were then used to generate a number of quantitative theorems. The actual mathematical formulae were derived from laboratory experimentation mainly with rats, although the theory was applied to complex human learning as well. Perhaps the most important aspect of his theory for the area of skill learning was his postulates and theorems concerning habit strength.

Learning was hypothesized by Hull to depend on contiguity between stimulus and response, when the response was closely followed by reinforcement. The learning curve was described by a simple growth function, such that habit strength was incremented by each reinforcement. Probably because these notions evolved from animal research, it was also predicted that learning would be maximized when there was little or no delay between the response and reinforcement. Along with these ideas, postulates concerning reactive and conditioned inhibition were also influential in skill learning research. Hull postulated that following each response, inhibition was generated, which acted to reduce the likelihood of that response being repeated. However, Hull believed that reactive inhibition spontaneously dissipated over time, thus allowing for an increase in performance following a rest period. This theoretical idea was incorporated by researchers to explain the reminiscence effect (i.e. an increase in performance after a rest period above the level seen just prior to the rest) typically seen in motor skill learning experiments.

As Hull continued to do research and to rethink his ideas, many of his postulates were changed. For example, Hull later hypothesized that delay of reinforcement produced less reactive potential and not less habit strength, as he originally believed (this idea was later emphasized by Adams as discussed below). Although Hull's theory was constantly cited in the 1950s and 1960s, as well as influencing the thinking of many researchers of that era, little mention is made of his theory today.

Information-processing models

At the time when Hull's theory began to wane in its influence, the information-processing paradigm appeared, which was to have a very dramatic effect on skill learning research. As concluded by Hilgard and Bower (1966, p. 387), 'The years 1955–1960 marked the major beginnings of modern information processing models', which were the cumulative result of two influences. Just prior to this shift in perspective, Shannon and Weaver (1949) published their book on the mathematical theory of communication (information theory), which, although not used extensively in skill learning research, provided a conceptual framework for many of the constructs used in this area (e.g. capacity, transmission, noise, etc.). The second factor was the advent of the computer, which provided both a metaphor for the human processor and programmed 'behavior' to simulate human performance and learning.

Much of the early 'information-processing' research was done under the rubric of cybernetics and involved the study of control processes in learning. For example, K.J.W. Craik published several articles (e.g. Craik, 1947) in which he described man as an intermittent correction servo, and indeed much of the tracking literature was aimed at questions posed by cybernetic theory. Research topics such as the study of knowledge of results also received added impetus from these considerations.

In 1964 Fitts published a chapter on perceptual-motor skill learning, within which he presented a model of the phases of skill learning. Although not stimulating a great deal of research, the model has affected the thinking of many researchers and is still quoted today as a conceptualization of the skill learning process. In the early or cognitive phase of skill learning the beginner tries to understand the task and what it demands. In the intermediate or associative phase old habits are associated in new ways and movement errors are corrected. This phase lasts for varying periods of time depending on the complexity of the skill to be learned. The final or autonomous phase unfolds as the skill becomes progressively more automatic (i.e. requires little or no attention to be performed).

This latter notion of 'automatization' has been very important to skill learning research and is related to the idea of the expert or skilled performer. A conception which is consistent across most skill learning theories today is that the skilled performer can execute relatively complex responses with very little mental effort, because the underlying information processing has become automatized. Indeed, Schmidt (1982) suggests that the measurement of attention demands during skilled performance represents an alternative measure of learning to the quantification of the performance itself. This is important because it provides a conceptualization and a measurement for learning when performance changes may be difficult to detect—something not handled well by earlier theories. Although introduced much earlier by Bryan and Harter (1899), the idea that skills are hierarchically and sequentially organized (e.g. Fitts and Posner, 1967) was emphasized by the information-processing models. It was hypothesized that as skill learning continues, conscious control shifts upwards in the hierarchy to a progressively more abstract level while most of the fine-grain aspects of the skill are controlled subconsciously by subroutines. The analogy given by Fitts and Posner (1967) is that of a company president issuing a command which is then organized and executed by progressively lower levels of the company workforce, without the president having to worry about the details of the job.

Fitts and Posner (1967, p. 19) also concluded that 'After the first few years of life, learning an entirely new skill is rare . . . the learning of skills is therefore largely a matter of transfer of prior habits to new situations.' This is a conceptually important idea because it has resulted in a virtual separation of research in 'adult' skill learning from skill learning in children. As a result, information-processing models of skill learning have been validated by laboratory research using college sophomores as subjects. This splitting of subject populations is rather arbitrary and ill-founded. Although it cannot be denied that the information-processing paradigm has been very influential in skill learning research, it is also true that these models have tended to be performance-oriented, with a resultant de-emphasis of learning.

Adams' closed-loop theory

It is perhaps ironic that Adams' (1971, p. 113) closed-loop theory of motor learning is being reviewed here in a chapter on skill learning, since Adams introduced his theory with the following remark: 'First, let us forget about the term skill which has been so blunted by colloquial usage and research practice that it lacks scientific value.' However, the theory was responsible for stimulating a great deal of research in this area and is therefore worthy of mention. The main constructs of the theory were the perceptual trace and memory trace; the former being responsible for determining the extent of movement, and the latter for the initiation and selection of the movement. Adams claimed that his theory dealt only with slow, graded responses, since he thought these movements represented the rudiments of skilled behavior and were therefore good grounds for a sound, basic, research program.

Perhaps most important to this review was Adams' view of knowledge of results, since it contrasted with Thorndike's and Hull's view for the role of reinforcement. Knowledge of results did not act by strengthening the bond between the stimulus and the response, but rather acted as error information during initial acquisition trials to allow the subject to make adjustments to the subsequent response. Indeed, the perceptual trace was strengthened by the accumulation of feedback traces over trials and the memory trace was a function of S–R contiguity. Unlike Thorndike and Hull, Adams proposed that delay of knowledge of results has no effect on movement acquisition.

In addition, it was hypothesized by Adams that performance improvement during acquisition depended on the presentation of knowledge of results and that withdrawal of knowledge of results would result in a deterioration of performance if the movement was poorly practised. Adams believed that there were two phases of skill learning, a verbal–motor stage during which acquisition was under verbal-cognitive control and a motor stage during which performance was relatively error-free and internally controlled (proprioceptive feedback). Perhaps the greatest strength and also weakness of Adams' theory was its rather narrow scope. This restricted range provided many testable hypotheses and thus spawned a great deal of research, but since other researchers were eager to generalize to other movement situations, interest in the theory dissipated rather quickly. Another difficulty in Adams' theory was its inability to deal with novel responses, and this partially motivated Schmidt to develop a motor schema theory.

Motor schema theory

In 1975 Schmidt published a schema theory of discrete motor skill learning, which built on schema theory in perception as well as the strengths of Adams' closed-loop theory. Schmidt (1975) hypothesized that information concerning the initial conditions, response outcome, sensory feedback, and response specifications were stored after each movement and that with experience, an abstract relationship among these information sources would evolve. More specifically, the recall schema was the relationship between the initial conditions, response specifications, and the response outcome (as primarily indicated through knowledge of results) and the recognition schema was the relationship among the initial conditions, sensory consequences (i.e. internal and external feedback), and response outcome. The recall schema was responsible for response production and the recognition schema assessed correctness of response. Both of these elements are part of the motor response schema, which, along with the other critical elements of the theory, can be seen in Figure 44.

Perhaps the most important thing to note is the role Schmidt gives knowledge of results, since it contrasts with the theories presented above. Here,

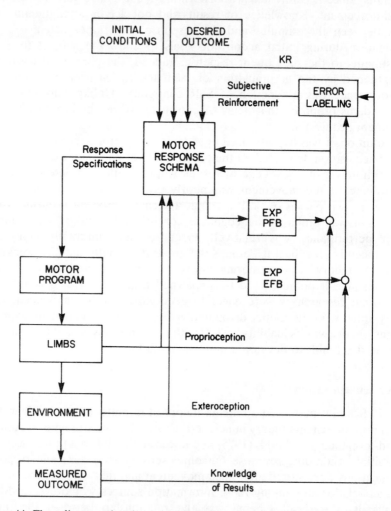

Figure 44. Flow diagram showing critical elements in a movement performance from the point of view of schema theory (EXP PFB = expected proprioceptive feedback; EXP EFB = expected exteroceptive feedback). (From Schmidt, 1975.) Reproduced by permission.

knowledge of results is directly responsible for incrementing the strength of both recall and recognition schema. The other important idea from Schmidt's theory was that practice variability is vital to provide a broad base of experience for a strong schema. This notion, perhaps more than any other aspect of schema theory, produced a great deal of research activity and was responsible for revitalizing interest in transfer of learning. Although both Adams' and Schmidt's theories have generated considerable research, their theoretical impact has been lessened I believe for two reasons. First, both theories presented ideas about learning at a time when learning was not in vogue in experimental psychology. Second, both theories emphasized constructs to explain the difference between recall and recognition and although valid ideas in their context, are presently of much less research interest. The present focus for skill learning has shifted to ideas about knowledge and concomitant interest in 'expert' performers, which to some degree represents a revitalization of interest in individual differences.

Anderson's ACT model

With the development of several artificial intelligence models, such as Anderson's (1976) ACT model, there has been a resurgence of interest in learning and more specifically in the acquisition of knowledge. The model has as its goal to explain the nature and development of adult competence. To do this the ACT model integrates a memory network (propositional or declarative knowledge) with a production system (procedural knowledge). The propositional network is a memory system whose job is to represent or store facts, and in so doing to record past memories, current goals, and current stimuli. The production system is a set of procedures which act on the memory system to control things like rehearsal, activation of relevant facts, and choice of the proper response goal. Each production consists of a condition (to satisfy) and an action (like rehearsal) to be carried out in memory if the condition is satisfied, much like an elaborate S–R model.

Although the ACT model was developed exclusively as a model of cognitive rather than motor skill, Anderson (1983, p. 215) has stated that 'Motor skills like riding a bike or typing are certainly instances of procedural knowledge, but they have not been the focus of the ACT theory.' As such, productions possess many similarities to motor programs, since their primary function is to provide the connection between declarative knowledge and behavior. Individual procedures are very specialized and are specific to a given condition. The ACT model assumes that the acquisition of productions is unlike the acquisition of facts, since procedural learning occurs only by doing, and its strength is only incremented through successful application. This characteristic partially explains why procedural learning is gradual.

The ACT model also predicts that learning is a shift from a declarative mode to a procedural mode, which in the skill domain means that the beginner will respond very slowly, having to move from fact to fact, where as the expert will respond very quickly, having developed a set of procedures to act automatically in a given situation. The strength of this model is the emphasis which it places on the knowledge structure supporting skilled performance, although it does not deal explicitly with the coordination of movement. In addition, it does not appear to provide a means of explaining current research in skill learning through vicarious factors such as observational learning, which will be reviewed next.

Bandura's model of observation learning

Bandura (1986) claims that views like Anderson's ACT model cannot explain skill attainment, since there must be a way of translating knowledge into skilled action and that physical enactment serves as the translating vehicle. Enactive (motor skill) learning is defined by Bandura (p. 110) as a process of extracting the basic structure of movement patterns from information conveyed by models, instructions, as well as extrinsic and/or intrinsic feedback resulting from movement. Indeed, Bandura sees enactive learning as a special case of observational learning, since he believes people construct conceptions of behavior from observing the effects of their actions during enactive learning.

Bandura hypothesizes that observational learning is governed by four processes (i.e. attentional, retention, production, and motivational processes), which are outlined in greater detail in Figure 45 below. As can be seen, the first production step is the development of a cognitive representation, which Bandura refers to as conception induction (i.e. the formation by observation of a conception of how constituent acts must be spatially and temporally organized to produce new forms of behavior). This is followed by centrally guided response initiation, feedback monitoring, and matching conception to action through movement corrections. In the early stages of learning these steps are transactional since the conception affects action, but action may also cause changes in the conception. These notions are very similar to Schmidt's motor schema, as Bandura, like Schmidt, believes that people learn generative rules of action rather than specific action patterns. As learning continues, control shifts to lower centres requiring little attention, as 'thought-governed behavior shifts to situationally prompted enactment of a fully integrated routine'.

The strength of Bandura's model for future research is the important role given to 'vicarious' factors in skill learning and this will be discussed further below. Its weakness seems to be Bandura's eclectic approach, which results in very few testable predictions. Indeed, Bandura's model represents a compilation of all those theories reviewed above.

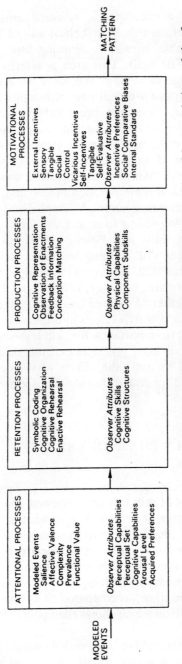

Figure 45. Subprocesses governing observational learning. (from Bandura, 1986.) Reproduced by permission. of the first author and Prentice-Hall, Inc.

Conclusions

In light of the theories above, specific research areas seem worthy of emphasis. First, because of the influence (behavioral) of Thorndike and Hull there has been considerable interest in learning how stimuli following a response affect response strength. This area is referred to most often in skill learning as knowledge of results. The early behavioral emphasis also popularized the study of transfer of learning, although with the exception of research in schema theory there has been little interest in this topic in recent times. With the advent of the information-processing paradigm and the disenchantment with the study of learning, a great deal of emphasis shifted to the study of retention of movements and more specifically to motor short-term memory research. Another notion which was revitalized by this paradigm was the hierarchical representation of skill and, more pertinent for skill learning, the idea of automatization. As emphasized by Fitts (1964), the highest level of skill learning seems to reflect a greatly minimized attention demand or mental effort. Fitts and Posner (1967) also at least partially legitimized the split between skill learning and motor development research by popularizing the idea that skill learning in the adult is mainly the recombination of old habits. There are, however, recent signs that these two areas may be growing back together. As stated above, an interest in learning has been rekindled through the research efforts and theorizing in the acquisition of knowledge. Perhaps more importantly for skill learning, this represents a renewed emphasis in individual differences and skill analysis. Lastly, researchers are beginning to study the effects of vicarious factors on skill learning, taking the lead provided largely by social psychologists like Bandura.

EARLY PHASE OF LEARNING

What gets learned?

If one peruses the theories of skill learning reviewed above it is evident that there is a considerable degree of consensus as to what is being accomplished by the learner during this phase. This fact is somewhat interesting because the consensus seems to be built more on practical experience than actual data, unless we were to assume that a majority of the research to date really only deals with the early phase of learning (i.e. most learning experiments use novel tasks and 50–150 trials, as compared to Crossman's famous cigar-making data published in 1959 which shows the results of >10,000,000 practice trials).

Adams (1971) called this phase the verbal–motor phase because he believed that movement was under verbal control, which places a heavy demand on 'cognitive' processing. (The term cognitive is used very loosely here since much of movement control is central in nature even in later phases of learning.) Fitts (1964) referred to this phase as the cognitive phase because he believed that the learner is trying to understand the task during this stage of the learning process. This latter idea sounds very much like the ACT model, since it assumes that the early stage of skill learning is the acquisition of declarative or factual knowledge. For example, in Newell's (1981) review, under the heading of information prior to movement, he stated, 'Before attempting any action, the performer ideally should have some knowledge about the goal of the act, together with some understanding of the ways through which the goal can be accomplished.' One must be careful not to overemphasize the terms knowledge and cognitive however, since it is not at all clear how much, if any, actual skill learning can accrue without actually moving. Fitts and Posner (1967) believe that the learner selects from existing subroutines to produce the initial movements and that through the diagnostic use of knowledge of results the initial aspects of the executive program are formulated. Bandura (1986) points out that a distinction must be made between skill and knowledge as he anecdotally concludes, 'A novice given complete information on how to ski, a set of decision rules, and then launched from a mountain top would most likely end up in an orthopedic ward . . .' Thus even though there is a degree of consensus as to what is gained during the early phase of learning there is only sparse research support for a direct link between this knowledge and skilled performance. For example, instructors usually use demonstrations to convey this knowledge and as Newell (1981) concluded, 'if we were to judge the effectiveness of demonstrations by the empirical literature one would wonder why they are generally accepted as facilitating the skill-learning process at all.'

Issues concerning the cognitive phase

What seems obvious is that a skill learner would need some type of translation mechanism to convert knowledge into action, however there is almost no research concerning the existence or ontogeny of such a mechanism. This idea has been studied under the rubric of intersensory integration and possibly the best-known research in this area was a study of children's drawing abilities by Birch and Lefford (1967). Children from the ages of 5 to 11 years were tested for abilities in visual recognition, visual analysis, visual synthesis, intersensory integration, and drawing figures (diamonds and triangles) from a model. Although all of these capabilities increased with age as expected, most interestingly only intersensory integration correlated with the ability to draw figures from a model. They argued that, although perceptual capabilities are present relatively early in life, intersensory integration skills (especially visual-kinesthetic) continue to improve until at least 11 years of age, and it is this translation skill which underlies improvements in movement skills such as drawing from a visual model. Thus, demonstrations and instructions to convey 'goal knowledge' may not be successful unless translation capabilities are well learned.

It is important to note that Birch's and Lefford's model is not totally supported by other research, and in particular a study by Millar (1975) does not appear to support the ontogeny of intersensory integration skills, since she was unable to show that stimulus complexity had any effect on cross-modal matching scores. However, only in her second experiment was age an independent variable and it is not clear that stimulus complexity affects only translation and not perceptual mechanisms as well. In fact, Millar found that perceptual complexity affected intersensory and intramodal matching equally, suggesting to me at least that complexity may be a perceptual problem.

An area of research which has rekindled an interest in the effectiveness of modeling to convey movement information during early skill acquisition is Bandura's ideas about observational learning. Bandura (1986) claims that both temporal and spatial aspects of movement can be gained through observation and indeed this has been shown to be the case with both adults and children and with both auditory and visual information. For example, Ross et al. (1985) showed that observing a perfect model paired with physical practice produced superior performance during withdrawal of knowledge of results than physical practice alone. These results are not inconsistent with Keele's (1977) idea that the model is stored as a template of ideal feedback, which can be used to correct the motor program. A study by Adams (1985) suggests that this may be over-simplistic however, since observers benefited from watching an unskilled performer learn a timing skill. In addition, Adams found that a group that heard the model receive knowledge of results was superior to a modeling group that did not have access to this information. These results are more in line with Bandura's claim that the modeled information is stored as an abstraction rather than as a physical copy of the ideal feedback.

There are many such issues concerning observational learning, and Scully and Newell (1985) have recently presented a review of observational learning and the acquisition of motor skills, in which they concluded that the area in general suffers from a lack of a comprehensive theoretical model. For example, they argued that more information is needed about what movement cues are picked up through observation, before principles can be developed. Scully and Newell also concluded that 'the effectiveness of modeling is task-specific and that novelty of the movement sequence mediates the impact of the demonstration', and that no operational definition of novelty exists. This latter point is only partially correct however, since Bandura (1986) claimed, in true behavioristic style, that a response is novel if there is a zero probability that the response in question could occur. (This definition must be treated more figuratively than literally since it is difficult to see how one could measure such a probability.) In contrast, to define novelty in terms of physical capability would lead one to conclude that an experienced pianist who has just mastered a 'new' piece has not learned anything. These ideas are in concert with Fitts' and Posner's notion reviewed above that nothing new is learned in adulthood and that most learning is simply the recombination of old habits in new ways. Thus, although it is clear that modeling can facilitate skill learning in some circumstances and not in others, it is not clear why this is the case.

Another way to communicate goal information is through verbal instructions, but as previously concluded by Newell (1981) little research has been done in this area in the last two decades. It does serve to point out, however, that a distinction may be made between knowledge about the goal of the response, which surely can be communicated by instructions and providing a feel for the correct response. A method often suggested to convey a 'feeling' for movement during the early phase of skill learning is physical guidance. In leafing through recent textbooks on motor learning, however, many books say nothing about guidance, and those that do, quote studies which were completed well before 1970. The most comprehensive review of this area seems to be a technical report completed by Armstrong (1970a). The problem with guidance research is that, like the research on observational learning, the results as to its benefits are mixed, and indeed Armstrong concluded that guidance seems to be task-specific and may be either better or worse than an equal amount of active physical practice. In addition, Holding (1965) concluded that guidance was most effective if it resembled the final form of the task and normal movement patterns. This latter point will be expanded later under transfer, but implies that if the guidance training leads the performer to learn an improper movement strategy then this could be detrimental rather than facilitatory to later performance.

It is perhaps interesting to note that in many respects much of the research on motor short-term memory could be considered under the topic of guidance, since quite often the criterion to be remembered was a constrained movement to a mechanical stop. In fact, studies like that of Adams and Dykstra (1966) could have been considered the study of the effects of guided practice on later movement performance. For example, a recent study by Hagman (1983) reported to be studying 'presentation- and test-trial effects on the acquisition and retention of distance and location'. A presentation-trial required the subject to make a constrained movement to a mechanical stop (linear positioning), whereas a test trial required a recall movement without a stop. A standard group alternated presentation- and test-trials in a one-to-one manner for 18 total trials. A test group had one presentation trial followed by five test trials, repeated three times and a presentation group had five presentation trials followed by one test trial, repeated three times. These trials were followed by a three-minute and then a 24-hour retention test. Not uncharacteristic of what one would predict for guidance, the test group was the worst during acquisition (for errors on comparable test trials) but the best during retention. It is not clear to me under what topic such results should be reviewed, but they do stand to point out the potential overlap among areas of research.

INTERMEDIATE OR ASSOCIATIVE PHASE OF LEARNING

What gets learned?

It is during this phase, according to Fitts and Posner (1967), that the learner begins work on diminishing the response errors which are inherent in the performance of a new skill. Once the performer understands the task require-ments he can begin to apply old habits to test their appropriateness under new conditions. The length of this error-reduction period will depend on the complexity of the task and what the learner is able to transfer from past experiences. If this is indeed the process under study during this period, then it would seem logical that areas of research such as knowledge of results, short-term or working memory, and transfer would be appropriate for discussion.

The role of knowledge of results

There have been several comprehensive reviews of this area over the years (i.e. Holding, 1965; Bilodeau, 1969; Newell, 1974; Salmoni et al., 1984) and thus no attempt will be made here to duplicate these works (see also Chapter 2, this volume). Rather, some concerns will be discussed, both from a prac-tical and theoretical perspective.

Probably one of the major theoretical problems in this area is the inconsist-ency with which knowledge of results has been defined. Bilodeau (1969) called knowledge of results 'information feedback' and defined it as those stimulus consequences under the experimenter's control; whereas Salmoni et al. (1984) defined it as verbal, terminal, augmented feedback. In contrast, Holding (1965) offered a classification system for the different categories of knowledge of results, which gives a much broader perspective for knowledge of results. This system can be seen below. The irony of this inconsistency is that some researchers view knowledge of results as the most important variable in promoting learning (e.g. Bilodeau, 1969), whereas other researchers have argued that knowledge of results is a research artifact and is irrelevant to learning in the natural environment (e.g. Fowler and Turvey, 1978).

KNOWLEDGE OF RESULTS

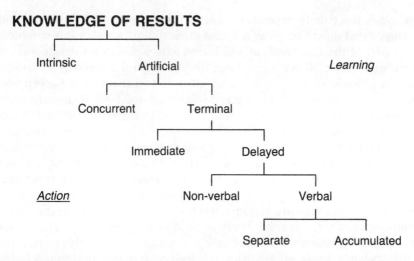

Figure 46. Different kinds of knowledge of results. (From Holding, 1965.) Reproduced by permission of Pergamon Press.

It is my contention that part of the problem is the definition and part is the experimental design that evolved to study knowledge of results (e.g. see Bilodeau, 1969). Indeed, Bilodeau (1969) claimed that the experimental task was irrelevant, and furthermore that the response goal and units of information feedback should be unknown to the subject to minimize transfer from past experience. However, if adult learning is largely a matter of using old habits in new ways, then this strategy hardly seems appropriate. In most natural learning situations the response goal and units of response error are well defined prior to the beginning of the learning experience. Indeed, Salmoni et al. (1983) have shown that the presence or absence of this information may potentially change the effect of the independent variable. In addition, Salmoni et al. (1985) produced data to show that the type of experimental task (e.g. timing, force production, or positioning) interacted with these sources of information in the determination of response accuracy. Since it is unlikely that consensus on a definition of knowledge of results can be reached, the next best strategy would be to study how information like knowledge of results interacts with different types of tasks (ballistic, slow positioning, complex, etc.) during learning.

A related topic is how to measure learning, which again suffers from definitional inconsistencies as well as a perspective problem. These definitional inconsistencies prompted researchers at the 1987 North American Society for the Psychology of Sport and Physical Activity meeting in Vancouver to argue that the no KR transfer design argued for by Salmoni et al. (1984) was incorrect. They argued that acquisition trials, with knowledge of results present are a valid measure of degree of task learning.

Obviously this debate depends on whether one defines knowledge of results as augmented information, as Salmoni et al. did, or whether it is considered to be part of the task itself, in which case a no KR transfer design does not seem appropriate. It was clear from the review in the theories section that interest in knowledge of results evolved from two theoretical backgrounds. On one hand, knowledge of results has been viewed by S–R investigators as similar in nature to a reinforcer which is added by the researcher to influence learning and which ultimately will be removed to see if performance is maintained in the absence of this augmented information. On the other hand, from an information-processing perspective, knowledge of results has been viewed as a type of feedback used for the assessment of response accuracy.

The former position seems to argue in favor of a no knowledge of results transfer design to measure learning, whereas the latter position argues against removing knowledge of results because feedback is present when performing most skills. (Obviously this contrast is oversimplified since there are certain instances were 'artificial' feedback is added to facilitate performance when the intrinsic feedback is impoverished.) A related consequence of these theoretical positions is that some topics, such as frequency and temporal locus of knowledge of results, seem more appropriate as 'reinforcement' topics than as 'feedback' topics. In addition, some researchers emphasize a feedback approach, whereas others emphasize the reinforcement aspect, while still others clearly combine both views. The problem is that when these positions are left unspecified, it is impossible to reconcile differences on logical grounds. Although Fowler and Turvey (1978) may argue that the feedback approach to the study of knowledge of results is not ecologically valid, there is no question that in many instances information is added for the learner's benefit (reinforcement approach) which can be validly studied using typical methodologies.

A consistent question in the literature has been whether learning can occur in the absence of knowledge of results. Certainly early research by Thorndike (1927) had shown that accuracy in drawing a line of a specified length while blindfolded could not be improved unless knowledge of results was present. However, more recent research concerning observational (e.g. Ross et al., 1985) learning has shown that this is not entirely true, and as long as some reference for correctness exists, whether it is externally provided through knowledge of results or internally stored as some type of memory representation, learning can occur. Indeed, Newell, Morris, and Scully (1985) argue that single-dimensional movements overestimate the value of knowledge of results because no other information besides the response goal is relevant. They argue that a more fruitful approach would be to study different modes of error information (e.g. kinematic and kinetic knowledge of performance) and their interaction with more complex movements. Although I agree with their point wholeheartedly, I also believe that an additional point is worth making. If the goal of KR research is to understand how feedback works, then the number of task dimensions and the type of information feedback may be completely irrelevant, unless it can be shown that kinetic and kinematic information acts in a qualitatively different way from traditional knowledge of results. In addition, using more complex movements is not necessarily more ecologically valid since kinematic and kinetic information are obviously artificially injected into the learning situation. Thus, this approach is aimed at seeing what type of information should be added to the natural setting to enhance learning.

A classic study in this area by Hatze (1976) required a subject to learn to make a leg extension movement as quickly as possible. For the first 120 trials the subject received knowledge of results concerning movement time, and as would be expected, movement time decreased. For a subsequent 100 trials the subject was shown a force-time trace of his response and the calculated optimal force-time curve. Learning continued beyond the level of the original knowledge of results trials, thus showing that learning of a more complex movement benefits from a different type of information from that traditionally provided. Newell, Sparrow, and Quinn (cited in Newell et al., 1985) have shown that graphically presented force-time traces facilitate the performance of an isometric force production task beyond the level achieved by a traditional knowledge of results group. Unfortunately, the evidence is not clear that the kinetic information produced a longlasting effect, since performance deteriorated when this information was removed (no feedback transfer trials). In addition, neither of these studies provides evidence that these information sources produce qualitatively different results from traditionally presented knowledge of results.

In summary, there seems to be a shift in the research in the areas of knowledge of results and performance, away from an emphasis on feedback toward an emphasis on the reinforcement or augmented nature of this information. This is probably true because of questions concerning the validity of this research area in terms of a model for feedback and because of the disagreements concerning the measurement of learning. This shift means that topics such as relative frequency of knowledge of results and long-term benefits of knowledge of results will receive increasing experimental attention.

The role of working memory in skill learning?

As was the case in other areas of experimental psychology, a great deal of research effort concentrated on the role of short-term memory for movements in the 1960s and 1970s. Since the intent of any practice session for skill learning is to enhance future movement reproduction, early attention focused on rehearsal of movement information in the hope of understanding how memory for movement becomes permanent. An influential study by Posner (1967) showed that whereas visual memory for movement could be maintained over an empty retention interval, kinesthetic information was lost, whether rehearsal was blocked or not. Thus, although these particular results were possibly an artifact of the methodology used (see Holding, 1968), much research concerning the rehearsal of kinesthetic memory codes followed. For example, Laabs (1973) subsequently demonstrated that movement location but not movement extent could be rehearsed. Thus, much of the research in this area dealt with how movement was encoded and the different encoding strategies employed by subjects (e.g. Roy and Diewert, 1975).

Unfortunately research evidence from the cognitive domain began to mount that cast considerable doubt on the distinction between short-term and long-term memory (see Crowder, 1982). Of greater concern however, was the fact that knowledge about short-term memory did not explain individual differences in certain skills. Most notably perhaps was the research on reading, since most people had hypothesized that reading skill should depend on short-term memory capacity. Indeed, no difference in capacity was found between good and poor readers. Another area where short-term memory was less than successful was in explaining developmental differences in cognition. Research in motor short-term memory has also largely been abandoned, partly because of the loss of interest for memory research in cognitive psychology and partly because the link between the memory research and learning research was difficult to make. For example, although a time delay was usually detrimental to movement reproduction, this did not seem to be the case for knowledge of results studies. Perhaps the only area within the memory domain that has received continued attention in cognitive psychology is working memory, although is not the case for movement retention.

Despite these problems there are at least two areas of continued interest in memory for movements that seem to have potential. One of the contributing factors in the abandonment of the long-term/short-term distinction was the levels of processing model of memory (see Craik and Craik, 1979), which emphasized strategies for encoding and retrieval of information. For example, Shea (1977) has shown that providing subjects with the hours on a clock-face aids memory recall for a curvilinear movement. Even though the levels of processing approach has since been dropped work on related areas like contextual interference (to be discussed below) continues.

A more recent, but largely unknown direction is to look at how cognitive styles might interact with encoding strategies in the memory for movement. Anshel and Ortiz (1986) identified subjects with verbal, visual, and tactual cognitive styles and provided learners with coding strategies to either match or not match these styles. Memory for movement extent was always best if the coding strategy matched the cognitive style of the subject. A note of caution is in order however, since other similar studies have not shown cognitive style to be a very powerful variable in movement learning. Still, this individual difference approach to the study of memory seems to have merit especially in an applied setting. For example, Meacci and Price (1985) found a cognitive intervention technique of relaxation, visualization, and body rehearsal to facilitate acquisition and retention of a golf putting stroke.

Another exciting direction for movement retention research comes from the present interest in knowledge structures, as discussed in Anderson's (1976) ACT model above. Ericsson's (1985) memory skill hypothesis claims that memory ability is a complex skill acquired through extensive practice, and that information is encoded in terms of knowledge structures. In addition, the speed of encoding and retrieval processes are dramatically improved with practice, giving these long-term memory processes the behavioral characteristics of what was once ascribed to short-term memory. The memory skill hypothesis predicts that memory is very specific to the skill being practised and this is important in the present context since it has long been accepted that motor skills are specific. These notions would lead one to do memory research with specific skill information and with skilled individuals. Indeed, Starkes (1987) has shown that national team field hockey players recall game-structured information better than lesser skilled players and non-players. What is not clear from this research, however, is whether recall is reconstructive or reproductive. In line with the above notions Starkes also found that skilled players were superior to unskilled players in all tests which were game-specific but that there were few significant differences when general ability measures were used (e.g. dynamic visual acuity). This research will be discussed further below under the topic of skill analysis.

Neisser (1985) concluded that past research suffered because the hypothetico-deductive model is not valid for behavioral research, and when this model was combined with a mentalistic approach, using artificial laboratory settings, memory for such materials was not representative of memory in general. In a Gibsonian fashion, Neisser argues that 'before we can theorize effectively about memory, we must get a better understanding of the sorts of things that are remembered'. He goes on to comment that it is possible that retention for motor skills could be different from other kinds of memory. Taken together these comments are rather disconcerting because they could be used to argue that all previous motor memory research has no ecological validity and that a completely new approach, as yet unidentified, needs to be developed. Thus, it is fair to conclude that the role of memory in the associative phase (or any phase) of skill learning is mostly hypothetical at this point in time.

Transfer of training

During the associative phase of learning the performer, according to Fitts (1964), begins to eliminate response errors and also to associate old habits in new ways to meet the new task demands. If this view is correct, transfer is of obvious importance to skill learning. Indeed, the topic of transfer is reviewed in most texts dealing with skill learning. Having said this however, it is also true, as noted by Newell (1981), that there has been little research interest in this area over the last fifteen years. Mackay (1982) concluded that despite the rather large amount of research on transfer (i.e. mostly in the 1940–65 era and much of this research in verbal learning), 'little is known about why transfer either occurs or fails to occur'. This serves to highlight the fact that skill research is still in its infancy and at the same time it is somewhat humbling for researchers, since it could be argued that transfer is potentially one of the most important issues in skill learning.

Why is it then, that little is known nor being done in this area? I believe that the main reason for this is that the two theoretical models that have dominated transfer research have been inadequate. Little new has happened since Thorndike (see Hilgard and Bower, 1966) proposed that transfer was the result of identical elements being transferred from one task to another. Indeed Osgood's (1949) transfer surface, which is based on S–R psychology notions, is still referred to today even though admittedly almost wholly inadequate for skill learning. This surface was designed to explain the findings for paired associate verbal learning and the early motor skill research on transfer was simply a derivative of this.

For example, Gagné and Foster (1949) looked at transfer from a two- to a four-choice reaction time condition, for which the two-choice S–R pairs were identical to the same two pairs found in the four-choice condition. Interestingly, although positive transfer was found, the researchers also noted that any amount of initial practice in the two-choice condition was not as efficient (in terms of total trials to criterion on the four-choice task) as practising the four-choice condition alone. On the other hand, the individual difference or motor abilities approach to transfer of skill learning has also been problematic, as the above results suggest, because skills seem to require specific abilities and thus a great deal of transfer is not predicted. Although this latter prediction is generally supported in the literature (e.g. see the discussion of memory skill above), it seems counterintuitive for many researchers and practioners. Thus what seems to be needed is a new approach.

Holding (1976) attempted to modify Osgood's transfer surface by incorporating some of the more recent findings from skill learning research. This surface can be seen in Figure 47 below. One of the important points that Holding made, was that intrusion errors rather than performance scores are

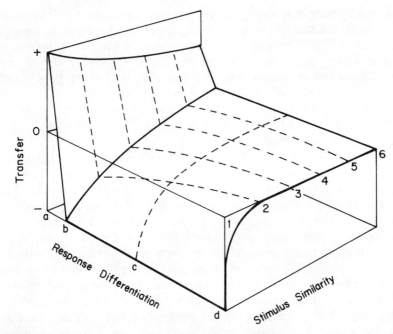

Figure 47. A transfer surface: expected interference between two tasks as dependent upon their input and output characteristics. (From Holding, 1976.) Reproduced by permission of Heldref.

the most appropriate measures for transfer research. In addition, the surface predicts that most transfer between skills will occur early in learning, since task differentiation increases with practice. As well, Holding concluded that both negative and positive transfer occurs in any skill learning situation, making the detection of transfer with global response measures difficult. Despite these improvements, as Holding admitted from the outset, the surface has several shortcomings and is thus only a slight improvement on Osgood's surface.

A slightly different view of transfer is offered by Mackay's (1982) model in which skill is represented as a hierarchically organized group of interconnected nodes. Since movement can be represented from a conceptual down to a muscle-specific level, transfer can also be mediated at several levels. In support of a conceptual level of transfer, Mackay discusses an intriguing experiment by himself and Bowman (cited in Mackay, 1982) dealing with the reading aloud of sentences first in one language (German) and then in a second language (English) by bilingual performers. Practice of a specific sentence in one language produced high positive transfer to the reading for speed in the other language even though the muscle commands would be entirely different in the two languages. Mackay claimed that these results supported transfer at a conceptual (in this case 'grammar' level) level, since there was no transfer when randomly organized words or sounds were practised. Newell (1981) argued that most support for positive transfer in skill learning comes from studies where the transfer involves simple metric changes from task A to task B (e.g. changes in speed of the pursuit rotor). On the other hand, he concluded that structural changes (e.g. changes in the rhythm of a musical piece) leads to negative transfer. It is not clear where Mackay's results would fit into this latter model, but it serves to exemplify the shortage of theoretical thinking in this area.

Most of the recent research discussion concerning transfer has centered not on the investigation of transfer *per se* but on how one should measure learning. Part of this debate was fueled by Schmidt's (1975) schema theory, since the theory predicted that appropriate practice during acquisition would allow the performer to transfer to a novel situation. This debate has also been fueled by the notion put forward by Salmoni et al. (1984) that the proper paradigm to measure the effectiveness of manipulating knowledge of results is by having all experimental groups transfer to a common no knowledge of results condition after a certain number of acquisition trials. As implied above, a transfer paradigm with withdrawal of knowledge of results makes sense from a learning theory perspective but does not necessarily make sense from a cybernetic or specificity perspective, since performance in the natural context is rarely without the aid of feedback and most learning situations appear to be task-specific. I believe that the best statement in this regard was made by Bransford et al. (1979), who claimed that the 'value of particular acquisition activities can be defined only in relation to the nature of the testing context', which I translated to mean only in the context of what is ultimately required of the performer. What is necessary then, is for the researcher to define the ultimate context for the performance and in so doing would rationalize the appropriate design. This would mean that several different paradigms are reasonable and all would provide interesting findings.

Since Bransford et al. (1979) argued that a transfer design was most appropriate for memory research, they discussed a concept they called 'transfer appropriate processing'. This concept means that what is important is not the level of performance during acquisition trials, but whether what is being learned or processed is beneficial for later performance or acquisition. A notion which has grown out of these ideas is that of contextual interference, which suggests that certain acquisition activities may facilitate transfer but debilitate performance during acquisition. For example, Shea and Morgan (1979) found that although a random presentation of test items (i.e. sequential movements) produced the worst performance during acquisition, the same group performed the best during transfer trials, which required making a novel sequence of movements. These results suggest that what is important for transfer is to maximize the generalizability or the flexibility of the performer during acquisition, such that later performance or learning can be most effective and efficient. The question still remains however as to how to maximize this effect and to what extent transfer can be expected if at all.

AUTONOMOUS PHASE OF LEARNING

Fitts (1964) hypothesized that during the autonomous or final phase of skill learning speed and efficiency of performance gradually improve. Indeed, Newell and Rosenbloom (1981) called this the 'ubiquitous law of practice', since plotting the logarithm of the time to perform a task against the logarithm of the trial number always yielded a straight line across a large range of tasks from cigar-making to card playing to sentence recognition. Thus, this final phase is by far the longest since improvements may continue indefinitely. A second result of practice according to Fitts (1964) was that tasks became less subject to cognitive control and to interference. Thus with practice, skills seem to require less processing. Although researchers may not agree with the exact phraseology used by Fitts in this regard, these latter changes are generally referred to today as changes towards automatization and it is this process which I shall discuss next.

Automatization

It is generally held that with practice the performance of a single skill becomes less effortful or that two or more skills can be performed simultaneously with a minimum of interference. These hypothesized changes seem very reasonable to most practitioners and researchers since this seems to be consistent with personal experience. Interestingly however, why this change occurs is still a mystery, although several theories have been espoused to explain its occurrence. Bahrick and Shelly (1958) defined automatization as the gradual change from exteroceptive to proprioceptive control during prolonged practice of a repetitive task, although they admitted that no operations were known which could define the process.

In their research, subjects received extensive practice on a sequential key press task (i.e. subjects were required to press keys with the four fingers of the right hand in the order of the onset of the four lights above the keys). Four groups of subjects learned this task under four conditions of sequential predictability, from a repetitive to a random order of lights. Subjects also practised a four-choice auditory reaction time task with the left hand. On certain training sessions subjects were required to perform the two tasks simultaneously. After several training sessions there were no differences among the groups in their performance of the tasks individually but there were significant differences in dual task performance. Specifically, interference between the tasks was inversely related to the predictability of the sequential visual task and this interference decreased with practice, although there was no change after session 14. This was a very rich experiment because it demonstrated clear automaticity.

As ubiquitous as the belief in the behavioral manifestations of automaticity appear to be, there is almost no consensus on what exactly allows this behavior to evolve. Thus, although most textbooks on skill learning mention automaticity, few authors do more than review the different theories that have been developed to try to explain the phenomenon (none satisfactorily) and to review the methodological issues inherent in dual task research. For example, Heuer and Wing (1984) have done a nice job of reviewing the theoretical notions behind dual task performance and Duncan (1980) and McLeod (1980) have offered valuable criticisms of the current research methodology.

Over the past fifteen years the most prominent explanation for the changes in task interference seen in experiments such as Bahrick's and Shelly's (1958), was the general capacity model. This model hypothesizes that a performer has a centrally limited processing capacity which is engaged to some degree by the task at hand. The degree of engagement is referred to as the attention demand or the mental effort required by the task. When a second task is performed it will interfere to the degree that both tasks require more capacity than is available. This conceptualization can be seen in Figure 48 below, which contrasts the attention demands (i.e. area of the circle) of a 'complex' and a 'simple' task. Interference is manifested as less than optimal performance on one or both tasks performed dually, as compared to single-task performance. Figure 48 depicts the complex task requiring more of the limited capacity than the simple task and thus the probe task (a reaction time task) will be performed faster when done in conjunction with the simple task than the complex task. This model would suggest that the predictable or redundant light sequences in Bahrick's and Shelly's experiment required less central capacity than the random sequences and thus allowed for superior dual-task performance. In addition, as subjects learned more about the sequential dependencies built into the visual task, the attention demands for that task would diminish resulting in less interference and better dual task performance.

These notions have been expanded as researchers have attempted to discover the degree to which different processes within a task require attention. These ideas are depicted in Figure 49, which shows the changes in available capacity (the part of the pie remaining) over the course of the task performance. One might reinterpret Bahrick's and Shelly's results to mean that the internalization of the movement control cues (i.e. exteroceptive to proprioceptive control) meant that movement became more automatic with practice because the processes required for control were less attention demanding. The general capacity model was not without its difficulties

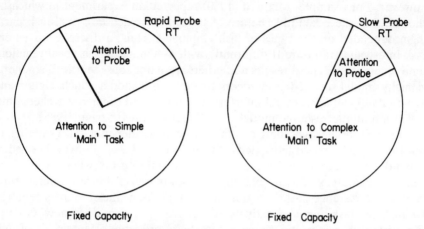

Figure 48. Assumptions of the probe-RT task: with fixed total capacity, attention to the probe decreases as the complexity of the main task increases. (From Schmidt, 1982). Reproduced by permission.

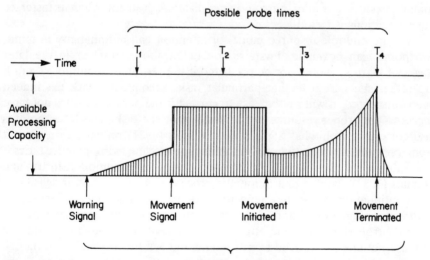

Figure 49. A possible distribution of processing capacity in a system common to both the probe and movement tasks during the time when a movement is being produced. (From McLeod, 1980.) Reproduced by permission of North-Holland Publishing Co.

however. For example, McLeod (1980) reported an experiment in which he showed that the qualitative nature of task interference in a dual-task paradigm depended on the types of task employed. Thus, a discrete movement task interacted (interfered) differently with a manual than a vocal reaction-time second task. These results and others were not consistent with a general capacity model and led researchers to develop a model which Heuer and Wing (1980) call a structural interference model, and other researchers have called a multiple resource model (e.g. Wickens, 1984; Logan, 1985).

This new model hypothesizes that performance depends on a number of resources, each limited in capacity. Since different tasks are hypothesized to depend on different resources, interference only occurs when tasks share common resources and the pairing of tasks is crucial in determining what type of interference pattern is obtained. In addition, the resources required by a certain task may qualitatively change with practice. This 'new' description of the processes underlying automaticity probably offers an air of *déjà vu* for the movement skills reader, as they sound very similar to hypotheses put forward for specificity three decades ago. Indeed, even though specificity was well documented in movement skills much earlier, this notion is now receiving considerable interest and support in cognitive psychology. For example, in Logan's review of skill and automaticity (and the multiple resource model) he concluded that 'the implication [of this model] is that automatization should result in very specific ways of performing a task, which should produce a rather narrow generalization gradient when transfer to other situations is tested.'

With the multiple-resource model of attention and automaticity in mind, two points can be made. First, as concluded above, transfer in the later stages of learning would not be predicted if the resources required by a task are rather specialized to that particular task. Second, if a task has indeed been automated, it will not be easy to correct if the performer does not have access to the proper resources while performing the task. This latter point is also consistent with what Shiffrin and Dumais (1981) referred to as a shift from controlled processing to automatic processing with practice. Error correction is not possible under automatic-processing conditions. Shiffrin and Dumais (1981) claimed that automatic processes have a certain indivisibility and continuation, since they tend to occur in units and run to completion before stopping. In addition, they argued that automatic processes tend not to be controlled directly, and often appear to be at an unconscious level. All of these notions are derived from research in cognitive psychology although they sound very similar to aspects of motor behavior explained presently by notions like the motor program.

The ideas concerning the evolution from controlled processing, which is slow, effortful, and capacity-limited or attention-demanding to automatic processing, which is fast, effortless, and not capacity-limited have been expanded by Schneider, Dumais, and Shiffrin (1985). There research has shown that automatic processing can only emerge after practice under consistent task conditions. For example, if a subject performs in a memory scanning task the target and distractor items can remain constant (i.e. constant mapping) or they may vary randomly over trials (varied mapping). It has been found that although conditions do not have to be totally consistent, a certain degree of consistency is necessary for automatic processing to develop. Under automatic processing conditions (i.e. extensive practice under consistent conditions) reaction time is not affected by positive set size, whereas under controlled processing (exhaustive serial search) reaction time is a positive function of set size. Schneider (1985b) has developed a computerized version of the change from controlled to automatic processing.

Although these ideas are still being formulated they appear to hold promise for motor skill learning. For example, past research has supported schema theory's (as reviewed above) prediction that varied practice should be superior to constant practice, as indicated by transfer performance on a novel skill. An alternative explanation is that varied practice (like practice under varied mapping) allows for controlled processing, whereas constant practice allows the development of automatic processing. Since controlled processing is necessary for novel tasks (as argued by Schneider et al., 1985) this could explain the superiority of varied practice on transfer. This argument would offer an alternative explanation for the contextual interference research also. Thus, under varied practice or contextual interference conditions it may not be that something unique is learned but rather that automatic processing does not develop. Some support for this notion comes from a study by Lee, Magill, and Weeks (1985), who studied practice schedules for schema learning. Not only was varied practice beneficial, as predicted by schema theory, but subjects in this condition also took significantly more time to prepare their response than subjects did under constant practice conditions.

Many of the findings concerning negative transfer in motor skills are also consistent with the controlled/automatic processing distinction. In transferring to a second task, subjects may be required to perform in a way which is incompatible with previously learned (on the first task) automatic processing. This then would provide an explanation for negative transfer in the later stages of skill learning. The above results emphasize the far-reaching nature that research in automatization could have. Thus Shiffrin and Dumais (1981) concluded, and it seems equally relevant now, that 'we think automatization is a major component of skill acquisition in both cognitive and motor domains and suggest that this factor be given prominent research attention.'

Knowledge acquisition

Neves and Anderson (1981) offered an alternative explanation for the development of automaticity, suggesting that automization in cognitive skills was the result of a change from declarative to procedural knowledge. They argued that encoding, proceduralization, and composition are the three major operations coinciding with Fitts' (1964) three stages of learning. Proceduralization refers to the conversion of declarative to procedural knowledge, and composition (occurring during the autonomous phase) is the pairing or chunking together of productions to form single productions. Since it is assumed that the time to execute a skill is proportional to the number of productions fired, the process of composition leads to a speeding-up of performance during the autonomous phase. Thus proceduralization and composition lead to both automatization and increased response speed. According to Neves and Anderson (1981) there is a cost involved however, and that is a loss in adaptability.

The argument is that because a single production is now doing the job of what during earlier phases might have been done by five productions, the skilled performer is less able to change his production. This does not sit well intuitively with our view of highly skilled athletes who seem to be extremely adaptable in game situations. I do not believe there is a contradiction, however. This loss of adaptability that Neves and Anderson are referring to is, I believe, that a highly learned production becomes more and more specific as practice continues and this particular production cannot easily be adapted to a new situation through learning. Thus a boxer or a chess player who has learned a certain style of attack cannot change that particular production easily. At the same time however, a skilled performer has gained many more productions than an unskilled performer and thus can choose among a number of productions. Thus, the skilled performer can choose from a large variety of highly learned productions, each one of which is not adaptable singly, but in total number make the skilled performer very flexible during an actual performance. For example, an Olympic freestyle swimmer may have 'perfected' a shallow, medium-depth, and a deep turn, any one of which he can decide to use for a given turn. An unskilled swimmer likely has only one turn to use during a race.

As mentioned earlier, memory research (and in particular short-term memory) formed the backbone of much of the research in cognitive psychology over the last three decades and cognitive development was no exception. When age changes in short-term memory proved less than successful in explaining cognitive development, researchers turned to meta-cognition and metamemory to find the answers. Unfortunately this did not produce the answers either and researchers began to look in other directions for cues as to how children become skilled in cognitive tasks. Some of the best-known research in this area looked at the performance of skilled versus novice chess players (e.g. Chi, 1978). It was found, for example, that skilled ten-year-old players could recall significantly more chess board positions than novice adults, even though the adults were superior to the children when tested under typical memory span conditions (i.e. number of digits recalled). More recent research in this area has begun to look at children's reasoning.

Gobbo and Chi (1986) compared the performance of expert and novice (in terms of dinosaur knowledge) children on a production task (i.e. generate information about dinosaurs) and a sort task (i.e. put dinosaurs into classes). They found that the experts' knowledge was more structured as well as focused on deeper-level concepts than the novices, who focused on surface-type features. In addition, the experts used their knowledge in a much more sophisticated fashion when reasoning about response choices. This type of research has focused on three important points for skill learning. First, skilled cognitive behavior seems to rely heavily on a person's experience (versus age) and second, knowledge, and therefore performance, seems to be domain-specific. Lastly, much of the retention performance displayed by experts appears to be reconstructive rather than reproductive. Although these ideas are not necessarily new to skill learning, the emphasis they are receiving in cognitive psychology is. It would seem that this could potentially pull all areas concerned with skill learning closer together. Recent studies on skill in sport are a good example of this.

What are the characteristics which distinguish a skilled performer in a given sport from a novice? Studies which have relied on an abilities approach to this problem have been less than successful. For example, Starkes (1987) has shown that general abilities tests such as dynamic visual acuity, simple visual reaction time and coincidence timing accuracy did not distinguish novice from skilled (national team members) field hockey players. On the other hand, tests such as shot prediction and strategic decision-making accuracy and speed, which are specific to field hockey, did afford discrimination. Indeed, Allard and Burnett (1985) in their review of skill in sport concluded that sports skills develop in much the same way as cognitive skills.

There are problems with this new approach, however. The first problem with the knowledge-based skill analysis technique is that it assumes that the knowledge is a determinant of game skill, when it could be just as logically the case (since these are non-causal studies) that this game-specific knowledge is a byproduct of experience in the sport. It should be noted that this is not a criticism of this exciting line of research, but rather a caution as to how these findings might be applied to the sports world. Perhaps a more serious problem is that the model assumes that skilled performers are those who have proceduralized the most declarative knowledge and that this procedural knowledge is non-verbal in nature. Yet, the tests being used to distinguish skilled from unskilled players are tapping declarative knowledge. Another issue is whether skill proceeds from declarative to procedural knowledge or vice versa. But despite these problems this approach to the study of skills is a very exciting advancement and it should lead to some worthwhile research findings.

CONCLUSIONS

In terms of science, skill learning is a very young field and indeed there are very few research findings that we would be willing to call laws of skill learning. However, Fitts' (1964) three stages of skill learning, although certainly not laws *per se*, seem to be just as pertinent in directing our thinking today as they were two decades ago. In fact, with the resurgent interest in skills in cognitive psychology during the 1980s this model perhaps has a greater following now then in the 1960s. As is probably the case in most areas of science, research interest in skill learning has been cyclic. Fueled by ideas from learning theory, there was an early interest in skill learning, led by people such as Thorndike and Hull. This largely theoretical interest was replaced by one of practical concern during the Second World War, when researchers actively explored issues concerning skill learning. With the lead of people like Adams and Posner, skill learning again gained a theoretical following in the 1960s and early 1970s. Recently however, there has been a swing away from skill learning toward an interest in human or skill performance. This shift is evident if one does a frequency count of the type of articles being published in the *Journal of Motor Behavior*. From 1969 to 1974 approximately 64% of the research articles dealt with skill learning, while 36% dealt with performance and motor control. From 1975 to 1980 the counts were 56% and 44% respectively. These figures show a continued decline in interest in skill learning from 1981 to 1986 as the numbers were 29% for skill learning and 71% for performance and control. I would guess there will be a shift back to a greater interest in skill learning as more researchers follow the lead in cognitive psychology.

So what do we know about motor skill learning? The best-known fact is what has been called the 'law of practice', which states that learning is a continuous, indefinite phenomenon following a power function. Equally accepted is the fact that skill learning is very specific. Other less concrete postulates include: much skill can be gained through observation, diagnostic error information is necessary to enhance skill, some transfer from old to new skills occurs, performance becomes increasingly automatic as practice continues.

SUMMARY

The first part of this chapter reviews those theories of learning which have been most influential in guiding the research thinking in the area of motor skill learning. Theories reviewed include: Thorndike's connectionism theory,

Hull's behavioral theory, Adams' closed-loop theory, Schmidt's schema theory, Bandura's observational learning theory, Anderson's ACT model, and information-processing models. Using Fitts' three stages of movement learning as a framework, the remainder of the chapter discusses topics which the author believes to be of primary concern for an overview of motor skill learning. Coinciding with the early phase of learning the topics discussed include: modeling, guidance and intersensory integration. Following this, topics such as transfer, motor short-term memory, and knowledge of results are presented. To parallel the final phase of learning, automatization and knowledge acquisition are discussed. Finally, the author attempts to draw some general conclusions about skill learning.

Chapter 9

Cognitive motor skills

Ann M. Colley

A substantial proportion of the motor skills literature focuses on the control of different types of movement such as discrete, sequential, ballistic, or slow positioning movements. Controversies over the organization and control of these various movement skills have arisen which have concentrated research effort on such issues as the relative merits of open- and closed-loop control (see, for example, Adams, 1976), and, more recently, on the divergent perspectives of the action systems/ecological and motor systems approaches to movement control (see, for example, Sheridan, 1988). The latter controversy has raised important questions concerning fundamental assumptions which are made in much of the skills literature, and in particular, the degree of involvement of higher level processes in the control of movement.

Cognitive motor skills are a class or 'family' (Shaffer, 1978) of skills, in which the involvement of higher-level processes is substantial and indisputable. These include speaking, writing, drawing, and musical performance. What they have in common is their requirement for the interpretation of symbolic material into a coordinated motor response sequence. Interest in these skills has arisen from two directions. First, it is of practical importance to know how they are acquired, and to know which factors facilitate their acquisition or contribute to their breakdown. With the exception of speaking (and even here there are a substantial number of special cases requiring therapy), they are taught. Second, and more important for the discussion which follows, it is of theoretical interest to know how control of these skills is organized.

When trying to understand and describe similarities and differences among the variety of human movement skills, one obvious dimension along which skills vary is in the amount of cognitive processing that they require prior to and during the execution of a movement. Many skills have a cognitive component of greater or lesser significance, and require decisions to be made for the selection and programming of a successful response. Not all of these

Human Skills. Edited by D. Holding © 1989 John Wiley & Sons Ltd

are very amenable to study because they take place in an environment which continually changes (open skills, Poulton, 1957a). Many sports skills fall into this category. These also differ from the cognitive motor skills already mentioned in several important respects: movements are made in response to perceptual information which could be perceived 'directly' in the Gibsonian sense (Gibson, 1979; Turvey and Carello, 1986); after the initial stages of acquisition, the involvement of cognitive processes in response selection may well be concerned entirely with strategy; the movements required in sports skills vary enormously, from ballistic aiming movements (for example, in darts) to slower sequences of interceptive movements (as in many ball games); the response made is neither an analog of the stimulus, nor does it necessarily translate physical characteristics of the stimulus into a different physical form (as occurs, for example, when writing to dictated speech, or sightreading music). They are, intuitively at least, a less coherent group of skills than typing, writing, musical performance, and speech, which, as Shaffer (1978) has argued, share important organizational features.

The issue of the partitioning of skills into areas of research which have evolved relatively independently will be taken up later in the chapter. The first part of the chapter will examine the individual skills of writing, typing, and speech and, by outlining models used to account for empirical findings, describe similarities in their organization.

HANDWRITING

The most comprehensive model of handwriting control has been presented by Ellis (1982), and the part of it which concerns response control is based upon a detailed study of his own writing errors over an eighteen-month period (Ellis, 1979). He proposes that there are three main representations for a letter. At the highest level is the *grapheme*, which is an abstract representation of a letter, which then has to be realized as an *allograph*, in which letter form has been selected (i.e. upper vs. lower case, etc.) and which is still in relatively abstract form since size and the muscle groups required to produce the letter are not specified. The spatial description provided by the allograph is then used to select the graphic motor pattern necessary to produce the *graph* which is the written realization of the allograph.

It is clear that there must be abstract representation of letter forms from the simple observation that it is possible to produce the same form when writing on a small piece of paper with a sharp pencil or with a spray can on a wall, or even with a different limb. It is clear also that there is a higher, more abstract representation which does not specify form because of the variety of letter forms used in different contexts. We not only use upper and lower case letter forms (A vs. a) but forms vary slightly between cursive handwriting and script, and also, as Ellis (1982) points out, according to the position of a letter within a word (the initial letter in a word is usually in script form, whereas the following letters are in cursive form; Wing, 1979), and formality (notes made for our own consumption are often barely legible to others). The analysis of writing errors undertaken by Ellis, served to confirm these observations and add detail to them. Most of the errors he found were omissions, intrusions or rearrangements in the letter sequences of words, which, by their nature, could be ascribed to a particular part of the conversion sequence from grapheme to graphic motor pattern. For example, one type of error confuses upper and lower case form, as in the example below from Ellis (1982, p. 129):

UNIVERSITY → UNi

This type of error must be localized prior to, or during, the selection of allographs. To give another example, letter substitution errors occur where a letter is replaced by one physically similar, but not in the immediate context, e.g.

Touch → touck

(from Ellis, 1982, p. 131). Ellis localizes these at the stage when the spatial code for a letter or allograph is used to select a graphic motor pattern for its execution. The wrong selection is made due to the physical similarity between the correct letter and the incorrect one.

Ellis's model gives a clear specification of the order and type of computations necessary between the specification of a letter to be written and the neuromuscular execution of the writing of that letter. The processes preceding the stages in Ellis's model will vary according to the mode of presentation of the word to be written. Some discussion of this is given in Ellis (1982). Ellis's model distinguishes between selection of a response as an abstract spatial code or allograph, and its execution in real time with size and temporal parameters fixed and appropriate muscular groups selected. Van Galen (1980) makes a similar distinction using the focal/ambient distinction first introduced by Trevarthen (1968) to account for phylogenetically older and more recent brain structures and associated information processing. Van Galen distinguishes between the focal stage of motor pattern retrieval and the ambient stage of parameter estimation for the execution of the movement. With the two stages are associated two types of memory. Motor patterns are stored as ordered sequences of movements described in terms of the relationship between temporal and spatial parameters. These are hierarchically organized, and frequently used or more recently used patterns have a lower threshold of activation. The temporal and spatial parameters used to execute the movement are computed in real time using general rules. (Van Galen acknowledges the similarities with Schmidt's schema theory here; Schmidt, 1975.) This is therefore a transient process which results in the rules rather than the parameters themselves being stored.

Van Galen distinguished between these two stages by examining latency of response and movement time separately in a serial drawing task with 4 to 6-year-old children. He assumed that latency provided a measure of the focal stage, whereas movement time would be affected by the ambient stage. Shape repetition, as predicted, decreased response latency but not movement time. He also examined repetition effects using two novel graphemes with adult subjects. Again, repetition reduced latency but not movement time. A control condition using a discrimination task confirmed that the effect was one of movement selection rather than stimulus repetition.

In subsequent work, Van Galen and collaborators have identified the need for three stages rather than two in response preparation: motor pattern retrieval or motor programming, parameter setting, and motor initiation, i.e. 'nerve impulses for specific muscles dependent on the actual anatomical and biomechanical context' (Van Galen and Teulings, 1983, p. 11). In an experiment which used a writing task, they manipulated three variables relating to the three stages: direction of execution of letters (motor pattern retrieval), size of the letter (parameter setting), and the orientation of letters with respect to a baseline (such that different anatomical and biomechanical conditions would prevail and so that motor initiation should vary). They found that all three variables affected response latencies, and that direction of execution and size were additive. Additive effects are usually taken as indicative of successive processing stages. The finding that direction of execution and orientation were not additive in their effects could be interpreted as pointing to the use of common processing resources for the two operations. However, a second possibility raised by Van Galen and Teulings is that the two processes may occur, at least partially, in parallel, i.e. that anatomical preselections can be made independently from other parts of the preparation process.

A second finding of some importance was that moment time increased for successive strokes in a grapheme in comparison with earlier ones, indicating that later strokes are unpacked during the execution of earlier ones. The same conclusion was drawn by Hulstijn and Van Galen (1983) from an experiment using a similar methodology. It therefore appears that only the first unit in a sequence is preprogrammed. The next and subsequent units are searched partly in parallel with the writing of previous units. This finding apparently generalizes to other orthographic forms, such as Chinese (Chau, Kao, and Shek, 1986). Some caution is necessary here in the assignment of the stroke as the basic programming unit. There have been a number of attempts to identify this unit (e.g. Wing, 1978; Hulstijn and Van Galen,

1983; Teulings, Thomassen, and Van Galen, 1983; Teulings, Mullins, and Stelmach, 1986; see also Hulstijn and Van Galen, 1988), which have looked at a number of possible candidates: individual strokes, stroke pairs, and individual letters. These will not be described in detail here as no clear picture has emerged from these studies. Indeed, support has been found in different studies for each of the aforementioned candidates. Because the writing tasks used in these studies have varied, it is possible that individual results reflect the nature of the task used, indicating perhaps, as Teulings, Mullins, and Stelmach (1986) have concluded, that 'there is no one single unit of programming in handwriting; instead, the production units may depend upon the form of the output' (p. 31). A similar conclusion has been drawn by Hulstijn and Van Galen (1988). There is also the possibility that output units may not only vary with task demands but also with level of practice. Studies comparing reaction times for writing familiar letters and novel symbols have been reported by Hulstijn (1987), and by Hulstijn and Van Galen (1988). For novel symbols, reaction time increases with the complexity, or number of strokes in the symbol. This effect is only very slight for familiar letters, indicating a larger output unit for familiar material.

Van Galen, Meulenbroek, and Hylkema (1986) have produced a model which describes the parallel and sequential processing which occurs during response execution. They point out that at the level of the unit, or micro-level, stages are sequential, but at the level of the writing task, or macro-level, some parallel processing occurs. This, they rightly argue, points to simultaneous representation of the movement task on a number of levels. Preparation precedes execution, with higher, more abstract, levels of preparation preceding lower levels. They manipulated the length of words in a writing task, and found that longer words resulted in longer latencies before writing of them commenced. They also manipulated the length of letters (1 vs. b) and found that before the longer letter (b), the movement time of the immediately preceding letter was increased. There was also some indication that the dynamics of the writing movement two letters back was affected. Thus they found support for a major prediction from their model: namely, that preparatory stages lower in the hierarchy of stages are processed closer to the time of execution of a handwriting response than those higher in the hierarchy. The simultaneous unpacking of higher levels of response programming during the execution of an earlier part of a serial response is a general characteristic of the skills described in this chapter.

TYPING

A relatively brief and selective synopsis of the extensive literature on typing will be given here, since an excellent recent review has been provided by Salthouse (1986). Typing reproduces the same symbolic material as writing, but in a sequence of discrete keystrokes. The problem for the motor system is not one of reproducing form, but rather of locating the correct spatial location and making an aiming response of sufficient force to depress a key. In writing, the process which translates input to output must include the conversion of a grapheme into a spatial code which represents its shape (the allograph). In typing, the translation process must specify a different kind of spatial code: the location of the appropriate key on the keyboard. This must involve some representation of the keyboard in the form of a space coordinate system. Although typing strokes are apparently simpler than handwriting in that they do not require the production of a complex shape, the control processes required to move the arm, hand and fingers of one of two limbs from one spatial location to the next, without visual feedback, are far from trivial.

As Long, Nimmo-Smith, and Whitefield (1983) point out, the unskilled and untrained typist locates keys by a 'hunt and peck' strategy, whereas a skilled touch typist reads ahead and types in a continuous sequence. The variation in the speed of production between novices and skilled typists is immense: to give some idea, a sample of subjects of different skill levels, used by West and Sabban (1982), had speeds ranging between 10 and 114 words per minute. An 'average' professional typist produces a rate of about 60 words per minute (Salthouse, 1986). Any comprehensive model of the typing process not only has to consider the control processes underlying performance, but must be able to produce a plausible explanation of how the way in which such processes are used, changes during skill acquisition to allow such large increases in speed of execution.

Models of the typing process share similar features in terms of the kinds of process they describe and their position within the necessary order of operations (e.g. Rumelhart and Norman, 1982; Salthouse, 1984, 1986). Salthouse (1986), for example, offers a four-component framework (see Figure 50) which distinguishes between input processes, parsing processes where text is divided into individual characters, a translation stage, where the specification of a given character is translated into a specification of a particular key press, and an execution stage, in which the keypress movement is implemented.

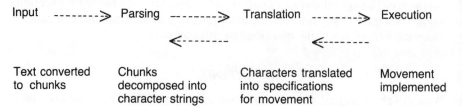

Figure 50. The four component processes of typing. (After Salthouse, 1986.)

Text must be 'chunked' at input; small portions of text are read at a time, and these are of sufficient length and available at an appropriate rate to ensure that continuous input is available for later processing stages. Information acquisition, then, would be expected to change as later processes of translation and execution speed up during skill acquisition. An indication that this indeed occurs comes from measures of the eye–hand span. This span is the number of characters which intervene between the fixation point of the eyes on the text, and the character which is simultaneously being typed. A similar span is found for the sightreading of music (Sloboda, 1974). For intermediate speeds of typing, the eye is approximately one second, or 6–8 characters ahead of the hand. The locus of this effect has been the focus of some controversy in the literature. However, since eye–hand span increases with skill level (Butsch, 1932; Salthouse, 1984), strong support is given to Salthouse's (1986) contention that 'it originates in the parsing process as a consequence of the need for a continuous flow of information to the translation and execution operations. From this perspective therefore, the eye-hand span is considered an adaptive mechanism whose purpose is to ensure efficient, uninterrupted processing concerned with the specification and execution of movement sequences' (p. 310).

The speed at which skilled typing is performed, together with the simple observation that skilled typists can read ahead and type at the same time, is suggestive of the same kind of output organization as for handwriting: serial processing on a micro-level, and parallel processing on a macro-level (Van Galen, Meulenbroek, and Hylkema, 1986).

Rumelhart and Norman (1982) have produced a model for typing execution, which has such properties, using their Activation Triggered Schema system (ATS) as a framework. The main features of the model are that it consists of interconnected schemata which each has an activation value equivalent to the amount of excitation received (resting value = 0). Excitation and inhibition result in an increase or decrease in activation respectively. Each schema contains 'instructions' for the performance of a particular operation, and can also initiate or call upon the operation of other schemata (parent schema) or be called upon by another schema (child schema). The hierarchical operation of this system in the control of typing of the word 'the' is illustrated in Figure 51.

The word schema 'the' is activated by the parser and acts as a parent schema for the 'child' keypress schemata for individual letters. Each of these schemata encodes position in terms of a 'keyboard-centered coordinate system' (p. 11), i.e. an abstract description of location on the keyboard. This stage of processing, then, is analogous to the allographic stage of handwriting execution. The keypress schemata in turn act as parent schemata for the child schemata of the response system, which specify and initiate the execution of the appropriate movements. The temporal order of keypresses is maintained

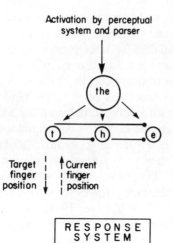

Figure 51. A simplified diagram of the interactions between schemata during typing of the word 'the'. (After Rumelhart, and Norman, 1982.)

through inhibition of successive keypress schemata, by the one currently activated. After the launch of a keypress, this inhibition is released by deactivation of the current keypress schema.

According to the model, each active schema pushes the relevant hand and finger toward their target keys at the same time. The final movement is a function of the competition between these forces: each schema has an effect proportional to its activation level, so that the movement is weighted by the most highly activated schema, i.e. the schema for the keypress which is next in line. When a keypress schema has the highest activation level, *and* has pushed the hand to within a criterion distance of its target key, the trigger conditions for initiation of a keypress are satisfied and the keypress is launched. After a short delay the schema is deactivated and the next most highly activated keypress schema takes over.

This model can account for the speed with which typing can occur, since there is a considerable amount of overlap in the processing for individual keystrokes. As Rumelhart and Norman point out, it neatly exploits the degrees of freedom 'problem' in movement (i.e. a number of different movements can usually achieve the same goal), by using extra degrees of freedom to allow the hand movement to move toward several goals (keys) at once.

The model and its computer simulation replicates phenomena commonly observed in typing, such as the shorter interstroke intervals across hands than between hands (e.g. Shaffer, 1978; Gentner, 1982; Ostry, 1983; Salthouse, 1984). In within-hand typing, preparation for launching one keystroke may move the hand away from the target position for the next keystroke. In between-hand typing this is not a problem, since the second keystroke will be the most highly activated on that hand and hence near its target. A second reason is based on a feature of the model designed to prevent deadlock, when two keystrokes are equally activated: subsequent strokes on the same hand are inhibited during the launching of a keystroke. The simulation of the model also produces a good explanation of some kinds of error which commonly occur in typing.

The scope of such a model is, however, limited as it simulates the performance of a *skilled* typist. It does not, as Long, Nimmo-Smith, and Whitefield (1983) point out, provide an explanation of how and why typists become faster and more fluent with practice. Long et al. examined distributions of inter-response times for keystrokes, and equated fluency with the peaks of the distributions (which were right skewed), and non-fluency with their tails (which contained the longer response times). They found that, with increased skill, inter-response time decreased for all responses, the number of non-fluent responses decreased, and the distribution of fluent responses became more peaked so that slower fluent responses and faster fluent responses became more alike. Long et al. note that an explanation of these effects can be provided using a number of different notions concerning skilled performance (e.g. controlled vs. automatic processing, open-loop vs. closed-loop control, etc.). This serves to emphasize the importance of providing an adequate theoretical framework, within which to consider the empirical data available. A first step towards that, is to identify and describe the necessary elements which comprise the skill. Rumelhart and Norman have done this with respect to execution. The next step is to say something about learning. One final point to consider is the lack of any comprehensive model of typing, that is, one which encompasses all stages of the production of each response from input to execution. Salthouse (1986) reviews the empirical phenomena that research in this area has uncovered to date in the context of his four component framework mentioned earlier. He concludes that:

Much of the contemporary research on typing has focused on output or motor processes, with processes of input, parsing, and translation largely neglected. This is unfortunate because transcription typing seems to involve a great many perceptual and cognitive aspects that may prove at least as interesting as those relating to purely motoric characteristics. (p. 316)

SPEECH

Speech is a ubiquitous skill which the majority of individuals accomplish at a high level of performance. Nevertheless, errors are common, and these have been studied and used as evidence of different stages in speech production (Fromkin, 1971; Garrett, 1982). Garrett (1982) has produced a model which has been developed from earlier models of Goldman-Eisler (1968) and Fromkin (1971), which have derived their evidence from speech hesitations and speech errors respectively. Garrett also considers evidence from the speech disorders of aphasic patients. Garrett's working model has five levels of representation: message level, functional level, positional level, phonetic level and articulatory level. Figure 52 shows these levels of representation and the procedures which are applied to them to construct the next (lower) level of representation.

The message level contains an abstract representation of the meaning of the utterance. The procedures applied to this level construct a syntactic representation at the functional level: the semantic contents of words are chosen and the logical and syntactic relationships between them are specified. The functional level still contains an abstract representation of the utterance, but with its semantic and functional relationships specified.

Procedures applied to the functional level construct the phonological (sound) representation of the positional level, which has strings of phonemes located in their correct positions within the utterance. This representation is in terms of the sounds of the constituents of the utterance. The phonetic level representation specifies the production characteristics (phonetics) of the utterance, and the articulatory level specifies the articulatory movements necessary to produce these. The abstract intention of 'what is to be said' is thus decomposed and specified in linguistic, phonological, and phonetic form, and lastly the muscular commands necessary to produce the correct configuration of the articulatory apparatus are specified.

The evidence used to support the detail of this model would require far too detailed an exposition to be given here. The interested reader is referred to Garrett (1982). The model focuses on the premotoric stage (MacNeilage, 1980), in which speech elements are selected and put into sequence. It describes the production of fluent speech, and accounts for the various forms of speech disorder upon which it is based. It is not a model of skill learning however. In common with models provided by Ellis, and Van Galen for handwriting, and Norman and Rumelhart, and Salthouse for typing it provides a useful description of the processing stages necessary to account for empirical phenomena observed at different levels of performance, but would need to incorporate additional features to deal with learning.

Mackay (1982, 1983) has produced a model of speech control which does cope with dynamic aspects of the skill. It takes as its starting point two

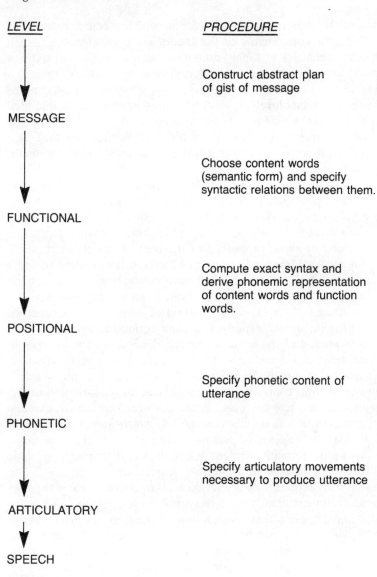

LEVEL   PROCEDURE

Construct abstract plan
of gist of message

MESSAGE

Choose content words
(semantic form) and specify
syntactic relations between them.

FUNCTIONAL

Compute exact syntax and
derive phonemic representation
of content words and function
words.

POSITIONAL

Specify phonetic content of
utterance

PHONETIC

Specify articulatory movements
necessary to produce utterance

ARTICULATORY

SPEECH

Figure 52. Garrett's (1982) five levels of representation during speech production.

characteristics of skilled performance: fluency, or the increase in speed and accuracy which results from practice of a skill, and flexibility, which allows transfer of performance from one skill to another similar skill, and also allows the same goal to be accomplished using different actions.

The theory consists of two independent systems: the mental system, which contains cognitive units which specify the components of an action and their relationship, and the muscle movement system, which specifies patterns of movement. The basic components of the theory are content nodes, which are hierarchically organized. A highly simplified example of the hierarchy of content nodes within the speech production system is shown in Figure 53. The mental system in this case is comprised of two subsystems—the conceptual system which contains levels of abstract representation of the intended utterance in terms of the meaning of the concept to be conveyed and the phrases and words which will be used; and the phonological system, which specifies phonological properties of the utterance such as syllabic, consonant and vowel pronunciation.

Mackay's model is an activation model. Activation theories, or the 'connectionist machine metaphor' (Stelmach and Hughes, 1987) have been popular in cognitive psychology for some time, and, as Stelmach and Hughes point out, have the advantage of some physiological realism. Dynamic aspects of speech are provided by three properties of the content nodes. First, serial activation of nodes at all levels of the control hierarchy must occur in order for a given action to be performed. Nodes are activated in an all-or-none fashion and the time for which they are activated can be specified. Second, simultaneous priming (sub-threshold activation) of other directly connected nodes occurs. Priming decays rapidly when the connected activated node ceases to be activated, and the level of priming depends on the number of activated connections and the length of time for which they apply. Priming in itself does not result directly in behavior. However, it does allow anticipation of activation from connected nodes higher in the hierarchy to occur, and may result in faster activation and hence performance. Third, practice increases the strength of linkage between nodes, which in activation terms means that the asymptotic level of priming increases, while the time taken to reach that asymptote remains constant, hence the sub-threshold asymptotic level of activation increases, as does the rate of priming.

Organization of the sequence of activation and triggering of content nodes is undertaken by independently stored syntax nodes, which connect to content nodes and organize them into a domain such as 'noun' or 'verb'. Words such as *dance* which can be used as either a noun or a verb belong to two domains. Syntax nodes are connected in a manner reflecting the ordinal constraints of a language (e.g. in English, adjectives precede nouns). When a syntax node is activated, it primes all connected nodes. The node within its domain with the greatest level of priming is activated. This node will have already received priming from a superordinate content node. Syntax nodes operate at each of the three levels of the systems shown in Figure 53: at the conceptual level, grammatical rules are applied; at the phonological level, rules concerning the order of syllables in words, and phonemes in syllables are applied; at the muscle movement level, rules concerning the order of articulatory movements are applied.

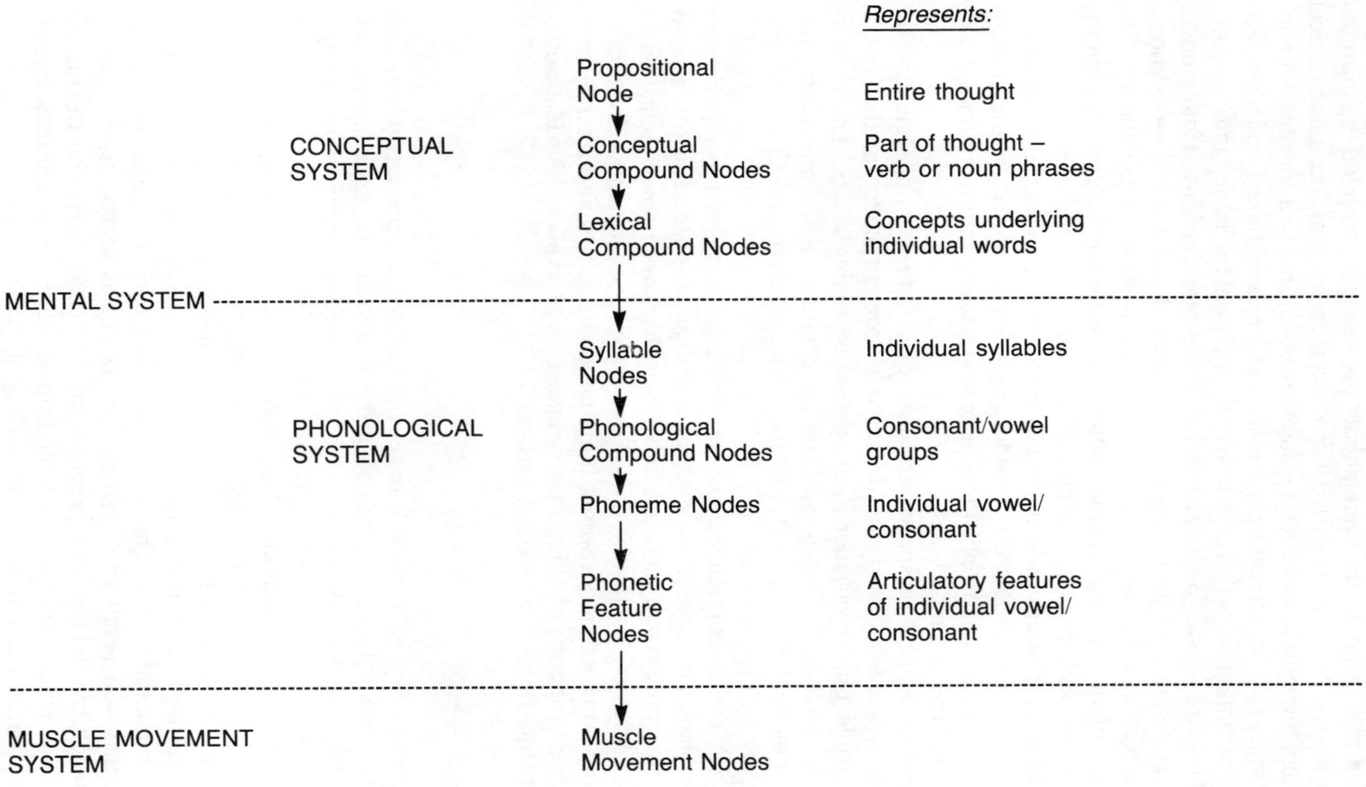

Figure 53. Content nodes in the conceptual, phonological, and muscle movement systems. (After Mackay, 1982.)

A third type of node, the timing node, provides the temporal organization for the theory. Syntax nodes for the conceptual system, the phonological system and the muscle movement system are connected to a concept/sentence timing node, a phonological timing node and a muscle timing node, respectively. The timing nodes organize syntax and content nodes into systems, while the syntax nodes organize content nodes into domains. Timing nodes activate syntax nodes by emitting pulses at a rate determined by motivational nodes, which are not described in current expositions of the theory. The pulse rate of the concept timing, phonological timing, and muscle timing nodes differs, with concept timing nodes emitting less frequent pulses than the phonological nodes, which in turn emit less frequent pulses than the muscle timing nodes. The three nodes are coupled, so that if the concept timing node speeds up, proportional increased rates of output occur in phonological and muscle timing nodes.

Expressive features of speech are also taken into account. Intensity (or stress or intonation) can be represented in content nodes in the mental system, while timing variations are applied by timing nodes. The issue of timing in movement, however, is more complex and contentious than Mackay's theory would suggest, and the reader is referred to Chapter 3, this volume, for an exposition of this.

Mackay's theory is intended to cover the empirical phenomena observed by researchers into speech production: for example, speech errors usually involve transposition or substitution of words or word components within the same level of his theory, and can be explained by the activation of extraneously-primed nodes within the same domain. It is also intended as a more general theory of skilled performance, and explains the features of flexibility and fluency mentioned earlier.

Flexibility

One aspect of flexibility is the transfer of practised components of one skill to another. In Mackay's theory this is attributed to the strengthening of node linkages with practice. At lower levels in the node hierarchy, some linkages will have been activated so many times that their connections will have reached a strength asymptote. This is more likely to be true of lower levels in the control hierarchy than higher levels: the same articulatory movements are required in many different word and sentence contexts, whereas at a higher level a given sentence may have been infrequently encountered or never encountered before. The use of established linkages between nodes in a novel task will result in a transfer of the effects of the practice which strengthened the linkage in a previous task. Further discussion of transfer findings, and empirical support for the transfer of lower, rather than higher, nodes is given in Mackay (1982, pp. 497–501).

A second aspect of flexibility is the ability to achieve the same goal with different actions (motor equivalence), which is a form of transfer, but this time of higher-level nodes in the hierarchy which specify the form of the action in abstract terms. These higher-level nodes will remain the same whatever the exact muscular commands required to enact the task.

Fluency

Increased speed in task performance with practice is a function of linkage strength between the nodes, and hence is intimately related to flexibility. The log-log linearity function which typically describes practice effects (i.e. a rapid increase in speed at first, followed by a much slower, more gradual increase), is accounted for by the mixture of practised and unpractised node linkages which will constitute the node hierarchy for a given new task. The initial rapid speed increase results from the strengthening of unpractised linkages. Later in practice, when all nodes are practised, learning rate slows considerably.

MUSICAL PERFORMANCE

As mentioned previously, Mackay's theory makes provision for the production of expressive features in speech. Such features are even more obvious in musical performance where the performer imposes his or her own interpretation upon the symbolic information provided by the composer. The thorough and careful studies of skilled pianists conducted by Shaffer (1980, 1981) demonstrate the consistent use of rhythm and intensity in their performance, and point to the importance of considering expressiveness as a major component of movement preparation. Shaffer's theory of motor programming, derived from his work on typing (Shaffer, 1975b, 1978) as well as from his observations of musicians contains two major levels of representation, a higher abstract level which specifies the structural aspects of the movement, including expressive features, and a command representation which contains specifications of movement targets. Timing constraints are imposed upon the structural representation or 'string' (Shaffer, 1980). This theory is similar in most respects to the theory described in more detail by Mackay.

In addition to emphasizing the expressive aspects of movements, consideration of musical performance draws attention to one further feature of certain cognitive motor skills. Skilled musicians can generate novel movement sequences within certain predetermined stylistic constraints. This generative ability may be regarded as one aspect of performance flexibility. Improvization in music is apparently enabled by knowledge of the particular musical genre concerned, the ability to be able to reproduce music composed in that genre, and by repeated attempts to improvise within that genre. As Johnson-

Laird (1987) points out, the skill of improvization is not accessible to consciousness, but before it can be accomplished, a set of basic structures (e.g. chord sequences in jazz) must be memorized. Johnson-Laird argues that musicians learn to improvize by acquiring a non-deterministic grammar which can be used to generate spontaneous and novel melodies within the structural and stylistic constraints imposed by the musical work being performed. Because of the speed with which improvized melodies must be produced, and the potential complexity of the decisions required to generate them, Johnson Laird proposes that the constraints of the genre are applied at the initial stages of generating the melody. This serves to reduce the computational requirements during the production of the melody in real time. The requirement of generative flexibility must be taken into account in any general theory or model of the performance of cognitive-motor skills.

A GENERAL FRAMEWORK FOR COGNITIVE MOTOR SKILLS?

Understanding skilled action, according to Allport (1980), starts from two basic ideas: multilevel, hierarchical control, and a library of stored specifications which need not be separate from the processing mechanisms themselves. These are features of the models which have been developed for cognitive motor skills. This chapter so far has presented models and theories of response organization in handwriting, speech, musical performance, and typing. Because these areas have developed more or less independently, a number of similar but different approaches have been taken to identifying empirical phenomena and placing them within a theoretical framework. This is true not only of cognitive-motor skills, but of the skills literature in general. Mackay (1982) has criticized what he calls the 'dichotimization strategy' which researchers have adopted in order to create manageable portions of the skills area for research. The partitioning of the area, he argues, has been based on practical or intuitive judgements rather than on theoretical considerations.

A second effect of this dichotomization he summarizes as follows:

> a concentration on the surface or muscle movement characteristics of different 'types' of skills, at the expense of the underlying mental processes that are involved in the control of muscle movements. As a consequence, important generalisations applying to all skills have been missed because . . . the major effects of practice on the flexibility and fluency of skilled behavior are usually taking place at the [this] mental level rather than at the muscle movement level. (p. 485)

There are two points made here which require qualification. First, in the area of cognitive-motor skills, in spite of the rather fragmentary nature of the literature, underlying mental processes have been discussed. The problem has been that, because of the fragmentary nature of the literature, such discussions have mostly not been at a general level: they have been provided to explain a limited set of phenomena observed for a particular skill. The models constructed have tended to be static rather than dynamic (in the sense of focusing on learning). The construction of dynamic models encourages the development of more general theories because of the generality of the learning phenomena which apply. Although researchers in the area of cognitive motor skills have frequently acknowledged the family resemblance of these skills and have assumed that their processing stages and acquisition are similar, there have been few discussions of such skills in the wider context of general learning phenomena. A detailed general framework, capable of generating testable predictions would provide a valuable basis for exploring the detail of these skills. In the broad area of cognitive skills, current theoretical approaches have been presented in a general form and applied to specific instances of skill learning. Anderson's ACT* theory (Anderson, 1982, 1983, 1987) is a procedural theory of skill acquisition based upon production rules or condition–action units. These specify an action to be performed if a given condition is fulfilled. For any task, a hierarchy of these rules will specify goals and subgoals to be achieved in a procedural description. Schema theories, such as that of Rumelhart and Norman, which have evolved in the artificial intelligence literature, are closely related to production rule theories. Schemata can be thought of as 'organised bundles of production rules' (Allport, 1980). Anderson's ACT* is stated in general terms, has a strong emphasis on changes in performance during learning, and has been applied with some success to skills such as the learning of geometry (Anderson, 1982) and LISP programming (Anderson, Farrell, and Sauers, 1984).

If one wishes to argue that a general theoretical framework for cognitive-motor skills would be useful, then Mackay's theory is one candidate, although its range of application encompasses all skills. He argues that the differences between skills such as piano-playing, typing, and speech are as numerous as the similarities, that the general node-structure approach can cope with these and encompass perceptual-motor skills such as tennis, as well as cognitive skills such as chess. This may well be true but there are other kinds of theory available, which can potentially have the same scope. For example, a production systems theory such as Anderson's ACT* has the potential for application in this area. It can cope with speedup and transfer effects. It has one advantage: it provides an explanation of how procedural information concerning the sequencing of operations in a given skill is acquired in the first place from the assemblage of general knowledge and from instruction. General problem-solving procedures are applied to this knowledge to generate domain-specific procedures, or production rules can transfer from one task to another (Anderson, 1987). It also has some potential for application in areas such as musical performance, where rules are applied to generate a novel product. The scope of Mackay's theory is limited to performance and practice effects, given the prior existence of syntax and content nodes.

Mackay's and Anderson's theories are both intended to encompass a wide range of skills. This is a consequence of their dynamic nature: consideration of learning phenomena in skilled performance which are generally applicable leads to the construction of theories with a broad scope. In the introduction to this chapter, cognitive motor skills were presented as a coherent family of skills, unlike other skills such as sports skills which have a cognitive, strategic component, but which are apparently much more heterogeneous. General theories, especially those which use production rules are of obvious utility in describing the performance of strategic as well as cognitive motor skills. There is, therefore, some scope for the further development and application of general cognitively-based theories using both empirically observable phenomena and computer simulation to test predictions.

A second qualification should be made to Mackay's point concerning the neglect of mental processes and the importance of these processes as a locus of learning phenomena. In skills with any significant motor component, kinematic and biomechanical analyses are crucial to understanding acquisition and there is a dearth of such analyses of cognitive motor skills. Not all skills require the translation of symbolic material into a motor response. There are compelling arguments for a direct linkage of perception with the motor system in 'natural' skills such as locomotion and stair climbing (Warren, 1984; Turvey and Carello, 1986). Skill acquisition and transfer phenomena in such skills may be understood, at least in part, by identifying the coordinative structures which constrain performance: analysis at the muscle movement level, therefore, is crucial. Mackay has advised that we must not neglect mental process. Neither must we neglect to examine the control which is exerted at lower levels. This is true not only for natural skills but also for 'cultural' cognitive motor skills. In several recent publications (e.g. Stelmach and Hughes, 1984) skills researchers have examined the difficulties created by excessive 'cognitivism'. Unless we can identify how much of the control of a given movement can be accomplished at lower levels of the central nervous system, we cannot attribute effects of learning, with certainty, to the premotoric level of response preparation. Current notions of distributed processing within the central nervous system stress the transfer of control between a number of levels, each of which can act relatively autonomously (Pew, 1984). For movement control these must include subcortical structures which respond to the biomechanical and environmental context of the movement (Turvey, 1977).

So far I have avoided using the term 'motor program', as many researchers in this field have done, to describe the hierarchy of control for the execution of cognitive-motor skills. Chapter 3, this volume, discusses the concept of the motor program in some detail. My reluctance to use the term in this chapter is due to the fact that it has been used in slightly different ways by different authors, and that it has often been taken to mean that all muscle commands are prepared prior to the execution of a skill. We do not have sufficient evidence to be able to support the notion that all of the muscle commands required for execution of the skill are specified in advance, and the ecological theorists contend that lower levels of the central nervous system supply detailed adjustments to movements, of which higher centres are ignorant (Bernstein, 1967; Turvey, 1977).

Consideration of the issues surrounding the use of the term 'motor program' focuses attention on an important omission from the accounts of cognitive motor skills described in this chapter, which I have already referred to less directly. All of these accounts contain a distinction, explicit or implicit, between premotoric and motor processes, to use MacNeilage's terms. The premotoric processes have been discussed at some length, but the lowest level of these processes, where commands are issued to muscles to execute the task, has received little attention. The ecological approach to the control of action would strongly suggest that such commands only specify how collectives of muscles should interact in task execution, and that a complete picture can only be obtained by considering which collectives or coordinative structures are involved, how these are established during acquisition, and how their action is modified and adjusted at lower levels in the central nervous system. Recent research is finding evidence for the use of coordinative structures in a wide range of motor tasks, and of particular relevance to this chapter is their role in the control of speech (e.g. Kelso et al., 1984). A good review of the ecological or action systems approach to speech production is given in Harris (1987).

From the point of view of model-building, it makes sense to approach the premotoric and motor processes separately. The premotoric processes can be modeled satisfactorily using activation and/or production systems models from cognitive psychology. Understanding the motor processes may require the production of biophysical models using biomechanical and kinematic analyses of movement. In order to obtain an adequate understanding of the nature and locus of learning effects, we need to look both ways. This prescription may do little to solve the identity crisis faced by motor skill scientists (Stelmach and Hughes, 1987): 'Those who seek a coherent theory of motor behavior are caught between . . . deciding whether we should focus on (neuro) motor control or on (psycho) motor behavior' (p. 190). However, it is probably far too early to look for coherent theories which encompass all levels of the control of complex skills, and it is unlikely that the same metaphor will prove appropriate for both response preparation and execution.

SUMMARY

The skills of typing, writing, speech, and musical performance have been treated as a family of skills in the literature because of their obvious similarities in sequential response execution and in the necessity for hierarchical, abstract response organization prior to movement execution. The models which have been developed to describe the output organization of these skills individually, have, for the most part, restricted their scope to an explication of the necessary levels of representation. They provide a useful description of skilled performance but have little to say about learning. Theories of skill learning are more broadly-based and can be potentially applied to a wide range of cognitive, cognitive motor, and perceptual motor skills.

The processes which precede the execution of each component of these sequential movements can be divided into premotoric processes, which specify the response in abstract form, and motor processes which issue the commands necessary for initiation and control of the movement. The ecological approach to the control of action contends that traditional notions of motor programming which assume that centrally-issued commands are sent to individual muscles are erroneous, and neglect the considerable contribution of lower centers in the central nervous system which respond to the immediate context of movement. The ecological view restricts the role of higher-level commands to the specification of the manner in which lower-level structures interact. One implication of this view is that cognitive theoretical metaphors which can be used to describe premotoric organization are unlikely to be of any use in describing the motor processes. Future developments in this area are likely to come from two directions: the further development of cognitive theories of response organization, and their computer simulation, and biomechanical and kinematic analyses of movement. Both approaches have much to offer, both to an understanding of cognitive motor skills, and more generally to the development of theories of the control of movement.

ACKNOWLEDGEMENTS

I would like to thank John Beech for comments on an earlier version of the chapter, and Wouter Hulstijn for providing valuable material.

Chapter 10

Handicap and Human Skill

Clark A. Shingledecker

A common characteristic of all skills is that they require coordinated physical and mental activity involving the entire chain of sensory, perceptual, and motor mechanisms which underlie behavior. When this organization is disrupted by some factor affecting one or more components of the chain, skilled performance deteriorates. Temporary decrements in human performance can often be attributed to task demands which exceed the inherently limited abilities of the individual, or to the actions of physiological, situational, and environmental stressors which can effectively reduce his capacities even further. In general, the acute breakdown of skill produced by these conditions can be alleviated or avoided by reducing the mental workload placed on the human operator or by protecting him from the stressor. Other deficits which arise from more enduring changes in the individual result in a chronic breakdown of skill. One example of this class of problems is the deterioration of skill caused by impairments of sensory and central capacities which accompany the normal aging process. The reader interested in the effects of aging on skill will want to consult the book by Charness (1985) which appears elsewhere in this series.

SENSORY AND MOTOR DISABILITY

This chapter is concerned with the chronic breakdown of skill which occurs when a receptor or effector component of the chain of mechanisms responsible for skill is lost or impaired because of disease, injury, or congenital malformation. Owing to the permanent nature of sensory and motor disability and to the fundamental way in which these conditions affect the organization of skill, many research efforts for the handicapped are aimed at the development of equipment which will permit them to acquire skill by some alternative

Human Skills. Edited by D. Holding © 1989 John Wiley & Sons Ltd

means. During the last 35 years the rapid development of technological capability has engendered the production of a number of prosthetic and orthotic devices intended to replace human limbs or to restore their function, as well as a large catalogue of sensory aids to supplement or replace defective visual and auditory systems. Unfortunately, sophisticated engineering solutions have often failed to alleviate the deficits in skill suffered by the handicapped because the design of sensory and motor devices has been undertaken with insufficient consideration of the human user, particularly with regard to the central mechanisms which underlie skill.

A general model of human performance has emerged from skills research which provides a framework for the understanding of the mechanisms of skill and which can serve as a useful conceptual approach to the problem of re-establishing skills that have been impaired by sensory or motor disability. Originally derived from theories of communication and control engineering, this model draws an analogy between the human operator and an information-processing device that receives inputs from the environment through a number of sensory channels and transmits information back to the environment via a group of effector mechanisms. Intervening between these input and output processes are a set of hypothesized mechanisms which select input channels, store and transform information, choose responses, provide commands for the motor system, and feed back response information.

Two global features of this man–machine analogy model illustrate important characteristics of human skill. First, like other processing devices, the human has a finite capacity to transmit information so that the speed and accuracy with which information is gathered, processed, and converted to an appropriate response is determined by the limited abilities of the sensory, perceptual, and motor processes that are responsible for skill. A second characteristic shared by human and inanimate information processors is that, when taken together, the individual processing mechanisms form an interdependent system. In the case of the human operator this implies that an alteration in a sensory or motor component may have considerable effects on the demands placed upon the central mechanisms and on the activities they will be required to perform.

These basic characteristics of the human as an information processor indicate that the structure and function of the mechanisms of skill should be given primary consideration when attempting to design motor or sensory aids. Unfortunately, surprisingly little is known about the way in which the human nervous system accomplishes the universal yet complex behaviors such as locomotion, manual control, speech perception, and reading which are most seriously affected by handicap. Nevertheless, in recent years there have been increasing numbers of attempts to apply contemporary theory and knowledge of the general nature of skill to the understanding of sensory-motor disability and to the development of suitable prostheses and aids.

Since the first edition of *Human Skills* was published, this trend has continued as biomedical engineers and rehabilitation specialists have become increasingly aware of the importance of perceptual and cognitive factors in the development of functionally useful devices. One of the goals of this chapter is to use this growing area of application of skills research to integrate some of the diverse topics considered in previous chapters of the book. In addition, because the technological capability to devise new aids for the physically impaired population continues to surpass current understanding of these fundamental determinants of skilled behavior, a second purpose of this chapter is to emphasize those areas where renewed efforts are needed in basic research to permit further progress toward the solution of the practical problems of both the handicapped and other groups of individuals.

MOTOR IMPAIRMENT

Persons impaired in motor function through the absence or loss of an extremity by amputation or by dysfunction of the motor system as a result of spinal injury, stroke, cerebral palsy, or neuromuscular diseases such as poliomyelitis represent one of the largest proportions of the severely handicapped population. Until approximately 35 years ago, such individuals had only a few body-powered aids available to them. These were both heavy and difficult to use, and were severely limited in their ability to restore the complex level of functioning observed in the normal arm or leg. The recent introduction of externally-powered devices has radically improved the potential utility of prosthetic equipment, but it also presented problems which call into play a number of skills variables. The initial difficulty that beset designers of electrically or pneumatically-powered devices concerned methods by which the equipment could be controlled by the disabled individual.

Motor control

The human upper extremity is a complex system of joints with a total of thirteen degrees of freedom of movement. Combined with the hand, this system permits rapid and accurate acquisition of objects in space and an almost infinite number of patterns of movement. Biomechanical research has shown that only two of the thirteen degrees of freedom could be eliminated without seriously affecting the performance of everyday manual skills (Hancock, 1970). With the complexity and versatility of this system in mind, it is not difficult to recognize that attempting to devise a method by which an amputee could control a prosthesis which even remotely approximates the capabilities of an intact arm is an exceedingly daunting task.

In order to eliminate the awkward body movements used to control conventional prostheses, two alternative types of control have been devised for externally-powered devices. One of these utilizes small movements in residual muscles to operate pull switches. Although sites for the location of these controllers are limited, this problem is often solved by using only a few muscle sites with multiple-position switches. The second type of control used for powered prostheses and orthoses is an electromyographic (EMG) potential derived from minute voluntary contractions of residual muscles. These myoelectric signals are detected by transducers mounted on the surface of the skin and are amplified to act as control sources for electric motors. EMG control of prostheses was originally suggested by Reiter (1948) and was first employed for this use in an experimental artificial hand displayed by Russian scientists at the 1958 World's Fair in Belgium.

Both switch and EMG methods of control have been used in systems to provide artificial hand prehension for below-elbow amputees and in more complex devices which replace elbow flexion and extension, humoral rotation, and sometimes limited shoulder movement. Comparisons of amputee performance with the two types of control have favored the EMG method. Carlson (1970) and Peizer et al. (1970) found that in tests of grasping objects and placing them in various positions, subjects with powered hand prostheses were able to perform more quickly and with fewer compression errors with EMG control. However, the latter study also showed that the advantage of EMG control diminishes with higher-level amputations where prosthetic hand and elbow components must be used together. Nevertheless, in all cases patients preferred EMG control because of reduced fatigue, and because the EMG control was less ambiguous than the switch control.

The control problems that arise with pull switches were delineated by Peizer, Wright, and Pirello (1970) in an evaluation of an electric elbow and mechanical hand prosthesis in which a single pull switch operated by shoulder flexion was used to control movement. Shoulder excursion of ⅛ inch with minimal force produced elbow extension while further movement of ⅛ inch produced elbow flexion. Continued pull bottomed the switch and operated the terminal device. Even after extensive training with the prosthesis, subjects found it difficult to avoid inadvertent operation and experienced considerable difficulty in hunting for control positions. Control discrimination with the EMG method appears to be better because a larger number of spatially separated sites can be used to provide signals. Rae and Cockrell (1971) found that many locations on upper trunk muscles were relatively free of unwanted EMG activity in the absence of voluntary contraction and were able to generate sufficiently high potential differences to provide control signals for an upper extremity prosthesis.

Discriminability is not the only factor influencing the ease with which prosthetic controls can be used. Regardless of the method of control, as the number of functions to be performed by the artificial limb increases, the total number of control locations or levels of control at a single site also increases.

Since the speed at which humans can respond is reduced as the number of equiprobable alternative responses increases (Hick, 1952), it is apparent that a multiple degree of freedom device with many control functions will tax the information-processing abilities of its user. This problem of multiple controls and the limited channel capacity of human operators was well illustrated in a review of a prosthesis which required the amputee to operate a system of nine control switches which had to be selected, actuated, and turned off individually (Groth and Lyman, 1961). Evaluation revealed that the decision load placed upon the user was excessive and that, even in simple tasks, performance was degraded.

Two general methods of EMG control have been used with externally powered prostheses. One of these, known as digital or on-off control, produces movement of the device in a single direction and at a fixed rate when EMG activity exceeds a preset threshold value. In the second type of EMG control system, individual muscle sites control different functions and the amplitude of activity at each site determines the force or rate of movement in a proportional manner (Staros and Peizer, 1972). Although a number of digital, proportional, and hybrid systems has been devised, little research has been conducted to determine an optimal system for the non-manual control of prostheses.

The skills literature provides fairly precise information regarding the capacities needed for manual control. An important source of limitation to motor output is the rate at which responses can be made. A number of studies indicates that the human motor system is capable of producing a maximum of ten responses per second (Fitts and Posner, 1967, p. 78). In most cases however this upper limit is not reached because the human operator is acting in a closed-loop fashion. That is, he is using information about the results of his ongoing actions to modify his responses. This activity introduces computational time-lags and reduces response rate. It appears that this lag is inherent to the human information-processing system and perhaps that a basic refractoriness or intermittency is responsible for the single-channel nature of skilled performance (Welford, 1968). Estimates derived from reaction-time studies (Hick and Bates, 1950), and from measurements of movement corrections in tracking performance (Hill, Gray, and Ellison, 1947), indicate that, for manual control, humans can generate approximately one control change per 0.33 second. In terms of information-theoretical measures, this indicates that the rate of information transmission from the manual system is 3.03 ($\log_2 n$) bits/second.

In comparison to the muscles of the intact arm and hand, the muscle sites available for the control of prostheses on the trunk and upper body would be expected to have coarser control and a lower capacity to transmit information because they are innervated by larger motor units, and because these muscles have less practice in the development of fine motor skill. This was confirmed by Lucaccini et al. (1967) in a study which showed that the upper trunk muscles display an average increase in reaction time of 0.25 seconds over the manual case. Assuming a proportional increase in the rate of generating control signals, this indicates that the maximum rate of information transfer for non-manual control is reduced to 1.72 bits/second. On the basis of these data, Freedy, Lucaccini and Lyman (1967) reviewed the information requirements of a number of possible control systems which could be used to operate an arm prosthesis capable of movement in three dimensions that would mimic the movement characteristics of the intact arm when transporting an object between two points in space. Analysis of position, velocity, and frequency controls indicated that the information demands for simultaneously controlling the three dimensions of movement in a trajectory similar to that observed in a normal arm would be excessive. The only system which appeared to fall within the capacity of non-manual control was a form of digital control that would require the user to discriminate three levels of muscle contraction. Using this system the operator would merely initiate an action and then supply a signal for deceleration at the appropriate time during the movement.

In more recent work aimed at overcoming the inherent imprecision of the EMG signal, researchers have increased the number of electrodes from more muscle groups and used sophisticated mathematical processing to yield finer control signals (Mann, 1981). Graupe et al. (1981) used a different approach in which more information is derived from fewer electrodes to achieve the same result. The basic hypothesis underlying this research was that different modes of muscle activation would result in different temporal patterns of signal at the same electrode site. Using a time-series analysis performed in real time on a microprocessor, discriminable spatio-temporal parameters were identified that can be learned by a patient with minimal practice to control up to six degrees of freedom of movement.

The actual rate at which information can be transferred in manual control is strongly influenced by the compatibility of the code which relates the way in which the control device is actuated to the observed results of the control change. Numerous studies of control–display compatibility have indicated that wide variations in the rate of information transmission can be produced with alternate stimulus–response codes (Fitts and Posner, 1967, pp. 104–6). Although prosthesis designers have often stressed the importance of 'naturalness' in device control, very little research appears to have been done to investigate compatibility in non-manual control. One obvious form of compatibility relevant to prosthesis control has been demonstrated in the reported naturalness of artificial hands controlled by residual muscles in the forearm that would normally control extension and flexion (Reswick, 1972). This compatibility principle has been adopted for a number of modern prostheses. Most available systems now use two muscle channels to control one degree of freedom (Childress, 1982). In the above elbow case the biceps and triceps muscles are used to control flexion and extension of the artificial elbow. With the below-elbow amputee, finger flexor and extensor muscle groups are used as signal sources to close and open the prosthetic hand. Each of these control modes is considered to be somewhat natural to the user since the muscles in both cases are involved in normal upper extremity activation.

Even in cases where this type of compatibility cannot be achieved however, it is likely that the investigation of alternative spatial configurations for control transducers and of various kinds of voluntary activity that can be generated at single sites will reveal differences in the ease with which handicapped persons can generate signals to control different dimensions of movement. It is also likely that compatibility effects are influenced by training and maturation variables. The reported Swedish success with acceptance of upper extremity prostheses by young children 2–5 years of age suggests that early experience promotes adaptation to the prosthesis as a natural system and permits it to be integrated into normal psychomotor development (Sorbye, 1977).

Sensory feedback

The provision of precise analogue control by EMG methods has been an elusive goal for the designers of prosthetic equipment. One factor which has contributed to the difficulty of this task has been that only a rough neurological relationship exists between EMG activity and voluntary muscle contraction (Mason, 1970). Devising a technique to overcome the inherent imprecision of the control signals that can be produced by the user of a prosthesis is a problem which demands some consideration of the manner in which the intact limb is normally controlled by the nervous system.

Two general theories have been put forward to describe the way in which movement control is achieved. In its strictest form, the outflow model suggests that proprioception plays no important role in motor control (see Chapter 3, this volume). Practice establishes learned patterns of motor impulses in the brain which are 'tuned' by experience to permit accurate movement. The inflow model (Chapter 2, this volume) states that feedback from both exteroceptors and interoceptors is necessary, and that it is the constant interplay between motor output and feedback information about the state of a limb which permits the performance of skilled movements. While neither model can account for all of the observed phenomena, in most cases the weight of the experimental evidence supports the inflow view. The profound effects of delay and spatial displacement of visual feedback conclusively demonstrate the necessity of this information in many skilled tasks (Smith, McCrary, and Smith, 1963). Although methodological problems limit the investigation of the role of kinesthetic feedback in movement control, numerous studies which have either partially blocked kinesthetic cues, or have enhanced them by the manipulation of control constants, illustrate its importance (see Trumbo and Noble, 1973).

Intact human limbs are richly supplied with muscle, tendon, and joint receptors as well as pressure receptors in the skin which can provide precise feedback information about the position of the limb in space and direct data on resistance and strain. Although all prosthetic devices severely degrade these sources of feedback, the problem is exacerbated in modern, externally-powered equipment. Earlier body-powered devices were cumbersome but they contributed direct feedback about the state of the prosthesis by muscle tension and force cues available to the amputee's stump. In contrast, electric-ally-powered devices transmit little or no information back to the user who is forced to rely upon vision and noise cues from the motor in order to function in a closed-loop fashion (Childress, 1980). Although these cues are useful, they cannot be monitored at a low level of awareness. Furthermore, complete reliance on vision and audition for feedback renders these systems unavailable for the reception of other task information. Finally, evidence which suggests that motor learning depends upon a shift from exteroceptive visual control to kinesthetic control indicates that the absence of proprioceptive feedback will retard normal skill development (Fleishman and Rich, 1963).

In view of the physiological and behavioral evidence for the importance of feedback in normal motor control, designers have endeavored to include substitute sensory feedback systems in powered prostheses and orthoses. These systems sense grasp force, hand position, or elbow position and display this information to the skin either by electrical stimulation or mechanical vibration. A number of experimenters have reported improvement in pros-thesis control when hand position and grasp force feedback were supplied. Rohland (1975) compared patients' ability to reproduce reference pressures on a pinch meter when using an artificial hand with and without supplemen-tary electrocutaneous feedback from a pressure detector located in the fingertips. Errors with feedback were shown to be ten times smaller than without. Nevertheless, these errors remained two to three times larger than those produced by the users with their intact hands. Prior and Lyman (1975) provided grasp force and hand position feedback to amputees' stumps via a single concentric electrode. Force was represented by the width of a constant current pulse while pulse repetition rate was used to code position. Tests of patients' ability to duplicate forces up to 15 lbs and to identify blocks of different sizes without vision indicated that the addition of electrocutaneous feedback substantially improved performance with the prosthesis. However, average performance with supplementary feedback was only 40–60 per cent as accurate as that obtained with the intact hand.

Just as compatibility is an important factor in control selection, a powerful factor influencing the effectiveness of artificial feedback in prostheses appears to be the coding of the information displayed to the user. An attempt at producing high physiological compatibility has involved the direct stimulation of afferent nerves which normally carry feedback from the intact limb. Clippinger, Avery, and Titus (1974) implanted several below-elbow amputees with stimulators located on the medial nerve of the forearm. A strain gauge in the terminal device was used to transform prehension force to an electrical signal which stimulated the nerve. Although no objective performance data were collected with the device, nearly all subjects reported perceptions of hand movement when the frequency of stimulation was varied.

Very little research exists to indicate which of the many possible forms of tactile display is most compatible for the presentation of feedback about limb position and movement. However, some inferences can be drawn from research on attempts to develop tactile communication codes. Geldard (1961) reviewed a number of possible codes for vibratory stimulation and found that the high spatial resolution of the skin made locus a desirable coding dimension. In addition, he indicated that cutaneous movement was a promising secondary dimension for tactile communication because of its vividness. Alles (1970) described a tactile display which incorporated both spatial and motion cues. The system made use of the phantom sensation which appears when two spatially separated vibrators mounted on the skin are modulated appropriately. The phantom position or motion of the vibratory display across a line segment of skin can be controlled by modulating the time of onset of the vibrators, their phase relationships, or their amplitudes. Alles found that the display was easily learned and the unimpaired subjects could use the system to match display position to elbow position with a high degree of precision. Results from a simple tracking task indicated that the display also provided accurate information on the direction and rate of movement. Mann and Reimers (1970) applied this system to the problem of presenting position feedback in an EMG-controlled elbow. Results from tasks in which unilateral amputees were required to match the position of the prosthetic elbow to that of their intact elbow and to locate targets on a panel without direct visual information revealed a 50 per cent reduction in errors over the no feedback condition and performance equal to, or better than, that achieved with a cable operated elbow. In more recent efforts, both mechanical and electrical stimulators have been used to provide feedback. Although both mechanisms have similar information-transmission capabilities, mechanical stimulation appears to be more acceptable to users (Shannon, 1976).

Motor programs and adaptive aiding

Figure 54 illustrates some of the artificial motor control and feedback connections which would have to be incorporated in a prosthesis that would provide the level of functioning observed in an intact arm. Although designers have begun to develop systems which approach this degree of sophistication, the user of such complex devices often finds that he must devote his full attentional capacity to the execution of a simple reaching movement. Hence, reducing the mental effort demands of operating an artificial limb is one of the greatest problems facing rehabilitation researchers (Wilson, 1965). It is likely that this problem will be solved in part by the continued development of more compatible control methods and displays for the provision of supplementary feedback. However, it is improbable that these improvements alone will be sufficient to permit disabled persons to achieve independent movement control at the low levels of effort experienced by non-handicapped individuals.

In addition to the fact that compatibility is neurologically 'hard-wired' into the sensory-motor system, other features of the unimpaired human

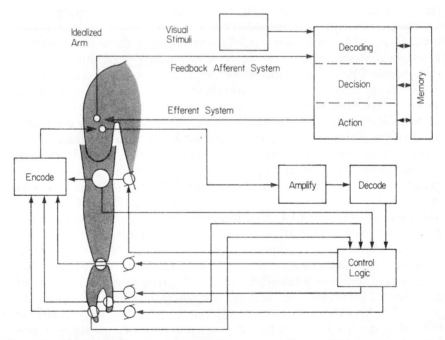

Figure 54. Idealized schematic representation of the machine and human components of a completely controlled arm prosthesis system. (From *Bulletin of Prosthetics Research*, BPR 10–8, 1967.)

information processor act to reduce the decision load of motor control. One way in which this is accomplished is by the presence of internal feedback and reflex loops in the peripheral nervous system (Geldard, 1972). These feedback loops regulate reflex responses and play an important role in the control of ongoing voluntary responses without the involvement of central processing mechanisms. A number of prosthetic devices have been designed to mimic this feature of the motor system. Pressure, force, position, and velocity have been automatically detected and used to stabilize the action of a prosthesis or to control secondary aspects of operation which would otherwise demand a portion of the user's limited channel capacity. An example of the use of this sort of local feedback is a system in which the incipient slip of an object held by an amputee in a prosthetic hand is detected and used to control prehension force. As the object begins to slip, a signal is fed back to cause the hand to grip tighter until the slip is prevented (Reswick, 1972). Several current systems now use such artificial, low-level feedback loops to improve the controllability of upper extremity prostheses and unburden the user (Cook, 1985).

Another reason why the unimpaired individual can engage in motor behavior while economizing on conscious effort is that his central processing mechanisms seem to be able to operate in both a closed-loop and an automatic mode. Highly overlearned movement patterns may be stored as motor programs which can be run off on command (see Chapter 3, this volume). This automatization reduces decision load by eliminating the need continuously to monitor feedback. The design of aiding subsystems to assume a portion of the decision and control load of a prosthesis is essentially an attempt to provide the handicapped user with an artificial motor program.

Freedy, Hull, and Lyman (1971) introduced an experimental computer control system for a prosthesis which worked to unburden the operator by 'learning' through observation of tasks being done and progressively assuming the majority of the responsibility for movement control. The system, based on a Maximum Likelihood Decision principle, is able to learn a variety of tasks and can predict unexperienced patterns of movement from rules extracted from redundant portions of a task. In the pilot evaluation a three degrees of freedom arm was controlled by EMG transducers mounted on the chest, abdomen, and shoulders of a normal subject. Two tasks requiring the movement of sixteen small blocks to specified locations on a table-top were chosen to test the performance of the aiding system. Measures of the system's effectiveness in unburdening the operator are shown in Figure 55. Following approximately two hours' practice on similar tasks, performance on the experimental tasks was recorded in terms of the proportion of trial time during which the machine and the user were in control of the arm. It is interesting to note that by substituting the labels *automatic control* and *feedback control* for *computer time* and *override time* in the figure, these data

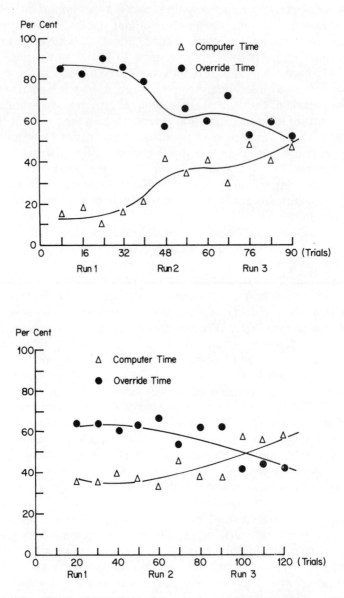

Figure 55. The shift in control from the operator to the computer as a function of practice on two manipulative tasks using an adaptive aiding system for artificial limb control. (From Freedy, Hull, and Lyman, 1971.)

present a feasible theoretical picture of the development of a motor program in normal skill acquisition.

SENSORY IMPAIRMENT

A mystique has always tended to surround popular conceptions of persons suffering from the major sensory disorders of deafness and blindness which is not apparent in attitudes concerning individuals with severe motor impairments. This view has been expressed in a number of ways, but in all cases it is characterized by the belief that the handicapped person somehow possesses supernatural or at least extraordinary sensory and cognitive abilities that automatically accrue to him by the loss of visual or auditory input. For the most part, these notions seem to be based on casual observations of successful deaf and blind persons who appear to be engaging in skilled behaviors thought to be impossible without the rich supply of information provided by the visual or auditory senses. Although the more bizarre beliefs that the blind and the deaf are endowed with powers of extrasensory perception or with especially high intelligence have been discounted on rational grounds, the general idea continues to survive in the form of the sensory compensation hypothesis.

Briefly stated, this hypothesis suggests that the deprivation of visual or auditory sensation produces a biological enhancement of the powers of residual sensory systems. Unfortunately, the experimental evidence has failed to confirm the hypothesis. In direct comparisons, the thresholds of sensitivity and powers of discrimination of the tactile and auditory senses of the blind have been shown to be equivalent to, and possibly even poorer than, those of the unimpaired population (Axelrod, 1959; Rice, 1970). At the neurophysiological level, Russian researchers, cited by McDaniel (1969), have presented evidence which indicates that the blind display reduced cortical excitability and disinhibition of subcortical structures in comparison to sighted subjects. Myklebust (1964) showed that a similar *negative* compensation may occur with deafness. Because persons with sensory deficits do not automatically acquire abilities which permit them to engage in skills normally served by audition or vision, considerable effort has been directed toward the development of efficient methods of employing alternative sensory systems. The following sections of this chapter discuss the profound effects of auditory and visual impairment on human performance, and examine the skills variables which contribute to the success of attempts to restore skill by the application of sensory aids.

Deafness

Auditory impairment is one of the least obvious yet most prevalent physical handicaps. In the United States alone it has been estimated that 8.5 million people have a significant degree of hearing loss and that there are over 900,000 people who cannot perceive speech without the use of some form of sensory aid (Levitt and Nye, 1971). Deafness is a broad term which encompasses a variety of hearing disorders. The most common symptom of most of these auditory impairments is an absolute loss of sensitivity of hearing either in specific frequency ranges or across the entire audible spectrum. However, additional deficits often include various forms of distortion of the acoustic signal, an abnormal growth of loudness with increases in signal amplitude, and the perception of buzzing or ringing in the ears.

Although audition plays an important background monitoring role in a number of skills, the overwhelming significance of language skill in nearly all aspects of human behavior has prompted rehabilitation researchers to focus the bulk of their attention on the improvement of speech perception in hearing-impaired persons. As in many perceptual-motor skills, the communication of ideas and concepts between individuals requires the use of a code. The listener's task is to decode the stream of sound waves produced by the speaker into the units of a language code and then to interpret the meaning which the speaker has intended to convey. The complexity of the listener's task is magnified by the fact there is no simple relationship between the phonemes, or basic units of spoken language, and the speech sounds which impinge upon the ear. The acoustic cues for successive phonemes are intermixed in the speech stream to such an extent that definable segments of sound do not correspond to segments at the phoneme level.

Despite its intricacy, the speech code is the most universal, efficient, and compatible code yet devised for the communication of ideas. Speech can be followed at rates as high as 400 words per minute (Orr, Friedman, and Williams, 1965). In addition, the perception of speech is highly resistant to disruption so that with normal hearing meaningful speech can often be recognized when embedded in noise of a greater intensity than the speech wave itself, when the speech signal is curtailed by filtering out its high or low frequency components, when it is distorted by various methods, and even when up to 50 per cent of an utterance is deleted by time sampling (Denes and Pinson, 1963).

If information was conveyed in speech only by the analysis of the cues present in the acoustic signal received by the ear, the speed and accuracy of the listening skills would be very poor indeed. Fortunately, the inherent limitations of the listener are circumvented by the fact that speech is perceived by the use of multiple cues. The speech signal itself contains multiple acoustic cues for the recognition of individual phonemes so that not all of the signal needs to be received for adequate comprehension. More importantly, a large part of the perception of speech is given by the knowledge of what the incoming signal *probably* is rather than by an exhaustive analysis of the stimulus itself. This knowledge is derived from a number of sources. In normal discourse the listener quickly builds up expectations about what is being conveyed by the speaker from the general speech situation and the context of the message. Furthermore, the listener normally has a detailed knowledge of the structure of the language in which the speaker has coded his message. Prior to receiving any signal the listener knows both the range of permissible phonemic units of the language and the rules which determine how these units can be combined to form words. Likewise, his knowledge of the grammar and syntax of the language restricts the way in which these words can be combined to form phrases and sentences. The multiple acoustic cues present in the speech signal added to those provided by the knowledge of language and those derived from the context of the speaker's message allow the listener to predict the content of connected speech quite accurately. In fact, the combined cues are far in excess of what is actually needed for the recognition of speech. However, it is this redundancy itself which permits the perception of speech at remarkable rates and under extremely variable listening conditions.

The congenitally deaf person has the primary disadvantage of being at least partially unable to make use of the basic structure of language to facilitate speech perception. Even when hearing loss is partial, the fact that these persons often have a deficient knowledge of the statistical, syntactic, and semantic properties of the language code limits their ability to anticipate the form and content of speech. Although the individual whose hearing loss occurs after he has acquired language skills is able to use the structure of the code, the redundancy of the speech stream is reduced because his impairment reduces the amount of relevant stimulation that he receives. Consequently, whether he relies on his residual hearing or the minimal cues available through lip-reading, the deaf individual is less likely to extract all of the information from the speech signal. This effect is cumulative so that the deaf person's uncertainty about contemporaneous input is raised even further by his inadequate knowledge of the situational information normally derived from preceding discourse. Finally, since the hearing-impaired person must recognize speech on the basis of degraded sensory evidence, a large part of his limited processing capacity must be devoted to retaining information in short-term memory while it receives more complete analysis than would be otherwise necessary. In combination with the other factors, this extra processing severely reduces the spare capacity that the deaf person has available to deal with the information currently arriving in the speech signal.

The most common approach to the problem has been to make use of residual hearing whenever possible. The conventional hearing aid is designed to overcome a loss in auditory sensitivity by linear amplification of the speech signal. Although this procedure seems to be simple enough, the choice of suitable levels of amplification for different frequency ranges is often quite difficult to make. For example, it is often found that the best speech perception is obtained when the greatest amount of amplification is provided for frequency regions where threshold elevation is least (Levitt and Nye, 1971). Furthermore, even when sufficient residual hearing appears to be available, simple amplification does not always result in an adequate improvement in speech perception.

Visual speech displays

In cases of profound hearing loss, methods must be devised to circument the damaged auditory system. Although a number of ongoing research efforts are exploring the possibility that hearing can be restored through direct electrical stimulation of the cochlea or even the auditory cortex (Bellahsene, 1985), the medical hazards and technical uncertainties of these approaches have focused the attention of many researchers on the concept of presenting speech to alternate sensory modalities. Visual displays of speech have existed for a number of years with the most common type consisting of some form of graphic array. These devices may indicate the presence of certain aspects of the acoustic signal such as the position of vowel sounds or certain high-frequency consonants, or they may present a picture of the entire frequency spectrum of the speech wave on a television screen (see Levitt and Nye, 1971, Chapter 3). Although these devices appear to be useful as speech training aids for the congenitally deaf, complex spectrographic representations are of little use for the perception of connected speech in real time. The eye excels at perceiving static spatial displays but tends to be unable to distinguish events occurring in rapid succession. Because of this it is not surprising that vision has difficulty in dealing with a complex graphic display designed for interpretation by repeated scanning when it continuously changes with the rapidly varying speech signal (Sherrick and Cholewiak, 1977).

Although complex visual displays have proved to be of limited value, it is clear that vision is capable of acting as an input channel for speech. Lip-reading is a skill acquired by many deaf individuals. Messages conveyed by lip-reading constitute an optical language encoded in the changing shape of the mouth and relative positions of the teeth, tongue, lips, and jaw which accompany the production of speech. The speechreader's task is complicated by the fact that only about one-third of the forty-odd meaningful sounds of spoken language are visible even to the careful observer. As a result, accurate lip-reading requires an extensive use of contextual and structural cues which can lead to an excessive processing load for the deaf individual (Pauls, 1964).

In order to reduce the effort of speechreading, Upton (1968) developed a device mounted in a spectacle frame which presents additional speech information via a seven-segment LED display projected on the speaker's face by virtual imagery. The signal processor of the device selects aspects of the speech signal which are not easily derived from the observation of the articulatory movements of the speaker and displays each feature as a flash of light from one of the LED segments. Tests of the aid indicate that dividing visual attention between the speaker's lips and the rapidly flashing display is a difficult perceptual task in itself. However, after extended training with one deaf subject, lip-reading scores were improved by 19 per cent when the aid was used (Gengel, 1977). Furthermore, the subject reported that communication was easier and more relaxed with the aid. Thus, although evidence for the efficiency of the Upton aid is meager, it appears that this device may reduce the processing demands of lip-reading by increasing the redundancy of the incoming signal.

Tactile speech displays

Any display designed to use vision to present speech to the deaf individual has the primary disadvantage of occupying a sensory channel which is important to the execution of numerous skills often performed in conjunction with speech perception. An alternative sensory substitute that does not suffer from this disadvantage is the tactile sense. The possibility of speech communication by touch has been an appealing notion to researchers because the skin shares some psychophysical properties with audition, including sensitivity to vibration and the ability to resolve temporal sequences of events. Unfortunately, over fifty years of research on this problem has failed to produce a method of presenting speech information to the skin by means of a vibratory display. Although a number of approaches have appeared promising in early work with limited test materials, none has been able to produce acceptable recognition of connected discourse.

One of the most obvious reasons why the development of tactile displays of speech has proved to be an extremely difficult task is that, in comparison to audition, the cutaneous sense is much more restricted in terms of vibratory sensitivity and power of discrimination. Although the range of frequencies over which the skin can respond is quite large, the absolute threshold of vibratory sensitivity rises sharply above 1000 Hz (Bekesy, 1959) and the skin's ability to discriminate frequencies deteriorates rapidly above 200 Hz (Goff, 1967). It has also been shown that the skin responds more slowly than the ear (Bekesy, 1959), and that in order to discriminate two successive events, it requires an interval at least five times longer than does the ear (Gescheider, 1970).

In an attempt to bypass these temporal limitations some researchers have coded the speech signal in a spatial form using devices based on the vocoder principle (Dudley, 1939). Vocoders divide the frequency spectrum of speech into a number of channels by means of a set of band pass filters. The output of each channel is a voltage proportional to the amount of acoustic energy fed into it. This apparatus has been used to drive a set of spatially separated vibrators at a frequency perceptible by the skin.

A variety of tactile vocoders have been developed which differ in the selection of pass bands and the number of channels into which the frequency spectrum is coded. However, none of the devices has proved to be adequate for more than learning simple discriminations among a restricted set of speech sounds. A limiting factor in the use of tactile vocoders has been the masking phenomenon which tends to occur when multiple skin loci are vibrated simultaneously. In their study with a ten-channel vocoder which stimulated each of the fingers of both hands, Pickett and Pickett (1963) found that simultaneous masking often prevented subjects from identifying speech sounds specified by vibrations on several fingers. Thus, problems of spatial discrimination must be added to the list of psychophysical limitations of the skin as an input channel for speech.

A second hypothesis which has been forwarded to explain the failure of both tactile and visual displays for speech is that speech perception is biologically tied to the auditory system. Liberman, et al. (1968) argued that the auditory channel contains a special mechanism for decoding phonemes from the complexly intermingled acoustic cues present in the speech wave, and that no such decoder is available to the other senses. Although this notion has had much influence on theoretical conceptions of speech perception, its practical validity is placed in doubt by considerable evidence that deaf-blind persons trained in the Tadoma method are able to perceive connected speech tactually by placing their hands on the face and neck of a speaker (Alcorn, 1945; Reed et al., 1977).

Kirman (1973) has suggested that the explanation both for the success of the natural tactile-kinesthetic display used by the deaf-blind and for the failure of artificial tactile displays of speech is that they differ in their ability to permit the skin to extract larger linguistic units from the speech stream. Kirman contended that techniques which seek to preserve the individual perceptual identities of the tactually coded elements by separating them spatially and temporally inevitably lead to slow communication rates because they reduce the probability that the skin will be able to organize the stimulus patterns produced by the speech wave into words and sentences. This argument indicates that a useful tactile display of speech would have to make use of aspects of tactile perception which facilitate the integration of information into meaningful perceptual entities.

A display which may satisfy this condition presents spatially-coded information which temporally unfolds across the surface of the skin. Research on the cutaneous display of letters (Bliss and Linville, 1967) and geometric forms (Bach-y-Rita, 1967) by matrices of vibrators has shown that when these stimuli are scanned so that they appear to move across the skin, identification is superior to the situation where the entire spatial pattern is presented statically. Kirman proposed that the phenomenon of tactile apparent movement could be used to provide the spatio-temporal framework for the perceptual integration of speech in the same way that the successive movements of the jaw and lips and the continuous variation of perceived laryngeal vibrations permit the perception of speech by the Tadoma method. Such an organizing framework could be achieved by using dynamic tactile patterns to represent such things as the continuous movement of formant resonances over time produced by changes in place of articulation during speech, or the continuous change in the amplitude envelope of the acoustic signal which reflects the segmentation of speech into syllables and patterns of stress. A limited device designed to present a Tadoma-like vibratory display to the fingertips was described by Miller et al. (1974). Using facially mounted accelerometers and microphones as sensors, these researchers showed that improvements of up to 30% could be obtained in lip-readers' recognition of randomly selected monosyllabic words.

Although no fully functional dynamic system appears to have been tested, the issues raised by Kirman (1973) indicate that the solution to the problem of developing compatible techniques of sensory substitution to restore receptive speech skill in the deaf will require a more complete understanding both of the way in which information is transmitted by speech and of the methods of coding and display which make the best use of the abilities of different sensory channels to integrate information into meaningful perceptual units.

Blindness

Vision's primacy among the human senses and its central role in the execution of the vast majority of skills, makes blindness potentially one of the most handicapping conditions that can be experienced. Reasonable estimates can be made of the prevalence of blindness in Western countries from statistics which have been shown that in the United States at least 1.7 million people suffer from severe visual impairment and that over 40 per cent of these people cannot read print or use vision to guide themselves during foot travel in the environment (Mann, 1974). The importance of these basic skills of reading and mobility to the rehabilitation of the blind cannot be underestimated. The blind individual who does not have access to the printed word or who is unable to travel independently often is relegated to a lifestyle characterized by passive reliance on others. In contrast, the visually impaired person who does acquire adequate reading and mobility skills enjoys a high degree of personal freedom and is able to pursue educational and vocational goals which otherwise would be unavailable to him.

Reading skills

The development of standardized non-visual alternatives for print began in France in the late eighteenth century with the introduction of the first embossed tactile codes. The earliest of these codes consisted of raised print letter shapes. Many simplified analogue alphabets were created to improve the legibility of individual characters, but by the late nineteenth century most of these printing systems were superseded by Louis Braille's punctiform code. Braille slowly gained universal acceptance as a substitute for print, partially because it appeared to be simpler to read, but primarily because it could be both read and written by the blind with comparative ease.

In modern braille the elements of printed language are coded as tangible characters composed of one to six raised dots arranged within a matrix of two columns and three rows. The most commonly used braille system, known as Grade 2 braille, contains 263 elements assigned to the 63 possible characters. In addition to the 24 letters of the alphabet, braille characters for numbers and contractions of certain letter groups are formed from the remaining 39 patterns and through the use of adjacent characters to modify the meaning of individual cells.

Despite its long history of acceptance and use by the blind, braille is by no means an ideal substitute for visually presented print. The reading rates attained by the majority of braille readers are disappointly slower than those of sighted print readers. Numerous studies have shown that typical average braille reading speeds range between 70 and 90 wpm depending on the experience of the reader and the difficulty of the test materials (e.g. Meyers, Ethington, and Ashcroft, 1958). Print is normally read by the sighted at rates four to five times faster than this.

One of the more obvious factors that may limit the rate of information transfer by the braille code is its low redundancy. Failure to perceive any of the dots in a character or to identify accurately the position of dot patterns in equivocal characters often leads to confusions among braille letters. In contrast, Kolers (1969) has shown that most print types are highly redundant so that the reader need not perceive an entire letter shape to identify it correctly.

A second problem with the braille code that has emerged from the important series of studies by Nolan and Kederis (1969) is that the visual print and tactual braille reading processes differ in a very basic way. Although both experienced print and braille readers are able to use their knowledge of the statistical constraints and grammar of written language as well as general context to identify the content of a passage, the unit of recognition for the braille reader is much smaller than that of the print reader. Recognition times for whole words printed in braille are longer than the sum of the recognition times for the individual letters which comprise the word. This result is in complete contrast to the comparable findings for print reading and indicates that most braille readers do not perceive whole words from the flow of dots which pass beneath the finger. Instead, larger linguistic units must be tediously constructed from an exhaustive analysis of individual braille cells. This mode of perception is time-consuming and forces the reader to retain the information acquired from individual characters in his limited-capacity short-term memory while further evidence is collected to identify a word. As a consequence, both the speed and accuracy of reading are likely to be impaired. Taenzer (1970) presented evidence in support of this explanation of the difficulties of braille reading by showing that when sighted readers are forced to perceive printed letters individually, reading rates similar to those of blind braille readers are obtained.

In addition to low reading speeds, braille has the disadvantage of providing only indirect access to print. Transcribers, in recent years aided by computers, must be employed to perform the translation, and this process inevitably limits the availability of braille reading material. The purpose of direct translating reading aids is to provide the blind with immediate access to print. These devices detect the light reflected from a page and present the reader with an auditory or tactual analogue of the patterns produced by printed letters. The Optophone provides an auditory display of the contours of a line of print as a probe consisting of a single vertical line of photodetectors is passed across individual letters (Coffey, 1963). The display is designed so that the presence of letter strokes in the beam of any of the detectors is coded as a unique tone. When the probe is scanned across a line of print the output of the Optophone is an intricate series of tonal patterns which uniquely specify individual letters.

Although several years of research have been invested in the development of the Optophone and other similar devices such as the Stereotoner (see Cook, 1982), only a small number of users have been able to achieve any measurable success at interpreting this sort of display. Considering the fact that the Optophone reader is required to make exceedingly difficult discriminations among complex tonal patterns it is not surprising that even after extended training reading rates rarely exceed 12 wpm.

The Optacon (Bliss and Linville, 1967; Bliss et al., 1970) is a direct translation device which displays a tactile image of printed text to the reader's fingertip. Although raised print letters were rejected in favor of braille long before the development of the Optacon, the results of a considerable amount of psychophysical research were taken into account in the design of this aid in order to maximize the accuracy and rate of reading tactually displayed letter forms. The Optacon display is a densely packed array of 144 vibrating points. Experiments conducted by the inventors showed that optimal legibility was obtained at a vibratory frequency of 200 Hz and when 24 stimulating points were used to represent the vertical dimension of print letters.

Bliss and his colleagues also found that reading speed was higher when letters flowed beneath the fingertip in a manner similar to the display presented by a Times Square lighted sign than when they were presented statically. The six-column width of the display was chosen on the basis of data which indicated that reading rate was enhanced when entire letters were within the field of view of the reader's fingertip. Typical reading rates with the Optacon in its present form range from 12 to 50 wpm after extended training and practice. However, speeds equivalent to those attained by average braille readers have been observed in some cases.

The relatively slow reading rates normally achieved with braille and available direct translation aids could be attributed to a basic inability of the cutaneous and auditory senses to make efficient use of the sort of information presented by written language. However, the apparent efficiency of these input channels for numerous other skills makes it more likely that the problem stems from a failure to display print information to the skin or the ear in an optimal manner. As a result of poor compatibility, the braille, Optaphone, or Optacon user is forced to engage in extra intellectual activities which place an excessive load on his limited information processing system. Since the task of gathering raw information from the display involves such a high degree of mental effort, the blind reader has little spare capacity to devote to the cognitive activities such as inference, anticipation, and interpretation which are the hallmark of the skilled print reader.

The problem of sensory substitution for reading skill is simplified by the fact that a compatible alternative for the print code is readily available in the speech code. Records and tapes presenting oral versions of written text have been used successfully by the blind for a number of years. Like braille, such recordings provide only indirect access to print. However, recent developments in optical character recognition and speech synthesis have made direct print-to-speech translation devices such as the Kurzweil reading machine a reality (Kurzweil, 1981). Although the reading rates of blind persons almost certainly will be improved by the design of such devices, it is doubtful that they will prove to be an ideal substitute for visual print reading. As Foulke (1970) has noted, one of the important features of skilled print reading is the reader's ability to control the rate of input and selectively to scan the textual material according to his informational needs. Because of the purely temporal nature of the speech display, the person who reads by listening cannot easily engage in the rapid skimming and selective scanning behaviors which enhance the efficiency of visual print reading. Such limitations make it apparent that any attempt to develop a device which will permit the blind to read as quickly and accurately as their sighted counterparts will not only have to optimize the compatibility of the code used to present print to an alternative sensory system, but also ensure that the format of the display allows the user to control his exposure to the reading materials.

Mobility skills

The difficulty with which reading skills are acquired and practised by the blind is undoubtedly a serious impediment to rehabilitation. However, the single greatest handicap that is produced by the absence of visual stimulation is the impairment of independent movement in the environment. Although a blind individual may gain a number of special intellectual and occupational skills, it is unlikely that they will be of significant value to him if he has insufficient travel skill to give him access to the places in which these abilities can be meaningfully exercised. Mobility, as this skill has been termed, can be defined as the ability to travel from one place to another safely, comfortably, gracefully, and independently (Foulke, 1970). Thus, mobility refers both to the ability to move through space without disruption because of accidental contact with obstacles, and to the ability to orient with the environment in order to achieve purposeful or goal-directed movement.

Efforts to assist the blind in acquiring mobility skill have consisted of the development of sensory aids and associated training techniques. The two most common mobility aids in regular use by blind pedestrians are the long cane (Hoover, 1950) and the dog guide (Ebeling, 1950). When properly used, the long cane acts as a tactual-kinesthetic extension of the traveler's arm which explores the surface of the path into which his next step will carry him. Dogs have been specifically trained as guides since 1916 and a limited number of blind persons who have the physical stamina and are able to tolerate the inconveniences of caring for an animal are able to use a dog guide to improve their mobility. Unfortunately, neither the dog nor the cane is an ideal mobility device. Not all blind persons are able to learn to use these aids effectively, and even when training is successful, the safety and efficiency of the performance of the blind traveler does not approach that of his sighted peer.

As a result, during the past 25 years, numerous designers have attempted to devise electronic sensory aids to enhance blind mobility skill. These devices emit ultrasound or coherent light and convert the energy reflected from objects in the environment to some form of auditory or tactual display. Most of these devices have never reached significant levels of development. However, a few have survived and are either in production or in the final stages of evaluation. The simplest electronic aids which indicate whether a clear path exists ahead of the pedestrian and provide some range information include the Pathsounder (Russell, 1971), and the Nottingham Obstacle Detector (NOD) (Armstrong and Heyes, 1975). More complex aids such as the Bionics Laser Cane (Benjamin, 1970) and the Sonic Guide (Kay, 1972) attempt to supply a more complete view of the environment by informing the traveler of specific environmental features or by providing a display enriched with azimuthal and textural cues. Regrettably, the electronic aids which have been subjected to thorough evaluation by blind pedestrians have failed to live up to the expectations of their creators.

An important reason why adequate solutions to the mobility problem have not yet been found is that relatively little research has been conducted to analyse the behavior of blind travelers or to investigate the perceptual processes which underlie mobility skill. Leonard (1972) noted that it is curious that experts in the field of human performance know very much about the behavior of astronauts in their working environment but very little about the performance characteristics of the common pedestrian. One reason for this disparity of knowledge is that, in many ways, the measurement and analysis of an astronaut's performance is a fairly simple problem. Essentially, he works in an enclosed, highly structured environment in which most of the stimuli presented to him and his responses are clearly observable and quantifiable. In contrast, mobility is a complex, open skill in which task demands continually change as the traveler enters new portions of space. The information displayed to his senses is not well constrained so that it is difficult to determine which environmental stimuli are important to his performance. In addition, response sequences in mobility tend to be highly integrated so that the quantification of output is an arduous task.

Because of these difficulties the problem of assessing and analysing the blind pedestrian's performance has been approached in a variety of ways. A large proportion of the research which has been conducted on blind mobility skill has been in the form of practical evaluations of mobility aids. Unfortunately, as noted by Shingledecker and Foulke (1978), because of inadequate experimental design, the use of device-specific indices of performance, and a reliance on subjective measurement, this purely applied work has provided only very meager insights into blind mobility.

An alternative approach which has made significant contributions to the understanding of blind mobility is represented by the body of research conducted to isolate various component subskills which contribute to overall performance. One of the most notable examples of this type of experimentation was a series of studies conducted to investigate the fabled 'facial vision' of the blind (Supa, Cotzin, and Dallenbach, 1944; Cotzin and Dallenbach, 1950). Results showed that this ability is attributable to the learned use of reflected, high-frequency acoustic cues usually produced by the traveler's footsteps and that the differential pitch of the original and reflected sounds is the important dimension of the cue. These results were extended by Kohler (1964) who replicated the earlier findings and described the way in which guiding sounds and sound shadows are used to complement echolocation. Other studies of the subskills underlying mobility have included Juurmaa's

(1973) preliminary work on spatial orientation skills and Cratty's (1971) psychophysical studies of the veering tendency displayed by blind subjects as they attempt to walk in a straight line and of their ability to detect gradients, path curvature, and geographical direction.

Although subskill studies have contributed much to our knowledge of the basic sources of information that the unaided blind pedestrian is able to call upon when walking, this approach cannot provide a complete description of the quality of overall mobility performance when traveling. A methodology for the assessment of mobility performance which permits whole-task measurement was described by Armstrong (1975). In this technique a number of behaviorally-defined objective measures derived from the task goals of safety and efficiency are used to evaluate the performance of blind subjects as they travel over prescribed routes. Safety measures include the frequency and nature of body contact with objects in the environment and the frequency of departures from the pathway. Measures of efficiency consist of the assessment of behaviors which lead to reasonably rapid progress and which provide the most accurate route to a destination. Such measures include walking speed, the continuousness of progress, and the accuracy of navigational decisions. This methodology has been used successfully to evaluate the contribution of several sensory aids to mobility performance.

A common starting point for the analysis of complex skills in human performance research is to attempt to assess the information-processing demands placed upon the individual. Upon initial consideration this approach may not appear to be meaningful for blind mobility because it is often thought that it is simply the lack of sufficient information which makes the blind pedestrian's task difficult. However, if the absence of visual input alters the mobility task so that extra processing activities are necessary to achieve safe and efficient performance, it is likely that the increased processing load or mental effort demanded by the task may be an important factor in accounting for deficient mobility performance.

Mental effort

The possible sources of excessive processing load for the blind traveler are numerous. For example, it is apparent that the increased difficulty of selectively attending to single sources of information presents an additional load for the blind pedestrian who must often rely on the relatively inefficient auditory system. Another process which is disproportionately loaded for the blind traveler is short-term memory. Unlike his sighted counterpart, he has few immediate cues available to permit him to monitor his present position in relation to the beginning and end of a route. Thus, he often must maintain a running memory span of the number of turns made or of the number of streets crossed in order to achieve orientation. An even more important difference between the blind and sighted pedestrian that may have an effect on the processing demands of mobility is that the blind traveler receives very little information about upcoming events while the sighted person normally has full knowledge of the near environment. Laboratory studies of tracking skill have shown that as subjects receive increased preview of the course that they are following, or as they gain practice on a course with recognizable regularities, performance improves (see Chapter 8, this volume). These results illustrate the importance of advance information in complex skills. When forthcoming stimulus events are unpredictable, processing overloads result because the performer's limited capacity decison-making mechanism lags behind the incoming information. However, when future events can be directly observed, or when they can be anticipated from memory, the decision-making apparatus can work ahead immediate motor output and thereby permit accurate performance.

The blind pedestrian is in much the same position as the subject in a tracking experiment with limited preview. Because he often receives only limited and degraded information about the space ahead, the blind person can experience momentary periods of overload during which large amounts of information are encountered. Instead of continuously working ahead of his immediate spatial position, the blind traveler tends to receive sporadic information that must be interpreted and acted upon within a very brief period of time if his performance is to remain both safe and efficient. Although with sufficient practice on a particular route the blind individual can begin to rely on a memorial representation to anticipate events, the success of this strategy depends on the questionable quality of the 'cognitive maps' that he has been able to construct, and on the problem of forgetting.

The validity of the notion that extra information-processing demands are placed upon the blind pedestrian and that these demands are partially responsible for poor blind mobility performance was tested in an experiment conducted by the author in which a secondary task (as discussed in Chapter 4, this volume) was used to assess processing load as blind and blindfolded sighted subjects walked over routes in a simulated travel environment (Shingledecker, 1978). The secondary task was a two-choice reaction time (RT) problem which required the subject to respond to vibratory pulses presented to his wrists by pressing the appropriate button on a panel carried in his left hand. After baseline mobility and RT performance had been recorded, the subjects were randomly divided into three groups and were then required to perform the mobility and RT tasks simultaneously.

In the dual-task condition one of the groups walked the same route on which they had received five practice trials. A second group walked an unfamiliar route of equivalent complexity. The third group walked the identical unfamiliar route but received preview of turns, steps, and curbs. Preview was presented in the form of brief verbal messages spoken to the subject by an experimenter who followed him over the route. It was hypothesized that subjects who had prior experience with a route and those who received preview of an unfamiliar route would produce better mobility performance than those who had no basis for anticipation. Furthermore, if the ability to anticipate reduces the momentary processing load of the mobility task, more 'spare channel capacity' should have been available to those subjects who had some form of advance information. Thus, it was expected that their performance on the RT task would show less impairment than that of the subjects who had no basis for anticipation.

The results of the experiment were in agreement with these predictions. Mobility performance as assessed by the measures outlined by Armstrong (1975) was improved under dual-task conditions by both practice and preview. More importantly, the effects of anticipation were clearly shown in the errors made by the subjects on the secondary task (see Figure 56). Subjects who were unable to anticipate upcoming events failed to respond to the vibratory stimuli significantly more often than those who received preview or those who could predict environmental events from memory. Secondary task performance was also shown to vary as a function of the momentary information processing demands of the travel environment. Decrements in RT performance for all of the groups tended to occur at points along the routes which required subjects to detect landmarks, locate changes in direction, and maintain a straight course while crossing a street. Barth (1979) confirmed these results using heart rate measures while varying the preview available to sighted pedestrians.

Both experiments provided objective evidence to support the hypothesis that human information-processing limitations are a significant impediment to blind mobility skill and that the provision of anticipatory information can reduce the extra processing load incurred by the loss of vision. The findings indicate that a major design criterion for mobility aids should be the incorporation of preview information. Although most designers have implicitly adopted this criterion, few of them have considered the problem of excess processing load when making decisions about the type and amount of advance information that should be gathered from the environment or about the way in which this information should be displayed to the blind pedestrian.

Aid design

An inspection of the characteristics of current mobility aids reveals two distinct design philosophies. The first of these contends that a viable mobility aid should gather very little information from the environment and should display that information to the user in a simple manner. The NOD and the Pathsounder were developed under this philosophy. Both are intended only

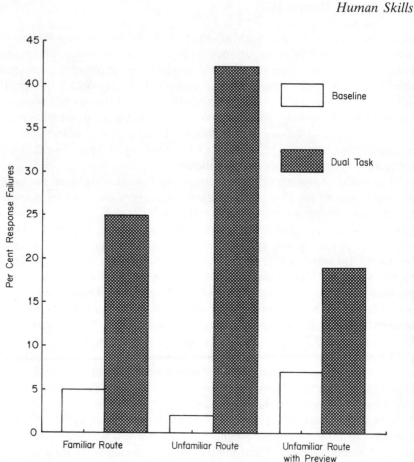

Figure 56. The effects of route familiarity and environmental preview on a secondary task performed during blind mobility. (Original figure from data presented by Shingle-decker, 1978.)

as supplementary sources of travel information and warn the user of objects in his path via an easily learned auditory display. The alternative approach to the design of mobility aids can be characterized by a belief that a device should gather a great deal of information and that as much of that raw information as possible should be displayed to enable the user's brain to select and interpret it as needed. Devices which have attempted to embody this principle include a prototype aid, the Tactile Visual Substitution System, which uses a television camera to drive an array of vibrators fixed on the user's abdomen or back (Bach-y-Rita, 1972), and the currently available Sonic Guide.

The potential problems associated with this form of mobility aid can be appreciated by examining the Sonic Guide, a binaural sonar system which is mounted in a spectacle frame. The distances of objects within its range are coded by the pitch of the auditory display, while azimuthal positions are coded by the relative intensity of the signals in the user's left and right ears. All of the objects which are simultaneously present within the wide beam of the device contribute to the display, and the reflective characteristics of these objects further modify the nature of the signal received by the user.

It is obvious that the output of the Sonic Guide is extremely rich in information about the traveler's world. Unfortunately, the expected improvement in mobility resulting from the use of this aid has not been fully realized. Although some blind persons have been able to achieve better performance, others have shown very little change or even a deterioration in travel skill (Airasian, 1972). Additional evidence has shown that long cane skills may suffer when, as recommended, the cane is used in conjunction with the Sonic Guide (Armstrong, 1972).

In a pilot study performed by Shingledecker (1983), the secondary task described previously was used to compare the mental load of a blind traveler using the long cane alone with that experienced when using the Sonic Guide or a similar complex mobility aid. While the results were derived from only one subject, the data indicated that both electronic aids offered a moderate improvement in travel performance over the long cane. However, secondary task performance was much poorer with the electronic devices than with the long cane.

Findings such as these are congruent with the results of the experiment described earlier in this section. Devices which attempt to display a complete and therefore complex view of the environment may, in fact, increase the already high cognitive processing load of the blind mobility skill. As shown above, the result may be a minimal enhancement in performance benefit with a disproportionate increase in mental cost.

The problem of limited processing capacity and the effective further reduction of this capacity by the absence of vision is one which must be a primary consideration in the design of future hardware to enhance mobility skill. Solutions to the problem may lie in an improved understanding of how spatial information is acquired and represented in the cognitive system of the blind pedestrian (Hollyfield and Foulke, 1983). However, it is also probable that significant advances will depend on the development of a better definition of the specific perceptual information needed to accomplish a wide variety of mobility tasks. Armed with knowledge of such critical environmental features, aids like the one described by Brabyn (1982) might preprocess environmental information and filter out irrelevant data, thereby providing the traveler with optimal cues at an acceptable mental cost.

FUTURE PROSPECTS

An overview of the advances in modern physical science which have made it possible to design and build the sorts of prostheses and sensory aids described in this chapter indicates that there are few insurmountable technological barriers to the development of any aid that a disabled person might require. In fact, it is not difficult to conceive of a time in the near future when our technical knowledge will be sophisticated enough to produce the equipment that would be needed to construct the Bionic Man of science fiction fame whose prosthetic receptors and effectors not only meet but exceed the functional capabilities of intact sensory and motor organs. Despite these immense technological resources, many devices intended to restore skill to the handicapped continue to have only limited value because designers often have been forced to rely on introspection and intuition to determine the appropriate characteristics of prosthetic equipment and sensory aids. As a result, the human user's information-processing capacities and limitations which are ultimately responsible for skill have not been sufficiently taken into account.

The problem is perhaps best illustrated by returning to an analogy presented in the introductory section of this chapter where the human operator was conceptualized as an information-processing device similar to a computer. Like a computer, the human operator can be described as a central information-processing device along with a set of peripheral input and output devices. The computer's input devices corresponding to human sensory systems might be a disk drive and a keyboard. Its output peripherals analogous to human limbs or vocal apparatus could be a line printer and a graph plotter. One task that the computer might be called upon to perform would be to receive some data via its disk drive, organize the data, and provide a frequency distribution of the data by drawing a curve on the graph plotter. A mechanical failure of the graph plotter would produce a breakdown of this 'skill'. A student who decides to substitute the line printer for the graph plotter in order to get his job done, simply by instructing the computer to address the printer rather than the plotter, is likely to be rather disappointed. Although the printer has the mechanical ability to plot a graph by printing a series of points to represent the data and axes of a figure, to do so it requires different instructions from those needed by the graph plotter. The eventual success with which this 'motor' substitution could be made would depend on the computer's ability to provide interpretable commands to the line printer, the availability of an appropriate program in the computer's memory, and the computer's capacity to meet the information-processing demands of the task.

In order to be successful at the task of restoring skilled performance, the designer of devices for the disabled, like the computer operator, must be aware of the mechanisms of skill and of the strategies of information processing that dictate the way in which these mechanisms are used. The development of efficient ways to use substitute sensory modalities and to design effective sensory and motor aids require consideration of the entire information-processing system. The sensitivity and powers of discrimination of sensory channels must be understood, the decision-making and memorial capacities of central processes must be taken into account, and the properties of attentional and motor control must be appreciated if useful solutions to the problems of handicap are to be found.

SUMMARY

This chapter reviews the relationship between research on human skilled performance and efforts to relieve handicaps caused by serious sensory and motor disabilities. Although the development of devices for the disabled traditionally has been guided by personal intuition, the limited success of such an approach is now leading designers to consider the basic human characteristics and limitations that determine the quality of skilled performance. Three handicapping conditions are discussed to illustrate the ways in which knowledge of perceptual and motor processes can be applied to rehabilitation engineering.

Motor impairments associated with the loss of a limb, and attempts to restore manual and locomotor skills with prosthetic devices, are considered in terms of requirements for control capacities, sensory feedback, and the need to develop normal automaticity in the use of artificial effectors. Deficits in receptive language skills caused by deafness are treated by examining the perceptual and cognitive problems underlying the use of alternative visual and tactile speech displays. Finally, the re-establishment of reading and travel skills affected by blindness is considered. Tactile and auditory substitutes for the printed page are evaluated and the cognitive information processing demand of non-visual mobility is implicated as a determinant of the travel behavior of blind pedestrians.

Chapter 11

Final Survey

Dennis H. Holding

It should now be possible to appreciate the general outlines that a description of skilled performance must follow. The previous chapters have covered a great many substantive issues, contributing between them nearly all the basic information needed to assemble a comprehensive account of human skills. It seems appropriate for this chapter to try to complete the picture in three different ways. First, the fact that the individual chapters have been written by different hands makes it more than usually important to provide a brief review of the most salient issues, with some attempt to exhibit the links between separately treated topics. Next, it seems necessary to introduce a little of the material which has been excluded from consideration so far. Probably the most relevant category of information not supplied in the previous chapters is material concerned with the breakdown of skills, since clues about the organization of skills are provided by the manner of their disintegration. Finally, there is a brief attempt to forecast the directions which research on skills seems likely to take.

SALIENT ISSUES

We have seen that feedback, whether or not it is consciously processed, is of central importance to the development and maintenance of complex skilled activities. An open-loop system, in which an input leads to a response output without reference to the consequences of any prior output, can operate well only in a highly predictable environment. It is only the highly skilled performer who can afford to 'go open-loop' since, for him, most action sequences are relatively predictable. Hence, skills tend to become more automatic as practice proceeds. As Winstein and Schmidt show in Chapter 2, the operation of feedback can be analysed in detail at the level of neural circuits such as the muscle spindle, at the level of visual and kinesthetic consequences of actions, or at the level of fully processed knowledge of results. We may expect to see continuing research exploring the contributions of feedback and knowledge of results to motor control and skill acquisition.

At the same time, it is now clear that humans operate in at least a temporarily open-loop fashion much more often than was once supposed, using motor control programs which specify in fair detail the characteristics of learned movement sequences. The evidence is that many coordinated movements can still be executed when feedback has been eliminated, either by direct intervention or by the speed demands of the task. We have also seen that there is evidence for the preprogramming of movements, even when feedback is available, from studies in which the preparation time for complex action is shown to exceed the times for simpler movements. As Summers suggests in Chapter 3, incorporating the motor program concept into a fuller account of skilled performance may require something along the lines of Schmidt's (1975) schema theory. This kind of concept calls for the representation in memory of integrated networks of information, relating the goals of human actions both to motor command sequences and to correlated data from the various sensory systems. The flexibility of this approach seems promising, although it remains to be seen whether the theory can be made sufficiently precise for explicit testing.

It should be stressed that the feedback and motor program concepts are complementary, rather than antithetical. In fact, even at the time when motor skills theory was primarily concerned with feedback mechanisms, Licklider (1960) drew attention to the possibilities of a 'conditional' servo system. Such a system contains predictor elements which allow for open-loop operation as long as the output is in line with the target or 'intention' of the activity, but will switch into corrective feedback whenever a significant discrepancy appears. Feedback is also viewed as functioning to adjust the overall parameters under which the system operates, which is fully compatible with current thinking. However, the practical problem for research is to determine exactly when the human operator is making use of feedback cues.

A useful example is given by Wilke and Vaughn (1976), who tried a reaction-time probe at various points during a dart-throwing movement. Reaction to a photographic flash bulb took 307 milliseconds during the period immediately before the movement, when most of the information-processing takes place, fell to 274 milliseconds as the subject's arm was drawn back ready for the throw, and continued to decline through successive segments of the movement down to 178 milliseconds immediately after the release of the dart. Notice that the greatest attention demand, as implied by the lengthened reaction time, arises at the stage when preprogramming is presumed to occur but, also, that the reaction times are still elevated while the movement is in progress. This in turn implies that monitoring of the movement, probably by proprioceptive feedback, is still taking place well after the initial motor commands have been formulated and the movement started. Subsequent research of this kind can be expected to clarify matters further.

The reaction-time method used in the dart-throwing experiment is a form of the secondary task technique discussed by Wickens in Chapter 4. The practical usefulness of this type of methodology is further underscored by the work on sharing reaction time with blind mobility (reported in Chapter 10). However, the use of a secondary task represents only one of many applications of the multiple task paradigm, which has also been used to generate research on the problems of time-sharing and mental workload. One finding of note is that operators can apparently learn, subject to memory limitations, to improve their strategies for switching attention between competing channels. The way in which attention is shared seems to depend on task difficulty, since more demanding tasks will compete for greater shares of the available resources. As a result, plotting the tradeoffs between different tasks in the form of performance operating characteristics often produces enlightening results. Of course, it is more difficult to share attention between tasks when misleading similarities exist between them, thus giving rise to task interference. In any case, people appear to differ in their performance at time-sharing activities, perhaps due to basic differences in ability.

Even when concentrating on a single task, the required control processes are complex. Thus, in the analysis of discrete movements, we see the application of both the motor programming and the feedback principles discussed in earlier chapters. Glencross makes it clear in Chapter 5 that discrete movements, whether simple or repetitive, are extensively preprogrammed. This is a necessity for really fast movements, although slower movements can be modified by various mechanisms of 'current control'. Changes in the time taken to amend ongoing responses might underlie the relationship expressed in Fitts' Law (1954), although there are several theoretical accounts of the mechanisms relating the speed, amplitude and tolerance limits of repeated movements. Many of the apparent conflicts may be resolved by noting that some formulations are appropriate to spatial and some to temporal precision, and that different formulations may address either accuracy or variability in responding. In any case, it appears necessary to distinguish between minor adjustments and the more major corrections needed for responses initiated in the wrong direction.

The instructions for quite long sequences of responses can be stored on long- or short-term memory. Accessing these instructions is one of the problems for sequential skills, typified by the many varieties of keyboard tasks, in which the analysis cannot neglect the role of verbal mediation. This is a developing area of research, involving issues which range from the thorough analysis of human errors and error detection to the elaboration of models of choice behavior. The particular contribution of Chapter 6 is to show how the concepts of control theory can deal with the constantly changing parameters of human performance. Serial choice reaction tasks and, in fact, all tasks that require continuous response selection, are subject to performance changes that are partially under the control of the operator. As Rabbitt shows, the effects of various stresses, practice, and learning effects are such that the human operator is clumsily represented by steady-state models. There is more promise for hierarchical models based on the assumption that humans monitor at a higher level the performance conducted at a lower level, although it remains to be seen what effect the recent work on reaction time distributions will have in determining the exact form of a workable model.

Analogous problems arise in tracking tasks, where attempts at transfer function analysis run foul of various non-linearities. However, Hammerton's job in Chapter 7 has been largely to explain the accumulated empirical data. A great deal is known about the advantage of pursuit over compensatory forms of tracking tasks, about the performance associated with different orders of control, and about the merits of various kinds of control design. Enough is known about the technology of tracking to produce extremely serviceable simulators when difficulty, danger, or expense makes training on live equipment undesirable. The crucial question for any simulator is how well its training transfers to the real task, although the issue is not simple. The scores on initial transfer may not reflect later performance and, as Holding (1976) illustrates, a transfer model for overall scores may be very different from a model predicting negative transfer in the form of intrusive errors.

Transfer of training is one of the central issues in learning, since it contributes toward the acquisition of skill, especially in the associative phase, and most skills must be generalized for practical use. However, Salmoni's exposition in Chapter 8 is organized around all three of Fitts' (1964) phases of learning. In the initial cognitive phase where the attempt is made to understand what is required, the techniques of modeling and guidance are prominent, but problems arise in relating words to actions. In the associative phase, the reshaping of old habits does raise the issues of transfer, and depends in various ways on the effectiveness of knowledge of results, although the latter issue is somewhat controversial. It is no longer possible, for example, to assert that terminal KR will affect learning while concurrent KR affects only performance, in view of findings like those of Patrick and Mutlusoy (1982) in which concurrent feedback produces a learning effect. The final, automatic phase of skill acquisition has been the subject of renewed interest in recent years, interacting with the multiple resource issues discussed above.

Many of the skills that are most readily applied in everyday tasks are also those with appreciable cognitive components. In Chapter 9, the skills of writing, typing, speaking, and music discussed by Colley all involve the translation of symbolic material into overt performance. In each case, the models proposed to account for these activities assume layered structures, with some degree of planning or preprogramming at higher levels coordinated with more direct control of action at lower levels. In other words, response preparation is viewed as preceding, or overlapping with, response execution. For the most part, however, these processes have been studied independently. There is an obvious need to delineate the ways in which different levels of these hierarchies interact, as well as to examine both the premotor and motor processes in greater detail.

In a different area of application, the growth of the knowledge needed to remedy physical handicaps seems reasonably promising. To some extent, engineering technology has outstripped the corresponding information on the sensory and motor control characteristics of the human user of various aids, but the gap may be closing. To some extent, piecemeal selection of aids is being replaced by remedial techniques which take into account the entire information-processing system. The formulation of research questions about the handicapped has been greatly helped by recent, more sophisticated approaches to skills analysis. Thus, for example, it is possible to ask whether blind mobility is hampered by requiring an overload of information-handling as much as by a deficit of stimulus information, and to answer the question by systematic use of the secondary task technique. Shingledecker raises many issues in Chapter 10, such as the importance of preview and anticipation, which exemplify in practical form the theoretical concerns of earlier chapters. In fact, considering and analysing handicaps can be seen to improve our general understanding of the ways in which skills function. Studying blind mobility, again as an example, has shown us a good deal about what is involved in normal travel from place to place.

THE BREAKDOWN OF SKILLS

Apart from the direct effects due to handicaps, skills may suffer deterioration as a result of drug action, because of fatigue or other stresses, or as a consequence of aging processes. Each of these areas has a considerable research literature, represented elsewhere in this series, but it is possible to give a brief indication of the kinds of skill difficulty suggested by breakdown under these different circumstances.

An example of a nervous system depressant, which tends to inhibit cortical function, is provided by nitrous oxide. Using this drug, Legge (1965) showed that handwriting became larger as the dose was increased, as shown in Figure 57. It seems that the perception of the movement of one's hand, by vision and by proprioception, is impaired by the drug; the increased size of writing compensates for this effect, perhaps because the new visual size is appropriate for a subjectively more distant visual stimulus. Legge's analysis of stylus

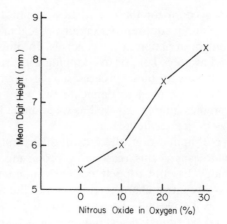

Figure 57. Handwriting size increases with drug dosage. (From Legge, 1965.) Reproduced by permission of the author and the British Psychological Society.

movements to a reference mark showed that the errors made were least when both the stylus and the target were perceived visually, and somewhat greater when both were perceived proprioceptively, but that the greatest variable error occurred with mixed modalities. Thus, combining visual and proprioceptive information seems to constitute an additional stage of processing for the subject, and one which is particularly sensitive to disruption by the drug.

Alcohol is also classified as a depressant drug, despite its use as a 'stimulant', and it, too, causes larger handwriting, together with other kinds of exaggerated movement. Drew, Colquhoun, and Long (1958) showed that heightened levels of blood alcohol produced successively greater amounts of steering-wheel movement in a simulated driving task. With high alcohol dosages, the subjects also tracked less accurately, often steering more toward the middle of the road in order to compensate for their variability, which was particularly evident in cornering. There were no consistent effects on driving speed, which seemed to depend on personality characteristics.

In addition, drugs and other substances may produce a number of toxic effects. Thus, the presence of lead in the blood tends to lengthen response times in vigilance tasks, and to slow down measures of eye-hand coordination (Morgan and Repko, 1974). Inhaling methylene chloride has the effect of impairing a wide range of performance measures, including indices of sensory functioning (Winneke, 1974), probably as a result of a general depressant effect. Evidence of this kind is accumulating, and will eventually contribute more fully toward the understanding of skills.

Stress and fatigue

Various environmental and individual stresses, such as heat, noise, or loss of sleep, have adverse effects on human performance. A volume surveying these effects, together with those due to fatigue, has been prepared by Hockey (1983). The consequences of many stresses may be linked in different ways to the concept of arousal.

Loss of sleep, for example, presumably results in a state of reduced arousal. It affects the rate of responding in many tasks like serial reaction, makes for errors or gaps in performance, and causes missed signals in watch-keeping. Of course, the opportunity for sleep will restore arousal and performance to normal levels. However, if arousal is further increased by some form of stimulation, performance may again deteriorate. Hence, it has been proposed that performance is related to arousal by an inverted U-shaped function, such that both under- and overarousal are detrimental (Corcoran, 1965).

This idea may explain some of the confusing effects of noise, which may in different circumstances be adverse, beneficial, or neutral (Loeb, 1986). Noise seems to be arousing, so that its use will improve performance after loss of sleep by raising arousal to an optimal level, whereas in other circumstances it may damage performance, perhaps by causing overarousal. Noise effects will also interact with the level of arousal as it varies during the normal day, and with other factors, in a complex way. Thus, Baker, Loeb, and Holding (1984) found no general effect of noise on a paced, serial addition task; however, noise made women react faster in the afternoon, and made men more accurate under fast pacing in the morning. Poulton's (1978) review suggests that the complexity of noise effects derives from the fact that noise provides distraction, in addition to masking auditory cues and to working through the arousal mechanism.

The effect of ambient heat seems to operate rather differently, tending to reduce accuracy directly rather than indirectly by reducing the amount of activity in the way which loss of sleep appears to do. Again, it is probably significant that heat and noise do not seem to interact. Bell (1978) recently used both of these stresses in an experiment with the secondary task technique, with rotary pursuit as the primary task and the comparison of auditory digits as the subsidiary task. More errors were made on the secondary task as the temperature was raised from 22°C to 35°C and also when background noise at 95 dB was introduced, but the two effects were independent (see Figure 58). This tends to confirm earlier suggestions that heat stress affects a different mechanism, separate from the arousal effect.

The effects of fatigue present a clearer picture of the breakdown of skills (Holding, 1983). Consideration must be given to two different aspects of fatigue, deterioration of performance on a prolonged task, and the more elusive results of earlier fatigue on subsequent tasks. Protracted performance

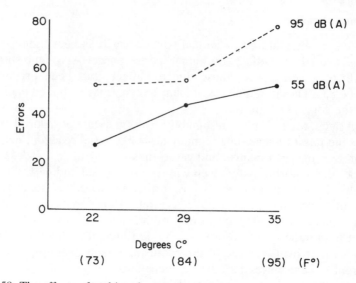

Figure 58. The effects of ambient heat and noise on pursuit rotor tracking. Both heat and noise seem to raise the error scores, but without interacting. (From Bell (1978) in the journal *Human Factors.*)

of a skilled task has a number of consequences, first outlined by Bartlett (1943) in describing experiments with an aircraft simulator. Progressively larger deviations of the instrument readings were tolerated, with a general deterioration in the operator's standards of performance. Lapses of attention occurred with increasing frequency, central aspects of the task were emphasized while peripheral elements were neglected, and operators became more easily distracted. Responses became much more variable, particularly in their timing, so that many correct actions were executed at the wrong time. Responding appeared to lose coherence, such that the overall pattern of action disintegrated into separated components. This kind of disintegration has also been observed in athletic movements, as when Bates, Osternig, and James (1977) analysed film records of the running cycle during fatigue. The times for components like foot strike and foot descent increased, while forward swing decreased and other measures remained constant, thus suggesting that the central control of timing had deteriorated.

On the other hand, generalized fatigue effects have always been difficult to measure on an interpolated or subsequent test, partly because people can usually compensate for any impairment on changing to a different task. Very often there is no direct carryover from a fatiguing task, although people's attitudes toward undertaking further effort are usually changed. Tired subjects will take chances and 'cut corners' in order to avoid effort. This may be seen in drivers' judgements of when to overtake (Brown, Tickner, and Simmons, 1970) and, with appropriate techniques (Holding, 1974), may be quantified in the laboratory. Thus it has been shown that subjects given the choice will elect to test fewer electrical components, at the risk of a lowered probability of finding a faulty item, after fatigue on a complex monitoring task (Shingledecker and Holding, 1974). Similarly, they will choose to crank an arm ergometer for shorter periods, at the risk of lowered success in the task, after a tiring run on the treadmill (Barth, Holding, and Stamford, 1976).

Aging

As people grow older they tend to become slower to decide and react, more hesitant and forgetful, and less inclined or able to change their ways. Charness (1985) examines these developments, which take place throughout adult life, in detail. The deterioration of sensory functions is well known, with steady drops in visual acuity and accommodation, and progressive changes in auditory thresholds and in the apparent loudness of the higher sound frequencies. There is some decrement in muscular output from the twenties onwards, although this is only of real significance when prolonged exertion is required. More important than these peripheral changes are the limitations on central mechanisms, which increasingly constrain the quality of performance when fast or complex processing is demanded.

Slowness of reaction is evidenced in many tasks, particularly those which pose difficult choices. Some early work by Szafran (1951), for example, required subjects to reach for a choice of visual targets. The movement times were approximately constant across different ages, but the 'preparation times', involving decisions before moving, rose steadily from 0.86 second for subjects in their twenties to 1.37 seconds for fifty year olds. The same series of experiments also showed that older subjects were much more seriously handicapped by having to wear dark goggles than were the younger subjects. Other lines of evidence may be adduced (Welford, 1958) which suggest that this finding is actually a partial example of three different generalizations concerning the effects of ageing. Thus, it illustrates a return to a dependence upon vision, which is normally a characteristic of the early stages of skill. Next, it serves to demonstrate that older subjects typically need more information in order to act, despite the fact that they can handle incoming information less well, with the result that they tend to hesitate. Finally, it shows an effect which has been replicated in a wide variety of tasks, such that any increase in complexity tends to widen the performance gap between older and younger subjects (see Figure 59).

The effect of task complexity may also be seen in the context of short-term memory load. A straightforward test of digit span shows little effect of age, but asking for the digits in reverse order increases the age differences.

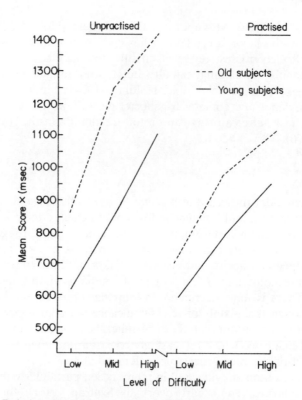

Figure 59. Relation between increasing difficulty (of transitions between choice responses) and the time taken to respond, before and after practice. The curves for older and younger subjects diverge significantly as the level of difficulty mounts. (From Jordan and Rabbitt, 1977.) Reproduced by permission of the authors and the British Psychological Society.

Having the subjects bear information in mind while carrying out some other manipulation such that, for instance, he has to respond by pressing a key which corresponds to a light which has appeared two or three items back in a series of lights at different positions, becomes an almost insuperable task for many of the older subjects. The same effect may be seen in tracking tasks (Griew, 1958), where masking off a preview of the target course imposes a load upon working memory for advance cues in a way which tends to defeat the older subjects. Long-term memory deficits are more difficult to demonstrate, except in cases of real senility. Thus, Franklin and Holding (1977) found that people aged up to the seventies all seemed to add steadily to their store of remembered events. However, the long-term effects of prior practice do tend to produce difficulties for transfer of training, so that veteran drivers of horse-drawn vehicles make poor students at bus driving (Entwisle, 1959).

Accumulated experience is an asset, when it is relevant, but is a burden when irrelevant.

PROBABLE TRENDS

Studies of the breakdown or deterioration of skills, such as those reviewed above, will obviously continue to provide useful information at many levels. The features of performance displayed under the influence of drugs, during stress or fatigue, or as aging proceeds, often mirror the earlier, clumsier stages of skill acquisition. Before any real breakdown has occurred, the effects of stress will tend to throw into prominence any discontinuities in the smooth performance of a skill. A steady stream of contributions to the skills area can be expected from these sources, much of it bearing on the cognitive problems of attention and arousal.

Applied work of various kinds will continue to provide a stimulus to investigate new problems, or to reconsider old problems in a new light. Theoretical research soon becomes sterile in the absence of the reinvigoration provoked by practical issues. A case in point is provided by the topics or preview and anticipation, which re-emerge alongside newer issues in the study of blind mobility. Similarly, vigilance studies were developed in response to the practical problem of submarine spotting, later received a theoretical overhaul with the advent of signal detection theory, and are now promising a resurgence in order to answer the questions posed by the problems of industrial inspection. Industrial problems in general, as represented by Holding (1969), are likely to orient toward the perceptual end of the skills continuum. Physical production processes have become far less important with the development of methods of automation, to be replaced by increasing concern for the inspection problems of quality control, the monitoring and selection problems of process control, and the strategy and decision problems of 'trouble-shooting' and maintenance.

In the mainstream of skills research, it is possible to detect two divergent trends. One direction of emphasis is toward the motor end of the skills continuum, toward the detailed analysis of athletic skills, and toward the elaboration of existing links with neurophysiology. The presence of a growing number of physical education specialists who are familiar with the methods of experimental psychology, and of psychologists with some knowledge of kinesiology and exercise physiology, ensures a steadily developing corpus of research concerning sports and physical skills. As with the applied, industrial work, facing the issues raised by physical education will stimulate further developments in pure research. One may also reasonably expect to see further work on neural mechanisms, more use of techniques such as electromyographic recording, and a better understanding of the ways in which kinesthesis functions, particularly with respect to the part it may play in the regulation of ongoing movements. The increasingly available background knowledge of physiological mechanisms will help to set clear limits to the kinds of theoretical speculation which are admissible.

The other major trend is toward the study of cognitive skills, as represented in the forthcoming volume by Colley and Beech (in press), and toward the development of cognitive models for the control of action. The earlier theoretical explanations of skilled behavior (Laszlo and Manning, 1970; Adams, 1971; Schmidt, 1975) already contained important cognitive components. These theories represent movement selection as a form of retrieval process, in which the appropriate movement features are extracted from long- or short-term storage for incorporation in an output program. Ongoing or completed movements are evaluated against an internal standard of some kind, which forms one step in an information flow sequence. Whether one refers to standards and programs, to perceptual traces, or to developing schemata, the general outlines are broadly similar. Later approaches such as the framework proposed by Turvey, Shaw, and Mace (1978) may attempt to place human action within the broader context of interaction with the environment, while as discussed above, there exists a variety of models for different cognitive skills. Such theories, as exemplified by Mackay's (1983) account of speech production, concentrate heavily on the higher levels of control and response preparation.

Clearly, these types of theory have all of the elements of contemporary cognitive models, and are cast in a form which is compatible with such models from other areas of research. Anderson's (1987) theory for the acquisition of problem-solving skills, for example, can also be applied to the skills of musical performance. Thus, as presaged in the first edition of this volume, the many parallels between verbal and nonverbal behavior have become more apparent in a number of ways. Despite following a separate course for several decades, skills research now enjoys the predicted integration with the remainder of experimental psychology. The new relationship continues to promise mutual benefits, both to the parent discipline and the field of sensori-motor skills.

SUMMARY

This final chapter briefly reviews the theoretical issues concerning feedback, motor programs, and time-sharing between dual tasks. It draws attention to some of the major features of discrete, sequential, and tracking skills, and surveys some aspects of motor learning, cognitive skills, and research on handicaps. The breakdown of skill is illustrated by outlining the effects of stimulant and depressant drugs, the effects of loss of sleep, noise, heat stress, and fatigue, and the effects of aging. An attempt is made to forecast the directions to be taken by future research into human skills.

References
and Author Index

(The numbers in parentheses at the end of each reference indicate the pages where the references are cited.)

Abbs, J. H., Gracco, V. L., and Cole, K. J. (1984) Control of multimovement coordination: Sensorimotor mechanisms in speech motor programming. *Journal of Motor Behavior*, **16**, 195–231. (65)

Adams, J. A. (1961) Human tracking behavior. *Psychological Bulletin*, **58**, 55–79. (171)

Adams, J. A. (1971) A closed-loop theory of motor learning. *Journal of Motor Behavior*, **3**, 111–150. (43, 49, 58, 200, 206, 292)

Adams, J. A. (1976) Issues for a closed-loop theory of motor learning. In G. E. Stelmach (ed.), *Motor Control: Issues and Trends*. New York: Academic Press. (49, 229)

Adams, J. A. (1977) Feedback theory of how joint receptors regulate the timing and positioning of a limb. *Psychological Review*, **84**, 504–523. (54)

Adams, J. A. (1984) Learning of movement sequences. *Psychological Bulletin*, **96**, 3–28. (50)

Adams, J. A. (1985) The use of a model of movement sequences for the study of knowledge of results and the training of experts. *Journal of Human Movement Studies*, **11**, 223–236. (208)

Adams, J. A. (1987) Historical review and appraisal of research on the learning, retention, and transfer of human skills. *Psychological Bulletin*, **101**, 41–74. (38)

Adams, J. A., and Dijkstra, S. (1966) Short-term memory for motor responses. *Journal of Experimental Psychology*, **71**, 314–318. (209)

Airaisian, P. W. (1972) *Evaluation of the Binaural Sensory Aid*. Washington, D.C.: National Academy of Sciences. (278)

Alcorn, S. (1945) Development of the Tadoma method for the deaf-blind. *Journal of Exceptional Children*, **11**, 117–119. (266)

Allard, F., and Burnett, N. (1985) Skill in sport. *Canadian Journal of Psychology*, **39**, 294–312. (225)

Alles, D. S. (1970) Information transfer by phantom sensations. *IEEE Transactions on Man-Machine Systems*, MMS-11 (1), 85–91. (257)

Allport, D. A. (1980) Patterns and actions: Cognitive mechanisms are content-specific. In G. Claxton (ed.), *Cognitive Psychology: New Directions*. London: Routledge & Kegan Paul. (244, 245)

Allport, D. A., Antonis, B., and Reynolds, P. (1972) On the division of attention: A disproof of the single channel hypothesis. *Quarterly Journal of Experimental Psychology*, **24**, 225–235. (14, 84)

Anderson, J. R. (1976) *Language, Memory, and Thought*. Hillsdale, N.J.: Lawrence Erlbaum Assoc. Publishers. (203, 215)

Anderson, J. R. (1982) Acquisition of cognitive skill. *Psychological Review*, **89**, 369–406. (245)

Anderson, J. R. (1983) *The Architecture of Cognition*. Cambridge, MA: Harvard University Press. (203, 245)

Anderson, J. R. (1987) Skill acquisition: Compilation of weak-method problem solutions. *Psychological Review*, **94**, 192–210. (245, 246, 292)

Anderson, J. R., Farrell, R., and Sauers, R. (1984) Learning to program in LISP. *Cognitive Science*, **8**, 87–129. (245)

Andre, A., and Wickens, C. S. (1988) The interaction of spatial and color proximity in aircraft stability information displays. Proceedings, 32nd Annual Meeting of the Human Factors Society. Santa Monica, CA: Human Factors.

Angel, R. W. (1976) Efference copy in the control of movement. *Neurology*, **26**, 1164–1168. (133)

Angel, R. W., and Higgins, J. R. (1969) Correction of false moves in pursuit tracking. *Journal of Experimental Psychology*, **82**, 185–187. (132)

Angel, R. W., Garland, H., and Fischler, M. (1971) Tracking errors amended without visual feedback. *Journal of Experimental Psychology*, **89**, 422–424. (133, 140)

Annett, J. (1969) *Feedback and Human Behaviour*. Harmondsworth, Middlesex: Penguin Books. (40, 45)

Annett, J., and Kay, H. (1957) Knowledge of results and 'skilled performance'. *Occupational Psychology*, **31**, 69–79. (40)

Anshel, M. H., and Ortiz, M. (1986) Effect of coding strategies on movement extent as a function of cognitive style. *Perceptual and Motor Skills*, **63**, 1311–1317. (214)

Appentung, K., Lund, J. P., and Seguin, J. J. (1982) Behavior of cutaneous mechano-receptors recorded in mandibular division of Gasserian ganglion of the rabbit during movements of the jaw. *Journal of Neurophysiology*, **47**, 151–166. (23)

Arbib, M. A. (1980) Interacting schemas for motor control. In G. E. Stelmach and J. Requin (eds), *Tutorials in Motor Behavior*, 71–81. Amsterdam: North-Holland. (64, 65)

Arbib, M. A. (1981) Perceptual structures and distributed motor control. In V. B. Brooks (ed.), *Handbook of Physiology, Vol. III: Motor Control*, 1449–1480. Bethesda, MD: American Physiological Society. (65)

Arbib, M. A., Iberall, T., and Lyons, D. (1985) Coordinated control programs for movements of the hand. In W. Goodwin and I. Darian-Smith (eds), *Hand Function and the Neocortex*, 111–129 (Experimental Brain Research Supplement, Vol. 10). Berlin: Springer. (65)

Armstrong, J. D. (1972) *An Independent Evaluation of the Kay Binaural Sensor*. Blind Mobility Research Unit, University of Nottingham. (278)

Armstrong, J. D. (1975) Evaluation of man–machine systems in the mobility of the visually handicapped. In R. M. Pickett and T. J. Trigg (eds), *Human Factors in Health Care*. Lexington, MA: Lexington Books. (274, 276)

Armstrong, J. D., and Heyes, A. D. (1975) The work of the Blind Mobility Research Unit. In E. Kwatny and R. Zuckerman (eds), *Devices and Systems for the Disabled*. Philadelphia, PA: Temple University Health Sciences Center, 161–165. (271)

Armstrong, T. R. (1970a) Feedback and perceptual-motor skill learning: A review of information feedback and manual guidance training techniques. *Technical Report No. 25*, Human Performance Center, University of Michigan. (209)

Armstrong, T. R. (1970b) Training for the production of memorized movement patterns. *Technical Report No. 26*, Human Performance Center, University of Michigan. (60)

Asatryan, D. G., and Feldman, A. G. (1965) Functional tuning of the nervous system with control of movement or maintenance of a steady posture—I. Mechanographic analysis of the work of the joint on execution of a postural task. *Biophysics*, **10**, 925–935. (63)

Atkeson, C. G., and Hollerbach, J. M. (1985) Kinematic features of unrestrained vertical arm movements. *Journal of Neuroscience*, **5**, 2318–2330. (63)

Audley, R. J. (1973) Some observations on theories of choice reaction time. In S. Kornblaum (ed.), *Attention and Performance IV*. New York: Academic Press. (148)

Audley, R. J., Caudrey, D. J., Howell, P., and Powell, D. J. (1975) Reaction time exchange functions in choice tasks. In P. M. A. Rabbitt and S. Dornic (eds), *Attention and Performance V*. London: Academic Press. (148)

Axelrod, S. (1959) Effects of early blindness: Performance of blind and sighted children on tactile and auditory tasks. American Foundation for the Blind. *Research Monograph No. 7*. (261)

Bach-y-Rita, P. (1967) Sensory plasticity: Applications to a visual substitution system. *Acta Neurologica Scandinavia*, **43**, 417–426. (266)

Bach-y-Rita, P. (1972) *Brain Mechanisms in Sensory Substitution*. New York: Academic Press. (277)

Baddeley, A. D., and Hitch, G. (1974) Working memory. In G. H. Bower (ed.), *The Psychology of Learning and Motivation*, Vol. 8. New York: Academic Press. (83)

Baddeley, A. D., and Lieberman, K. (1980) Spatial working memory. In R. S. Nickerson (ed.), *Attention and Performance VIII*. Hillsdale, N.J.: Lawrence Erlbaum Assoc. Publishers. (83)

Bahrick, H. P., and Shelly, C. (1958) Time-sharing as an index of automation. *Journal of Experimental Psychology*, **56**, 288–293. (80, 219, 220)

Baker, M. A. (ed.) (1987) *Sex Differences in Human Performance*. Chichester: John Wiley. (7)

Baker, M. A., Holding, D. H., and Loeb, M. (1984) Noise, sex and time of day effects in a mathematics task. *Ergonomics*, **27**, 67–80. (287)

Bandura, A. (1986) *Social Foundations of Thought and Action: A Social Cognitive Theory*. Englewoods Cliffs, N.J.: Prentice Hall, Inc. (204, 207, 208)

Barnett, B. J., and Wickens, C. D. (1987) Display proximity in multicue information integration: The benefit of boxes. *Human Factors*, **30**, 15–24. (94, 95)

Baron, S., Kleinman, D., and Levison, W. (1970) An optimal control model of human response. *Automatica*, **6**, 357–369. (164)

Barrett, N. C., and Glencross, D. J. (1988) Double-step analysis of rapid manual aiming movements. *Quarterly Journal of Experimental Psychology*, **40A**, 299–322. (137, 139)

Barth, J. L. (1979) The effects of preview constraint on perceptual motor behavior and stress level in a mobility task. Unpublished Doctoral Dissertation, University of Louisville. (276)

Barth, J. L., Holding, D. H., and Stamford, B. A. (1976) Risk versus effort in the assessment of motor fatigue. *Journal of Motor Behavior*, **8**, 189–194. (289)

Bartlett, F. C. (1943) Fatigue following highly skilled work. *Proceedings of the Royal Society, Series B*, **131**, 247–257. (288)

Bartlett, F. C. (1958) *Thinking: An Experimental and Social Study*. London: Allen and Unwin. (1)

Bates, B. T., Osternig, L. R., and James, S. L. (1977) Fatigue effects in running. *Journal of Motor Behavior*, **9**, 203–207. (288)

Beatty, J. (1982) Task-evoked pupillary responses, processing load, and the structure of processing resources. *Psychological Bulletin*, **91**, 276–292. (79)

Becker, W. (1976) Do correction saccades depend exclusively on retinal feedback: A note on the possible role of non-retinal feedback. *Vision Research*, **16**, 425–427. (130)

Becker, W., and Jurgens, R. (1975) Saccadic reactions to double-step stimuli: Evidence for model feedback and continuous information uptake. In G. Lenner-strand and P. Bach-y-Rita (eds), *Basic Mechanisms of Ocular Motility and Their Clinical Implications*. Oxford: Pergamon Press. (137)

Becker, W., and Jurgens, R. (1979) An analysis of the saccadic system by means of double-step stimuli. *Vision Research*, **19**, 964–983. (127, 137, 139, 140, 141)

Beggs, W. D. A., and Howarth, C. I. (1970) Movement control in a repetitive motor task. *Nature*, **225**, 752–753. (120, 126, 128)

Beggs, W. D. A., and Howarth, C. I. (1972a) The accuracy of aiming at a target. Some further evidence for a theory of intermittent control. *Acta Psychologica*, **36**, 171–177. (126)

Beggs, W. D. A., and Howarth, C. I. (1972b) The movement of the hand towards a target. *Quarterly Journal of Experimental Psychology*, **24**, 448–453.

Bekesy, G. V. (1959) Similarities between hearing and skin sensations, *Psychological Review*, **66**, 1–22. (126, 265)

Belenkii, V. Ye., Gurfinkel, V. S., and Paltsev, Ye, I. (1967) Elements of control of voluntary movements. *Biophysics*, **12**, 154–161. (56)

Bell, P. A. (1978) Effects of noise and heat stress on primary and subsidiary task performance. *Human Factors*, **20**, 749–752. (287, 288)

Bellahsene, B. E. (1985) Hearing aids. In J. G. Webster, Albert M. Cook, Willis J. Tompkins, and Gregg C. Vonderheiden (eds), *Electronic Devices for Rehabilitation*. New York: John Wiley, 116–147. (264)

Benjamin, J. M. (1970) The bionics instruments C-4 laser cane. Paper to the National Academy of Engineering, Committee on the Interplay of Engineering with Biology and Medicine, Subcommittee on Sensory Aids, Warrenton, VA. (271)

Bernstein, N. (1967) *The Coordination and Regulation of Movements*. Oxford: Pergamon Press. (18, 66, 144, 247)

Bertelson, P. (1965) Serial choice reaction time as a function of response versus signal-and-response repetition. *Nature*, **206**, 217–218. (148)

Bertelson, P. (1966) Central intermittency twenty years later, *Quarterly Journal of Experimental Psychology*, **18**, 153–163. (129, 141)

Bilodeau, E. A., and Bilodeau, I. M. (1958) Variable frequency knowledge of results and the learning of a simple skill. *Journal of Experimental Psychology*, **55**, 379–383. (41)

Bilodeau, E. A., and Bilodeau, I. McD. (eds) (1969) *Principles of Skill Acquisition*. New York: Academic Press. (3)

Bilodeau, E. A., Bilodeau, I. M., and Schumsky, D. A. (1959) Some effects of introducing and withdrawing knowledge of results early and late in practice. *Journal of Experimental Psychology*, **58**, 142–144. (39)

Bilodeau, I. M. (1966) Information feedback. In E. A. Bilodeau (ed.), *Conference on Acquisition of Skill, New Orleans, 1965*, 255–296. New York: Academic Press. (38)

Bilodeau, I. M. (1969) Information feedback. In E. A. Bilodeau (ed.), *Principles of Skill Acquisition*, 255–285. New York: Academic Press. (43, 210, 211)

Bilodeau, I. M., and Jones, M. B. (1970) Information feedback in positioning problems and progress. In L. E. Smith (ed.), *Psychology of Motor Learning*, 1–23. Chicago, IL: The Athletic Institute. (46)

Binder, M. D., Kroin, J. S., Moore, G. P., and Stuart, D. G. (1977) The response of Golgi tendon organs to single motor unit contractions. *Journal of Physiology*, **271**, 337–349. (22)

Birch, H. G. and Lefford, A. (1967) Visual integration, intersensory integration and voluntary motor control. *Monographs of the Society for Research in Child Development*, No. 32. (207)

Birmingham, H. P., and Taylor, F. V. (1954) A design philosophy for man-machine systems. *Proceedings of the I. R. E.*, **42**, 1748–1758. (187)

Birren, J. (1977) Introduction to J. Birren and J. W. Schaie (eds), *Handbook of Aging and the Individual*. US Public Health Service. (158)

Bizzi, E., and Abend, W. (1983) Posture control and trajectory formation in single- and multi-Joint arm movements. In J. E. Desmedt (ed.), *Motor Control Mechanisms in Health and Disease*, 31–45. New York: Raven. (51, 63)

Bizzi, E., Dev. P., Morasso, P., and Polit, A. (1978) Effect of load disturbances during centrally initiated movements. *Journal of Neurophysiology*, **41**, 542–556. (62)

Bizzi, E., Polit, A., and Morasso, P. (1976) Mechanisms underlying achievement of final head position. *Journal of Neurophysiology*, **39**, 435–444. (62, 63, 143)

Bjork, R. A. (1987) Personal Communication, UCLA. (46)

Bliss, J. D., and Linvill, J. G. (1967) A direct translation reading aid. In R. Dufton (ed.), *Proceedings of the International Conference on Sensory Devices for the Blind*. London: St Dunstan's. (266, 269)

Bliss, J. D., Katcher, M. H., Rogers, C. H., and Shephard, R. P. (1970) Optical-to-tactile image conversion for the blind. *IEEE Transactions on Man-Machine Systems*, **11**, 58–65. (269)

Boles, D., and Wickens, C. D. (1987) Task integration between processing codes. *Human Factors*, **29**, 395–406. (94)

Bossom, J. (1974) Movement without proprioception. *Brain Research*, **71**, 285–296. (51)

Bouisset, S., and Zattara, M. (1981) A sequence of postural movements precedes voluntary movement. *Neuroscience Letters*, **22**, 263–270. (56)

Bowditch, H. P., and Southard, W. F. (1880) A comparison of sight and touch. *Journal of Physiology*, **3**, 232–245. (2)

Brabyn, J. A. (1982) Mobility aids for the blind. *Engineering in Medicine and Biology*, December, 36–38. (278)

Bransford, J. D., Franks, J. J., Morris, C. D., and Stein, B. S. (1979) Some general constraints on learning and memory research. In L. S. Cermak and F. I. M. Craik (eds), *Levels of Processing in Human Memory*. Hillsdale, N.J.: Lawrence Erlbaum Assoc. Publishers. (46, 218)

Braune, R., and Wickens, C. D. (1985) The functional age profile: An objective decision criterion for the assessment of pilot performance capacities and capabilities. *Human Factors*, **27**, 681–694. (100)

Braune, R., and Wickens, C. D. (1986) Time-sharing revisited: Test of a componential model for the assessment of individual differences. *Ergonomics*, **29**, 1399–1414. (100, 103, 104)

Bridgeman, B., Kirch, M., and Sperling, A. (1981) Segregation of cognitive and motor aspects of visual information using induced motion. *Perception and Psychophysics*, **29**, 336–342. (35)

Bridgeman, B., Lewis, S., Heit, G., and Nagle, M. (1979) Relation between cognitive and motor-oriented systems of visual position perception. *Journal of Experimental Psychology: Human Perception and Performance*, **5**, 692–700. (35)

Briggs, G. C., and Swanson, J. M. (1970) Encoding, decoding and central functions in human information processing. *Journal of Experimental Psychology*, **86**, 296–308. (149)

Broadbent, D. E. (1958) *Perception and Communication*. London: Pergamon Press. (3, 193)

Broadbent, D. E. (1972) *Decision and Stress*. London: Academic Press. (160)

Broadbent, D., and Broadbent, M. H. (1980) Priming and the passive/active model of word recognition. In R. Nickerson (ed.), *Attention and Performance VIII*. New York: Academic Press. (93)

Brooks, V. B. (1979) Motor programs revisited. In R. E. Talbott and D. R. Humphrey (eds), *Posture and Movement: Perspective for Integrating Sensory and Motor Research on the Mammalian Nervous System*, 13–49. Raven Press. (65, 123)

Brown, G., and Campbell, D. (1948) *Principles of Servomechanisms*. London: Chapman and Hall. (186)

Brown, I. D., Tickner, A. H., and Simmons, D. C. (1970) Effect of prolonged driving on overtaking criteria. *Ergonomics*, **13**, 239–242. (289)

Brown, J. S., and Slater-Hammel, A. T. (1949) Discrete movements in the horizontal plane as a function of their length and direction. *Journal of Experimental Psychology*, **2**, 84–95. (114)

Brunia, C. H. M., Haagh, S. A. V. M., and Scheirs, J. G. M. (1985) Waiting to respond: Electrophysiological measurements in man during preparation for a voluntary movement. In H. Heuer, U. Kleinbeck, and K.-H. Schmidt (eds), *Motor Behavior: Programming, Control and Acquisition*, 35–78. Berlin: Springer-Verlag. (56)

Bryan, W. L., and Harter, N. (1897) Studies in the physiology and psychology of the telegraphic language. *Psychological Review*, **4**, 27–53. (2)

Bryan, W. L., and Harter, N. (1899) Studies on the telegraphic language: The acquisition of a hierarchy of habits. *Psychological Review*, **6**, 345–375. (107, 200)

Burgess, R. R., and Clark, F. J. (1969) Characteristics of knee joint receptors in the cat. *Journal of Physiology*, **203**, 317–335. (23)

Burke, D. (1985) Muscle spindle function during movement. In E. V. Evarts, S. P. Wise, and D. Bousfield (eds), *The Motor System in Neurobiology*, 168–172. Amsterdam: Elsevier. (22)

Burns, J. T. (1965) The Effect of Errors on Reaction Time in a Serial Reaction Task. Unpublished Ph.D. thesis, University of Michigan. (156)

Burton, A. W. (1986) The effect of age on relative timing variability and transfer. *Journal of Motor Behavior*, **18**, 323–342. (63)

Butsch, R. L. C. (1932) Eye movements and the eye-hand span in typewriting. *Journal of Educational Psychology*, **23**, 104–121. (235)

Carlson, L. E. (1970) Below-elbow control of an externally powered hand. *Bulletin of Prosthetics Research*, **10–14**, 43–61. (252)

Carlton, L. G. (1981) Processing visual feedback information for movement control. *Journal of Experimental Psychology: Human Perception and Performance*, **7**, 1019–1030. (119, 127, 128, 129, 130, 141)

Carlton, M. J. (1983) Amending movements: The relationship between degree of mechanical disturbance and outcome accuracy. *Journal of Motor Behavior*, **15**, 39–62. (54, 144)

Caro, P. W., Isley, R. N., and Jolley, O. B. (1975) Mission suitability testing of an aircraft simulator. *HumRRO Technical Report*, 75–12. (191)

Carroll, W. R., and Bandura, A. (1982) The role of visual monitoring in observational learning of action patterns: Making the unobservable. *Journal of Motor Behavior*, **14**, 153–167. (57)

Carroll, W. R., and Bandura, A. (1985) Role of timing of visual monitoring and motor rehearsal in observational learning of action patterns. *Journal of Motor Behavior*, **17**, 269–281. (57)

Carswell, C. M., and Wickens, C. D. (1987) Information integration and the object display: An interaction of task demands and display superiority. *Ergonomics*, **30**, 511–527. (94)

Carter, M. C., and Shapiro, D. C. (1984) Control of sequential movements: Evidence for generalized motor programs. *Journal of Neurophysiology*, **52**, 787–796. (61)

Casey, E. J., and Wickens, C. D. (1986) *Visual Display Representation of Multidimensional Systems: The Effect of Information Correlation and Display Integrality*. University of Illinois Cognitive Psychophysiology Laboratory (Tech. Rep. CPL 86–2). Champaign, IL: Department of Psychology. (94)

Chambers, J. W., and Schumsky, D. A. (1978) The compression block technique: Use and misuse in the study of motor skills. *Journal of Motor Behavior*, **10**, 301–311. (29)

Charness, N. (1985) *Aging and Human Performance*. Chichester: John Wiley. (7, 249, 289)

Chau, A. W. L., Kao, H. S. R., and Shek, D. T. L. (1986) Writing time of double-character Chinese words: Effects of interrupting writing responses. In H. S. R. Kao, G. P. Van Galen, and R. Hoosain (eds), *Graphonomics: Contemporary Research in Handwriting*. Amsterdam: North-Holland. (232)

Chernikoff, R., and Lemay, M. (1963) Two-dimensional tracking with identical and different control dynamics in each coordinate. *Journal of Experimental Psychology*, **66**, 95–99. (91)

Chernikoff, R., and Taylor, F. V. (1952) Reaction time to kinaesthetic stimulation resulting from sudden arm displacement. *Journal of Experimental Psychology*, **43**, 1–8. (133)

Chernikoff, R., Duey, J. W., and Taylor, F. V. (1960) Effect of various display-control configurations on tracking with identical and different coordinate dynamics. *Journal of Experimental Psychology*, **60**, 318–322. (91, 180)

Chi, M. T. H. (1978) Knowledge structures and memory development. In R. S. Siegler (ed.), *Children's Thinking: What Develops?* Hillsdale, N.J.: Lawrence Erlbaum Assoc. Publishers. (225)

Childress, D. S. (1980) Closed-loop control in prosthetic systems: Historical perspective. *Annals of Biomedical Engineering*, **8**, 293–303. (256)

Childress, D. S. (1982) Myoelectric control of powered prostheses. *Engineering in Medicine and Biology*, December, 23–25. (255)

Christina, R. W. (1970) Minimum visual feedback processing time for amendment of an incorrect movement. *Perceptual and Motor Skills*, **31**, 991–994. (128)

Christovich, L. A. (1960) Vospriyatie zvukovoi posledovatel' nosti. *Biofizika*, **5**, 671–676. (153)

Christovich, L. A., and Klauss, Lu. A. (1962) Kamalizy skritovo perioda 'proizvol' noi reakstii na zvukovor signal. *Fiziologicheskii Zhurnal SSSR*, **48**, 899–906. (153)

Churchland, P. M. Cognitive neurobiology. Cited in Churchland, P. S. (1986) *Neurophilosophy* (Cambridge: MIT) Ch. 10. (188)

Clark, F. J., and Horch, K. W. (1986) Kinesthesia. In K. R. Boff, L. Kaufman, and J. P. Thomas (eds), *Handbook of Perception and Human Performance: Sec. 3. Basic Sensory Processes II: Vol. 1. Sensory Processes and Perception*, 1–62. New York: John Wiley. (20)

Clark, F. J., Burgess, R. C., and Chapin, J. W. (1983) Human's lack of sense of static-position of the fingers. *Society for Neuroscience Abstracts*, 1033. (24)

Clark, F. J., Horch, K. W., Bach, S. M., and Larson, G. R. (1979) Contribution of cutaneous and joint receptors to static knee-position sense in man. *Journal of Neurophysiology*, **42**, 877–888. (24)

Clippinger, F. W., Avery, R., and Titus, B. R. (1974) A sensory feedback system for upper-limb amputation prosthesis. *Bulletin of Prosthetics Research*, **10–22**, 247–258. (257)

Coffey, J. L. (1963) The development and evaluation of the Batelle aural reading device. In L. L. Clark (ed.), *Proceedings of the International Congress on Technology and Blindness*. New York: American Foundation for the Blind. (269)

Cole, K. J., and Abbs, J. H. (1983) Intentional responses to kinesthetic stimuli in orofacial muscles: Implications for the coordination of speech movements. *Journal of Neuroscience*, **3**, 2660–2669. (27)

Colley, A. M., and Beech, G. (eds) (1988) *Acquisition of Cognitive Skills*. Chichester: John Wiley. (14)

Connelly, J. G., Jr, Wickens, C. D., Lintern, G., and Harwood, K. (1987) Attention theory and training research. *Proceedings, 31st Annual Meeting of the Human Factors Society*. Santa Monica, CA: Human Factors. (96)

Cook, A. M. (1982) Sensory and communication aids. In A. M. Cook and J. G. Webster (eds), *Therapeutic Medical Devices: Application and Design*. Englewood Cliffs, N.J.: Prentice-Hall. (269)

Cook, A. M. (1985) Electrically-controlled upper extremity prosthetic devices. In J. G. Webster, Albert M. Cook, Willis J. Tompkins, and Gregg C. Vonderheiden (eds), *Electronic Devices for Rehabilitation*, 319–342. New York: John Wiley. (259)

Cooke, J. D., and Diggles, V. A. (1984) Rapid error correction during human arm movements: Evidence for central monitoring. *Journal of Motor Behavior*, **16**, 348–363. (133)

Cooke, J. D., Brown, S., Forget, R., and Lamarre, Y. (1985) Initial agonist burst duration changes with movement amplitude in a deafferented patient. *Experimental Brain Research*, **60**, 184–187. (51)

Corcoran, D. W. J. (1965) Personality and the inverted-U relation. *British Journal of Psychology*, **56**, 267–273. (287)

Corcos, D. M. (1984) Two-handed movement control. *Research Quarterly for Exercise and Sport*, **55**, 117–122. (61)

Cotzin, M., and Dallenbach, K. M. (1950) 'Facial vision': The role of pitch and loudness in the perception of obstacles by the blind. *American Journal of Psychology*, **64**, 485–515. (273)

Crago, P. E., Houk, J. C., and Hasan, Z. (1976) Regulatory actions of the human stretch reflex. *Journal of Neurophysiology*, **39**, 925–935. (29, 33, 34)

Craik, F. I. M. (1979) Human memory. *Annual Review of Psychology*, **30**, 63–102. (214)

Craik, K. J. W. (1947) Theory of the human operator in control systems. I. The operator as an engineering system. *British Journal of Psychology*, **38**, 56–61. (2, 113, 128, 172, 199)

Craik, K. J. W. (1948) Theory of the human operator in control systems. II. Man as an element in a control system. *British Journal of Psychology*, **38**, 142–148. (113, 128, 172)

Craske, B., and Craske, J. D. (1986) Oscillator mechanisms in the human motor system: Investigating their properties using the aftercontraction effect. *Journal of Motor Behavior*, **18**, 117–145. (64)

Cratty, B. J. (1971) *Movement and Spatial Awareness in Blind Children and Youth*. Springfield, IL.: Charles C. Thomas. (274)

Crosby, J. V., and Parkinson, S. R. (1979) A dual-task investigation of pilot's test skill level. *Ergonomics*, **22**, 1301–1313. (99)

Crossman, E. R. F. W. (1956) The Measurement of Perceptual Load in Manual Operations. Unpublished Ph.D. Thesis, University of Birmingham. (148)

Crossman, E. R. F. W. (1959) A theory of the acquisition of speed skill. *Ergonomics*, **2**, 153–166. (154, 155, 206)

Crossman, E. R. F. W., and Goodeve, P. T. (1983) Feedback control of hand movement and Fitts' Law. *Quarterly Journal of Experimental Psychology*, **35A**, 251–278. (120, 121, 122, 125, 126, 127, 139)

Crowder, R. G. (1982) The demise of short-term memory. *Acta Psychologica*, **50**, 291–323. (214)

Cruse, H., Dean, J., Heuer, H., and Schmidt, R. A. (1988) Information for motor control. In O. Neumann and W. Prinz (eds), *Relations Between Perception and Action: Current Approaches*. Berlin: Springer. (18)

Damos, D. (1978) Residual attention as a predictor of pilot performance. *Human Factors*, **20**, 435–440. (99)

Damos, D., and Wickens, C. D. (1980) The acquisition and transfer of time-sharing skills. *Acta Psychologica*, **6**, 569–577. (89, 96)

Davis, R. (1957) The human operator as a single channel information system. *Quarterly Journal of Experimental Psychology*, **9**, 119–129. (152, 162)

Delcomyn, F. (1980) Neural basis of rhythmic behavior in animals. *Science*, **210**, 492–498. (51)

Denes, P. B., and Pinson, E. N. (1963) *The Speech Chain*. Murray Hill, N.J.: Bell Telephones. (262)

Denier van der Gon, J. J., and Wieneke, G. H. (1969) The concept of feedback in motorics against that of programming. In L. D. Proctor (ed.), *Biocybernetics of the Central Nervous System*, 287–304. Boston: Little Brown. (32)

Derrick, W. L., and Wickens, C. D. (1984) *A Multiple Processing Resource Explanation of the Subjective Dimensions of Operator Workload*. University of Illinois Engineering Psychology Laboratory Technical Report EPL-84-2/ONR-84-1. (79, 84)

Deubel, H., Wolf, W., and Hauske, G. (1984) The evaluation of the oculomotor error signal. In A. G. Gale and F. Johnson (eds), *Theoretical or Applied Aspects of Eye Movement Research*, 55–62. Amsterdam: Elsevier/North-Holland. (139)

Dietz, V. (1986) Afferent and efferent control of posture and gait. In W. Bles, and Th. Brandt (eds), *Disorders of Posture and Gait*, 69–81. Amsterdam: Elsevier. (29)

Dietz, V., Quintern, J., and Berger, W. (1984) Corrective reactions to stumbling in man: functional significance of spinal and transcortical reflexes. *Neuroscience Letters*, **44**, 131–135. (29)

Dietz, V., Schmidtbleicher, D., and Noth, J. (1979) Neuronal mechanisms of human locomotion. *Journal of Neurophysiology*, **42**, 1212–1222. (29, 30)

Donders, F. C. (1868) Die Schnelligkeit psychischer Processe. *Archiv Anatomie u. Physiologie*, Leipzig, 657–681. (148)

Drew, G. C., Colquhoun, W. P., and Long, H. A. (1958) Effect of small doses of alcohol on a skill resembling driving. *British Medical Journal*, **5103**, 993–999. (286)

Drury, C. G. (1975) Application of Fitts' Law to foot-pedal design. *Human Factors*, **17**, 368–373. (123)

Dudley, H. W. (1939) The vocoder. *Bell Laboratories Record*, **18**, 122–126. (265)

Duncan, J. (1979) Divided attention: the whole is more than the sum of its parts. *Journal of Experimental Psychology: Human Perception and Performance*, **5**, 216–228. (90, 95)

Duncan, J. (1980) The demonstration of capacity limitation. *Cognitive Psychology*, **12**, 75–96. (220)

Easton, T. A. (1972) On the normal use of reflexes. *American Scientist*, **60**, 591–599. (64)

Easton, T. A. (1978) Coordinative structures—The basis for a motor program. In D. M. Landers and R. W. Christina (eds), *Psychology of Motor Behavior and Sport*. Champaign, IL.: Human Kinetics. (64)

Ebeling, W. H. (1950) The guide dog movement. In P. A. Zahl (ed.), *Blindness*. Princeton, N.J.: Princeton University Press. (271)

Ellis, A. W. (1979) Slips of the pen. *Visible Language*, VIII, 265–282. (230)

Ellis, A. W. (1982) Spelling and writing (and reading and speaking). In A. W. Ellis (ed.), *Normality and Pathology in Cognitive Functions*. London: Academic Press. (230, 231)

Ellis, W., Burrows, A. A., and Jackson, K. F. (1953) Presentation of air speed while deck-landing. *Flying Personnel Research Committee, Report No. 841*. (183)

Ells, J. G. (1973) Analysis of temporal and attentional aspects of movement control. *Journal of Experimental Psychology*, **99**, 10–21. (116)

Entwistle, D. G. (1959) Aging: Effects of previous skill on training. *Occupational Psychology*, **33**, 238–243. (290)

Ericsson, K. A. (1985) Memory skill. *Canadian Journal of Psychology*, **39**, 188–231. (215)

Evarts, E. V. (1968) Relation of pyramidal tract activity to force exerted during voluntary movement. *Journal of Neurophysiology*, **31**, 14–27. (65)

Evarts, E. V. (1973) Motor cortex reflexes associated with learned movements. *Science*, **179**, 501–503. (54)

Evarts, E. V. (1981) Sherrington's concepts of proprioception. *Trends in Neurosciences*, **4**, 44–46. (55)

Evarts, E. V. (1984) Neurophysiological approaches to brain mechanisms for preparatory set. In S. Kornblum and J. Requin (eds), *Preparatory States and Processes*, 137–153. Hillsdale: Lawrence Erlbaum Assoc. Publishers. (56)

Evarts, E. V., and Tanji, J. (1974) Gating of motor cortex reflexes by prior instruction. *Brain Research*, **71**, 479–494. (54)

Eysenck, H. J., and Thompson, W. (1966) The effects of distraction on pursuit rotor learning, performance, and reminiscence. *British Journal of Psychology*, **57**, 99–106. (98)

Falmagne, J. C. (1965) Stochastic models for choice reaction times with application to experimental results. *Journal of Mathematical Psychology*, **2**, 77–124. (148)

Farmer, E. W., Berman, J. V., and Fletcher, Y. L. (1986) Evidence for a visual-spatial scratch pad in working memory. *Quarterly Journal of Experimental Psychology*, **38**, 675–688. (83)

Feldman, A. G. (1986) Once more on the equilibrium—point hypothesis (Model) for motor control. *Journal of Motor Behavior*, **18**, 17–54. (63)

Fentress, J. C. (1973) Development of grooming in mice with amputated forelimbs. *Science*, **179**, 704–705. (51)

Festinger, L., and Canon, L. K. (1976) Information about spatial location based on knowledge about efference. *Psychological Review*, **72**, 373–384. (54)

Findlay, S. M., and Harris, L. R. (1984) Small saccades to double-stepped targets moving in two dimensions. In A. G. Gale and F. Johnson (eds), *Theoretical and Applied Aspects of Eye Movement Research*, 71–78. Amsterdam: North-Holland. (139)

Fitts, P. M. (1951) Engineering psychology and equipment design. In S. S. Stevens (ed.), *Handbook of Experimental Psychology*. New York: John Wiley. (2)

Fitts, P. M. (1954) The information capacity of the human motor system in controlling the amplitude of movement. *Journal of Experimental Psychology*, **47**, 381–391. (119, 120, 123, 283)

Fitts, P. M. (1964) Perceptual-motor skill learning. In A. W. Melton (ed.), *Categories of Human Learning*. New York: Academic Press. (206, 207, 216, 219, 224, 226, 284)

Fitts, P. M. (1966) Cognitive aspects of information processing: III. Set for speed versus accuracy. *Journal of Experimental Psychology*, **71**, 849–857. (11)

Fitts, P. M., and Peterson, J. R. (1964) Information capacity of discrete motor responses. *Journal of Experimental Psychology*, **67**, 103–112. (119, 122, 123, 127)

Fitts, P. M., and Posner, M. I. (1967) *Human Performance*. Belmont, CA: Brooks/ Cole. (32, 79, 200, 206, 210, 253, 254)

Fitts, P., Jones, R. E., and Milton, E. (1950) Eye movements of aircraft pilots during instrument landing approaches. (74)

Fleishman, E. A. (1958) Dimensional analysis of movement reactions. *Journal of Experimental Psychology*, **55**, 438–453. (5)

Fleishman, E. A. (1966) Human abilities and the acquisition of skill. In E. A. Bilodeau (ed.), *Acquisition of Skill*. New York: Academic Press. (5)

Fleishman, E. A., and Rich, S. (1963) Role of kinesthetic and spatial-visual abilities in perceptual-motor learning. *Journal of Experimental Psychology*, **66**, 6–11. (256)

Fletcher, C. (Ben), and Rabbitt, P. M. A. (1978) The changing pattern of perceptual analytic strategies and response selection with practice in a two-choice reaction time task. *Quarterly Journal of Experimental Psychology*, **30**, 417–427. (154)

Flexman, R. E., Matheny, W. G., and Brown, E. L. (1950) Evaluation of the Link and special methods of instruction etc. University of Illinois, *Aeronautics Bulletin No. 8*. (191)

Flückiger, M. (1987) Human body sway in an optical flow. *Society for Neuroscience Abstracts*, **13**, 347. (36)

Forget, R., and Lamarre, Y. (1987) Rapid elbow flexion in the absence of propriocep- tive and cutaneous feedback. *Human Neurobiology*, **6**, 27–37. (51)

Forssberg, H. (1979) Stumbling corrective reaction: A phase-dependent compensa- tory reaction during locomotion. *Journal of Neurophysiology*, **42**, 936–953. (33)

Forssberg, H., Grillner, S., and Rossignol, S. (1975a) Phase dependent reflex reversal during walking in the chronic spinal cats. *Brain Research*, **85**, 103–107. (31)

Forssberg, H., Grillner, S., and Rossignol, S. (1975b) Phasic gain control of reflexes from the dorsum of the paw during spinal locomotion. *Brain Research*, **132**, 121–139. (52)

Foulke, E. (1970) The perceptual basis for mobility. *American Foundation for the Blind, Research Bulletin*, **23**, 1–8. (270, 271)

Fowler, C. A., and Turvey, M. T. (1978) Skill acquisition: An event approach with special reference to searching for the optimum of a function of several variables. In G. E. Stelmach (ed.), *Information Processing in Motor Control and Learning*, 1–40. New York: academic Press. (38, 210, 212)

Fracker, M. L., and Wickens, C. D. (1988) Resources, confusions, and compatibility in dual axis tracking: Displays, controls, and dynamics. *Journal of Experimental Psychology: Human Perception and Performance*, 14, 545–553. (89, 90, 91)

Franklin, H. C., and Holding, D. H. (1977) Personal memories at different ages. *Quarterly Journal of Experimental Psychology*, 29, 527–533. (290)

Freedy, A. Hull, F., and Lyman, J. (1971) Adaptive aiding for artificial limb control. *Bulletin of Prosthetics Research*, 10–16, , 3–15. (259, 260)

Freedy, A., Lucaccini, L. F., and Lyman, J. (1967) Information and control analysis of externally powered artificial arm systems. *Bulletin of Prosthetics Research*, 10–8, 112–131. (254)

Friedman, A., and Polson, M. C. (1981) The hemispheres as independent resource systems: Limited capacity processing and cerebral specialization. *Journal of Experimental Psychology: Human Perception and Performance*, 7, 1031–1058. (82, 83)

Friedman, A., Polson, M. C., and Dafoe, C. G. (1988) Dividing attention between the hands and the head: Performance tradeoffs between rapid finger tapping and verbal memory. *Journal of Experimental Psychology: Human Perception and Performance*, 14, 60–68. (82, 83)

Friedman, A., Polson, M. C., Dafoe, C. G., and Gaskill, S. J. (1982) Dividing attention within and between hemispheres: Testing a multiple resources approach to limited-capacity information processing. *Journal of Experimental Psychology: Human Perception and Performance*, 8, 625–650. (83)

Frith, C. D., and Lang, R. J. (1979) Learning and reminiscence as a function of target predictability in a two-dimensional tracking task. *Quarterly Journal of Experimental Psychology*, 31, 103–109. (4)

Fromkin, V. A. (1971) The non-anomalous nature of anomalous utterances. *Language*, 47, 27–52. (238)

Fuchs, A. F., and Kornhuber, H. H. (1969) Extraocular muscle afferents to the cerebellum of the cat. *Journal of Physiology*, 200, 713–722. (54)

Gagne, R. M., and Foster, H. (1949) Transfer of training from practice on component parts in a motor skill. *Journal of Experimental Psychology*, 39, 47–68. (216)

Garrett, M. F. (1982) Production of speech: Observations from normal and pathological language use. In A. W. Ellis (ed.), *Normality and Pathology in Cognitive Functions*. London: Academic Press. (238, 239)

Garvey, W. D. (1960) A comparison of the effects of training and secondary tasks on tracking. *Journal of Applied Psychology*, 44, 370–375. (187)

Geldard, F. A. (1961) Cutaneous channels of communication. In W. A. Rosenblith (ed.), *Sensory Communication*, 73–88. New York: John Wiley. (257)

Geldard, F. A. (1972) *The Human Senses*. New York: John Wiley. (259)

Gengel, R. W. (1977) *Research With Upton's Visual Speech Reading Aid*. Paper presented at the Research Conference on Speech-Processing Aids for the Deaf, Gallaudet College, Washington, D.C., May 24–26. (265)

Gentile, A. M. (1972) A working model of skill acquisition with application to teaching. *Quest*, 17, 3–23. (38)

Gentner, D. R. (1982) Evidence against a central control model of timing in typing. *Journal of Experimental Psychology: Human Perception and Performance*, 8, 793–810. (63, 237)

Gentner, D. R. (1987) Timing of skilled motor performance: Tests of the proportional duration model. *Psychological Review*, **94**, 255–276. (63)

Georgopoulos, A. P., Kalaska, J. F., and Massey, J. T. (1981) Spatial trajectories and reaction times of aimed movements: Effects of practice, uncertainty, and change in target location. *Journal of Neurophysiology*, **46**, 725–743. (137, 139, 140, 141)

Gescheider, G. A. (1970) Some comparisons between touch and hearing. *IEEE Transactions on Man-Machine Systems, MMS-11*, 28–35. (265)

Gibbs, C. B. (1965) Probability learning in step-input tracking. *British Journal of Psychology*, **56**, 233–242. (131, 133)

Gibson, J. J. (1966) *The Senses Considered as Perceptual Systems*. Boston: Houghton Mifflin. (25, 35)

Gibson, J. J. (1979) *The Ecological Approach to Visual Perception*. Boston: Houghton Mifflin. (25, 35, 230)

Gielen, C. C. A. M., van der Heuvel, P. J. M., and Denier van der Gon, J. J. (1984) Modifications of muscle activation patterns during fast goal-directed arm movements. *Journal of Motor Behavior*, **16**, 2–19. (137, 139, 141)

Glencross, D. J. (1972) Latency and response complexity. *Journal of Motor Behavior*, **4**, 251–256. (114)

Glencross, D. J. (1977) Control of skilled movements. *Psychological Bulletin*, **84**, 14–29. (53)

Glencross, D. J. (1979) Output and response processes in skilled performance. In G. C. Roberts and K. M. Newell (eds), *Psychology of Motor Behavior and Sport*. Champaign, IL: Human Kinetic Publishers. (129, 130)

Glencross, D. J. (1980a) Response planning and the organization of speed movements. In R. S. Nickerson (ed.), *Attention and Performance VIII*. Hillsdale: Lawrence Erlbaum Assoc. Publishers. (116)

Glencross, D. J. (1980b) Levels and strategies of response organization. In G. E. Stelmach and J. Reguin (eds), *Tutorials in Motor Control*. Amsterdam: North-Holland. (59, 134)

Glencross, D. J., and Barrett, N. C. (1983) Programming precision in repetitive tapping. *Journal of Motor Behavior*, **15**, 191–200. (119, 121)

Gobbo, C., and Chi, M. (1986) How knowledge is structured and used by expert and novice children. *Cognitive Development*, **1**, 221–237. (225)

Goff, G. D. (1967) Differential discrimination of frequency of cutaneous mechanical vibration. *Journal of Experimental Psychology*, **74**, 294–299. (265)

Goldman-Eisler, F. (1968) *Psycholinguistics*. London: Academic Press. (238)

Goldsmith, T., and Schvanveldt, R. (1984) Facilitating multi-cue judgments with integral information displays. In J. Thomas and M. Schneider (eds), *Human Factors in Computer Systems*. New Jersey: Ablex. (94)

Goodman, D., and Kelso, J. A. S. (1980) Are movements prepared in parts? Not under compatible (naturalized) conditions. *Journal of Experimental Psychology: General*, **109**, 475–495. (118)

Goodwin, G. M., McCloskey, D. I., and Matthews, P. B. C. (1972) The contribution of muscle afferents to kinesthesia shown by vibration-induced illusions of movement and by the effects of paralyzing joint afferents. *Brain*, **95**, 705–748. (22)

Gopher, D. (1982) A selective attention test as a prediction of success in flight training. *Human Factors*, **24**, 173–184. (100)

Gopher, D. (1986) Energetics and resources. In R. Hockey, A. Gaillard, and M. Coles (eds), *Energetics and Human Information Processing*. Dordrecht, Netherlands: Martinus Nijhoff. (78)

Gopher, D., and Braune, R. (1984) On the psychophysics of workload: Why bother with subjective measures? *Human Factors*, **26**, (5), 519–532. (79)

Gopher, D., and Brickner, M. (1980) On the training of time-sharing skills: An attention viewpoint. In G. Corrick, M. Hazeltime, and R. Durst (eds), *Proceedings, 24th Annual Meeting of the Human Factors Society*. Santa Monica, CA: Human Factors. (86)

Gopher, D., and Kahneman, D. (1971) Individual differences in attention and the prediction of flight criteria. *Perceptual and Motor Skills*, **33**, 1335–1342. (100)

Gopher, D., and Sanders, A. F. (1984) S-Oh-R? Oh stages! On resources! In W. Prinz, and A. F. Sanders (eds), *Cognition and Motor Behaviour*. Heidelberg: Springer. (82)

Gopher, D., Weil, M., and Siegel, D. (1986) Is it only a game? Using videogames as surrogate instructors for the training of complex skills. *Proceedings of the 1986 IEEE International Conference of systems, Man, & Cybernetics*. (86)

Gottsdanker, R. M. (1956) The ability of human operators to detect acceleration of target motion. *Psychollogical Bulletin*, **53**, 367–375. (181)

Gottsdanker, R. (1966) The effect of superseding signals. *Quarterly Journal of Experimental Psychology*, **18**, 236–249. (120, 137)

Gottsdanker, R. (1973) psychological refractoriness and the organization of step tracking responses. *Perception and Psychophysics*, **14**, 60–70. (137)

Gottsdanker, R. M., and Kent, K. (1978) Reaction time and probability on isolated trials. *Journal of Motor Behavior*, **10**, 233–238. (10)

Gracco, V. L., and Abbs, J. H. (1985) Dynamic control of the perioral system during speech: Kinematic analyses of autogenic and nonautogenic sensorimotor processes. *Journal of Neurophysiology*, **54**, 418–432. (31)

Graupe, D., Salahi, J. and Kohn, K. H. (1981) Control of limb prostheses and powered braces via EMG temporal signature identification. In H. S. Eden and M. Eden (eds), *Microcomputers in Patient Care*. Park Ridge, N.J.: Noyes Medical Publication. (254)

Greene, P. H. (1972) Problems of organization of motor systems. In R. Rosen and F. Snell (eds), *Progress in Theoretical Biology, Vol. 2*. New York: Academic Press. (134)

Greene, P. H. (1982) Why is it easy to control your arms? *Journal of Motor Behavior*, **14**, 260–286. (64)

Griew, S. (1958) Age changes and information loss in performance of a pursuit tracking task involving interrupted preview. *Journal of Experimental Psychology*, **55**, 486–489. (290)

Grigg, P.. (1976) Response of joint afferent neurons in cat medial articular nerve to active and passive movements of the knee. *Brain Research*, **118**, 482–485. (23)

Grillner, S. (1975) Locomotion in vertebrates: Central mechanisms and reflex interaction. *Physiological Reviews*, **55**, 247–3–4. (18, 31)

Grillner, S. (1981) Control of locomotion in bipeds, teptrapods, and fish. In V. Brooks (ed), *Handbook of Physiology: Sec. 1,: Vol. 2. Motor Control*, 1179–1236. Bethesda, MD: American Physiological Society. (18)

Grillner, S. (1985) Neurobiological bases of rhythmic motor acts in vertebrates. *Science*, **228**, 143–149. (52, 53, 64)

Grillner, S., and Wallen, P. (1985) Central pattern generators for locomotion, with special reference to vertebrates. *Annual Review of Neuroscience*, **8**, 233–261. (51, 52, 54)

Groth, H., and Lyman, J. (1961) Control problems in externally powered arm prostheses. *Orthopedic and Prosthetic Appliance Journal*, **15**, 174–177. (253)

Gurfinkel, V. S., Lipshits, M. I., and Popov, K. Y. (1974) Is the stretch reflex the main mechanism in the system of regulation of the vertical posture of man? *Biophysics*, **19**, 744–748. (29)

Hagman, J. D. (1983) Presentation- and test-trial effects on acquisition and retention of distance and location. *Journal of Experimental Psychology: Learning, Memory, & Cognition*, **9**, 334–345. (209)

Hallett, M., Shahani, B. T., and Young, R. R. (1975) EMG analysis of stereotyped voluntary movements in man. *Journal of Neurology, Neurosurgery, and Psychiatry*, **38**, 1154–1162. (51)

Hammerton, M. (1963) The components of acquisition time. *Ergonomics*, **7**, 91–93. (179)

Hammerton, M. (1967) Visual factors affecting transfer of training from a simulated to a real control situation. *Journal of Applied Psychology*, **51**, 46–49. (190, 191)

Hammerton, M., and Tickner, A. H. (1966) An investigation into the comparative suitability of forearm, hand and thumb controls in an acquisition task. *Ergonomics*, **9**, 125–130. (181)

Hammerton, M., and Tickner, A. H. (1970) Structured and blank backgrounds in a pursuit tracking task. *Ergonomics*, **13**, 719–722. (188)

Hancock, R. P. (1970) Interfacial couplings for man–machine systems. *Bulletin of Prosthetics Research*, **10–14**, 78–101. (251)

Hansen, R. M., and Skavenski, A. A. (1977) Accuracy of eye position information for motor control. *Vision Research*, **17**, 919–926. (35)

Hanson, C., and Lofthus, G. K. (1978) Effects of fatigue and laterality on fractionated reaction time. *Journal of Motor Behavior*, **10**, 177–184. (10)

Harris, K. S. (1987) Action theory as a description of the speech proceeess. In H. F. M. Peters and W. Hulstijn (eds), *Speech Motor Dynamics in Stuttering*. Vienna: Springer-Verlag. (247)

Harris, R. L., and Christhilf, D. M. (1980) What do pilots see in displays? In G. Corrick, E. Hazeltine, and R. Durst (eds), *Proceedings, 24th Annual Meeting of the Human Factors Society*. Santa Monica, CA: Human Factors. (74)

Harris, R., and Spady, A. (1985) Visual scanning behavior. *Proceedings of NAECON*. New York: IEEE. (74, 78)

Hart, S. G., and Hauser, J. R. (1987) In-flight applications of the pilot workload measurement techniques. *Aviation, Space and Environmental Medicine*, **58**, 402–410. (79)

Harwood, K., Wickens, C. D., Kramer, A., Clay, D., and Liu, Y. (1986) Effects of display proximity and memory demands of the understanding of dynamic multidimensional information. *Proceedings of the 30th Annual Meeting of the Human Factors Society*. Santa Monica, CA. (94)

Hatze, H. (1976) Biomechanical aspects of a successful motion optimization. In P. V. Komi (ed.), *Biomechanics V-B*. Baltimore, MD: University Park Press. (213)

Hayes, K. C. (1978) Supraspinal and spinal processes involved in the initiation of fast movements. In D. M. Landers and R. W. Christina (eds), *Psychology of Motor Behavior and Sport*. Champaign, IL.: Human Kinetics. (66)

Henderson, S. E. (1977) Role of feedback in the development and maintenance of a complex skill. *Journal of Experimental Psychology: Human Perception and Performance*, **3**, 224–233. (26)

Hendrickson, G., and Schroeder, W. H. (1941) Transfer of training in learning to hit a submerged target. *journal of Educational Psychology*, **32**, 205–213. (192)

Henmon, V. A. C. (1911) The relation of time of judgment for accuracy. *Psychological Review*, **18**, 186–201. (148)

Henry, F. M. (1958) Specificity vs. generality in learning motor skills. *61st Annual Proceedings of the College of Physical Education*, Washington, D.C.

Henry, F. M. (1968) Specificity vs. generality in learning motor skills. In R. C. Brown and G. S. Kenyon (eds), *Classical Studies on Physical Activity*, 328–331. Englewood Cliffs, NJ: Prentice-Hall. (45)

Henry, F. M. (1986) Development of the motor memory trace and control program. *Journal of Motor Behavior*, **18**, 77–100. (58)

Henry, F. M., and Harrison, J. S. (1961) Refractoriness of a fast movement. *Perceptual and Motor Skills*, **13**, 351–354. (26, 128)

Henry, F. M., and Rogers, D. E. (1960) Increased response latency for complicated movements and a 'memory drum' theory of neuromotor reaction. *Research Quarterly*, **31**, 448–458. (26, 114)

Henson, D. B. (1978) Corrective saccades: Effects of altering visual feedback. *Vision Research*, **18**, 63–67. (130)

Herdman, C. M., and Friedman, A. (1985) Multiple resources in divided attention: A cross-modal test of the independence of hemispheric resources. *Journal of Experimental Psychology: Human Perception and Performance*, **11**, 40–49. (84)

Heuer, H. (1984) Binary choice reaction time as a function of the relationship between durations and forms of responses. *Journal of Motor Behavior*, **16**, 392–404. (56, 61)

Heuer, H. (1986) Intermanual interactions during programming of aimed movements: Converging evidence on common and specific parameters of control. *Psychological Research*, **48**, 37–46. (61)

Heuer, H. and Wing, A. M. (1984) Doing two things at once: Process limitations and interactions. In M. M. Smyth and Wing, A. M. (eds), *The Psychology of Human Movement*. New York: Academic Press. (220, 222)

Hick, W. E. (1952) On the rate of gain of information. *Quarterly Journal of Experimental Psychology*, **4**, 11–26. (2, 10, 26, 129, 253)

Hick, W. E., and Bates, J. A. (1950) The human operator of control mechanisms. London: *Ministry of Supply. Permanent Records of Research and Development*, 17024. (253)

Higgins, J. R., and Angel, R. W. (1970) Correction of tracking errors without sensory feedback. *Journal of Experimental Psychology*, **84**, 412–416. (120, 131, 132, 133, 134, 135)

Higgins, J. R., and Spaeth, R. K. (1972) Relationship between consistency of movement and environmental condition. *Quest*, **17**, 61–69. (59)

Hilgard, E. R., and Bower, G. H. (1966) *Theories of Learning*. New York: Meredith Publishing Corporation. (197, 198, 199, 216)

Hill, H., Gray, F., and Ellision, D. G. (1947) *Wavelength and Amplitude Characteristics of Tracking Error Curves*. AAF-AMC Engineering Report, TSEAA-694-2D, Wright Field, Ohio. (253)

Hinton, G. (1984) Parallel computations for controlling an arm. *Journal of Motor Behavior*, **16**, 171–194. (64)

Hirst, W. (1984) Aspects of divided and selective attention. In J. LeDoux and W. Hirst (eds), *Mind and Brain*. New York: Cambridge University Press. (89, 92)

Ho, L., and Shea, J. B. (1978) Effects of relative frequency of knowledge of results on retention of a motor skill. *Perceptual and Motor Skills*, **46**, 859–866. (41, 46)

Hockey, G. R. J. (1983) *Stress and Fatigue in Human Performance*. Chichester: John Wiley. (287)

Hockey, R., Gaillard, A., and Coles, M. (1986) *Energetics and Human Information Processing*. Dordrecht: Martinus Nijhoff. (79)

Holding, D. H. (1962) Transfer between difficult and easy tasks. *British Journal of Psychology*, **53**, 397–407. (190)

Holding, D. H. (1965) *Principles of Training*. London: Pergamon. (40, 45, 67, 209, 210, 211)

Holding, D. H. (1968) Accuracy of delayed aiming responses. *Psychonomic Science*, **17**, 125–126. (214)

Holding, D. H. (ed.) (1969) *Experimental Psychology in Industry*. London: Penguin Books. (291)

Holding, D. H. (1970) Learning without errors. In L. E. Smith (ed.), *Psychology of Motor Learning*. Chicago: Athletic Institute. (40)

Holding, D. H. (1974) Risk, effort and fatigue. In M. G. Wade and R. Martens (eds), *Psychology of Motor Behavior and Sport*. Champaign, IL.: Human Kinetics. (289)

Holding, D. H. (1976) An approximate transfer surface. *Journal of Motor Behavior*, **8**, 1–9. (216, 217, 284)

Holding, D. H. (1983) Fatigue. In G. R. J. Hockey (ed.), *Stress and Fatigue in Human Performance*. Chichester: John Wiley. (287)

Holding, D. H. (1985) *The Psychology of Chess Skill*. Hillsdale, N.J.: Lawrence Erlbaum Assoc. Publishers. (1)

Holding, D. H., and Dennis, J. P. (1957) An unexpected effect in sound localization. *Nature*, **180**, 1471–1472. (11)

Holding, D. H., and Macrae, A. W. (1964) Guidance, restriction and knowledge of results. *Ergonomics*, **7**, 289–295. (8)

Hollyfield, R. L. and Foulke, E. (1983) The spatial cognition of blind pedestrians. *Journal of Visual Impairment and Blindness*, **77**, 204–210. (278)

Hoover, R. E. (1950) The cane as a travel aid. In P. A. Zahl (ed.), *Blindness*. Princeton, N.J.: Princeton University Press. (271)

Horner, D. G. (1982) Can vision predict baseball players' hitting ability? *American Journal of Optometry and Physiological Optics*, **59**, 695. (6)

Houk, J. C. (1979) Regulation of stiffness by skeletomotor reflexes. *Annual Review of Physiology*, **41**, 99–114. (23)

Houk, J. C., and Rymer, W. Z. (1981) Neural control of muscle length and tension. In V. B. Brooks (ed.), *Handbook of Physiology: Sec. 1: Vol. 2. Motor Control*, 257–323. Bethesda, MD: American Physiological Society. (34)

Howarth, C. I., Beggs, W. D. A., and Bowden, J. (1971) The relationship between speed and accuracy of movement aimed at a target. *Acta Psychologica*, **35**, 207–218. (126)

Hulstijn, W. (1987) Programming of speech and nonspeech motor activity. In H. F. M. Peters and W. Hulstijn (eds), *Speech Motor Dynamics in Stuttering*. Vienna: Springer-Verlag. (233)

Hulstijn, W., and Van Galen, G. P. (1983) Programming in writing: Reaction time and movement time as a function of sequence length. *Acta Psychologica*, **54**, 23–49. (232)

Hulstijn, W., and Van Galen, G. P. (1988) Levels of motor programming in writing familiar and unfamiliar symbols. In A. M. Colley and J. R. Beech (eds), *Cognition and Action in Skilled Behaviour*. Amsterdam: North-Holland. (233)

Hunt, E., and Lansman, M. (1982) Individual differences in attention. In R. J. Sternberg (ed.), *Advances in the Psychology of Human Intelligence*, Vol. 1, 207–254. Hillsdale, NJ: Lawrence Erlbaum Assoc. Publishers. (101)

Hyman, R. (1953) Stimulus information as a determinant of reaction time. *Journal of Experimental Psychology*, **45**, 188–196. (26)

Institute of Measurement and Control (1977) *Human Operators and Simulation*. London. (189)

Ivry, R. B. (1986) Force and timing components of the motor program. *Journal of Motor Behavior*, **18**, 449–474. (56)

Jagacinski, R. J., Hartzell, E. S., Ward, S., and Bishop, K. (1978) Fitts' Law as a function of system dynamics and target uncertainty. *Journal of Motor Behavior*, **10**, 123–131. (123)

Jagacinski, R. J., and Monk, D. L. (1985) Fitts' Law in two dimensions with hand and head movements. *Journal of Motor Behavior*, **17**, 77–95. (123)

James, W. (1890) *The Principles of Psychology*, vol. 1. New York: Holt. (32)

Jeannerod, M. (1981) Intersegmental coordination during reaching at natural objects. In J. Long and A. Baddeley (eds), *Attention and Performance*, IX, 153–169. Hillsdale: Lawrence Erlbaum Assoc. Publishers. (60)

Johansson, R. S., and Westling, G. (1987) Signals in tactile afferents from the fingers eliciting adaptive motor responses during precision grip. *Experimental Brain Research*, **66**, 141–154. (24, 34)

Johnson, R. W., Wicks, G. G., and Ben-Sira, D. (1981) *Practice in the Absence of Knowledge of Results: Motor Skill Retention*. Unpublished manuscript, University of Minnesota. (41)

Johnson-Laird, P. N. (1987) Reasoning, imagining and creating. *Bulletin of the British Psychological Society*, **40**, 121–129. (244)

Jones, B. (1971) Is there any proprioceptive feedback? Comments on Schmidt (1971). *Psychological Bulletin*, **79**, 386–390. (135)

Jones, B. (1974) Is proprioception important for skilled performance? *Journal of Motor Behavior*, **6**, 33–45. (135)

Jones, R. V. (1978) *Most Secret War*. London: Hamilton. (183)

Jordan, T. C., and Rabbitt, P. M. A. (1977) Response times of increasing complexity as a function of ageing. *British Journal of Psychology*, **68**, 189–201. (290)

Julesz, B. (1981) Textons, the elements of texture perception. *Nature*, **290**, 91–97. (189)

Juurmaa, J. (1973) Transposition in mental spatial manipulation: A theoretical analysis. *American Foundation for the Blind Research Bulletin*, **26**, 87–134. (273)

Kahneman, D. (1973) *Attention and Effort*. Englewood Cliffs, NJ: Prentice-Hall. (15, 72)

Kahneman, D., and Chajezyk, D. (1983) Tests of the automaticity of reading: Dilution of Stroop effects by color-irrelevant stimuli. *Journal of Experimental Psychology: Human Perception and Performance*, **9**, 497–501. (79, 89)

Kalikow, D. N. (1974) Information processing models and computer aids for human performance: Final report second language learning. *Technical Report No. 2841*, Bolt, Beranek and Newman, Cambridge, MA. (67)

Kalsbeek, J. W., and Sykes, R. W. (1967) Objective measurement of mental load. *Acta Psychologica*, **27**, 253–261. (79)

Kantowitz, B. H. (1974) Double stimulation. In B. H. Kantowitz (ed.), *Human Information Processing: Tutorials in Human Performance and Cognition*. New York: John Wiley. (117)

Kantowitz, B. H. (1985) Channels and stages in human information processing: A limited analysis of theory and methodology. *Journal of Mathematical Psychology*, **29**, 135–174. (72)

Karlin, L. (1966) Development of readiness to respond during short foreperiods. *Journal of Experimental Psychology*, **72**, 505–509. (152)

Kay, L. (1972) *Evaluation of the Ultrasonic Binaural Sensory Aid for the Blind*. Paper presented at the Conference on Evaluation of Sensory Aids for the Visually Handicapped, National Academy of Sciences, Washington, D.C. (273)

Keele, S. W. (1968) Movement control in skilled motor performance. *Psychological Bulletin*, **70**, 387–403. (18, 50, 57, 120, 121, 122, 125, 126)

Keele, S. W. (1972) Attention demands of memory retrieval. *Journal of Experimental Psychology*, **93**, 245–258. (88)

Keele, S. W. (1973) *Attention and Human Performance*. Pacific Palisades, CA: Goodyear. (72, 113)

Keele, S. W. (1977) Current status of the motor program concept. In D. M. Landers and R. W. Christina (eds), *Psychology of Motor Behavior and Sport*, Vol. 1. Champaign, IL: Human Kinetics. (67)

Keele, S. W. (1980) Behavioral analysis of motor control. In V. B. Brooks (ed.), *Handbook of Physiology, Vol. III: Motor Control*. New York: American Physiological Society. (126)

Keele, S. W. (1981) Behavioral analysis of movement. In V. B. Brooks (ed.), *Handbook of Physiology, Vol. II: Motor Control*, 1391–1413. Bethesda, MD: American Physiological Society. (59, 62, 66)

Keele, S. W. (1982) Learning and control of coordinated motor patterns: The programming perspective. In J. A. S. Kelso (ed.), *Human Motor Behavior*, 161–186. Hillsdale: Lawrence Erlbaum Assoc. Publishers. (67)

Keele, S. W. (1986) Motor control. In K. Boff, L. Kaufman, and J. Thomas (eds), *Handbook of Perception and Human Performance: Sec 5. Information Processing: Vol. 2. Cognitive Processes and Performance*, 1–60. New York: John Wiley. (18)

Keele, S. W., and Hawkins, H. L. (1982) Explorations of individual differences relevant to high level skill. *Journal of Motor Behavior*, **14**, 3–23. (5, 100)

Keele, S. W., and Posner, M. I. (1968) Processing of visual feedback in rapid movement. *Journal of Experimental Psychology*, **77**, 155–158. (122, 128)

Keele, S. W., and Summers, J. J. (1976) The structure of motor programs. In G. E. Stelmach (ed.), *Motor Control: Issues and Trends*. New York: Academic Press. (55, 57, 58, 67)

Kelly, C. (1962) Predictor instruments look into the future. *Control Engineering*, **9**, 86–90. (177)

Kelso, J. A. S. (1977) Motor control mechanisms underlying human movement reproduction. *Journal of Experimental Psychology: Human Perception and Performance*, **3**, 529–543. (143)

Kelso, J. A. S. (1981) Contrasting perspectives in order and regulation of movement. In J. Long and A. Baddeley (eds), *Attention and Performance IX*, 437–457. Hillsdale: Lawrence Erlbaum Assoc. Publishers. (66)

Kelso, J. A. S. (ed.) (1982) *Human Motor Behaviour: An Introduction*. Hillsdale, NJ: Lawrence Erlbaum Assoc. Publishers. (110, 118, 135)

Kelso, J. A. S., and Holt, K. G. (1980) Exploring a vibratory systems analysis of human movement production. *Journal of Neurophysiology*, **43**, 1183–1196. (143)

Kelso, J. A. S., and Kay, B. A. (1987) Information and control: A macroscopic analysis of perception-action coupling. In H. Heuer and A. F. Sanders (eds), *Perspectives on Perception and Action*, 3–32. Hillsdale: Lawrence Erlbaum Assoc. Publishers. (18)

Kelso, J. A. S., and Stelmach, G. E. (1976) Central and peripheral mechanisms in motor control. In G. E. Stelmach (ed.), *Motor Control: Issues and Trends*, 1–40. New York: Academic Press. (18, 134)

Kelso, J. A. S., and Tuller, B. (1981) Toward a theory of apractic syndromes. *Brain and Language*, **12**, 224–245. (64)

Kelso, J. A. S., Holt, K. A., Rubin, P., and Kugler, P. N. (1981) Patterns of human interlimb coordination emerge from the properties of non-linear, limit cycle oscillatory processes: Theory and data. *Journal of Motor Behavior*, **13**, 226–261. (61)

Kelso, J. A., Southard, D. L., and Goodman, D. (1979) On the coordination of two-handed movements. *Journal of Experimental Psychology: Human Perception and Performance*, **5**, 229–259. (61, 91)

Kelso, J. A. S., Tuller, B., Vatikoitis-Bateson, E., and Fowler, C. A. (1984) Functionally specific articulatory cooperation following jaw perturbations during speech: Evidence for coordinative structures. *Journal of Experimental Psychology: Human Perception and Performance*, **10**, 812–832. (31, 247)

Kerr, B. (1973) Processing demands during mental operations. *Memory and Cognition*, **1**, 401–412. (72, 88)

Kerr, B. (1975) Processing demands during movements. *Journal of Motor Behavior*, **7**, 15–27. (116)

Kerr, B. (1978) Task factors that influence selection and preparation for voluntary movements. In G. E. Stelmach (ed.), *Information Processing in Motor Control and Learning*, 55–69. New York: Academic Press. (56)

Kerr, B., and Langolf, G. D. (1977) Speed of aimed movements. *Quarterly Journal of Experimental Psychology*, **29**, 475–481. (123)

Kerr, R. (1973) Movement time in an underwater environment. *Journal of Motor Behavior*, **5**, 175–178. (123)

Kerr, R. (1978) Diving, adaptation, and Fitts' Law. *Journal of Motor Behavior*, **10**, 255–260. (123)

Kinsbourne, M. (1981) Single channel theory. In D. H. Holding (ed.), *Human Skills*. New York: John Wiley. (15, 71, 82, 83)

Kinsbourne, M., and Hicks, R. E. (1978) Functional cerebral space: A model for overflow, transfer and interference effects in human performance. In J. Requin (ed.), *Attention and Performance VII*. Hillsdale: Lawrence Erlbaum Assoc. Publishers. (83)

Kirman, J. H. (1973) Tactile communication of speech: A review and analysis. *Psychological Bulletin*, **80**, 54–74. (266, 267)

Klapp, S. T. (1975) Feedback versus motor programming in the control of aimed movements. *Journal of Experimental Psychology: Human Perception and Performance*, **104**, 147–153. (114)

Klapp, S. T. (1979) Doing two things at once: The role of temporal compatibility. *Memory and Cognition*, **7**, 375–381. (61)

Klapp, S. T. (1981) Motor programming is not the only process which can influence RT: Some thoughts on the Marteniuk and Mackenzie analysis. *Journal of Motor Behaviour*, **13**, 320–328. (56)

Klapp, S. T., and Erwin, C. I. (1976) Relation between programming time and duration of the response being programmed. *Journal of Experimental Psychology: Human Perception and Performance*, **2**, 591–598. (26)

Klapp, S. T., and Greim, D. M. (1979) Programmed control of aimed movements revisited: The role of target visibility and symmetry. *Journal of Experimental Psychology: Human Perception and Performance*, **5**, 509–521. (56, 61)

Klein, G. S. (1964) Semantic power measured through the interference of words with color naming. *American Journal of Psychology*, **77**, 576–588. (89)

Klemmer, E. T. (1956) Time uncertainty, in simple reaction time. *Journal of Experimental Psychology*, **72**, 505–509. (152)

Knibestol, J. (1975) Stimulus-response functions of slowly adapting mechanoreceptors in the human glabrous skin area. *Journal of Physiology*, **245**, 63–80. (23)

Knight, A. A., and Dagnall, P. R. (1967) Precision in movements. *Ergonomics*, **10**, 327–330. (123)

Kohler, I. (1964) Orientation by aural cues. American Foundation for the Blind, *Research Bulletin*, **14–53**. (273)

Kolers, P. A. (1969) Clues to a letter's recognition: Implications for the design of characters. *Journal of Typographic Research*, **3**, 145–168. (268)

Konishi, M. (1985) Birdsong: From behavior to neuron. *Annual Review of Neuroscience*, **8**, 125–170. (57)

Kramer, A. F., Wickens, C. D., and Donchin, E. (1985) Processing of stimulus properties: Evidence for dual-task integrality. *Journal of Experimental Psychology: Human Perception and Performance*, **11**, 393–408. (79)

Kristofferson, M. W. (1977) The effects of practice with one positive set in a memory scanning task can be completely transferred to a new set. *Memory and Cognition*, **5**, 177–186. (154)

Kurzweil, R. C. (1981) Kurzweil reading machine for the blind. *Proceedings of the Johns Hopkins First National Conference on Applications of Personal Computing to Aid the Handicapped*, **1**, 236–241. (270)

Laabs, G. J. (1973) Retention characteristics of different reproduction cues in motor short-term memory. *Journal of Experimental Psychology*, **100**, 168–177. (217)

Laabs, G. J., and Simmons, R. W. (1981) Motor memory. In D. H. Holding (ed.), *Human Skills*, 119–151. Chichester: John Wiley. (62)

LaBerge, D., VanGelder, P., and Yellott, S. (1971) A cueing technique in choice reaction time. *Journal of Experiment Psychology*, **87**, 225–228. (77, 86)

Labuc, S. (1978) A comparison of pursuit tracking performance using thumb movement and thumb pressure controls with high and low gains. *Army Personnel Research Establishment Report No. 17/77*. (180)

Lacquanti, F., Terzuolo, C., and Viviani, P. (1984) Global metric properties and preparatory processes in drawing movements. In S. Kornblum and J. Requin (eds), *Preparatory States and Processes*, 357–370. Hillsdale: Lawrence Erlbaum Assoc. Publishers. (60)

Laming, D. R. J. (1968) *An Information Theory of Choice Reaction Times*. New York: Academic Press. (148)

LaMotte, R. H., and Mountcastle, V. B. (1975) Capacities of humans and monkeys to discriminate between vibratory stimuli of different frequency and amplitude: A correlation between neural events and psychophysical measurements. *Journal of Neurophysiology*, **38**, 539–559. (24)

Langley, D., and Zelaznik, H. N. (1984) The acquisition of time properties associated with a sequential motor skill. *Journal of Motor Behavior*, **16**, 275–301. (63)

Langolf, G. D., Chaffin, D. B., and Foulke, J. A. (1976) An investigation of Fitts' Law using a wide range of movement amplitudes. *Journal of Motor Behavior*, **8**, 113–1128. (123, 130)

Lansing, R. W., and Myerink, L. (1981) Load compensating responses of human abdominal muscles. *Journal of Physiology*, **320**, 253–268. (27)

Lansman, M., and Hunt, E. (1982) Individual differences in secondary task performance. *Memory and Cognition*, **10**, 10–24. (101, 102)

Lansman, M., Poltrock, S., and Hunt, E. (1984) Individual differences in the ability to focus and divide attention. *Intelligence*, **7**, 299–312. (100)

Lashley, K. S. (1917) The accuracy of movement in the absence of excitation from the moving organ. *The American Journal of Physiology*, **43**, 169–194. (18, 50)

Lashley, K. S. (1951) The problem of serial order in behavior. In L. A. Jeffress (ed.), *Cerebral Mechanisms in Behavior*. New York: John Wiley. (53, 113)

Laszlo, J. I. (1967) Training of fast tapping with reduction of kinaesthetic, tactile, visual and auditory sensations. *Quarterly Journal of Experimental Psychology*, **19**, 344–349. (29)

Laszlo, J. I., and Manning, L. C. (1970) The role of motor programming, command and standard in the central control of skilled movement. *Journal of Motor Behavior*, **2**, 111–124. (292)

Lavery, J. J. (1962) Retention of simple motor skills as a function of type of knowledge of results. *Canadian Journal of Psychology*, **16**, 300–311. (43)

Lee, D. N. (1978) The functions of vision. In H. L. Pick, Jr, and E. Saltzman (eds), *Modes of Perceiving and Processing Information*. Hillsdale: Lawrence Erlbaum Assoc. Publishers. (25)

Lee, D. N. (1980) The optic flow field: The foundation of vision. *Philosophical Transactions of the Royal Society of London, B 290*, 169–179. (25, 35, 37)

Lee, D. N., and Aronson, E. (1974) Visual proprioceptive control of standing in human infants. *Perception and Psychophysics*, **15**, 527–532. (35, 36)

Lee, D. N., and Lishman, J. R. (1975) Visual proprioceptive control of stance. *Journal of Human Movement Studies*, **1**, 87–95. (36)

Lee, D. N., Lishman, J. R., and Thomson, J. A. (1982) Regulation of gait in long jumping. *Journal of Experimental Psychology: Human Perception and Performance*, **8**, 448–459. (37)

Lee, D. N., and Reddish, P. E. (1981) Plummeting gannets: A paradigm of ecological optics. *Nature*, **293**, 293–294. (37)

Lee, D. N., and Young, D. S. (1985) Visual timing of interceptive action. In D. Ingle, M. Jeannerod, and D. N. Lee (eds), *Brain Mechanisms and Spatial Vision*, 1–30. Dordrecht: Martinus Nijhoff. (19)

Lee, D. N., and Young, D. S. (1986) Gearing action to the environment. In H. Heuer, and C. Fromm (eds), *Generation and Modulation of Action Patterns*, 217–230. Berlin: Springer-Verlag. (36)

Lee, T. D. (1988) Testing for motor learning: A focus on transfer-appropriate processing. In O. G. Meijer and K. Roth (eds), *Complex Motor Behavior: The Motor-Action Controversy*. Amsterdam: Elsevier Science. (46)

Lee, T. D., and Carnahan, H. (1985) Unpublished data, McMaster University. (45)

Lee, T. D., Magill, R. A., and Weeks, D. J. (1985) Influence of practice schedule on testing schema theory predictions in adults. *Journal of Motor Behavior*, **17**, 283–299. (223)

Legge, D. (1965) Analysis of visual and proprioceptive components of motor skill by means of a drug. *British Journal of Psychology*, **56**, 243–254. (285, 286)

Leibowitz, H. W., and Post, R. B. (1982) The two modes of processing concept and some implications. In J. Beck (ed.), *Organization and Representation in Perception*. Hillsdale: Lawrence Erlbaum Assoc. Publishers. (85)

Lenneberg, E. H. (1967) *Biological Foundations of Language*. New York: John Wiley. (53)

Leonard, J. A. (1953) Advanced information in sensorimotor skills. *Quarterly Journal of Experimental Psychology*, **5**, 141–149. (13)

Leonard, J. A. (1959) Tactual choice reactions: I. *Quarterly Journal of Experimental Psychology*, **11**, 76–83. (26)

Leonard, J. A. (1972) Studies in blind mobility. *Applied Ergonomics*, March, 37–46. (273)

Levitt, H., and Nye, P. W. (1971) Sensory training aids for the hearing impaired. Proceedings of a conference 15–17 November 1970, Easton, Maryland, National Academy of Engineering, Washington, D.C. (262, 264)

Liberman, A. M., Cooper, F. S., Shankweiler, D. P., and Studdert-Kennedy, M. (1968) Why are speech spectrograms hard to read? *American Annals of the Deaf*, **113**, 127–133. (266)

Licklider, J. C. R. (1960) Quasi-linear operator models in the study of manual tracking. In R. D. Luce (ed.), *Developments in Mathematical Psychology*. Glencoe, IL.: Free Press. (282)

Lintern, G., and Gopher, D. (1978) Adaptive training of perceptual motor skills: Issues, results, and future directions. *International Journal of Man–Machine Studies*, **10**, 521–551. (99)

Lintern, G., and Wickens, C. D. (1987) *Attention Theory as a Basis for Training Research*. University of Illinois Aviation Research Laboratory (Tech. Rep. ARL-87-2NASA-87-3). Savoy, IL: Institute of Aviation. (95, 98)

Lippman, R. P. (1982) A review of research on speech training aids for the deaf. In N. J. Lass (ed.), *Speech and Language: Advances in Basic Research and Practice*, Vol. 7, 105–133. New York: Academic Press. (67)

Loeb, M. (1986) *Noise and Human Behavior*. New York: John Wiley. (287)

Logan, G. D. (1985) Skill and automaticity: Relations, implications and future directions. *Canadian Journal of Psychology*, **39**, 367–386. (79, 222)

Long, J. (1976) Visual feedback and skilled keying: Differential effects of masking the printed copy and the keyboard. *Ergonomics*, **19**, 93–110. (156)

Long, J., Nimmo-Smith, I., and Whitefield, A. (1983) Skilled typing: A characterization based on distribution of times between responses. In W. E. Cooper (ed.), *Cognitive Aspects of Skilled Typewriting*. New York: Springer-Verlag. (234, 237)

Loveless, N. E., and Holding, D. H. (1959) Reaction time and tracking ability. *Perceptual and Motor Skills*, **9**, 134. (10)

Lucaccini, L. F., Freedy, A., Rey, P., and Lyman, J. (1967) Sensory motor control system for an externally powered artificial arm. *Bulletin of Prosthetics Research*, **10–8**, 92–111. (254)

Lund, J. P., Drew, T., and Rossignol, S. (1984) A study of jaw reflexes of the awake cat during mastication and locomotion. *Brain Behavior Evolution*, **25**, 146–156. (31)

Mackay, D. G. (1982) The problems of flexibility, fluency and speed–accuracy trade-off in skilled behavior. *Psychological Review*, **89**, 483–506. (216, 217, 238, 241, 242, 244)

Mackay, D. G. (1983) A theory of the representation and enactment of intentions. In R. A. Magill (ed.), *Memory and Control of Action*. Amsterdam: North-Holland. (14, 238, 292)

Mackenzie, C. L., and Marteniuk, R. G. (1985b) Bimanual coordination. In E. A. Roy (ed.), *Neuropsychological Studies of Apraxia and Related Disorders*, 345–358. Amsterdam: North-Holland. (65)

MacNeilage, P. F. (1980) Distinctive properties of speech motor control. In G. E. Stelmach and J. Requin (eds), *Tutorials in Motor Behavior*. Amsterdam: North-Holland. (238)

McDaniel, J. W. (1969) *Physical Disability and Human Behavior*. New York: Pergamon. (261)

McGill, W. J. (1967) Stochastic latency mechanisms. In R. D. Luce, R. R. Bush, and E. Galanter (eds), *Handbook of Mathematical Psychology*. New York: John Wiley. (148)

McGuigan, F. J. (1959) The effect of precision, delay, and schedule of knowledge of results on performance. *Journal of Experimental Psychology*, **58**, 79–84. (39)

McLeod, P. D. (1977) A dual task modality effect: Support for multiprocessor models of attention. *Quarterly Journal of Experimental Psychology*, **29**, 651–668. (14, 85, 193)

McLeod, P. D. (1980) What can probe RT tell us about the attentional demands of movement? In G. E. Stelmach and J. Requin (eds), *Tutorials in Motor Behavior*. Amsterdam: North-Holland. (117, 220, 221, 222)

McLeod, P. D., Poulton, C. E., du Ross, H., and Lewis, W. (1986) The influence of ship motion on manual control skills. MRC Applied Psychology Unit, Cambridge. (194)

McRuer, D., Graham, D., and Krendel, E. (1967) Manual control of single-loop systems. *Journal of the Franklin Institute*, **283**, 1–29, 145–168. (187)

Mane, A. M. (1984) Acquisition of perceptual-motor skill: Adaptive and part-whole training. In *Proceedings of the Human Factors Society 28th Annual Meeting*, 522–526. Santa Monica, CA: Human Factors Society. (99)

Mann, R. W. (1974) Technology and human rehabilitation: Prostheses for sensory rehabilitation and/or sensory substitution. *Advances in Biomedical Engineering*, **4**, 209–353. (267)

Mann, R. W. (1981) Cybernetic limb prosthesis. *Annals of Biomedical Engineering*, **9**, 1–43. (254)

Mann, R. W., and Reimers, S. D. (1970) Kinesthetic sensing for the EMG controlled 'Boston arm'. *IEEE Transactions on Man–Machine Systems*, MMS-11, 110–115. (257)

Marsden, C. D., Merton, P. A., and Morton, H. B. (1972) Servo action in human voluntary movement. *Nature*, **238**, 140–143. (21, 28, 54)

Marteniuk, R. G., and MacKenzie, C. L. (1980) Information processing in movement organization and execution. In R. S. Nickerson (ed.), *Attention and Performance VIII*, 29–57. Hillsdale: Lawrence Erlbaum Assoc. Publishers. (56)

Marteniuk, R. G., and MacKenzie, C. L. (1981) Methods in the study of motor programming: Is it just a matter of simple vs. choice reaction time? A comment on Klapp et al. (1979). *Journal of Motor Behavior*, **13**, 313–319. (56)

Marteniuk, R. G., and Romanow, S. K. E. (1983) Human movement organization and learning as revealed by variability of movement, use of kinematic information and fourier analysis. In R. A. Magill (ed.), *Memory and Control of Action*, 167–198. Amsterdam: North-Holland. (63)

Marteniuk, R. G., Mackenzie, C. L., and Baba, S. M. (1984) Bimanual movement control: Information processing and interaction effects. (61)

Mason, C. P. (1970) Practical problems in myoelectric control of prostheses. *Bulletin of Prosthetics Research*, **10–13**, 39–45. (255)

Matthews, P. B. C. (1981) Muscle spindles: Their messages and their fusimotor supply. In V. B. Brooks (ed.), *Handbook of Physiology. Section 1: The Nervous System (Vol. 2)*. Bethesda, MD: American Physiological Society. (28)

Meacci, W. G., and Price, E. E. (1985) Acquisition and retention of golf putting skill through the relaxation, visualization and body rehearsal interaction. *Research Quarterly for Exercise and Sport*, **56**, 176–179. (215)

Megaw, E. D. (1972) Direction and extent uncertainty in step-input tracking. *Journal of Motor Behavior*, **4**, 171–186. (131, 133, 134)

Mehr, M. (1970) *Newsletters*. Measurement Systems Incorporated. (181)

Meyer, D. E., Smith, J. E. K., and Wright, C. E. (1982) Models for the speed and accuracy of aimed movements. *Psychological Review*, **89**, 449–482. (125, 126, 130)

Meyers, E., Ethington, D., and Ashcroft, S. (1958) Readability of Braille as a function of three spacing variables. *Journal of Applied Psychology*, **42**, 163–165. (268)

Millar, S. (1975) Effects of input conditions on intramodal and cross-modal visual and kinesthetic matches by children. *Journal of Experimental Child Psychology*, **19**, 63–78. (208)

Miller, G. A., Galanter, E., and Pribram, K. H. (1960) *Plans and the Structure of Behavior*. New York: Henry Holt. (66)

Miller, J. D., Engebretson, A. M., and DeFilippo, C. L. (1974) Preliminary research with a three channel vibrotactile speech reception aid for the deaf. *Proceedings of the 1974 Seminar on Speech Communications*, 341–347. (267)

Monsell, S. (1986) Programming of complex sequences: Evidence from the timing of rapid speech and other productions. In H. Heuer and C. Fromm (eds), *Generation and Modulation of Action Patterns*, 72–86. Berlin: Springer-Verlag. (55, 67)

Monster, A. W. (1973) Loading reflexes during two types of voluntary muscle contractions. In R. B. Stein, K. G. Pearson, R. S. Smith, and J. B. Redford (eds), *Control of Posture and Locomotion*, 347–362. New York: Plenum. (28)

Moore, S. P., and Marteniuk, R. G. (1986) Kinematic and electromyographic changes that occur as a function of learning a time-constrained aiming task. *Journal of Motor Behavior*, **18**, 397–426. (59, 63)

Morasso, P., Bizzi, E., and Dichgans, J. (1973) Adjustments to saccadic characteristics during head movements. *Experimental Brain Research*, **16**, 492–500. (54)

Moray, N. (1978) The strategic control of information processing. In G. Underwood (ed.), *Strategies of Information Processing*. London: Academic Press. (164)

Moray, N. (1981) Feedback and the control of skilled behaviour. In D. H. Holding (ed.), *Human Skills*. Chichester: John Wiley. (17)

Moray, N. (1984) Attention to dynamic visual displays in man–machine systems. In R. Parasuraman anf R. Davies (eds), *Varieties of Attention*, 485–512. New York: Academic Press. (76)

Moray, N. (1986) Monitoring behavior and supervisory control. In K. Boff, L. Kaufman, and J. Thomas (eds), *Handbook of Perception and Performance*, Vol. 2. New York: John Wiley. (74, 75, 78)

Moray, N., Richards, M., and Low, J. (1980). *The Behaviour of Fighter Controllers* (Tech. Rep.). London: Ministry of Defence. (75)

Morgan, B. B., and Repko, J. D. (1974) Evaluation of behavioral functions in workers exposed to lead. In C. Xintaras, B. L. Johnson, and I. de Groot (eds), *Behavioral Toxicology*. Washington, DC: DHEW. (286)

Morris, R. (1981) Error correction paradigms: A possible confounding. In G. C. Roberts and D. M. Landers (eds), *Psychology of Motor Behavior*. Champaign, IL.: Human Kinetics. (133)

Moscovitch, M. (1979) Information processing and the cerebral hemispheres. In M. S. Gazzaniga (ed.), *The Handbook of Behavioral Biology: Volume on Neuropsychology*. New York: Plenum. (82)

Mowbray, G. H., and Rhoades, M. U. (1959) On the reduction of choice reaction-times with practice. *Quarterly Journal of Experimental Psychology*, **11**, 16–23. (26, 148)

Mulder, G., and Mulder, L. J. (1981) Information processing and cardiovascular control. *Psychophysiology*, **18**, 392–401. (79)

Mulder, T., and Hulstijn, W. (1985) Sensory feedback in the learning of a novel motor task. *Journal of Motor Behavior*, **17**, 110–128. (39)

Murdock, B. B. (1957) Transfer designs and formulas. *Psychological Bulletin*, **54**, 313–326. (190)

Myklebust, H. R. (1964) *The Psychology of Deafness*. New York: Grune and Stratton. (261)

Nashner, L. M. (1977) Fixed patterns of rapid postural responses among leg muscles during stance. *Experimental Brain Research*, **30**, 13–24. (34)

Nashner, L. M., and Berthoz, A. (1978) Visual contribution to rapid more responses during postural control. *Brain Research*, **150**, 403–407. (36)

Nashner, L. M., and Forssberg, H. (1986) Phase-dependent organization of postural adjustments associated with arm movements while walking. *Journal of Neurophysiology*, **55**, 1382–1394. (31)

Nashner, L. M., Black, F. O., and Wall III, C. (1982) Adaptation to altered support and visual conditions during stance: Patients with vestibular deficits. *Journal of Neuroscience*, **2**, 536–544. (24)

Nashner, L. M., Wollacott, M., and Tuma, G. (1979) Organization of rapid responses to postural and locomotor-like perturbations of standing man. *Experimental Brain Research*, **36**, 463–476. (31)

Navon, D. (1984) Resources: A theoretical soupstone. *Psychological Review*, **91**, 216–234. (72, 88)

Navon, D., and Gopher, D. (1979) On the economy of the human processing system. *Psychological Review*, **86**, 254–255. (72)

Navon, D., and Miller, J. (1987) The role of outcome conflict in dual-task interference. *Journal of Experimental Psychology: Human Perception and Performance*, **13**, 435–448. (72, 88, 89)

Naylor, J. C., and Briggs, G. E. (1963) Effects of task complexity and task organization on the relative efficiency of part and whole training methods. *Journal of Experimental Psychology*, **65**, 217–224. (97)

Neisser, U. (1985) The role of theory in the ecological study of memory: Comment on Bruce. *Experimental Psychological Review*, **84**, 272–276. (215)

Neves, D. M., and Anderson, J. R. (1981) Knowledge compilation: Mechanisms for the automatization of cognitive skills. In J. R. Anderson (ed.), *Cognitive Skills and Their Acquisition*. Hillsdale: Lawrence Erlbaum Assoc. Publishers. (224)

Newell, A., and Rosenbloom, P. S. (1981) Mechanisms of skill acquisition and the law of practice. In J. R. Anderson (ed.), *Cognitive Skills and Their Acquisition*. Hillsdale: Lawrence Erlbaum Assoc. Publishers. (219)

Newell, K. M. (1974) Knowledge of results and motor learning. *Journal of Motor Behavior*, **4**, 235–244. (39, 210)

Newell, K. M. (1976) Knowledge of results and motor learning. In J. Keogh, and R. S. Hutton (eds), *Exercise and Sport Sciences Reviews: Vol. 4*, 195–228. Santa Barbara, CA: Journal Publishing Affiliates. (38)

Newell, K. M. (1981) Skill learning. In D. H. Holding (ed.), *Human Skills*. New York: John Wiley. (67, 207, 209, 216, 218)

Newell, K. M. (1985) Coordination, control and skill. In D. Goodman, R. B. Wilberg, and I. M. Franks (eds), *Differing Perspectives in Motor Learning, Memory, and Control*, 295–317. Amsterdam: North-Holland. (38)

Newell, K. M., Morris, L. R., and Scully, D. M. (1985) Augmented information and the acquisition of skill in physical activity. In R. L. Terjung (ed.), *Exercise and Sport Sciences Review*. New York: Macmillan. (212, 213)

Newell, K. M., Sparrow, W. A., and Quinn, J. T. (1985) Kinetic information feedback for learning isometric tasks. *Journal of Human Movement Studies*, **11**, 113–123. (213)

Nickerson, R. S. (1965) Response time for the second of two successive signals as a function of absolute and relative duration of inter signal interval. *Perceptual and Motor Skills*, **21**, 3–10. (152, 162, 164)

Nickerson, R. S., Kalikow, D. N., and Stevens, K. N. (1976) Computer-aided speech training for the deaf. *Journal of Speech and Hearing Disorders*, **41**, 120–132. (67, 68)

Nissen, M. J., and Bullemer, P. (1987) Attention requirements of learning: Evidence from performance measures. *Cognitive Psychology*, **19**, 1–32. (97)

Noble, C. E. (1978) Age, race and sex in the learning and performance of psychomotor skills. In R. T. Osborne, C. E. Noble, and N. Weyl (eds), *Human Variation*. New York: Academic Press. (7)

Noble, M. E., and Trumbo, D. A. (1967) The organization of skilled response. *Organizational Behavior and Human Performance*, **2**, 1–25. (13)

Noble, M. E., Trumbo, D. A., and Fowler, F. (1967) Further evidence on secondary task interference in tracking. *Journal of Experimental Psychology*, **73**, 146–149. (98)

Nolan, C. Y., and Kederis, C. J. (1969) Perceptual factors in Braille word recognition. American Foundation for the Blind, *Research Series No. 20*. (268)

Norman, D. A. (1968) Toward a theory of memory and attention. *Psychological Review*, **75**, 522–536. (72)

Norman, D. A., and Bobrow, D. G. (1975) On data-limited and resource-limited processes. *Journal of Cognitive Psychology*, **7**, 44–60. (72, 80)

Nottebohm, F. (1970) The ontogeny of bird song. *Science*, **167**, 950–956. (51)

Ogden, G. D., Levine, J. W., and Eisner, E. J. (1979) Measurement of workload by secondary tasks. *Human Factors*, **21**, 529–548. (80)

Ollman, R. T. (1966) Fast guesses in choice reaction time. *Psychonomic Science*, **6**, 155–156. (150)

Orr, D. B., Friedman, H. L., and Williams, J. C. (1965) Trainability of listening comprehension of speeded discourse. *Journal of Educational Psychology*, **56**, 148–156. (262)

Osgood, C. E. (1949) The similarity paradox in human learning: A resolution. *Psychological Review*, **56**, 132–143. (216)

Ostry, D. J. (1983) Determinants of interkey times in typing. In W. E. Cooper (ed.), *Cognitive Aspects of Skilled Typewriting*. New York: Springer-Verlag. (237)

Pachella, R. G., and Pew, R. W. (1968) Speed–accuracy trade-off in reaction times: Effect of discrete criterion times. *Journal of Experimental Psychology*, **76**, 19–24. (150, 156)

Parks, T. E., Kroll, N. E., Salzberg, P. M., and Parkinson, S. R. (1972) Persistence of visual memory as indicated by decision time. *Journal of Experimental Psychology*, **92**, 437–438. (87)

Patrick, J., and Mutlusoy, F. (1982) The relationship between types of feedback, gain of a display and feedback precision in acquisition of a simple motor task. *Quarterly of Experimental Psychology*, **34A**, 171–182. (284)

Pauls, M. D. (1964) Speechreading. In H. Davis and S. H. Silverman (eds), *Hearing and Deafness*. New York: Holt, Rinehart and Winston. (264)

Pearson, K. G., and Duysens, J. (1976) Function of segmental reflexes in the control of stepping in cockroaches and cats. In R. M. Herman, S. Grillner, P. S. G. Stein, and D. G. Stuart (eds), *Neural Control of Locomotion*, 519–537. New York: Plenum. (26)

Peizer, E., Wright, D. W., and Pirello, T. (1970) Perspectives on the use of external power in upper-extremity prostheses. *Bulletin of Prosthetics Research*, **10–13**, 25–38. (252)

Peizer, E., Wright, D. W., Pirello, T., and Mason, C. P. (1970) Current indications for upper-extremity powered components. *Bulletin of Prosthetics Research*, **10–14**, 22–42. (252)

Pellionisz, E., and Llinas, R. (1982) Space–time representation in the brain. *Neuroscience*, **7**, 2249–2970. (188)

Peters, M. (1977) Simultaneous performance of two motor activities: The factor of timing. *Neuropsychologia*, **15**, 461–465. (91)

Peters, W., and Wenborne, A. A. (1936) The time pattern of voluntary movements. *British Journal of Psychology*, **26**, 388–396. (112)

Pew, R. W. (1966) Acquisition of hierarchical control over the temporal organization of a skill. *Journal of Experimental Psychology*, **71**, 764–772. (32, 128)

Pew, R. W. (1969) The speed-accuracy operating characteristic. *Acta Psychologica*, **30**, 16–26. (11, 150, 156)

Pew, R. W. (1974) Levels of analysis in motor control. *Brain Research*, **71**, 393–400. (98)

Pew, R. W. (1984) A distributed processing view of motor control. In W. Prinz and A. F. Sanders (eds), *Cognition and Motor Processes*. Amsterdam: North-Holland. (65, 66, 246)

Pew, R. W., and Rupp, G. L. (1971) Two quantitative measures of skill development. *Journal of Experimental Psychology*, **90**, 1–7. (13, 17)

Pickett, J. M., and Pickett, B. M. (1963) Communication of speech sounds by a tactual vocoder. *Journal of Speech and Hearing Research*, **6**, 207–222. (266)

Pierce, J. R. (1962) *Symbols, Signals and Noise*. London: Hutchinson. (188)

Pike, A. R. (1973) Response latency models for signal detection. *Psychological Review*, **80**, 53–68. (148)

Polit, A., and Bizzi, E. (1979) Characteristics of motor programs underlying arm movements in monkeys. *Journal of Neurophysiology*, **42**, 183–194. (62)

Polson, M., Wickens, C. D., Colle, H., and Klapp, H. (1987) Interactive processes: Task interference, independence, and integration. In M. Chignell and P. A. Hancock (eds), *Intelligent interfaces: Theories, research and design*. Amsterdam: North-Holland. (83)

Pomerantz, J. R. (1981) Perceptual organization in information processing. In M. Kubovy and J. R. Pomerantz (eds), *Perceptual Organization*. Hillsdale: Lawrence Erlbaum Assoc. Publishers. (95)

Posner, M. I. (1967). Characteristics of visual and kinestheric memory codes. *Journal of Experimental Psychology*, **75**, 103–107. (214)

Posner, M. I. (1979) *Chronometric Explorations of Mind*. Hillsdale: Lawrence Erlbaum Assoc. Publishers. (113)

Posner, M. I., and Keele, S. W. (1969) Attention demands of movement. *Proceedings of the XVth International Congress of Applied Psychology*. Amsterdam: Swets and Zeitlinger. (116)

Possemai, C. A., Granjon, M., Reynard, G., and Requin, J. (1975) High order sequential effects and the negative gradient of the relationship between simple reaction time and foreperiod duration. *Acta Psychologica*, **39**, 263–270. (152)

Poulton, E. C. (1950) Perceptual anticipation and reaction time. *Quarterly Journal of Experimental Psychology*, **2**, 99–112. (187)

Poulton. E. C. (1952) Perceptual anticipation in tracking with two-pointer and one-pointer displays. *British Journal of Psychology*, **43**, 222–229. (174)

Poulton, E. C. (1957a) On the stimulus and response in pursuit tracking. *Journal of Experimental Psychology*, **53**, 57–65. (3, 230)

Poulton, E. C. (1957b) On prediction in skilled movements. *Psychological Bulletin*, **54**, 467–478. (7, 12)

Poulton, E. C. (1957c) Learning the statistical properties of the input in pursuit tracking. *Journal of Experimental Psychology*, **54**, 28–32. (178)

Poulton, E. C. (1973) Unwanted range effects from using within-subject experimental designs. *Psychological Bulletin*, **80**, 113–121. (180)

Poulton, E. C. (1974) *Tracking Skill and Manual Control*. London: Academic Press. (173, 174, 179, 181, 183, 185, 187)

Poulton, E. C. (1978) A new look at the effects of noise: A rejoinder. *Psychological Bulletin*, **85**, 1068–1079. (287)

Povel, D. J., and Wansink, M. (1986) A computer-controlled vowel corrector for the hearing impaired. *Journal of Speech and Hearing Research*, **29**, 99–105. (67)

Prather, D. C. (1971) Trial-and-error versus errorless learning: Training, transfer, and stress. *American Journal of Psychology*, **84**, 377–386. (40)

Pribram, K. H., and McGuinness, D. (1975) Arousal, activation and effort in the control of attention. *Psychological Review*, **82**, 116–129. (82)

Prinz, W. (1984) Modes of linkage between perception and action. In W. Prinz and A. F. Sanders (eds), *Cognition and Motor Processes*, 185–193. Berlin: Springer-Verlag. (58)

Prior, R. E., and Lyman, J. (1975) Electrocutaneous feedback for artificial limbs. *Bulletin of Prosthetics Research*, **10–24**, 3–37. (256)

Rabbitt, P. M. A. (1965) Response facilitation on repetition of a limb movement. *British Journal of Psychology*, **56**, 303–304. (166)

Rabbitt, P. M. A. (1966a) Errors and error-correction in choice-response tasks. *Journal of Experimental Psychology*, **71**, 264–272. (156)

Rabbitt, P. M. A. (1966b) Error correction time without external error signals. *Nature*, **212**, 438. (156)

Rabbitt, P. M. A. (1968a) Repetition effects and signal classification strategies in serial choice response tasks. *Quarterly Journal of Experimental Psychology*, **20**, 232–240. (148)

Rabbitt, P. M. A. (1968b) Three kinds of error-signalling responses in a serial choice task. *Quarterly Journal of Experimental Psychology*, **20**, 179–188. (156)

Rabbitt, P. M. A. (1969) Psychological refractory delay and response-stimulus interval in serial, choice-response tasks. In Koster, W. (ed.), *Attention and Performance 11*, 195–219. Amsterdam: North-Holland. (152, 156, 162)

Rabbitt, P. M. A. (1971) Times for analyzing stimuli and relating responses. *British Medical Bulletin*, **27**, (3), 259–265. (149)

Rabbitt, P. M. A. (1978a) Hand dominance, attention and the choice between responses. *Quarterly Journal of Experimental Psychology*, **30**, 407–416. (166)

Rabbitt, P. M. A. (1978b) Detection of errors by skilled typists. *Ergonomics*, **21**, 945–958. (156)

Rabbitt, P. M. A. Cumming, C. G., and Vyas, S. M. (1978) Some errors of perceptual analysis in visual search can be detected and corrected. *Quarterly Journal of Experimental Psychology*, **30**, 319–332. (156)

Rabbitt, P. M. A. Cumming, C. G., and Vyas, S. M. (1979a) Improvement, learning and retention of skill at visual search. *Quarterly Journal of Experimental Psychology*, **31**, 441–460. (152, 154, 156, 163)

Rabbitt, P. M. A. Cumming, C. G., and Vyas, S. M. (1979b) Modulation of selective attention by sequential effects in visual search tasks. *Quarterly Journal of Experimental Psychology*, **31**, 305–317. (152, 163)

Rabbitt, P. M. A., and Rogers, M. (1965) Age and choice between responses on a self-paced repetitive task. *Ergonomics*, **8**, 435–444. (165)

Rabbitt, P. M. A., and Vyas, S. M. (1970) An elementary preliminary taxonomy of errors in choice reaction time tasks. *Acta Psychologica*, **33**, 56–76. (150, 151, 156, 157)

Rabbitt, P. M. A., and Vyas, S. M. (1979) Selective anticipation for events in old age. *Journal of Gerontology*, **35**, 913–919. (157, 158)

Rae, J. W., and Cockrell, J. L. (1971) Applications in myoelectrical control. *Bulletin of Prosthetics Research*, **10–16**, 24–37. (252)

Raibert, M. H. (1977) Motor control and learning by the state–sapce model. Technical Report, Artificial Intelligence Laboratory, MIT. (59)

Reed, C. M., Durlach, N. I., Braida, L. D., Norton, S. J., and Schultz, M. C. (1977) Experimental results on Tadoma. Paper to Research Conference on Speech-Processing Aids for the Deaf, Gallaudet College, Washington, D. C. (266)

Regan, J. J. (1959) Tracking performance related to display-control configurations. *U.S. NAVTADEVCEN Technical Report No. 322–1–2*. (181)

Reiter, R. (1948) Eine neue Elektrokunsthand. *Grenzgebiete der Medizin*, **4**, 133. (252)

Requin, J., Lecas, J.-C., and Bonnet, M. (1984) Some experimental evidence for a three-step model of motor preparation. In S. Kornblum and J. Requin (eds), *Preparatory States and Processes*, 259–284. Hillsdale: Lawrence Erlbaum Assoc. Publishers. (56, 57)

Requin, J., Semjen, A., and Bonnet, M. (1984) Bernstein's purposeful brain. In H. T. A. Whiting (ed.), *Human Motor Actions—Bernstein Reassessed*, 467–504. Amsterdam: North-Holland. (18)

Reswick, J. B. (1972) Prosthetic and orthotic devices. In J. H. U. Brown and J. D. Dickson (eds), *Advances in Biomedical Engineering*, Vol. 2. London: Academic Press. (254, 259)

Rice, C. E. (1970) Early blindness, early experience and perceptual enhancement. American Foundation for the Blind, *Research Bulletin*, **22**, 1–22. (261)

Richter, F., Silverman, C., and Beatty, J. (1983) Response selection and initiation in speeded reactions: A pupillometric analysis. *Journal of Experimental Psychology: Human Perception and Performance*, **9**, 360–370. (79)

Rieck, A., Ogden, G. D., and Anderson, N. S. (1980) An investigation of varying amounts of component task practice on dual task performance. *Human Factors*, **22**, 373–388. (96)

Rohland, T. A. (1975) Sensory feedback for powered limb prostheses. *Medical and Biological Engineering*, **13**, 300–301. (256)

Rolfe, J. M. (1971) The secondary task as a measure of mental load. In W. T. Singleton, J. G. Fox, and D. Whitfield (eds), *Measurement of Man at Work*, 135–148. London: Taylor and Francis. (80)

Rosenbaum, D. A. (1980) Human movement initiation: Specifications of arm, direction and extent. *Journal of Experimental Psychology: General*, **109**, 444–474. (118)

Rosenbaum, D. A. (1983) The movement precuing technique: Assumptions, applications and extensions. In R. A. Magill (ed.), *Memory and Control of Action*, 231–274. Amsterdam: North-Holland. (56)

Rosenbaum, D. A. (1985) Motor programming: A review and scheduling theory. In H. Heuer, U. Kleinbeck, and K.-M.Schmidt (eds), *Motor Behavior: Programming Control, and Acquisition*, 1–33. Berlin: Springer-Verlag. (62, 65)

Rosenbaum, D. A. Inhoff, A. W., and Gordon, A. M. (1984) Choosing between movement sequences: A hierarchical editor model. *Journal of Experimental Psychology: General*, **113**, 372–393. (55, 56, 61, 67)

Ross, D., Bird, A. M., Doody, S. G., and Zoeller, M. (1985) Effects of modeling and videotape feedback with knowledge of results on motor performance. *Human Movement Science*, **4**, 149–157. (208, 212)

Rothwell, J. C., Traub, M. M., Day, B. L., Obeso, J. A., Thomas, P. K., and Marsden, C. D. (1982) Manual motor performance in a deafferented man. *Brain*, **105**, 515–542. (18, 51)

Roy, E. A., and Diewert, G. L. (1975) Encoding of kinesthetic extent information. *Perception and Psychophysics*, **17**, 559–564. (214)

Rubin, W. M. (1978) Application of signal detection theory to error detection in ballistic motor skills. *Journal of Experimental Psychology: Human Perception and Performance*, **4**, 311–320. (46)

Rumelhart, D. E., and Norman, D. A. (1982) Simulating a skilled typist: A study of skilled cognitive-motor performance. *Cognitive Science*, **6**, 1–36. (63, 234, 235, 236)

Russell, L. (1971) *Evaluation of Mobility Aids for the Blind. Pathsounder Travel Aid Evaluation*. Washington, D. C.: National Academy of Engineering. (271)

Salmoni, A. W., Ross, D., Dill, S., and Zoeller, M. (1983) Knowledge of results and perceptual-motor learning. *Human Movement Science*, **2**, 77–89. (211)

Salmoni, A. W., Ross, D., and Williams, I. D. (1985) Goal uncertainty and knowledge of results. Unpublished data. (211)

Salmoni, A. W., Schmidt R. A., and Walter, C. B. (1984) Knowledge of results and motor learning: A review and critical reappraisal. *Psychological Bulletin*, **95**, 355–386. (38, 39, 40, 41, 42, 45, 210, 211, 218)

Salthouse, T. A. (1984) Effects of age and skill on typing. *Journal of Experimental Psychology: General*, **113**, 345–371. (234, 235, 237)

Salthouse, T. A. (1986) Perceptual, cognitive, and motoric aspects of transcription typing. *Psychological Bulletin*, **99**, 303–319. (233, 234, 235, 237)

Saltzman, E., and Kelso, J. A. S. (1987) Skilled actions: A task-dynamic approach. *Psychological Review*, **94**, 84–106. (66, 144)

Sanders, A. F. (1983) Towards a model of stress and human performance. *Acta Psychologica*, **53**, 61–97. (82)

Sanders, A. F. (1986) Energetical states underlying task performance. In G. R. J. Hockey, A. W. K. Gaillard, and M. G. H. Coles (ed), *Energetical states underlying task performance. In G. R. J. Hockey, A. W. K. Gaillard, and M. G. H. Coles (eds), Energetics and Human Information Processing*, 139–154. Amsterdam: Martinus Nijhoff. (82)

Schmidt, R. A. (1975) A schema theory of discrete motor skill learning. *Psychological Review*, **82**, 225–260. (43, 60, 66, 135, 201, 202, 218, 232, 282, 292)

Schmidt, R. A. (1976a) The schema as a solution to some persistent problems in motor pearing theory. In G. E. Stelmach (ed.), *Motor Control: Issues and Trends*, 41–65. New York: Academic Press. (55, 135)

Schmidt, R. A. (1976b) Control processes in motor skills. In J. Keogh and R. S.

Hutton (eds), *Exercise and Sport Sciences Reviews, Vol. 4*, 229–261. Santa Barbara: Journal Publishing Affiliates. (29, 55, 60, 66)

Schmidt, R. A. (1982) *Motor Control and Learning: A Behavioural Emphasis*. Champaign, IL: Human Kinetics. (55, 60, 62, 67, 129, 221)

Schmidt, R. A. (1984) The search for invariance in skilled movement behavior. *Research Quarterly for Exercise and Sport*, **56**, 188–200. (60, 62)

Schmidt, R. A. (1987) The acquisition of skill: Some modifications to the perception-action relationship through practice. In H. Heuer, and A. F. Sanders (eds), *Perspectives on Perception and Action*, 77–103. Hillsdale: Lawrence Erlbaum Assoc. Publishers. (32)

Schmidt, R. A. (1988) *Motor Control and Learning: A Behavioral Emphasis* (2nd edn). Champaign, IL: Human Kinetics. (18, 34, 35, 38, 45)

Schmidt, R. A., and Gordon, G. B. (1977) Errors in motor responding, 'rapid' corrections, and false anticipations. *Journal of Motor Behavior*, **9**, 101–111. (135, 136)

Schmidt, R. A., and McGowan, C. (1980) Terminal accuracy of unexpectedly loaded rapid movements: Evidence for a mass-spring mechanism in programming. *Journal of Motor Behavior*, **12**, 149–161. (63)

Schmidt, R. A., Shapiro, D. C., Winstein, C. J., Young, D. E., and Swinnen, S. (1987) *Feedback and Motor Skill Training: Relative Frequency of KR and Summary KR (Tech. Rep. Contract No. MDA903–85–K–0225)*. Alexandria, VA: US Army Research Institute. (43, 44)

Schmidt, R. A., Sherwood, D. E., Zelaznik, H. N., and Leikind, B. J. (1985) Speed–accuracy trade-offs in motor behavior: Theories of impulse variability. In H. Heuer, U. Kleinbeck, and K.-H. Schmidt (eds), *Motor Behavior: Programming, Control, and Acquisition*, 79–123. Berlin: Springer-Verlag. (62)

Schmidt, R. A., Young, D. E., Shapiro, D. C., and Swinnen, S. (1987) *Summary Knowledge of Results and Skill Acquisition*. Manuscript submitted for publication. (43, 46)

Schmidt, R. A., Zelaznik, H. N., and Frank, J. S. (1978) Sources of inaccuracy in rapid movement. In G. E. Stelmach (ed.), *Information Processing in Motor Control and Learning*. New York: Academic Press. (123, 124, 125, 128, 129, 130)

Schmidt, R. A., Zelaznik, H. N., Hawkins, B., Frank, J. S., and Quinn, J. T., Jr (1979) Motor output variability: A theory for the accuracy of rapid motor acts. *Psychological Review*, **86**, 415–451. (62, 127)

Schneider, G. E. (1969) Two visual systems. *Science*, **163**, 895–902. (25)

Schneider, W. (1985a) Training high performance skills: Fallacies and guidelines. *Human Factors*, **27**, (3) 285–300. (80, 99)

Schneider, W. (1985b) Toward a model of attention and the development of automatic processing. In M. Posner and O. S. Marin (eds), *Attention and Performance XI*, 475–492. Hillsdale: Lawrence Erlbaum Assoc. Publishers. (223)

Schneider, W. (1986) Theoretical development in automatic/controlled processing. Unpublished presentation at the 30th Annual Meeting of the Human Factors Society. (98)

Schneider, W., and Fisk, A. D. (1982a) Concurrent automatic and controlled visual search: Can processing occur without cost. *Journal of Experimental Psychology: Learning, Memory, and Cognition*, **8**, 261–278. (32, 80, 86)

Schneider, W., and Fisk, A. D. (1982b) Degree of consistent training: Improvements in search performance and automatic process development. *Perception and Psychophysics*, **31**, 160–168. (32)

Schneider, W., and Fisk, A. D. (1983) Attention theory and mechanisms for skilled performance. In R. A. Magill (ed.), *Memory and Control of Action*, 119–143. Amsterdam: North-Holland. (27, 32, 33)

Schneider, W., and Shiffrin, R. M. (1977) Controlled and automatic human information processing I: Detection, search, and attention. *Psychological Review*, **84**, 1–66. (80, 99)

Schneider, W., Dumais, S. T., and Shiffrin, R. M. (1985) Automatic and control processing and attention. In R. Parasuraman and D. R. Davies (eds), *Varieties of Attention*, 1–27. New York: Academic Press. (80, 99, 223)

Schouten, J. F., and Bekker, J. A. M. (1967) Reaction time and accuracy. *Acta Psychologica*, **27**, 143–153. (150)

Scully, D. M. and Newell, K. M. (1985) Observational learning and the acquisition of motor skills: Toward a visual perception perspective. *Journal of Human Movement Studies*, **11**, 169–186. (208)

Selverston, A. I. (1980) Are central pattern generators understandable? *Behavioral and brain Sciences*, **3**, 535–571. (18)

Senders, J. W. (1966) A reanalysis of the pilot eye-movement data. *IEEE Transactions on Human Factors in Electronics*, **HFE-7**, 103–106. (74, 75, 76)

Senders, J. W. (1983) Visual scanning processes. Netherland: University of Tilburg Press. (75, 78)

Shaffer, L. H. (1973) Latency mechanisms in transcription. In S. Kornboum (ed.), *Attention and Performance IV*. New York: Academic Press. (153, 155)

Shaffer, L. H. (1975a) Multiple attention in continuous verbal tasks. In P. M. A. Rabbitt and S. Dornic (eds), *Attention and Performance V*. London: Academic Press. (153)

Shaffer, L. H. (1975b) Control processes in typing. *Quarterly Journal of Experimental Psychology*, **27**, 419–432. (14, 243)

Shaffer, L. H. (1978) Timing in the motor programming of typing. *Quarterly Journal of Experimental Psychology*, **30**, 333–345. (53, 229, 230, 237, 243)

Shaffer, L. H. (1980) Analysing piano performance: A study of concert pianists. In G. E. Stelmach and J. Requin (eds), *Tutorials in Motor Behavior*. Amsterdam: North-Holland. (243)

Shaffer, L. H. (1981) Performances of Chopin, Bach, and Bartok: Studies in motor programming. *Cognitive Psychology*, **13**, 326–376. (243)

Shaffer, L. H. (1982) Rhythm and timing in skill. *Psychological Review*, **89**, 109–122. (59, 62)

Shaffer, L. H. (1984) Timing in solo and duet piano performances. *Quarterly Journal of Experimental Psychology*, **36A**, , 577–595. (59, 62)

Shaffer, L. H., and Hardwick, J. (1970) The basis of transcription skill. *Journal of Experimental Psychology*, **84**, 424–440. (153)

Shannon, C. E., and Weaver, W. (1949) *The Mathematical Theory of Communication*. Urbana, IL: University of Illinois Press. (113, 199)

Shannon, G. F. (1976) A comparison of alternative means of providing sensory feedback on upper limb protheses. *Medical and Biological Engineering*, **14**, 289–294. (257)

Shapiro, D. C. (1977) A preliminary attempt to determine the duration of a motor program. In D. M. Landers and R. W. Christina (eds), *Psychology of Motor Behavior and Sport*. Champaign, IL.: Human Kinetics. (61)

Shapiro, D. C., and Schmidt, R. A. (1982) The schema theory: Recent evidence and developmental implications. In J. A. S. Kelso and J. E. Clark (eds), *The

Development of Movement Control and Co-ordination, 113–150. New York: John Wiley. (60, 63)

Shapiro, D. C., Zernicke, R. F., Gregor, R. J., and Diestal, J. D. (1981) Evidence for generalized motor programs using gait pattern analysis. *Journal of Motor Behavior*, **13**, 33–47. (60)

Shea, J. B. (1977) Effects of Labeling on motor short-term memory. *Journal of Experimental Psychology: Human Learning and Memory*, **3**, 92–99. (214)

Shea, J. B., and Morgan, R. L. (1979) Contextual interference effects on the acquisition, retention, and transfer of a motor skill. *Journey of Experimental Psychology: Human Learning and Memory*, **5**, 179–187. (218)

Sheridan, M. R. (1979) A reappraisal of Fitts' Law. *Journal of Motor Behavior*, **11**, 179–188. (127)

Sheridan, M. R. (1988) Movement metaphors. In A. M. Colley and J. R. Beech (eds), *Cognition and Action in Skilled Behaviour*. Amsterdam: North-Holland. (229)

Sheridan, T. B. (1972) On how often the supervisor should sample. *IEEE Transactions on Systems, Sciences, and Cybernetics*, **SSC-6**, 140–145. (76)

Sherrick, D. E., and Cholewiak, R. W. (1977) Matching speech to vision and touch. Paper to Research Conference on Speech-Processing Aids for the Deaf, Gallaudet College, Washington, D.C. (264)

Sherrington, C. S. (1906) *The Integrative Function of the Nervous System*. New Haven: Yale University Press. (20)

Sherwood, D. E. (1988) Effect of bandwidth knowledge of results on movement consistency. *Perceptual and Motor Skills*, **66**, 532–542. (44)

Shiffrin, R. M., and Dumais, S. T. (1981) The development of automatism. In J. R. Anderson (ed.), *Cognitive Skills and Their Acquisition*. Hillsdale: Lawrence Erlbaum Assoc. Publishers. (222, 223)

Shiffrin, R. M., and Schneider, W. (1977) Controlled and automatic human information processing: II. Perceptual learning, automatic attending and a general theory. *Psychological Review*, **84**, 127–190. (4, 32)

Shik, M. L., Severin, F. V., and Orlovsky, G. N. (1966) Control of walking and running by means of electrical stimulation of the mid-brain. *Bifzika*, **11**, 659–666. (52)

Shingledecker, C. A., (1978) The effects of anticipation on performance and processing load in blind mobility. *Ergonomics*, **21**, 355–371. (275, 277)

Shingledecker, C. A., and Foulke, E. (1978) A human factors approach to the assessment of the mobility of blind pedestrians. *Human Factors*, **20**, 273–286. (273)

Shingledecker, C. A., and Holding, D. H. (1974) Risk and effort measures of fatigue. *Journal of Motor Behavior*, **6**, 17–25. (289)

Shingledecker, C. A. (1983) Measuring the mental effort of blind mobility. *Journal of Visual Impairment and Blindness*, **77**, 7, 334–339. (278)

Siddall, G. J., Holding, D. H., and Draper, J. (1957) Errors of aim and extent in manual point to point movement. *Occupational Psychology*, **31**, 185–195. (11)

Sittig, A. C., Denier van der Gon, J. J., and Gielen, C. C. A. M. (1985) Separate control of arm position and velocity demonstrated by vibration of muscle tendon in man. *Experimental Brain Research*, **60**, 445–453. (22)

Skoglund, S. (1956) Anatomical and physiological studies of the knee joint innervation in the cat. *Acta Physiologica Scandinavica*, **36**, (Suppl. 124), 1–101. (23)

Slater-Hammel, A. T. (1960) Reliability, accuracy and refractoriness of a transient reaction. *Research Quarterly*, **31**, 217–228. (26)

Sloboda, J. A. (1974) The eye-hand span: An approach to the study of sight-reading. *Psychology of Music*, **2**, 4–10. (235)

Smith, G. A. (1977) Studies in compatibility and a new model of choice reaction times. In S. Dornic (ed.), *Attention and Performance VI*. Hillsdale: Lawrence Erlbaum Assoc. Publishers. (10)

Smith, J. L., Roberts, E. M., and Atkins, E. (1972) Fusimotor neuron block and voluntary arm movement in man. *American Journal of Physical Medicine*, **5**, 225–239. (18)

Smith, W. M., and Bowen, K. F. (1980) The effects of delayed and displaced visual feedback on motor control. *Journal of Motor Behavior*, **12**, 91–101. (142)

Smith, W. M., McCrary, J. R., and Smith, K. U. (1963) Delayed and space-displaced sensory feedback and learning. *Perceptual and Motor Skills*, **16**, 781–796. (255)

Smyth, M. M. (1978) Attention to visual feedback in motor learning. *Journal of Motor Behavior*, **10**, 185–190. (8)

Snodgrass, J. A., Luce, R. D., and Galanter, E. H. (1967) Some experiments on simple and choice reaction time. *Journal of Experimental Psychology*, **75**, 1–17. (148)

Sorbye, R. (1977) Myoelectric controlled hand prostheses in children. *International Journal of Rehabilitation Research*, **1**, 15–25. (255)

Sperry, R. W. (1950) Neural basis of the spontaneous optokinetic response produced by visual neural inversion. *Journal of Comparative and Physiological Psychology*, **43**, 482–489. (135, 136)

Starkes, J. L. (1987) Skill in field hockey: The nature of the cognitive advantage. *Journal of Sport Psychology*, June. (215, 225)

Staros, A., and Peizer, E. (1972) Veterans Administration Prosthetics Center Research Report. *Bulletin of Prosthetics Research*, **10–17**, 202–233. (253)

Stein, R. B. (1982) What muscle variable(s) does the nervous system control in limb movements? *Behavioral and Brain Sciences*, **5**, 535–541. (63)

Stelmach, G. E., and Diggles, V. S. (1982) Control theories in motor behavior. *Acta Psychologica*, **50**, 83–105. (64, 65)

Stelmach, G. E., and Hughes, B. G. (1984) Cognitivism and future theories of action: Some basic issues. In W. Prinz, and A. F. Sanders (eds), *Cognition and Motor Processes*. Berlin: Springer-Verlag. (246)

Stelmach, G. E., and Hughes, B. G. (1987) The cognitivist orientation: The Problem of system reduction. *European Bulletin of Cognitive Psychology*, **7**, 190–194. (66, 240, 247)

Stelmach, G. E., Mullins, P. A., and Teulings, H.-L. (1984) Motor programming and temporal patterns in handwriting. In J. Gibbon and L. Allan (eds), *Timing and Time Perception*, 144–157. New York: Annals of the New York Academy of Sciences, Vol. 423. (60)

Sternberg, S. (1969) The discovery of processing stages: Extensions of Donders' method. *acta Psychologica*, **30**, 276–315. (149)

Sternberg, S. (1975) Memory scanning: New findings and current controversies. *Quarterly Journal of Experimental Psychology*, **27**, 1–32. (149)

Sternberg, S., Monsell, S., Knoll, R. L., and Wright, C. E. (1978) The latency and duration of rapid movement sequences: Comparisons of speech and typewriting. In G. E. Stelmach (ed.), *Information Processing in Motor Control and Learning*. New York: Academic Press. (55, 56, 66)

Stetson, R. H., and Bouman, H. D. (1935) The coordination of simple skilled movements. *Archives Neerlander de Physiologie*, **20**, 177–254. (110, 111, 112)

Stone, M. (1960) Models for choice reaction time. *Psychometrika*, **25**, 251–260. (148)

Stroop, J. R. (1935) Studies of interference in serial verbal reactions. *Journal of Experimental Psychology*, **18**, 643–662. (88)

Stull, G. A., and Kearney, J. T. (1978) Effects of variable fatigue levels on reaction-time components. *Journal of Motor Behavior*, **10**, 223–232. (10)

Sugden, D. A. (1980) Movement speed in children. *Journal of Motor Behavior*, **12**, 125–132. (123)

Summers, J. J. (1975) The role of timing in motor program representation. *Journal of Motor Behavior*, **7**, 229–241. (61)

Summers, J. J. (1977a) The relationship between the sequencing and timing components of a skill. *Journal of Motor Behavior*, **9**, 49–59. (61)

Summers, J. J. (1977b) Adjustments to redundancy in reaction time: A comparison of three learning methods. *Acta Psychologica*, **41**, 205–223. (68)

Summers, J. J. (1981) Motor programs. In D. H. Holding (ed.), *Human Skills*, 41–64. Chichester: John Wiley. (59)

Summers, J. J., Sargent, G. I., and Hawkins, S. (1984) Rhythm and the timing of movement sequences. *Psychological Research*, **46**, 107–119. (61)

Supa, M., Cotzin, M., and Dallenbach, K. M. (1944) 'Facial vision': The perception of obstacles by the blind. *American Journal of Psychology*, **57**, 133–183. (273)

Szafran, J. (1951) Changes with age and exclusion of vision in performance at an aiming task. *Quarterly Journal of Experimental Psychology*, **3**, 111–118. (289)

Taenzer, J. C. (1970) Visual word reading. *IEEE Transactions on Man-Machine Systems*, **11**, 44–53. (269)

Taub, E. (1976) Movement in nonhuman primates deprived of somatosensory feedback. In J. Keogh and R. S. Hutton (eds), *Exercise and Sport Sciences Reviews, Vol. 4*, 335–373. Santa Barbara: Journal Publishing Affiliates. (18, 51)

Teasdale, A., and Reynolds, J. (1955) Two ways to get frequency response from transient data. *Control Engineering*, **10**, 55–63. (186)

Terzuolo, C. A., and Viviani, P. (1979) The central representation of learned motor programs. In R. E. Talbott and D. R. Humphrey (eds), *Posture and Movement*, 113–121. New York: Raven Press. (60)

Terzuolo, C. A., and Viviani, P. (1980) Determinants and characteristics of motor patterns used for typing. *Neuroscience*, **5**, 1085–1103. (60)

Teuber, H. L. (1972) Unity and diversity of frontal lobe functions. *Acta Neurobiologiae Experimentalis*, **32**, 615–656. (135)

Teulings, H. L., Mullins, P. A., and Stelmach, G. E. (1986) The elementary units of programming in handwriting. In H. S. R. Kao, G. P. Van Galen, and R. Hoosain (eds), *Graphonomics: Contemporary Research in Handwriting*. Amsterdam: North-Holland. (233)

Teulings, H. L., Thomassen, A. J., and Van Galen, G. P. (1983) Preparation of partly precued handwriting movements: The size of movement units in handwriting. *Acta Psychologica*, **54**, 165–177. (233)

Theios, J., Smith, P. G., Haviland, S. E., Traupmann, J., and McCoy, M. C. (1973) Memory scanning as a serial, self-terminating process. *Journal of Experimental Psychology*, **97**, 323–336. (148)

Thelen, E. (1987) We think; therefore, we move. *Cahiers de Psychologie Cognitive*, **7**, 195–198. (53)

Thelen, E., and Fisher, D. M. (1982) Newborn stepping: An explanation for a disappearing reflex. *Developmental Psychology*, **18**, 760–775. (53)

Thelen, E., Bradshaw, G., and Ward, J. A. (1981) Spontaneous kicking in month-old infants: Manifestation of a human central locomotor program. *Behavioral and Neural Biology*, **32**, 45–53. (53)

Thelen, E., Kelso, J. A. S., and Fogel, A. (1987) Self-organizing systems and infant motor development. *Developmental Review*, **7**, 39–65. (53)

Thorndike, E. L. (1903) *Educational Psychology*. New York: Lemcke and Buechner. (192)

Thorndike, E. L. (1927) The law of effect. *American Journal of Psychology*, **39**, 212–222. (2, 43, 212)

Townsend, J. T. (1974) Issues and models concerning the processing of a finite number of inputs. In B. Kantowitz (ed.), *Human Information Processing*, 133–185. Hillsdale: Lawrence Erlbaum Assoc. Publishers. (72, 78)

Treisman, A. (1964) The effect of irrelevant material on the efficiency of selective listening. *American Journal of Psychology*, **77**, 533–546. (89)

Treisman, A. (1969) Strategies and models of selective attention. *Psychological Review*, **76**, 282–299. (72)

Trevarthen, C. B. (1968) Two mechanisms of vision in primates. *Psychologische Forschung*, **31**, 299–337. (25, 231)

Trowbridge, M. H., and Cason, H. (1932) An experimental study of Thorndike's theory of learning. *Journal of General Psychology*, **7**, 245–260. (39, 40, 198)

Trumbo, D., and Noble, M. (1973) Motor skill. In B. B. Wolman (ed.), *Handbook of General Psychology*. Englewood Cliffs, N.J.: Prentice-Hall. (256)

Tsang, P., and Wickens, C. D. (1988) The structural constraints and strategic control of attention allocation. *Human Performance*, **1**, 45–72. (84, 87)

Tulga, M. K., and Sheridan, T. B. (1980) Dynamic decisions and workload in multitask supervisory control. *IEEE Transactions on Systems, Man, and Cybernetics*, **SMC-10**, 217–232. (77)

Tuller, B., Kelso, J. A. S., and Harris, K. S. (1982) Interarticulator phasing as an index of temporal regularity in speech. *Journal of Experimental Psychology: Human Perception and Performance*, **8**, 460–472. (60)

Tuller, B., Turvey, M. T., and Fitch, H. (1982) The Bernstein perspective: II. The concept of muscle linkages or coordinative structures. In J. A. S. Kelso (ed.), *Human Motor Behavior: An Introduction*. Hillsdale: Lawrence Erlbaum Assoc. Publishers. (18)

Tulving, E., and Thomson, D. M. (1973) Encoding specificity and retrieval processes in episodic memory. *Psychological Review*, **80**, 352–373. (45)

Turvey, M. T. (1977) Preliminaries to a theory of action with reference to vision. In R. Shaw and J. Bransford (eds), *Perceiving, Acting, and Knowing*, 211–265. Hillsdale: Lawrence Erlbaum Assoc. Publishers. (19, 64, 246, 247)

Turvey, M. T., and Carello, C. (1986) The ecological approach to perceiving and acting: A pictorial essay. *Acta Psychologica*, **63**, 133–155. (230, 246)

Turvey, M. T., and Kugler, P. N. (1984) An ecological approach to perception and action. In H. T. A. Whiting (ed.), *Human Motor Actions—Bernstein Reassessed*, 373–412. Amsterdam: North-Holland. (18)

Turvey, M. T., Shaw, R. E., and Mace, W. (1978) Issues in the theory of action. In J. Requin (ed.), *Attention and Performance VII*. Hillsdale: Lawrence Erlbaum Assoc. Publishers. (13, 64, 144, 292)

Tustin, A. (1944) An investigation of the operator response in manual control of a power-driven gun. Metro-Vickers Electric, C. S. Memo. 169. (172, 186)

Upton, H. W. (1968) Wearable eyeglasses speechreading aid. *American Annals of the Deaf*, **113**, 222–229. (264)

Vallbo, Å. B. (1971) Muscle spindle response at the onset of isometric voluntary contractions in man. Time difference between fusimotor and skeletomotor effects. *Journal of Physiology*, **318**, 405–431. (21)

Van Galen, G. P. (1980) Handwriting and drawing: A two stage model of complex motor behavior. In G. E. Stelmach and J. Requin (eds), *Tutorials in Motor Behavior*. Amsterdam: North-Holland. (231)

Van Galen, G. P., Meulenbroek, R. G. J., and Hylkema, H. (1986) On the simultaneous processing of words, letters and strokes in handwriting: Evidence for a mixed linear and parallel model. In H. S. R. Kao, G. P. van Gallen, and R. Roosain (eds), *Graphonomics: Contemporary Research in Handwriting*. Amsterdam: North-Holland. (233, 235)

Van Galen, G. P., and Teulings, H.-L. (1983) The independent monitoring of form and scale factors in handwriting. *Acta Psychologica*, **54**, 9–22. (232)

Vickers, D. (1970) Evidence for an accumulator model of psychophysical discrimination. *Ergonomics*, **13**, 37–58. (148)

Vidulich, M. A., and Wickens, C. D. (1986) Causes of dissociation between subjective workload measures and performance. *Applied Ergonomics*, **17**, 291–296. (79)

Vince, M. A. (1948) Corrective movements in a pursuit task. *Quarterly Journal of Experimental Psychology*, **1**, 85–103. (113)

Viviani, P., and Terzuolo, C. (1980) Space–time invariance in learned motor skills. In G. E. Stelmach and J. Requin (eds), *Tutorials in Motor Behavior*, 525–533. Amsterdam: North-Holland. (60)

von Holst, E. (1954) Relations between the central nervous system and the peripheral organs. *British Journal of Animal Behavior*, **2**, 89–94. (135)

Wade, M. G., Newell, K. M., and Wallace, S. A. (1978) Cited in Schmidt, R. A., Zelaznik, H. N., and Frank, J. S. (1979) Sources of inaccuracy in rapid movement. In G. E. Stelmach (ed.), *Information Processing in Motor Control and Learning*. New York: Academic Press. (123)

Wallace, S. A., and Newell, K. M. (1983) Visual control of discrete aiming movements. *Quarterly Journal of Experimental Psychology*, **35**, 311–321. (130)

Warm, J. S. (ed.) *Sustained Attention and Human Performance*. Chichester: John Wiley. (7)

Warren, W. H. (1984) Perceiving affordances: The visual guidance of stair climbing. *Journal of Experimental Psychology: Human Perception and Performance*, **10**, 683–703. (246)

Warren, W. H., Young, D. S., and Lee, D. N. (1986) Visual control of step length during running over irregular terrain. *Journal of Experimental Psychology: Human Perception and Performance*, **12**, 259–266. (37)

Weiskrantz, L., Warrington, E. K., Sanders, M. D., and Marshall, J. (1974) Visual capacity in the hemianopic field following a restricted cortical ablation. *Brain*, **97**, 709–728. (25)

Welford, A. T. (1958) *Aging and Human Skill*. London: Oxford University Press. (289)

Welford, A. T. (1968) *Fundamentals of Skill*. London: Methuen. (10, 13, 119, 148, 253)

Welford, A. T., Norris, A. H., and Shock, N. W. (1969) Speed and accuracy of movement and their changes with age. In W. G. Koster (ed.), *Attention and Performance II*. Amsterdam: North-Holland. (123)

West, L. J., and Sabban, Y. (1982) Hierarchy of stroking habits at the typewriter. *Journal of Applied Psychology*, **67**, 370–376. (234)

Westling, G., and Johansson, R. S. (1984) Factors influencing the force control during precision grip. *Experimental Brain Research*, **53**, 277–284. (34)

Westling, G., and Johansson, R. S. (1987) Responses in glabrous skin mechanoreceptors during precision grip in humans. *Experimental Brain Research*, **66**, 128–140. (34)

Wetherell, A. (1979 Short-term memory for verbal and graphic route information. *Proceedings, 1979 Meeting of the Human Factors Society*, Santa Monica, CA: Human Factors. (83)

Wickelgren, W. A. (1977) Speed–accuracy tradeoff and information processing dynamics. *Acta Psychologica*, **41**, 67–85. (11)

Wickelgren, W. A. (1979) *Cognitive Psychology*. Englewood Cliffs, N.J.: Prentice-Hall. (93)

Wickens, C. D. (1980) The structure of attentional resources. In R. Nickerson (ed.) *Attention and Performance VIII*, 239–257. Hillsdale: Lawrence Erlbaum Assoc. Publishers. (81)

Wickens, C. D. (1984) Processing resources in attention. In R. Parasuraman and R. Davies (eds), *Varieties of Attention* 63–101. New York: Academic Press. (75, 81, 82, 222)

Wickens, C. D. (1986a) Gain and energetics in information processing. In R. Hockey, A. Gaillard, and M. Coles (eds), *Energetics and Human Information Processing*. Dordrecht: Martinus Nijhoff. (74, 78)

Wickens, C. D. (1986b) *The Object Display: Principles and a Review of Experimental Findings*. University of Illinois Cognitive Psychophysiology Laboratory (Tech. Rep. CPL 86–6). Champaign, IL: Department of Psychology. (94)

Wickens, C. D., and Goettl, B. (1985) The effect of strategy on the resource demands of second order manual control. In R. Eberts and C. Eberts (eds), *Trends in Ergonomics and Human Factors*. Amsterdam: North-Holland. (88)

Wickens, C. D., and Kessel, C. (1980) The processing resource demands of failure detection in dynamic systems. *Journal of Experimental Psychology: Human Perception and Performance*, **6**, 564–577. (83)

Wickens, C. D., Kramer, A., Vanasse, L., and Donchin, E. (1983) The performance of concurrent tasks: A psychophysiological analysis of the reciprocity of information processing resources. *Science*, **221**, 1080–1082. (79)

Wickens, C. D., and Liu, Y. (1988) Codes and modalities in multiple resources: A success and a qualification. *Human Factors*, **30**, 381–387. (83, 85)

Wickens, C. D., Sandry, D., and Vidulich, M. (1983) Compatibility and resource competition between modalities of input, output, and central processing. *Human Factors*, **25**, 227–248. (85)

Wickens, C. D., Webb, J., and Fracker, L. (1987) *Cross-Modality Interference: A Resource, Preemption, or Switching Phenomenon?* University of Illinois Engineering Psychology Laboratory Technical Report (EPL-87-1/NASA-87-1). Champaign, IL: Institute of Aviation and Department of Psychology. (85)

Wickens, C. D., and Weingartner, A. (1985) Process control monitoring: The effects of spatial and verbal ability and current task demand. In R. Eberts and C. Eberts (eds), *Trends in Ergonomics and Human Factors*. Amsterdam: North-Holland. (83, 103)

Wickens, C. D., Zenyuh, J., Culp, V., and Marshak, W. (1985) Voice and manual control in dual task situations. *Proceedings, 29th Annual Meeting of the Human Factors Society*. Santa Monica, CA: Human Factors. (83)

Wiener, N. (1948) *Cybernetics*. New York: John Wiley. (113)

Wilke, J. T., and Vaughn, S. C. (1976) Temporal distribution of attention during a throwing motion. *Journal of Motor Behavior*, **8**, 83–88. (282)

Wilkinson, R. T. (1959) Rest pauses in a task affected by loss of sleep. *Ergonomics*, **2**, 373–380. (159)

Williams, L. R. T., and Churchman, P. (1986) Timing accuracy, precision and rhythm in serial movement. *Journal of Human Movement Studies*, **12**, 35–49. (61)

Wilson, A. B. (1965) Control of external power in upper-extremity rehabilitation. *Bulletin of Prosthetics Research*, **10–13**, 57–59. (258)

Wilson, D. M. (1961) The central nervous control of flight in a locust. *Journal of Experimental Biology*, **38**, 471–490. (51)

Wing, A. M. (1978) Response timing in handwriting. In G. E. Stelmach (ed.), *Information Processing in Motor Control and Learning*. New York: Academic Press. (232)

Winneke, G. (1974) Behavioral effects of methylene chloride and carbon monoxide as assessed by sensory and psychomotor performance. In C. Xintaras, B. J. Johnson, and I. de Groot (eds), *Behavioral Toxicology*. Washington, D.C.: DHEW. (286)

Winstein, C. J. (1988) *Relative Frequency of Information Feedback in Motor Performance and Learning*. Unpublished doctoral dissertation, University of California, Los Angeles. (42, 46)

Woodworth, R. S. (1899) The accuracy of voluntary movement. *Psychological Review*, **23**, 1–114. (2, 8, 107, 108, 109, 110, 112, 119, 122)

Wright, C. E., and Meyer, D. E. (1983) Conditions for a linear speed–accuracy trade-off in aimed movements. *Quarterly Journal of Experimental Psychology*, **35A**, 279–296. (126)

Wynne, A. L. (1984) Neuromotor synergies as a basis for coordinated intentional action. *Journal of Motor Behavior*, **16**, 135–170. (64)

Yamanishi, J., Kawato, M., and Suzuki, R. (1980) Two coupled oscillators as a model for the coordinated finger tapping by both hands. *Biological Cybernetics*, **37**, 219–225. (61)

Yeh, Y., and Wickens, C. D. (1988) Dissociation of performance and subjective measures of mental workload. *Human Factors*, **30**, 111–120. (79).

Yellott, J. T. (1967) Correction for fast guessing in choice reaction time. *Psychonomic Science*, **8**, 321–322. (150)

Young, L. R., and Stark, L. (1963) Variable feedback experiments testing a sampled data model for eye tracking movements. *IEEE Transactions of the Professional Technical Group on Human Factors in Electronics*, **4**, 38–51. (129)

Zanone, P. G., and Hauert, C. A. (1987) For a cognitive conception of motor processes: A provocative standpoint. *Cahiers de Psychologie Cognitive*, **7**, 109–129. (60, 64)

Zattara, M., and Bouisset, S. (1986) Chronometric analysis of the posturo-kinetic programming of voluntary movement. *Journal of Motor Behavior*, **18**, 215–223. (57)

Zelaznik, H. N. (1986) Issues in the study of human motor skill development: A reaction to John Fentress. In M. G. Wade and H. T. A. Whiting (eds), *Motor Development in Children: Aspects of Coordination and Control*, 125–132. Dordrecht: Martinus Nijhoff. (63)

Zelaznik, H. N., Hawkings, B., and Kisselburgh, L. (1983) Rapid visual feedback processing in single-aiming movements. *Journal of Motor Behavior*, **15**, 217–236. (133, 140, 142)

Zelaznik, H. N., and Larish, D. D. (1986) Precuing methods in the study of motor programming. In H. Heuer and C. Fromm (eds), *Generation and Modulation of Action patterns*, 55–63. Berlin: Springer-Verlag. (56)

Ziegler, P. N., Reilly, R., and Chernikoff, R. (1966) The use of displacement, flash and depth-of-flash coded displays. US Navy Research Laboratory, *Report No. 6412*. (183)

Subject Index

acceleration control, 176
accuracy, 11, 18, 107–146, 147–151
age effects, 148, 158–162, 249, 289–291
aids, sensorimotor, 264–267, 269–271
alternative displays, 182–184
amplitude, tracking, 137, 173
anticipation, 9–13, 56, 76, 136, 164, 274
arousal, 287
attention, 13–15, 71–105, 166, 288
augmented displays, 177
automatic processing, 4, 27, 32, 55, 79, 99, 142, 200, 219, 259

ballistic movements, 8, 110, 114, 166
blindness, 267–277
Braille, 268–271

central pattern generation, 52–53
channel capacity, 14, 193, 259, 274
closed-loop control, 2, 17, 32, 49, 58, 69, 186, 201, 253, 256, 259, 282
cognitive control, 13, 64, 166, 207
cognitive skills, 3, 229–248, 292
compatibility, 90–94, 147, 181, 255, 257
compensatory tracking, 174, 177, 184
control characteristics, 175–182
controlled/automatic processing, 4, 32, 127, 219–223
coordinative structures, 13, 18, 64, 144
corollary discharge, 135
current control, 108, 118–130
cybernetics, 113, 199

deafferentation, 18, 50, 62
deafness, 68, 261–267
discrete movements, 3, 6, 107–146, 234
display/control ratio, 178–182

displays, 177–184, 264–267
drugs, 148, 160, 285
dual-task performance, 14, 71–105, 283
dynamic acuity, 5

efference copy, 58, 127, 135, 141
effort, 15, 72, 223, 259, 273, 288
errors, 11, 17, 37–46, 73, 90, 109, 119, 129, 131–136, 140–144, 149, 156–162, 174, 184, 202, 216, 231, 238, 256, 288
eye movements, 54, 130

facial vision, 272
factor analysis, 5
fatigue, 10, 158, 187, 287
feedback, 7, 17–47, 49–55, 65, 255, 281
feedforward, 65
frequency, tracking, 173

goals, 38, 209
guidance techniques, 8, 40, 45

handicaps, 249–280
handwriting, 59, 230–233, 286
hierarchical control, 14, 54, 64, 200, 231, 240, 244, 284

impairment, 249–280
impulse timing, 62, 124–126, 144
index of difficulty, 120
individual differences, 7, 99–104, 216, 225, 289
information processing, 3, 5, 72, 113, 199, 212, 275
information theory, 2, 10, 188, 194
interference, 72, 83, 90, 220